SOCIAL DEMOCRACY IN NEOLIBERAL TIMES

Social Democracy in Neoliberal Times

The Left and Economic Policy since 1980

Edited by
ANDREW GLYN

OXFORD
UNIVERSITY PRESS

OXFORD
UNIVERSITY PRESS

Great Clarendon Street, Oxford OX2 6DP

Oxford University Press is a department of the University of Oxford.
It furthers the University's objective of excellence in research, scholarship,
and education by publishing worldwide in

Oxford New York

Athens Auckland Bangkok Bogotá Buenos Aires Cape Town
Chennai Dar es Salaam Delhi Florence Hong Kong Istanbul Karachi
Kolkata Kuala Lumpur Madrid Melbourne Mexico City Mumbai Nairobi
Paris São Paulo Shanghai Singapore Taipei Tokyo Toronto Warsaw

with associated companies in Berlin Ibadan

Oxford is a registered trade mark of Oxford University Press
in the UK and in certain other countries

Published in the United States
by Oxford University Press Inc., New York

British Library Cataloguing in Publication Data
Data available

Library of Congress Cataloging in Publication Data
Data available

ISBN 0-19-924137-6 (hbk.)
ISBN 0-19-924138-4 (pbk.)

1 3 5 7 9 10 8 6 4 2

Printed in Great Britain
on acid-free paper by
Biddles Ltd., Guildford & King's Lynn

Contents

Contributors   vii

1   Aspirations, Constraints, and Outcomes   1
    Andrew Glyn

2   Understanding Swedish Social Democracy: Victims of
    Success?
    Juhana Vartiainen   21

3   The Austrian Experience
    Alois Guger   53

4   Social Democracy and Market Reform in Australia and
    New Zealand
    John Quiggin   80

5   The Logic and Limits of *Désinflation Compétitive*
    Frédéric Lordon   110

6   The Political Economy of Social Democratic Economic
    Policies: The PASOK Experiment in Greece
    Euclid Tsakalotos   138

7   The Spanish Socialists in Power: Thirteen Years of
    Economic Policy
    Albert Recio and Jordi Roca   173

8   New Labour's Economic Policy
    Andrew Glyn and Stewart Wood   200

9   Why the Social Democratic Option Failed:
    Poland's Experience of Systemic Change
    Tadeusz Kowalik   223

10   The Choices for Scandinavian Social Democracy in
     Comparative Perspective
     Torben Iversen   253

11   The Social Democratic Welfare State
     Evelyne Huber and John D. Stephens   276

12   How Many Ways Can Be Third?
     Adam Przeworski   312

Bibliography   334

Index   367

Contributors

Andrew Glyn
Andrew Glyn is Fellow in Economics at Corpus Christi College, Oxford. His publications cover the political economy of advanced capitalist economies, especially unemployment, inequality, and profitability, and include *Capitalism Since 1945* (with Philip Armstrong and John Harrison).

Alois Guger
Alois Guger is Deputy Director of the Austrian Institute of Economic Research, Vienna, and Lecturer in Economics at the University of Economics in Vienna. His key areas of research include income distribution, social policy, income and wage policy, industrial relations, and corporatism. He has had visiting fellowships at the universities of Cambridge, Harvard, New South Wales, and Curtin University, WA.

Evelyne Huber
Evelyne Huber is Morehead Alumni Professor of Political Science at the University of North Carolina, Chapel Hill. Her current research interests are in the politics of welfare states/social policy in advanced industrial societies and Latin America. Among her most recent publications, co-authored with John D. Stephens, are *Development and Crisis of the Welfare State: Parties and Policies in Global Markets* (University of Chicago Press, in press) and 'The Political Economy of Pension Reform: Latin America in Comparative Perspective' (Geneva: UNRIDS, 2000). She is also the editor of *Models of Capitalism: Lessons for Latin America* (Pennsylvania State University Press, forthcoming).

Torben Iversen
Torben Iversen is Associate Professor of Government at Harvard. He is the author of *Contested Economic Institutions: The Politics of Macroeconomics and Wage Bargaining in Advanced Democracies,* and co-editor (with Jonas Pontusson and David Soskice) of *Unions, Employers and Central Banks: Macroeconomic Coordination and Institutional Change in Social Market Economies.* He is currently completing a book on the intersection

of the welfare state and the production system, and has written numerous articles on electoral politics and political economy.

Tadeusz Kowalik

Tadeusz Kowalik is Professor of Economics and Humanities at the Institute of Economics, Polish Academy of Sciences, Warsaw, and a Dean of the Faculty of Economics, Social and Economic School. His publications cover history of economic thought and comparative economic systems. He was the editor of Oskar Lange's works and co-editor of Michal Kalecki's works.

Frédéric Lordon

Frédéric Lordon is Researcher at CNRS-CEPREMAP and Professor at the Institut d'Etudes Politiques. His main research areas are economic policy, financial markets, shareholder value, and pension funds. His publications include *Les Quadratures de la Politique Economique* (Albin Michel, 1997) and *Fonds de Pension, Piège à Cons?* (Raisons d'Agir, 2000).

Adam Przeworski

Adam Przeworski is the Carrol and Milton Petrie Professor of Politics at New York University and a Fellow of the American Academy of Arts and Sciences. Formerly, he was the Martin A. Ryerson Distinguished Service Professor at the University of Chicago. He has taught and researched at scholarly institutions in Chile, France, Germany, India, Poland, Switzerland, and Spain. His recent books include *Democracy and Development* (co-author; New York, Cambridge University Press, 2000), *Democracy, Accountability, and Representation* (co-editor; New York, Cambridge University Press, 1999), *Sustainable Democracy* (co-author; New York, Cambridge University Press, 1995), *Economic Reforms in New Democracies: A Social-Democratic Approach* (co-author; New York, Cambridge University Press, 1993), and *Democracy and the Market: Political and Economic Reforms in Eastern Europe and Latin America* (Cambridge, Cambridge University Press, 1991).

John Quiggin

John Quiggin is an Australian Research Council Senior Fellow based at the Australian National University and Queensland University of Technology. He is prominent both as a research economist and as a commentator on Australian economic policy. He has published over 400 research articles, books, and reports in fields including risk analysis, production economics, and the theory of economic growth. He has also written on policy topics including unemployment policy, microeconomic reform, privatization, and competitive tendering.

Albert Recio

Albert Recio teaches economics at the Universitat Autònoma de Barcelona. He has published on different topics, mainly in labour economics, industrial relations, and economic institutions. He is the author of *Capitalismo y formas de contratacion laboral* (1988) and *Trabajos, personas y mercados* (1997).

Jordi Roca

Jordi Roca teaches economics at the Universitat de Barcelona. He has published on several topics, but mainly labour economics, ecological economics, and environmental policy. He is the author of *Pactos sociales y política de rentas* (1993) and (with J. Martínez Alier) *Economía ecológica y política ambiental* (2000).

John D. Stephens

John D. Stephens is Gerhard E. Lenski Professor of Political Science and Sociology at the University of North Carolina, Chapel Hill. His main current research interests are in the political economy of advanced industrial societies. He is the co-author (with Evelyne Huber) of *Development and Crisis of the Welfare State: Parties and Policies in Global Markets*, and 'Internationalization and the Social Democratic Model', *Comparative Political Studies*, **31**(3), 1998. He is also co-editor (with Herbert Kitschelt, Peter Lange, and Gary Marks) of *Continuity and Change in Contemporary Capitalism* (Cambridge University Press, 1999).

Euclid Tsakalotos

Euclid Tsakalotos is currently an Associate Professor in the Department of International and European Economic Studies at Athens University of Economics and Business. His research interests include political economy, the impact of institutions (including labour and financial) on economic performance, and European integration. He has published widely in journals including *Oxford Economic Papers, Journal of Industrial Economics, The Manchester School, Oxford Bulletin of Economics and Statistics* and the *Cambridge Journal of Economics*.

Juhana Vartiainen

Juhana Vartiainen has worked at the University of Helsinki, the Labour Institute for Economic Research, Helsinki (his current employer), and the Trade Union Institute for Economic Research, Stockholm. His research interests include labour economics, wage bargaining, variants of capitalism, the political economy of economic policy. He is the author of *History of Economic Policy in Finland* (with Jukka Pekkarinen, in Finnish, 1995), *Capital Accumulation in a Corporatist Economy*, Lecture

Notes in Economics and Mathematical Systems (Springer, 1992), and 'The Economics of Successful State Intervention in Industrial Transformation', in Woo-Cumings (ed.), *The Developmental State* (Cornell University Press, 1999).

Stewart Wood

Stewart Wood is a Fellow in Politics at Magdalen College, Oxford. His interests and published work concern contemporary political economy, welfare state retrenchment, and public policy in Western Europe. Currently he is completing a book comparing the politics behind economic reform initiatives in the Federal Republic of Germany and Great Britain during the post-war period.

1

Aspirations, Constraints, and Outcomes

ANDREW GLYN*

At the turn of the century more parties of the Left were in government in advanced capitalist countries than ever before, including, for the first time ever, those of the four largest West European countries. Does this make a substantial difference to the conduct of economic policy? Even 20 years ago the answer would have been clear. Mitterrand had just been elected to the presidency of France on a radical programme including extensive nationalization and he then proceeded with 'a barrage of reforms without precedent in post-reconstruction Europe' (Jensen and Ross, 1994, p. 172). By contrast, the Left's spectacular election victories in the UK and France in 1997 and then in Germany in 1998 brought far more modest shifts in economic policy. Labour promised a tougher attitude to inflation, ruled out the restoration of state benefits and abandoned its interventionist approach to industry. The French socialists have privatized at a faster rate than the right-wing governments they replaced. Oscar Lafontaine's attempt to push the Bundesbank into a more expansionary stance collapsed within 6 months. Within left parties generally there have been policy shifts in the same direction. How has this come about?

The majority of the chapters which follow approach this question by examining the experience of individual countries in the 1980s and 1990s. While not every country which had a left government is surveyed, a broad range of experience is covered. In Sweden and Austria the Left had long been dominant and had produced quite distinct social democratic 'models' of economic policy; in France, Greece, and Spain government by the Left was historically rather exceptional; Australia and New Zealand were in an intermediate position. In the UK the Left did not

* Corpus Christi College, Oxford.
I would like to thank the following for very helpful comments and suggestions: Chris Allsopp, Andrea Boltho, Wendy Carlin, David Soskice, Bob Sutcliffe, Frank Vandenbroucke, and the contributors to this volume.

regain power until 1997, much later than the other countries considered here, and after 18 years of hard-core conservative rule. The role played by Solidarity in the overthrow of communism seemed to mark Poland out as the 'transition economy' where social democratic forces would be strongest, and Tadeusz Kowalik's chapter examines why a strong alternative social democratic economic policy did not develop there. Analysing these experiences brings out common factors behind the trend towards conservative orthodoxy. While economic constraints play a prominent role in the stories recounted in the papers, it is important to remember that these governments had many priorities other than narrowly economic ones. For example, consolidation of democratic rule or desire to join the EU helped shape economic policy in Southern Europe and Poland especially.

The three final chapters take a broader comparative view. Evelyne Huber and John Stephens analyse the evolution of the social democratic welfare states, arguably the one sphere in which social democratic parties can still claim a distinctive approach. Torben Iversen discusses the policy dilemmas in terms of employment, taxation, and inequality which Northern European social democracy faces. Finally, Adam Przeworski sets the current evolution of social democratic policy in an historical and ideological perspective.

Particular national histories and institutions, and their influence on options and outcomes, are a recurrent theme in the country studies. In this introduction, however, these national specificities are submerged in order to outline, first, the common aspirations of 'social democracy' or the parties of the Left (terms that will be used interchangeably), and then the economic trends which provided the context for social democratic rule in the 1980s and 1990s. Finally, a brief assessment is given of what was achieved.

1. Aspirations

The reference to 'social democracy' in the title of this volume indicates that the focus is on governments in the broad 'reformist socialist' tradition. Historically, this has encompassed parties envisaging a long process of transformation of capitalism into a socialist system, based on common ownership of the means of production, as well as parties accepting the authority and ownership structures of capitalism but pressing for reforms to increase economic efficiency and to reduce inequality (see Przeworski's chapter). The latter, revisionist, position has been associated with the 'social democracies' of Northern Europe (and the labour parties of Australasia); the former, 'socialist' approach was strongest in 'Southern Europe' including France (see Sassoon, 1996, for a masterly survey). The last 20 years witnessed some jumbling of these distinctions. Sweden, the archetypal reformist social democracy, saw a range of challenges to the prerogatives of capital, culminating in the proposal for wage-earner funds in the early 1980s (see Juhana Vartiainen's chapter and Pontusson, 1992*b*). Conversely economic orthodoxy was embraced as rapidly and wholeheartedly by the Spanish socialists as by any party of the Left in Europe (see the chapter by Albert Recio and Jordi Roca). In the early 1980s, when most of the governments analysed here came to power, the core aspirations of the Left were full employment, enhancing the welfare state and redistribution, and, finally, supply-side interventions aimed at guiding or controlling capital.

(a) *Full Employment*

Maintaining full employment has been the centrepiece of social democratic programmes since the 1930s as Fritz Scharpf (1991, p. 22) explains:

> As long as capitalist crises could happen at any moment, whatever gains unions and social democratic parties might have achieved in the redistribution of incomes or the expansion of public services must have seemed extremely insecure. Indeed the unions had been helpless during the Great Depression of the early 1930s, as the welfare state collapsed under the burden of mass unemployment. Social democrats could thus make their reluctant peace with capitalism only if they could also hope to avoid its recurrent crises.

The achievement of full employment in the 1950s and 1960s could hardly be credited as a uniquely social democratic achievement. Germany, for example, had 1 per cent unemployment in 1960 before the Sozialdemokratische Partei Deutschlands (SPD) tasted power at the national level. The specifically social democratic dimension to full employment came to be its inclusive nature; full employment for 'core' workers (traditionally male) should not be achieved at the cost of joblessness or very low pay for other sections (women, less qualified workers, youth, the non-unionized). Sweden had 57 per cent of women participating in the labour force as early as 1968, as compared to 46 per cent in the USA or, at the other extreme, 28 per cent in the Netherlands (where the measured unemployment rate was just as low as in Sweden). The ratio of earnings of workers at the 90th and 10th percentiles (men and women) was 2.1 in Sweden, 3.3 in France, and 5.0 in USA in 1973 (OECD Employment Outlook, 1993, table 5.2). It should be noted that not all the strongly social democratic countries achieved this inclusive form of full employment. As Rowthorn (1992) showed, only the Nordic

countries achieved both high employment and low wage dispersion;
Austria, in particular, had quite an unequal wage distribution and only
moderate labour-force participation (see the discussion in Alois Guger's
chapter).

The fundamental problem in sustaining high employment concerns
the distributional conflict, which prolonged full employment was
always likely to engender. Keynes put the matter succinctly in 1943: 'the
task of keeping efficiency wages [wages per unit of output] reasonably
stable . . . is a political rather than an economic problem'. In the
following year he wrote, 'I do not doubt that a serious problem will
arise as to how wages are to be restrained when we have a combination
of collective bargaining and full employment' (quoted by Winch, 1988,
p. 107). 'Full employment capitalism', Kalecki said in his famous article
on the political aspects of full employment, 'will, of course, have to
develop new social and political institutions which will reflect the
increased power of the working class. If capitalism can adjust to full
employment a fundamental reform will have been incorporated in it'
(1990 [1943], p. 356).

The social democratic version of Kalecki's 'fundamental reform' was
coordinated wage bargaining by the trade-union movement, with
centralized negotiations able to take account of the impact of wage
demands on employment for the whole work-force (Calmfors and
Driffill, 1988; Soskice, 1990). With the problem of containing wage
pressure endemic to high employment, the solution had to be an
enduring system for disciplined wage determination, rather than a
government inspired incomes policy imposed in a situation of balance
of payments or inflationary crisis. Employer disenchantment and
differences of interest between sections of the work-force pose major
difficulties with sustaining these systems, as Vartiainen and Iversen
show. But no other solution to wage pressure was on offer which could
hope to meet social democracy's egalitarian objectives.

Social democratic priorities for welfare, discussed below, implied a
relatively high share of public spending in GDP. The expansion of
government spending, even when covered by taxation, sustained
demand through balanced budget multiplier effects. In addition, the
larger the share of government spending, the greater the automatic
stabilizer effect of budget deficits in bolstering demand in recessions.
Beyond that, in the 1950s and 1960s private investment was sufficiently
buoyant for additional, discretionary deficits to play only a temporary
'pump-priming' role; Scandinavian social democracies, in particular,
ran budget surpluses. Full employment was never maintained by
sustained budget deficits, so the collapse of full employment cannot be
attributed to pressures from international capital markets to stop

running them.[1] Sustained deficits to cover current spending are a sign of weakness—the government is either incapable of levying the tax rates necessary to cover demands for public spending or is forced by weak private investment to run deficits to sustain demand. The PASOK government in Greece in the 1980s, described in the chapter by Euclid Tsakalotos, illustrates such unsustainable, populist attempts to redistribute and boost employment.

(b) *Equality, the Welfare State, and Redistribution*

The dogma that equality necessarily undermines economic efficiency, always disputed by the Left, has taken a terrible battering in recent econometric work on economic growth. A comprehensive survey concludes that regressions 'run over a variety of data sets and periods and with many different measures of income distribution, deliver a consistent message: initial inequality is detrimental to long-run growth' (Benabou, 1996, p. 2). Another author reported that the impact of the marginal tax rate on growth 'is positive and highly significant rather than negative as the theory would predict. This finding . . . is difficult to rationalize with most of the existing theories which emphasize the distortionary effects of government expenditure and taxation'; he also found that 'not only taxation but also redistributive expenditures are positively associated with growth' (Perotti, 1996, pp. 170–1). If the range of opportunities open to poor people is expanded their incentives to deploy their potential to best advantage will be increased. Thus reduced incentives for the rich may be outweighed by increased incentives for the poor in a 'well designed' redistribution policy (see Aghion and Howitt, 1998, ch. 9, for a review of recent theoretical analysis of this issue). If children from poor areas participate much less in higher education than their abilities would allow, then this is a failure to accumulate human capital where its return would be greatest, involving a cost to society as well as unfairness to the people concerned. So taxation of the better off to fund improvements to schools in such areas is very likely to have beneficial effects on efficiency as well as equity, and similar, if less direct effects, could be expected from much other welfare expenditure (see Richard Wilkinson's (1994) claim that more equal societies display better health throughout all the population).

[1] One interpretation of the full employment period (Matthews, 1968; Boltho, 1989) emphasizes private-sector confidence that demand could and would be sustained which in turn bolstered investment and rendered persistent deficits unnecessary. Such confidence rested on a number of conditions, such as adequate profits, stable industrial relations, and a predictable international environment, as well as demand-management policies.

The socialist tradition would not confine redistributions to those which enhanced efficiency through expanding equality of opportunity (Cohen, 1997). The Left has traditionally argued for much more than a minimal safety net for those incapable of looking after themselves and, by extension, for redistribution to offset the disadvantages of those who, even with equal opportunity, suffer from a weak position in the market.

The welfare states inherited by the Left varied enormously, both in terms of resources and character. Sweden stands out as the exemplary social-democratic welfare state, promoting 'an equality of the highest standards' (Esping-Andersen, 1990, p. 27) and characterized by high replacement rates, extensive state provision of services, and maximum participation in the labour force (see the detailed discussion on the distinctive features of social democratic welfare states by Huber and Stephens).

It should be emphasized that the differences between the most and least egalitarian OECD countries have been and remain huge. In Sweden in the early 1990s, 4.9 per cent of single-parent households lived in poverty (less than half average income) compared to nearly 60 per cent in the USA and Canada (and around 30 per cent in France and Germany — OECD, 1997b, table 24). Pensioners in the UK are four times as likely to be in the worst-off 20 per cent of the population as in the best-off 20 per cent; in France the ratio is 1.5:1 (Tsakloglou, 1996). Unexciting-sounding differences in Gini coefficients measuring income inequality mask really enormous differences in distributive patterns. Egalitarians in the more unequal countries really do have something to emulate and in the more equal countries something to fear.

(c) Supply-side Intervention (or the Transformation of Capitalism)

Full employment and consolidation and extension of the welfare state were regarded as irreversible reforms to capitalism by the social democratic revisionists of the 1950s (Crosland, 1956; Sassoon, 1996). Where there was a more or less explicit post-war settlement between capital and labour, in Sweden for example, the government pursued full employment, extended the welfare state, but guaranteed managerial prerogatives over organization of production and the allocation of capital (Gustafsson, 1995). At the other extreme, in countries such as France, the 'stabilization' which had occurred at the end of the 1940s inflicted defeats on the labour movement depriving them of the power to make anything approaching an explicit deal (see Armstrong et al., 1991); however, a similar, if less developed, pattern of welfare capitalism evolved even in the countries dominated by the Right, such as Germany.

From around the mid-1960s two developments threatened such an 'historic compromise'. First, the labour movement grew in organizational strength and confidence as a result of the achievement and maintenance of full employment. This bred demands for further protection of conditions of employment, for an extension of union influence over corporate decision-making, and for measures to redistribute wealth, comprising a 'shift in the balance of power and wealth in favour of working people and their families', as the UK Labour Party's 1974 manifesto put it. Second, there was a belief that economic growth could be faster if government intervention could overcome coordination problems that were thought to be holding back investment.

The range of initiatives and interventions developed during the 1970s was reflected in left governments coming to power in the 1980s with programmes including:

- selective nationalization (France)
- planning agreements between governments and large firms (Greece)
- industry plans (Australia)
- co-determination of corporate decision-making (industrial democracy) (France, Sweden)
- wage-earner funds (Sweden)
- extension of employment rights (France)

The common idea behind these rather disparate proposals was to shift influence or even power over decision-making from private capital to government and/or workers (and, in the case of wage-earner funds and nationalization, to redistribute capital in addition). The transfer of economic power was seen as a democratic advance in and of itself; it would represent a form of economic democracy to complement the 'social' democracy achieved through full employment and the welfare state (Pontusson, 1992*b*). In the case of employment rights — restrictions on dismissals, and so forth — the purpose was to curtail unilateral exercise of economic power. But the justification for intervention in corporate decision-making usually rested on expected improvements in economic performance as well.

Such proposals as these faced formidable obstacles to their successful implementation. First, there was the political opposition from those whose freedom to manage and allocate capital would be circumscribed. Even if this could be surmounted, governments of the Left were obviously vulnerable to the economic effects of the uncertainty and loss of confidence involved. 'Strikes of capital' could develop quite spontaneously as owners and managers felt threatened. Second, even where sensible objectives could be set out, such as increasing the investment rate in order to improve productivity and trade performance, the mechanisms for inducing private firms to respond to the stimuli frequently lacked plausibility. For example, Stuart Holland, one of the foremost proponents of intervention (Holland, 1972), argued that private firms could be pressurized into higher investment by the competition from firms taken into public ownership; but lack of competition could hardly be taken as the general explanation for poor performance. It should be noted, however, that the enthusiasm for interventionism developed before the economic failures of centralized planning had become so glaring or the difficulties in contriving effective systems of enterprise governance had been seriously analysed.

2. Context

The starting point from which governments of the Left began to conduct economic policy in the early 1980s was far from favourable. The mid-1970s brought much slower growth rates in the OECD as a whole, combined with high inflation, squeezed profits, industrial strife, high government deficits, unstable exchange rates, weak investment, and very low levels of employer confidence. The particular economic inheritance faced by governments of the Left in the early 1980s contained many of these elements:

- unemployment was very high in Spain and rather high in France;
- inflation was particularly high in Greece and Spain and above the OECD average except in Austria;
- profitability had been squeezed more than the OECD average in France, Australia, and, especially, Greece;
- the budget deficit was particularly large in Sweden;
- investment had been growing more slowly even than the modest average OECD growth rate, except in Australia.

As explained in the chapter by Glyn and Wood, the Blair government faced a much more favourable macroeconomic pattern as the UK economy recovered from the severe recession of the early 1990s.

Developments in the international economy have always had a strong influence on the economic performance of individual capitalist economies, especially the middle-sized and smaller ones. Over the 1980s and 1990s the most significant trends across OECD countries, which influenced the capacity of social democratic governments to fulfil the aspirations of their supporters were as follows.

(a) *The Stagnation of Output Growth*

GDP growth in the OECD slowed from 4.9 per cent per year over the years 1960–73, to 2.6 per cent per year from 1979 to 1989, and 1.8 per cent per year from 1979 to 1995. Attempting to grow faster than the average would tend to bring balance-of-payments problems as imports were sucked in. Exports could grow correspondingly faster if the real exchange rate depreciated, but this in turn would reduce real wages. Many discussions of globalization have emphasized the increasing importance of trade, but after rising in the 1970s and early 1980s there has been no further increase in the share of exports in European GDP (see Sutcliffe and Glyn, 1999). Over the 1980s and 1990s the external constraint was the *slow* growth of export markets rather than the growing weight of exports in the economy.

(b) *The Productivity Slow-down*

The growth rate of OECD labour productivity declined in line with output growth to reach 1.4 per cent per year in the 1980s and below 1 per cent per year in the 1990s. The implication is that real wages have necessarily grown slowly, constraining the political feasibility of further redistribution—in the EU real wage growth has averaged only slightly more than 1 per cent per year since 1979.

(c) *The Decline in Inflation*

The OECD inflation rate, measured by the GDP deflator, fell from 8.6 per cent per year over 1973–9 to 3.1 per cent in 1987, and (after a hiccup) to 2 per cent per year by the mid-1990s. The growth of international capital flows has made it more difficult to manage persistently a higher inflation rate than competitors, given the growing weight of speculation against overvalued currencies. So governments of the Left were under severe pressure to conform.

Initially, most of the social democratic governments presided over substantial currency depreciations. During the first 4 years in government effective exchange rates fell by between about 18 per cent (Sweden and France) and 38 per cent (Greece and Australia); only Austria (and the UK more than a decade later) bucked this pattern. By the early 1990s all the governments of the Left had abandoned depreciation and opted for hard-currency policies. Since Mitterrand's programme had been the most radical, his conversion in 1983 to the *franc fort* policy was the most dramatic, as discussed in Frédéric Lordon's chapter. Just as significant was the falling into line of the Swedish Social Democrats in 1991 with their budget statement that

in the longer run it is not possible to safeguard employment in an economy
which has a higher inflation rate than the surrounding world. In order to
protect employment and prosperity economic policies in the next few years
... will have to aim for a permanent reduction in inflation. This task must take
priority over all other aims and ambitions. (quoted by Notermans, 1993)

Coordinated wage bargaining could bring the inflation rate down in
line with OECD-wide trends — disinflation by agreement rather than
by the fear of unemployment. But coordinated reductions in the
inflation rate are tricky as they require systematic acceptance of wage
increases below the going rate of inflation plus productivity growth.
Moreover, maintaining a very low rate of inflation once achieved may
bring additional problems for coordinated bargaining systems, as
Juhana Vartiainen explains. The Swedish system actually involved a
number of levels of bargaining (centre, industry, firm), and a very low
inflation rate compromises the ability of negotiators at each level of the
wage-bargaining process to deliver money-wage increases to their
constituencies. The implication is that, even with a coordinated system,
higher unemployment may be required to impose necessary real wage
restraint if the inflation rate is very low (see Akerlof et al., 1996, for an
alternative explanation of why the non-accelerating inflation rate of
unemployment (NAIRU) may be higher at low inflation rates). Nevertheless Torben Iversen's chapter argues that the alternative of accommodating inflation with periodic devaluations brings worse results in
the end.

(d) Financial Deregulation and Domestic Instability

Violent swings in demand swamp the capacity of any bargaining system
to maintain high employment. In the 1980s financial deregulation
unleashed a series of destructive consumer booms and slumps. Surprisingly perhaps, governments of the Left did not escape these pressures.
Consumer booms were as strong in Sweden (fall of 7 percentage points
in the savings ratio between 1985 and 1988) or France (fall of 6
percentage points between 1983 and 1987) as in the notorious case of the
Lawson boom in the UK (fall of 7 percentage points between 1983 and
1988) and considerable also in Australia, Spain, and New Zealand.
Austria stands out, again, with stable or even rising savings at the end
of the 1980s. The reaction to the consumer boom, in the form of rising
savings ratios as policy was tightened, was even fiercer in Sweden than
in the UK (a rise of 13 points between 1989 and 1993 as compared to 8
points in the UK). This was the immediate factor behind the disastrous
rise in Swedish unemployment (see Calmfors, 1993). No plausible
degree of wage flexibility could offset a demand 'shock' of this
magnitude.

Perhaps an expansion of consumer credit was especially seductive in a context where take-home pay had been squeezed over an extended period. But such macroeconomic mismanagement seriously compounded the underlying problems in the bargaining system in Sweden and John Quiggin makes a similar case against Labor in Australia. Precipitate deregulation of domestic financial markets was more a question of aping international fashions than an inevitable consequence of globalization. Many countries avoided such excesses — Germany, for example. The obsessive focus on macroeconomic stability of the Blair government can be traced to these damaging experiences.

(e) *Declining Demand for the Unskilled*

It was pointed out earlier that the Left has believed, or at least come to believe, in an inclusive pattern of full employment. The past two decades have seen a strong shift in the demand for labour away from those with few qualifications; in the race between declining demand and declining supply the former has emerged the stronger (Machin and Van Reenen, 1998). In most countries, either their relative pay, or their chances of being in work, and frequently both, have worsened considerably in the 1980s and 1990s (Glyn and Salverda, 2000). Again globalization has been in the dock. However, the evidence suggests that North–South trade has so far been a relatively minor contributor to this trend; more significant influences have been the bias of technical progress and institutional changes, including the weakening of trade unions which had been particularly effective in defending the jobs and pay of less qualified industrial workers (Howell, 2000). Although high employment overall appears to bring disproportionately great benefits to the least qualified, it may be insufficient to ensure the position of the least qualified, and deliberate policies to boost demand for their labour may very well be necessary (such as in-work benefits, labour subsidies, or the expansion of public services targeted regionally on the areas of lowest employment — see Iversen's discussion of the dilemmas posed over how to increase demand for the less qualified). Such measures in turn require higher taxation. Thus the possibility of an egalitarian pattern for full employment is closely linked to the broader issue of welfare and redistribution.

(f) *Taxation and the Welfare State*

There is a general presumption that it became increasingly difficult during the 1980s to raise the taxation necessary to fund further increases in the share of government spending. One common explanation is that globalization limits taxation, especially taxes on profits and interest income, as countries compete for direct investment and to retain portfolio funds. The EU's Expert Committee (CEC, 1992) did find less variability of tax systems across member countries in the 1980s, but a decline in corporation tax rates was balanced by cuts in the value of investment incentives so that the overall impact of corporation tax did not decline. Top rates of tax were reduced in the 1980s in all the countries considered in this issue (OECD, 1989, table 5.11). However, taxes were cut on relatively less mobile labour as well as on unearned income. Contagion of ideas about incentives may well have been more important than tax competition between countries. Taxation of capital has been rising only a bit slower than taxation of labour over the past 20 years (Rodrick, 1997). Squeezing business investment, as in the profits crisis of the 1970s, or running balance-of-payments deficits which provide resources in excess of current production, cannot support a sustainable redistribution, as the Greek experience in the 1980s, recounted by Euclid Tsakalotos, shows very clearly. In the longer term, wage and salary earners have to pay for a large part of redistribution (though the taxation may be more or less progressive).

A more significant constraint on redistribution than overseas tax competition has been the slow-down in the growth of productivity and, therefore, living standards. An example from Sweden illustrates this. At the end of the golden age of growth (1965–73), consumption out of earned income per worker was growing about 1.2 per cent per year. This was 2.6 per cent per year slower than labour productivity growth in the market sector, as increased taxation was required to finance growing transfer payments and an expansion of state services. Over the subsequent 6 years, consumption out of earned income per worker *fell* by 1.7 per cent per year (Glyn, 1992). More than half of this slow-down in consumption growth (as compared to the previous period) reflects slower productivity growth, and less than half the greater weight of redistribution as transfers grew more rapidly. A given increase in the share of public spending and taxation in GDP may be far less burdensome if it occurs when productivity growth is rising rapidly, since then it is the growth rate, rather than the absolute level of consumption, which is held back. So the 1960s were the ideal time politically for a radical extension of the welfare state; for the latecomers in Southern Europe the 1980s, with much slower productivity growth, made matters much more difficult.

A further trend militating against redistribution is raised by Vandenbroucke (1998):

> to the extent that skill has become more important as an explanatory factor
> of quite visible wage inequalities such inequalities come to have more of a

biographical character: they seem to be more related to personal history and qualifications than to class as traditionally understood.

Greater differentiation of pay, deliberately fostered as a strategy to increase incentives by management, may have had the unintended impact at the social level of justifying market outcomes. In similar vein, Przeworski suggests that increasing differentiation of the risks faced by individuals encourages private insurance catering for specific risks rather than much broader pooling of risks through state insurance. Such trends may have squeezed support for an egalitarianism going beyond a narrow conception of equality of opportunity.

This brief overview shows that the circumstances under which governments of the Left were attempting to meet the aspirations of their supporters were far from ideal. General trends *within* the world economy — growth slow-down, declining demand for less qualified workers, the epidemic of neo-liberal ideas in response to these problems — seem to have been more significant than globalization in the sense of *increasing* openness, although greater capital mobility undoubtedly played an important role in enforcing inflation convergence. The next section summarizes how the Left fared.

3. The Record

The chapters which follow give a rich picture of the diverse circumstances faced by, and the uneven results achieved by the social democratic governments surveyed; what follows is a bald overview.[2]

(a) *The Employment Record*

Employment was accorded such centrality by the Left that it is reasonable to take it as the key indicator of macroeconomic success.

Sweden's very favourable employment record during the period of Social Democrat rule in the 1980s is misleading. The collapse of its strategy meant that by 1994 the employment rate had fallen by 9 percentage points. If the Swedish record up to 1990 showed that unemployment *could* be kept at very low levels, despite the internal and external pressures, the subsequent collapse of employment showed how vulnerable high employment had become. Australia's record appears better; the rise in unemployment was small and both the employment rates and female participation rose at a time when population of working age was growing very fast. Moreover, this was

---

[2] Detailed tables with supporting data are given in Glyn (1998*a*).

achieved without much rise in wage inequality; the weakening of the
Accord allowed wage inequality to increase in the early 1990s, but there
was little change over the period as a whole. Unfortunately, unemployment stayed high as the number of jobs created still fell short of those
needed to reduce it. The pattern for Austria is somewhat similar, except
that unemployment remained relatively low. A very large rise in
women's participation rather belies Austria's reputation for a low
degree of inclusiveness; there was a moderate rise in earnings inequality, however. For the remainder of the countries the employment
record was very poor — substantial rises in unemployment and/or falls
in employment. The rapid increases in women's participation in Spain
is rather misleading in that female unemployment rose nearly as much.
As Albert Recio and Jordi Roca emphasize, the employment problem
was especially daunting in Spain, where rapid decline in agriculture and
restructuring of industry coincided with this surge in women's participation. In France, the minimum wage retained its value in relation to
average earnings in contrast to the decline in Greece and Spain and most
OECD countries (OECD, 1997a, chart 1.2) and wage dispersion (although rather high) did not grow. The one really sharp rise in pay
dispersion was in New Zealand.

As discussed earlier, governments of the Left found little alternative
but to bring inflation down in line with other countries. How successful
were they in minimizing the unemployment cost? Reducing inflation by
as much as the OECD average, while suffering a lesser rise in unemployment, would constitute success of a sort. Most of the left governments
presided over noticeably larger increases in unemployment than the
average for the OECD over the same period. Inflation was typically
reduced by more than the average fall in OECD countries, but from
higher starting points. However, the disinflation exacted a heavy toll
in terms of lost jobs. France exemplifies this pattern; over the period
1980–93, unemployment rose 3.8 per cent more than the OECD average,
while the fall in the inflation rate was 4.1 per cent more. Only Austria
stands out as having resisted the tide of rising unemployment, with the
Left benefiting from the low inflation it had inherited from the 1970s.

Austria also ranks consistently as having the most centralized and
coordinated wage-bargaining structures (see OECD, 1997a). In Sweden, however, the centralization and coordination of wage-bargaining
was decreasing, which Vartiainen blames partly on the unrealistically
egalitarian ambitions of the unions. The Australian Accord, an unexpected corporatist development in reaction to the problems faced by
the earlier Whitlam Labor government in the mid-1970s (Archer, 1992),
was widely regarded as rather effective for most of the 1980s. It
atrophied from the end of the 1980s, as centralization of bargaining

declined. Recio and Roca describe how the attempts at a social pact in Spain soon broke down, culminating in a successful general strike against the government's welfare reforms. In Greece, Tsakalotos concludes that the trade-union movement was too divided along party lines and without sufficient independence from the state, for a corporatist solution to the problem of wage-bargaining ever to have had much chance of enduring success. The histories recounted in this volume underline how difficult coordinated wage bargaining is to sustain. However, the Left has no alternative proposal for the containment of distributive conflict (see Boyer *et al.*, 1994), and the hostility of the Blair government, for example, towards anything which smacks of corporatism may prove difficult to sustain if high employment is maintained.

(b) *Equality and the Welfare State*

Sweden had the most equal distribution of household income of all the OECD countries at the beginning of the 1980s, with a household 10 per cent from the top having 2.45 times as much income as one 10 per cent from the bottom (Atkinson *et al.*, 1995, ch. 4). Austria (90/10 ratio around 3), New Zealand and France (3.5), and Australia and Spain (4 and slightly over) span the central and lower range of the inequality ranking (the ratio in the USA at the time was nearly 5). Income inequality rose very sharply under Labor in New Zealand. In Australia, Sweden (and probably Austria) there were smaller increases in inequality, similar to the rise in the USA (Atkinson *et al.*, 1995, ch. 5; Gottschalk and Smeeding, 1997, Appendix table B; OECD, 1997b). In France, the distribution of income was very stable (true also of Germany, Italy, the Netherlands, and Canada). In Spain — according to the analysis reported by Recio and Roca — and Greece, there seem to have been modest declines in inequality (Tsakloglou, 1996).

Huber and Stephens conclude that cuts in welfare entitlements and services have generally been modest as the popularity of the welfare state has made attempting deep cuts very unpopular. They suggest that differences between Left and Right in this respect have diminished (with the Left becoming less willing to raise taxation).

(c) *Supply-side Interventions*

Some of the proposals for supply-side intervention discussed earlier were implemented in full, but in circumstances which seemed to dictate an abandonment of original objectives (nationalization in France); others were watered down (wage-earner funds in Sweden); and some allowed to atrophy (planning agreements in Greece). There has been relatively little legacy from all this effort. Instead, the main thrust of policy shifted to the restoration of profitability as the basic condition for securing an investment recovery. By the end of the 1980s there had been a rather dramatic recovery of manufacturing profitability in France, Australia, and Sweden (7–12 percentage point increase in the profit share of value added—see Glyn, 1997a), with Greece, exceptionally, showing a fall. Investment rose rapidly in the later 1980s but from the very low level reached after a decade of stagnation. Only in Australia and Sweden was the share of investment in GDP higher at the end of the 1980s boom than during 1974–9, and in those two countries it fell by 4–5 per cent of GDP in the ensuing recessions.

Moreover, the brief burst of investment at the end of the 1980s was concentrated in the service sectors, suggesting that the Left's focus on the manufacturing sector, because of its significance for international trade, had little impact, or at least was swamped by other influences. Here again, financial deregulation, sharply criticized by Quiggin for its baneful influence in Australia, probably played an important part.

The SPD Chancellor, Helmut Schmidt, had made the case for relying on profitability in 1976: 'The profits of enterprises today are the investments of tomorrow and the investments of tomorrow are the employment of the day after' (quoted by Bhadhuri, 1993). Having done all that could be expected of them in terms of ensuring profitability, social democrats discovered that it was far from being a sufficient condition for a high level, and appropriate distribution of investment.

Nevertheless, confidence on the left that governments and unions could interfere purposefully to reshape the pattern of production evaporated. Ensuring that the playing field slopes in the appropriate direction (infrastructure, education, corporate taxation) is seen as a legitimate, even necessary role for the government, but giving directions on tactics, let alone picking the team, is decidedly not. Most of the governments discussed in this volume ended up by accepting the privatization of state industry and assets.

While the economic legacy of the attempts by the labour movement in the 1970s and early 1980s to constrain the power of capital has been meagre indeed, the political legacy has been extremely important. The prominent Swedish economist Erik Lundberg wrote in 1985, 'The fall of the Swedish model is, at bottom, a political development. The present *political crisis* [his emphasis], which has involved intense confrontation between socialist and non-socialist parties, since the middle seventies, has created a stage of uncertainty and bewilderment' (1985, pp. 31–2). Assar Lindbeck (1997, p. 1277) put it thus:

> The unions' ambitions to gain power peaked in the second half of the 1970s, when they proposed the creation of union controlled, tax financed wage-

earner funds designed to take over the bulk of ownership of Swedish corporations on the stock market. The proposal may, more generally, be seen as a unilateral cancellation of the implicit cooperative contract between labor and capital.

Lindbeck goes on to refer to the subsequent employers' offensive which was described in graphic terms by Robert Taylor (*Financial Times*, 8 November 1990) under the headline 'Business plans five-year campaign to end Swedish economic model'. He reported that this was a plan to 'transform social-democratic Sweden into a robust free-market economy', aiming to 'destroy the vestiges of the famed Swedish economic model, with its collectivist values of equality and solidarity'.

If the proposals from social democracy to control capital can be seen as flowing from the extended period of high employment, then the political offensive by the employers bears out Kalecki's remarkable prediction in 1943:

> the *maintenance* [Kalecki's emphasis] of full employment would give new impetus to the opposition of business leaders. Indeed, under a regime of permanent full employment, the 'sack' would cease to play its role as a disciplinary measure. The social position of the boss would be undermined, and the self-assurance and class consciousness of the working class would grow. Strikes for wage increases and improvements in conditions of work would create political tensions. . . . 'discipline in the factories' and 'political stability' are more appreciated than profits by business leaders. Their class instinct tells them that lasting full employment is unsound from their point of view, and that unemployment is an integral part of the 'normal' capitalist system. (1990 [1943], p. 351)

The one respect in which the labour movement's offensive had a lasting impact on the 'supply side' of the economy concerned employment rights. In many countries in the 1970s and early 1980s employment rights were strengthened or extended (to part-time workers, for example). Coverage of collective bargaining agreements was generally maintained, and in France it increased to 95 per cent (even though union membership declined to 9 per cent).[3] While less threatening than planning agreements, let alone nationalization, extension of employment rights did represent a constraint on managerial prerogatives, limiting 'labour-market flexibility' from the point of view of employers. The OECD has been engaged in a militant campaign to reverse these developments. Ironically, in Spain, limitations on dismissal were inher-

[3] Sweden and Spain, with union membership at 80 per cent and 9 per cent of the work-force in 1980 respectively were exceptional in recording increases in membership (about 10 per cent of the work-force in each case) over the 1980s and early 1990s (OECD, 1997a, table 3.3).

ited from the Franco period. Recio and Roca dispute the common perception that these were unreasonably draconian and take the Partido Socialista Obrero Español (PSOE) government to task for accepting the widespread use of temporary contracts in order to circumvent them.[4]

Shifts in the state of relations between capital and labour are not susceptible of precise measurement, but comparing share prices with average wages gives some indication of the balance of advantage. Between 1973 and the Left's accession to power, stock-market prices fell by one-half compared to wages in several countries, and much more in Spain. There was a general recovery of share prices under the left governments under review here, with the exception of Greece and New Zealand. Relative to wages, share prices rose by about one-half in Austria and Spain (similar to the rise in Germany over the period 1980–95), nearly doubled in France and Australia (as in the UK), and tripled in Sweden (matching the rise in the USA). Despite the restoration of profitability and confidence the investment response remained anaemic throughout the countries surveyed here.

4. Conclusions

This introduction has examined the record of left governments during the 1980s and 1990s in the light of their aspirations to maintain or achieve full employment, to ensure an egalitarian distribution of welfare, and to enhance democratic control over the allocation of capital and the organization of work places.

Macroeconomic starting points were unpromising; inflation was high and profits squeezed in many countries and there was a need to cope with rapid structural change (run-down in agriculture in Southern Europe, increase in women's participation). The context was difficult — slow growth throughout the OECD and the pressures favouring disinflationary policies. There were some bright spots in the employment record. During the 1980s employment grew very rapidly in Australia, including a major increase in women's participation, and without an increase in wage inequality; unemployment stayed very low in Sweden, and in Austria high employment was preserved and made more inclusive as women's participation rose. But elsewhere unemployment rose rapidly and/or employment rates fell, and in New Zealand wage inequality shot up as well. Overall, the cost of reducing

[4] The failure to find a robust effect of more employment protection on unemployment (see Nickell, 1997; OECD, 1999; Blanchard and Wolfers, 2000) suggests that its impact is dependent on other features of the economy.

inflation from higher inherited rates than the OECD average was a greater increase in unemployment than in the OECD as a whole. Given the priority accorded to employment, this record must be reckoned as extremely disappointing.

The context of slow productivity growth was unfavourable for an extension of welfare spending and redistribution, which would squeeze take-home pay, and the record of left governments was mixed. Important expansions of welfare were achieved in those countries with the weakest welfare states. New Zealand is really the anomalous case, with inequality rising as fast during the short period in office of Labor as in the UK under Thatcher. In Australia, Sweden (and probably Austria) inequality rose as fast as the rise in the USA (though from very much less unequal starting points). Income inequality fell somewhat in Greece and Spain, but this seems typical of Southern European countries, where structural change was rapid. In France, income inequality was stable (with a heavy cost in public spending) but non-socialist governments brought a similar outcome in Germany and Canada, for example. Perhaps the best summary is that the range of outcomes for the group of countries here was not much different from that of OECD countries as a whole; again social democrats might have expected better.

The measures to plan, control, widen the ownership of, or nationalize private firms, so prominent in the discussions of the 1970s on the left, have sunk with little trace, except for a legacy of business hostility towards the whole social democratic model which governments of the Left, such as UK Labour, have been at pain to dispel. A high level of investment implies that demand can be kept high without budget deficits and that the capital stock will increase rapidly and provide the resources to accommodate wage pressure and fund improvements in the welfare state. Having abandoned the often half-hearted attempts to pressurize private capital into such investment, governments of the Left had little option but to rely on a restoration of profitability to do the trick. Wage restraint was indeed achieved, through rising unemployment or coordinated bargaining or both, but the investment response was erratic and especially weak in manufacturing which is still of central importance for trade and for jobs. Here again the experience of countries under social democratic rule was not untypical of OECD countries (Glyn, 1997a). Capital did not deliver high investment in return for high profits, but social democratic governments have seen no alternative but to redouble their efforts to create even more favourable conditions.

An optimistic interpretation of this experience would emphasize that the circumstances of the 1980s and 1990s — slow growth, the pressure for disinflation, excessively tight macroeconomic policy in

Europe, private investment still hesitant after the previous decades of instability—were extremely unfavourable for governments of the Left. Coordinated bargaining, though subject to many pressures and vulnerable to ill-judged macroeconomic policy, survives as an alternative to unemployment as a regulator of social conflict, and one whose relevance will grow if the more favourable macroeconomic conditions persist and unemployment rates decline. With the exception of New Zealand, wholesale capitulation to conservative economic policies was avoided by governments of the Left and retreats on income inequality and welfare-state provision have been limited. The generalized claim that equality involves too high a cost in terms of efficiency has been shown to be ill-founded and neo-liberalism is on the defensive against growing demands for financial and environmental regulation. On the basis of a renewed appeal to social solidarity, employment can be raised, employment rights extended, environmental concerns addressed, and egalitarian shifts in the distribution of welfare preserved or extended. However, regaining such a position requires above all that the costs (wage restraint and tax increases) are openly canvassed and campaigned for, a task that social democracy has clearly ducked for the present. If higher employment could be sustained for an extended period, however, then bargaining power would tilt back towards labour and the issue of democratizing ownership and control in the economy, submerged in the 1980s and 1990s, would surely return to revitalize the Left's agenda.

An alternative interpretation, closer to the position of a majority of the contributors to this volume, would see governments of the Left succumbing to remorseless pressure, both ideological and from the economic constraints they faced, to accept orthodox policies—priority to inflation control, limitation of overall tax burdens, labour-market deregulation. The Left can still intervene in valuable ways to stem the tide of rising inequality—more in-work benefits for the low-paid, protection of the most vulnerable when welfare states are reformed, targeting the extremes of inequality of opportunity which are obviously economically inefficient. However valuable in themselves, these are strictly limited objectives and if they really represent the limits to social democracy's vision, then as Perry Anderson put it: 'what kind of movement will it change into?' (1994, p. 16).

2

Understanding Swedish Social Democracy: Victims of Success?

JUHANA VARTIAINEN*

1. Introduction: Success or Failure?

Has the 'Swedish model' been a success or a failure? Such a formulation of the question suggests a view of economic and social policy models as a set of specific policy programmes, the success of which is evaluated by using criteria such as economic growth and employment. In terms of such criteria, the Swedish model has lost its international appeal and is increasingly seen as a failure. In particular, the relatively poor growth performance of the Swedish economy during the last 20 years and the high unemployment of the 1990s have contributed to this lack-lustre picture.

The Swedish model has generated an enormous research literature and there is no shortage of analyses and surveys — ranging from apologetic to sympathetic, sceptical, critical, or even inimical — of the Swedish experience. Among recent contributions, Lindbeck (1997) suggests an enlightened analysis of the Swedish experience and the volume by Freeman *et al.* (1997) contains a variety of useful economic analyses of the Swedish welfare state.

This paper suggests an economic and historical analysis of Swedish social democracy and its economic policies in particular. Taking the large literature on the Swedish welfare state as a starting point, we will emphasize the following insights.

First, we focus explicitly on the social democratic determinants of the Swedish model. We see Swedish social democratic economic policies as a series of political projects that reflect a strong underlying ideology of egalitarianism and a continuous and 'heroic' endeavour to

* Labour Institute for Economic Research, Helsinki.

I am grateful to Andrew Glyn, Jukka Pekkarinen, Bob Rowthorn, and two referees for very useful comments.

make the two ends of radical socialism and successful capitalism meet. Swedish social democrats form a political movement with extremely egalitarian political preferences. Much of the history of Swedish social democracy can be understood as a series of remarkable political interventions seeking to make these preferences materialize in society's economic outcomes. With hindsight, many of these political initiatives have been failures. Yet they were introduced at times when hindsight was not available and the structural constraints of the market economy were less understood than now.

A striving for an egalitarian outcome can thus be seen as a super-ideology that has motivated Swedish economic and social policies, at different times and in different circumstances. A neoclassical interpretation of such a political programme could be that it reflects a very strong aversion to risk: in a society where all 'slots' imply a decent standard of living, any individual knows that he or she will not be exposed to extreme poverty. An alternative interpretation could run in Rawlsian terms: maximize society's overall welfare behind a veil of ignorance, which leads to a social weighting function that is biased towards the well-being of the least advantaged. Whatever one's analytical conceptualization of these political preferences, taking them as basic data is a useful starting point for understanding social democratic policies in Sweden. Thus, although it is customary to identify a 'model' such as the Swedish one with a set of specific programmes and policies, such programmes can ultimately be seen in instrumental terms, as devices designed to realize a set of underlying preferences.

Second, the commonplace view of Sweden as a 'model' tends to obscure the fact that most of the policies were not the product of a centralized intellectual authority, but, rather, a series of compromises influenced by several political actors, such as the trade unions, the social democratic government, and the business community. We try to show why these policies arose and give an assessment of their success, in terms both of their own objectives and of overall economic performance. In particular, the Swedish social democratic hegemony was not a hegemony of an enlightened technocracy but that of a labour movement which sought to conquer state power while remaining an autonomous political actor. This reflected the character of Swedish society, which, like its Nordic neighbours, was already strongly organized and mobilized in the 19th century. Popular social movements, such as the labour movement, the sports movements, the temperance movement, and various autonomous churches and revivalist religious movements, had contributed to a culture where it was natural for individuals to engage and express themselves within organizations.

A concrete expression of these traditions is the fact that the Swedish trade unions have been an active and equal partner in the formulation of economic policies. This observation questions the simplistic view of the political process where a centralized enlightened authority maximizes the common good by manipulating the typical agent's behaviour. In Swedish social democratic ideology, the trade unions are not an external agent whose behaviour should be influenced by appropriate incentive structures, but, instead, are seen as an organic part of the decision-making body. This constrains the set of feasible policy measures to combat the structural labour-market problems of the 1990s.

The paper is organized as follows. Sections 2–4 describe three crucial areas of Swedish policies: the expansion of the public sector, the labour-market model, and macroeconomic management. The labour-market model will get most attention, since, at least at this stage, it seems to be the most critical issue in Swedish economic management. Section 5 binds the threads together and suggests an assessment of the Swedish experience as well as some speculations on the future of Swedish social democratic economics. I argue there that the Swedish social democrats are a victim of their own success; many of their policies were rational and sustainable until they were pushed too far. On the other hand, although the Swedish welfare state is in need of economic reform, the ultimate test of a political movement is whether it can impose its own preferences on the majority of the electorate, and in that sense the Swedish social democracy's achievement has been remarkable.

2. The Welfare State

The great structural achievement of Swedish social democracy is the growth of the world's largest public sector within a market economy. Evaluated by social democratic standards, it is a success story. The public sector has grown steadily during social democratic rule. The GDP share of total public expenditure and some of its components in years 1950–95 are depicted in Figure 1. In the span of 45 years, the GDP share of total public expenditure grew from about 25 per cent to over 60 per cent. Since the end of the 1980s, it has just about stabilized. The impact of public-sector growth on the allocation of labour has been quite dramatic as well. As shown in Figure 2, the public sector has absorbed most of the growth in the labour force in the years 1950–95. From the 1960s onwards, all significant employment growth has occurred in services provided by the local government. During the latter half of the 1990s, as economic growth has resumed and a programme of budget consolidation has been carried out, the GDP

Figure 1
Public-sector Expenditure as a Share of GDP, in Current Prices

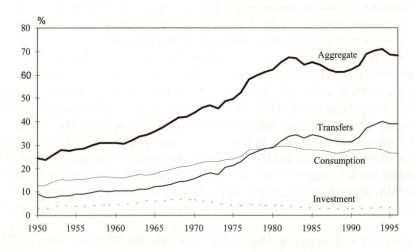

Source: Statistics Sweden.

Figure 2
Cumulative Change in Public Employment, Private Employment, and Population in Sweden, 1950–92

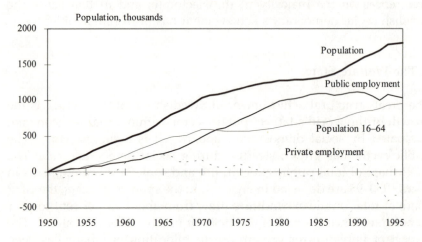

Source: Statistics Sweden, Magnus Henrekson, and Gunnarsson and Lindh (1997).

share of general government expenditure has shrunk by about 5 per cent, mainly because of transfer cuts.

The objective of this expansion has been the provision of basic public services and income redistribution, both as a goal in itself and as insurance against unemployment, sickness, and old age. Thus, an evening out of the distribution of well-being has relied both on socialized consumption of services and on redistribution of incomes through progressive taxation and transfers. This redistribution has been effective. Whatever measure of income equality one chooses, Sweden usually emerges as the one, among developed nations, with least income inequality, or among the two or three most egalitarian economies.[1] By international standards, the distribution of wages is even, and the high participation in work of women further increases equality in wage incomes. The redistribution system makes the distribution of disposable income even more egalitarian, and, on top of an even distribution of disposable income, the Swedish public sector provides a large amount of socialized consumption.

These structural developments were qualitatively no different from those of other developed countries, but they went furthest in Sweden. As pointed out by Lindbeck (1997), it is only from the late 1960s and early 1970s onwards that Sweden begins to stand out internationally for the size of its welfare state provision. It also seems clear that this expansive phase of the welfare state is now over, as suggested by Figure 1. This does not necessarily imply that an ideological realignment and a comprehensive retreat of the welfare state are likely. Although many critics have recently pointed out potential economic problems associated with such an extensive supply of income transfers and public services, there is no reason to assume that they do not correspond to the political preferences of the Swedish electorate. Indeed, most surveys tend to indicate that political support for extensive public services and redistribution has not eroded in Sweden. For example, Svallfors (1995) compares questionnaire data from the years 1981, 1986, and 1992 and shows that the popular support for welfare state arrangements remains robust. Although people are critical of extensive bureaucracy and suspicious of misuse of welfare benefits, their commitment to the welfare state remains strong (see also Svallfors, 1996). Even the extensive austerity programme enacted by the Göran Persson government — budget savings amounting to about 8 per cent of GDP — was motivated by fiscal reasons instead of being inspired by a fundamental political reorientation.

As to the political aspects of the Swedish welfare state, it is clear that the growth of the public sector and public-sector employment has cemented the social democrats' position of power. It has created political preferences that favour social democracy: since more than half of the economy's wage-earners work either directly or indirectly

[1] For different kinds of comparisons, see Björklund and Freeman (1997).

within the realm of the public economy, electoral support for public transfers and services is going to be robust. Any visitor to Sweden is struck by the high degree of public support for the extensive welfare state and high taxation.[2] As pointed out by Lindbeck (1997), the ratio of 'tax-financed' to 'market-financed' individuals had risen to 1.83 (highest of all countries) in 1995, from 1.51 in 1990 and 0.38 in 1960. This means that the incomes of the majority of Swedish people are determined in political processes.

The experience of the Swedish welfare state has generated a large body of critical economic literature; for surveys, see Lindbeck (1997) and Freeman et al. (1997). This discussion has focused either on incentive problems and economic efficiency or on the relatively poor growth performance and low productivity growth of the Swedish economy.

As to economic efficiency, the studies have indicated complex and mutually counteracting mechanisms. The tax-benefit system encourages participation in work, since benefit levels are closely related to earnings (Aronsson and Walker, 1997). After a first tax reform in the early 1970s, incomes were assessed individually rather than on a family basis, so that work became more attractive for spouses. Furthermore, female labour supply has been encouraged by heavily subsidized child care and care for the elderly outside the household. Thus, participation in the labour force is encouraged in general and for women in particular. The Swedish model has socialized and drawn into the public production sphere many such activities that would in other societies be taken care of by the family or the household. This has resulted in a female participation rate of about 75 per cent. Such characteristics are a direct consequence of Swedish social democracy's political aspirations: equality between genders has been seen to require that men and women participate on an equal footing in the world of work. As emphasized in Rosen (1997), there is a strong gender dimension to the Swedish public economy. Free or subsidized child-care services are an important advantage for Swedish women, and an attempt to dismantle these systems would probably fail because of women's resistance.

However, many individual aspects of the transfer and benefit system have probably worked against labour supply. According to many studies, the high marginal tax rates of the 1970s and 1980s produced substantial welfare losses. Such distortions were addressed and to some extent rectified in the comprehensive tax reform of the early 1990s (see Agell et al., 1995). Similarly, there was a large increase in the use and possible misuse of sickness benefits once these became

---

[2] On attitudes, see Svallfors (1996).

more generous (the replacement ratio had risen to over 90 per cent in the late 1980s) and their monitoring less stringent.

It has also been argued that the high level of transfers and benefits increases reservation wages. Indeed, it is the advent of substantial unemployment that has raised the question of whether the Swedish social safety net is compatible with an efficient labour market and high employment. In a nutshell, the Swedish labour-market policy regime has been characterized by high replacement ratios, limited duration of unemployment benefits, and large investments in such active measures as vocational counselling, support for job mobility, and retraining (Forslund and Krueger, 1997). One obvious hypothesis has been that the high replacement ratio of Swedish unemployment benefits[3] lowers search activity and prolongs unemployment. Aronsson and Walker (1997) argue that high unemployment and sickness benefits do keep the reservation wage at a high level.

However, it has also been characteristic of Swedish active labour-market policy that an unemployed person is eligible for generous unemployment benefit for a limited time period only. This combination of benefits that are generous but strictly limited in time and of active retraining worked well in conditions of low unemployment, but when the supply of jobs is limited anyway, the costs of the system become quite high in relation to benefits (Lindbeck, 1997; Aronsson and Walker, 1997; Forslund and Krueger, 1997). Again, such a system is a direct consequence of the social democrats' political preferences: the trade unions were obviously in favour of generous unemployment compensation, and the way to combine generosity with efficiency was to use public resources to enhance the search and retraining process for the individual worker.

Finally, it has been asked to what extent the size of the public sector can be blamed for the sluggish growth performance of the Swedish economy during the last 20 years. Swedish growth is discussed by Korpi (1996), Henrekson (1996), Agell (1996), and Dowrick (1996). This discussion has not produced an ultimate proof of the claim that the extensive welfare state has slowed down growth, but, as pointed out by Agell (1996), it is clear that the Swedish welfare state has needed and needs reforming.

---

[3] The replacement ratio was 90 per cent in the 1980s, and it was subsequently decreased to 80 per cent by the Bildt government (1991–4) and to 75 per cent by the social democratic Persson government (1994–). however, it was again increased to 80 per cent in September 1997.

3. The Labour-market Model

The main goals of the Swedish trade union movement have been associated with (i) full employment, (ii) technical progress, (iii) an egalitarian distribution of wage income, (iv) an active labour-market policy, and (v) collective capital formation. The trade unions and, especially, the blue-collar central trade union federation, LO, have been active partners in the shaping of social democratic policies in Sweden and generators of ideas on economic policy. About 90 per cent of Swedish wage-earners belong to labour unions and the trade unions played an important role in the labour movement's ascent to power. The basic historical compromise between the labour-market partners was established in the 1930s, after an earlier history of turbulent industrial relations and costly work stoppages. When the social democrats had gained effective control of the state, the labour-market parties signed the Basic Agreement of Saltsjöbaden 1938. They thereby agreed to try to settle their differences without using such mutually harmful and costly procedures as strikes and lockouts. That reflected a reorientation of LO strategy: as the trade union movement had grown stronger and its twin sister, the political labour movement, had gained control of the state, the trade unions recognized that they could not exercise their power without regard to general macroeconomic objectives. This implied that they should play down the importance of specific group interests and look at the interests of workers in general. It also led to an emphatic approval of technical progress and rationalization.[4] This accords with Katzenstein's (1984, 1985) interpretation of corporatism in small open economies: the labour movement in such countries must recognize that its members' welfare depends on the economy's successful adaptation to a competitive world market.

(a) *The Rehn–Meidner Model*

The 1950s presented the parties to the labour market in Sweden with the question of how to reconcile full employment with price stability. During that decade, the idea that a striving for full employment by Keynesian means might run into inflationary problems gained general acceptance in Europe. The proposed solution was incomes policy, a direct intervention into the process of wage formation by the govern-

---

[4]See Tilton (1991, pp. 191–2). Tilton cites the 'committee of 15' of LO: 'In a democratic state the working class cannot separate its fate from the nation's. The working class is a significant part of contemporary society. The workers must accept their responsibility, but with suitable economic and political means they must also strongly emphasize and powerfully assert their demands and their rights' (p. 192).

ment, or a voluntary policy of moderation exercised by the labour-market parties.

Direct negotiation of wage rates by the peak organizations had been used in wartime Sweden, but all parties had interpreted them as exceptional emergency measures. During the 1950s, social democratic authorities became keen on getting the LO to endorse a coordinated policy of wage restraint. The LO and its member unions were concerned with their internal cohesion and their ability to mobilize workers and were reluctant to tailor their policies to the Social Democratic Party's economic policy. Yet the challenge of inflation had to be taken seriously, since the very objective of full employment would otherwise be jeopardized.

The LO's alternative, conceived by its brilliant non-academic economist, Gösta Rehn, was to focus on the sources of unemployment and inflationary pressures.[5] General fiscal demand management was indeed to be cautious enough to avoid an inflationary tightening of the labour market. Low aggregate demand would lead to the threat of unemployment in those firms in which productivity was below average. General fiscal expansion would lead to bottlenecks in other firms and thus to inflation.

With a tight fiscal policy, full employment requires that new job opportunities exist elsewhere in the economy. This would be ensured by two means: first, an active manpower policy that encouraged geographical and professional mobility, and, second, a wage-setting system that prevented the workers of the better-than-average firms from extracting the rents that their productivity generated. That meant imposing a uniform wage level on all firms.

Thus, the famous Rehn–Meidner model was originally conceived as a functional solution to the problem of inflation, given that full employment was a prime policy objective. Gösta Rehn regarded even the 'solidaristic' element of the model as an instrument for attaining price stability. If the structure of wages was generally considered as just, inter-union wage rivalry would be dampened and no inflationary price–wage spiral would arise to hamper inflation control, as had happened in the 1940s.

Such a centralized wage-setting would create extra profits in the best firms and allow them to expand their activities. This mechanism would encourage structural transformation. High profits were supposed to encourage the growth of the most competent firms, while less productive firms would be compelled either to increase their productivity or get out of business. That would create structural unemployment in the

[5] See Martin (1984) and Tilton (1991) for these discussions.

shrinking sectors of the economy. That problem would be addressed by the government, which had to develop new programmes to minimize the costs of transition and maximize labour mobility. In the 1960s, the Swedish government indeed developed a network of training centres and started subsidizing the moving expenses of migrating workers.[6]

Inasmuch as the policy would decrease the average profits of the industry and thus decrease the supply of funds for new investment, there was a role for the state as well; a part of the increase in wages was to be channelled to new investment through public saving. The concrete institutional arrangement was provided by a pension fund associated with a new old-age pension scheme (see Scharpf, 1991, p. 92).

(b) *Rehn–Meidner at Work: Macroeconomic and Microeconomic Evaluation*

The Rehn–Meidner model was actively debated during the 1950s, but ultimately accepted as the rules of the game at the end of the decade. By that time, the main trade union federations, as well as the employers, had accepted the principles of coordinated wage formation. The Swedish employers were at that time supporters of the idea of coordination, since it seemed to offer a way of mitigating the effects of inter-union rivalry on aggregate wages (de Geer, 1992). The institutions of wage bargaining were threefold. The central organizations concluded so-called *frame agreements* (*ramavtal*) that specified the scope for wage increases. The individual unions would then negotiate the *collective agreements* that have the status of binding contracts under Swedish labour law. These collective agreements were finally applied in plant-level negotiations.

The actual outcome of the labour-market model can be evaluated from two points of view: the microeconomics of wage differentials and the macroeconomics of inflation and employment. As to the latter, the main achievement of full employment was attained. In that sense, the goods were delivered at least from the 1950s through the 1980s, although it is more difficult to say to what extent that was due to the labour-market model. Labour mobility, both geographical and between firms, was also high in Sweden by international standards throughout the 1960s and 1970s (Faxén *et al.*, 1988).

The inflation record, too, was satisfactory in the 1960s, when Sweden's inflation rate was equal to the OECD average. However, accelerating inflationary tendencies started to surface in the 1970s, at increasing intensity. The solidaristic outcome was increasingly 'bought'

[6] The 1960s indeed became a period of high internal mobility, although it is questionable how much of this was due to the labour-market model (see Edin and Topel, 1997).

with high nominal increases, and the role of local wage drift became gradually decisive in boosting wages.

Wage drift, i.e. wage increases in excess of the collectively agreed contract increases, have been an essential element of all collective wage arrangements in the Nordic countries. Wage drift would, even in the best of Swedish worlds, provide a necessary safety valve within a centralized bargaining system. It provides an element of flexibility that otherwise would be missing and without which the task of enforcing a centralized agreement might have been even more difficult. If economic policy allows a moderate but positive rate of inflation, the manager of the firm is also provided with some discretionary room to remunerate the performance of the best workers.

It has been argued on theoretical grounds that a multi-tier bargaining system such as Sweden's has a built-in inflationary bias (see Holden, 1990, 1991). The argument goes as follows. In a typical wage round, the central bargainers agreed on a general wage increase, which was followed in each industry-wide collective agreement. This contract must then be applied locally, at the plant level. Formally, the local discussions were to be conducted under an industrial peace clause, as collective agreements in Sweden (as in the other Nordic countries) have the force of law. In practice, however, the collective agreement treats the local bargaining parties asymmetrically. The firm must anyway pay out the increased wages, since doing otherwise would be a verifiable breach of the collective contract. The workers, however, can work inefficiently or protest in other ways that cannot be contested in a court, until they get an extra wage increase. Thus, there will always be positive drift. If that drift is foreseen by the central bargainers, it need not jeopardize the employment objective since the central bargainers can adjust their own preferred wage increase by the amount of predicted drift. If inflation is low, however, attaining the goals of full employment and low inflation may require that the central bargainers write nominal wage cuts into their agreement, which is probably not feasible.[7] It has become a common view in Sweden that the multi-tier bargaining structure as such is inflationary.

One interesting aspect of Swedish wage drift concerns the role of local bargaining. In Swedish labour law, collective agreements are binding after they have been signed by the union and the corresponding employer federation. However, the collective agreements have usually been formulated in such a way that a part of the general wage increase is explicitly deferred to local negotiations. Thus, with an

[7] See Holden (1990, 1991) for a fully fledged game-theoretic argument.

overall increase of 5 per cent, say, it could be agreed that 3 per cent would be guaranteed to everybody while the remaining 2 per cent would be allocated in local bargains. This opens a new bargaining front at the company and work-place level. In Finland and Germany, other fairly corporatistic countries, the system is 'tighter' in the sense that, as a rule, no local bargains are assumed to take place. In Finland, once the collective agreement has been signed, the employers have the right to apply this agreement unilaterally by just increasing everyone's wage by the specified amount and resuming normal business management. With no additional local bargaining front, one would expect that drift would be lower, too, and this has, in fact, been the case throughout the 1970s and 1980s, as the studies of Eriksson *et al.* (1990) and Calmfors and Forslund (1990) indicate.

The 'microeconomic' part of the Rehn–Meidner model, i.e. the evening out of relative wage differentials, seems to have been effective in carrying out its stated objectives. Studies of worker flows and productivity increases lend support to the argument that the evening out of wages indeed contributed to an accelerated structural transformation and an associated increase in productivity growth.[8] Edin and Topel (1997) have shown that inter-sector worker flows in the 1960s and 1970s indeed followed a clear pattern: the most productive sectors expanded while less productive sectors decreased their work-force. As to actual productivity, Hibbs and Locking (1995, 1997) have produced tentative estimates which show that the evening out of wage differentials between firms and between sectors was associated with higher productivity growth. Yet a large part of that growth was to be 'eaten' by the subsequent forced evening out of differentials even within firms and between tasks and competence levels, as we argue below.

(c) *Hitting the Limits of Political Intervention: Radical Wage Policy and Wage-earner Funds*

The Rehn–Meidner principles of coordinated wage settlements and equal remuneration for equal work were not at odds with the requirements of a successful market economy.[9] However, the late 1960s saw the Swedish trade unions starting to embark on an ambitious extension of this policy. First, the solidaristic wage policy, originally conceived as 'same pay for similar work' was increasingly transformed into 'same

---

[8] Moene and Wallerstein (1993, 1995) construct theoretical models of vintage capital which clarify these mechanisms.

[9] As has been pointed out by many economists, the idea of 'equal pay for equal work' corresponds in principle to the outcome of a competitive process (Ramaswamy, 1992; Moene and Wallerstein, 1993, 1995; Edin and Topel, 1997).

Table 1
Changes in the Coefficient of Variation of Swedish Wage-earners' Wages

	Phase I 1962–70	Phase II 1970–83	Breakdown 1983–93
Total variation	–0.34	–0.61	+0.49
Within industry	–0.26	–0.63	+0.39
Within firm	n.a.	–0.60	+0.41
Between industries	–0.50	–0.58	+0.76
Between firms	n.a.	–0.46	+0.56

Source: Hibbs and Locking (1997).

pay for all work'.[10] Second, the LO launched its controversial initiative for wage-earner funds.

The transformation of the LO's wage policy towards a more radicalized version of solidarism reflected the strength of left-wing objectives in the 1960s and the 1970s. With hindsight, it can be characterized as a policy 'mistake' that has led to many subsequent difficulties, as we shall see below. Yet it was a genuine reflection of the preferences of LO membership and a movement towards such a version of solidarism was the only way of implementing – albeit very imperfectly – *some* kind of coordinated wage moderation in the radicalized political atmosphere of the 1960s and 1970s, when an upward push for the low wage groups came to be seen as a legitimate objective in its own right. The radicalized phase seems to have made a real impact on wage differentials. Whereas the original phase of the model resulted in a clear evening out of wage differentials between firms and between industries, the latter phase led to a dramatic equalization of wages within firms and between tasks and competence levels. A comprehensive picture of the evolution of wage differentials is presented in Table 1, borrowed from Hibbs and Locking (1997). The table reports changes in a measure of wage dispersion for three phases of the Swedish labour-market model. We see that intra-firm differentials narrowed considerably during the radicalized phase of the 1970s.

As described by Pontusson and Swenson (1993) and de Geer (1992), this striving for a radical evening out of all wage differentials was the most important factor that contributed to the Swedish employers' rejection of coordinated bargaining. From the early 1980s onwards, the employers strove consistently to change the collective wage-bargaining practices. Moreover, as has been shown by Hibbs and Locking (1996),

[10] See Meidner (1974).

the radical solidarism boosted *average* wage drift: since all firms were compelled to pay out the higher wage increases of low-wage workers and some firms and workers would resist the change in the distribution of wages implied by the solidaristic wage settlements, they would agree on higher wage increases for those workers whose relative position would otherwise deteriorate. Thus, the solidaristic policies contributed to a higher wage drift that partly annihilated the overall moderating effect of coordinated bargaining.[11] Furthermore, according to the estimates of Hibbs and Locking (1995, 1997), the narrowing of wage differentials probably slowed down productivity growth as well. Their results indicate that the narrowing of intra-firm differentials slowed down productivity growth, whereas productivity growth increased with narrower inter-firm and inter-sector wage differentials.

From the point of view of employers, radical solidaristic policy was an unacceptable political opening which hindered their profit objectives. The wage-earner funds were another initiative that they would not accommodate. As of now, the failed fund project is most often seen as a left-wing whim, and the publication of Meidner's report on wage-earner funds indeed represented the high-water mark of egalitarianism in the Swedish labour movement.[12] Yet even the fund project was originally conceived as a logical repercussion of the labour-market model. A solidaristic wage policy left high profits in those companies which had been able to increase their productivity more than the average. This had left the LO with the problem of justifying these 'extra profits' to workers. The idea of those firms and sectors being able to use these internal funds to invest and expand had been present all along, but in the radical political atmosphere of the 1960s it had led to the discussion of increased concentration of Swedish corporate ownership.[13] Seen from this perspective, the funds provided a working solution. They would keep the sound principle of 'equal pay for equal work' and thereby preserve the Rehn–Meidner engine of structural transformation. As they would increase state ownership in the most efficient part of the economy, they presented an operational way of meeting the radical and socialist aspirations of a large part of the social democratic electorate. According to Meidner's original projections, the

---

[11] During many years in the 1970s and 1980s, the centrally agreed wage increases would not even have guaranteed existing real wages. Thus, drift became increasingly the most important element in wage increases.

[12] This is the assessment of, for example, Tilton (1991) in his careful study of social democratic ideology.

[13] Concentration of corporate ownership had indeed taken place, and it could to some extent even be blamed on the labour-market model.

recommended rate of growth of the funds' assets implied that they would control about half of the value of Swedish companies' shares within 20 years.[14]

From the outset, the policy debate on the wage-earner funds was bitter. The proposal aroused a fierce opposition within the business community but even the labour movement was divided. The project was launched in a diluted form, and the fund project was subsequently cancelled by the Bildt government of 1992–5.

(d) *Employers on the Offensive – Breakdown of the Model*

The coordinated wage bargaining system was plagued by internal and political contradictions from its very beginning, but by and large it worked during the 1950s and 1960s. The radicalized solidaristic policies of the 1970s, however, led to accentuated contradictions that finally brought down peak-level wage negotiations.[15] Such contradictions appeared between labour and employers as well as within each side. The LO member unions remained mostly loyal to the principles of coordination, but the white-collar and public-sector unions gradually became tired of adjusting their wages according to the wage claims of others. Already by the end of the 1960s, they had renounced LO leadership in wage setting (Scharpf, 1991).

The decisive offensive against peak-level bargaining, however, arose from the employers spearheaded by the influential Verkstadsföreningen, the metal industry's employer confederation. Engineering employers began to call into question the system as early as the beginning of the 1970s. From the point of view of technically advanced open-sector firms, the radical version of the centralized model had many flaws. First, the centralized system provided these firms with little discretion on wage differentials and incentive pay systems. Second, the levelling of all wages started to decrease the supply of skilled workers for technologically advanced tasks within manufacturing. And, finally, there was the question of the relative wage increases in the open and sheltered sectors of the economy, which also for a long time divided the employers' position. The open-sector employers felt that the centralized agreements reflected too much the ability to pay of the sheltered-sector firms and employees, especially

---

[14] Meidner's idea drew inspiration from the literature on profit-sharing, too.

[15] See Pontusson and Swenson (1993), de Geer (1992), Flanagan *et al.* (1983), and Martin (1984) for historical and analytical accounts of the erosion of the centralized model.

retailing, a sector in which it was easier to pass increased costs on to product prices.[16]

These attitudes were exacerbated by the wage explosion of 1974–6, which to a large extent reflected inter-union rivalry and the attempt of some unions to receive compensation for the higher drift of other industries. 'Wage-drift guarantees', frequently negotiated between the unions, were a clear symptom of the crisis of the model.

The centralized bargaining system finally broke down in 1983, when the Swedish metal industry's employer association was able to conclude a separate agreement with its workers. That reflected the employers' disillusionment with the centralized and solidaristic wage-setting practice. From that year onwards, wage-setting has been characterized by varying arrangements and a see-saw between peak-level and industry-level negotiations. The central employers' confederation, SAF, effectively dismantled its negotiating organization in 1992.

(e) The 1990s: from disarray to reform?

During most of the 1990s, Swedish industrial relations were in a bind. With the exception of the so-called Rehnberg wage contract of 1992, wage bargaining has been conducted on a decentralized basis. The conditions for successful coordination have been absent. As suggested above, employers have sought to decentralize wage bargaining, and the authority of the LO and other central trade union organizations does not suffice to coordinate the claims of their member unions. Since it is part of the Swedish political rules of the game that the government does not interfere with wage bargains, there has been no effective political power centre which would have taken care of the coordinating function.

With respect to unemployment, the outcome of the tumultuous[17] 1995 bargaining round was particularly problematic. It generated, for years 1995 through 1997, contractual wage increases of the order of 4.5 per cent across the board, which together with drift obviously ex-

---

[16] The question of price competitiveness of exports and the traded–non-traded sector relative price was addressed by a joint expert group of the employers and the trade unions. The outcome was the well-known EFO model which, in principle, could be used to generate an estimate of a rational pay norm associated with full employment and price stability. The EFO model is described in the next section of this chapter.

[17] Altogether 600,000 workdays were then lost in conflicts; with an employed labour force of about 4m, this is approximately equivalent to 3 per cent of the workers striking for a week; such figures are very high by post-Saltsöbaden standards.

ceeded the pace compatible with a real improvement in employment.[18] The upward shift of the wage-setting curve after coordination broke down is clearly shown in Figure 3, which depicts yearly nominal (upper panel) and real (lower panel) wage increases together with unemployment in the years 1990–2000. Since the mid-1990s were, anyway, a time of fiscal consolidation, it is hardly surprising that unemployment did not shrink at all in the years 1993–7. The next bargaining round that took place in 1998 was again an uncoordinated one, but this time there was a more general feeling of the necessity of wage moderation. It resulted in wage increases that were about 1 per cent lower than those of the previous agreement (see Figure 3). They were more in line with the macroeconomic situation but still exceeded those of most other European countries (SOU, 1998).

Whatever the future evolution of industrial relations, Swedish social democracy is presented with a dilemma. Politically, it is essential for social democracy to restore full employment. The history of social democratic labour-market policy — the radical striving for a more equal distribution of wages plus the Meidner fund project — has made Swedish employers suspicious of any active labour-market intervention short of radical liberalization of wage bargaining. The wage-earner fund project, in particular, demonstrated that the Swedish labour movement did not stop at having established a working compromise with capital, but, instead, strove to reach a partisan outcome in which the capital owners' rights would be severely affected. Such grievance effects are not emphasized in rational economic models where bygones are bygones. Yet it is possible to construct game-theoretic arguments which support the importance of such factors. It is precisely in models of labour and capital that game-theoretic ideas of long-term threshold strategies have found an interesting field of applications. In many such models, it is shown that politically powerful labour and capital-owners can coexist on a mutually beneficial, dynamically efficient path of capital accumulation, if both parties play long-term strategies that allow the build-up of mutual trust.[19] Once trust is broken, a 'punishment' must be inflicted on the party that deviated from the cooperative solution.

At the same time, ambitious solidaristic wage policy still seems to correspond to the preferences of a large section of Swedish organized

[18] With productivity growth at about 2 per cent and the Swedish central bank's inflation target of 2 per cent, the *long-term* norm for overall wage increases would be 4 per cent at full employment. Figure 3 shows that this norm was clearly exceeded in 1996 and 1998. Furthermore, inflation was below the target rate for most of the mid-1990s, which implies that real wages have increased too fast.

[19] See Lancaster (1973) and Kaitala and Pohjola (1990) for bench-mark models.

Figure 3
Wage Increases and Unemployment, Sweden 1990–2000

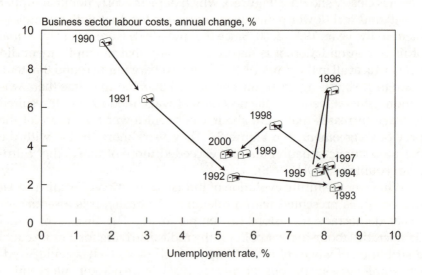

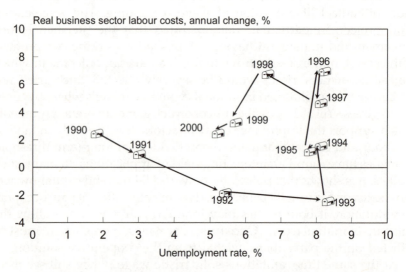

Source: OECD. The unemployment rate is the non-standardized rate which is lower than the standardized rate since, *inter alia*, the Swedish national unemployment figure does not include students. The real labour-cost change has been obtained by subtracting the rate of change of the consumer price index (CPI) from the rate of change of nominal business-sector labour costs. The CPI increase for years 1999 and 2000 is taken from the forecast of the Konjunkturinstitutet.

labour. Such collective valuations are out of tune with the market-oriented policies of the 1990s. By now most economists probably agree that it is difficult to influence the wage structure in the long run by bargaining mechanisms alone. A collectively agreed wage structure will affect the relative demands for various kinds of labour inputs as well as the incentives to improve one's productivity. Furthermore, the Swedish state today redistributes a large part of the market-generated incomes, so that the *ex-ante* distribution of wages is, anyway, transformed by the welfare state.

In contrast, it was a natural and practical policy step in the 1930s or in the 1960s to try to use the trade union movement's bargaining mandate directly to influence relative wages and thereby the final distribution of income. In the 1950s, the public redistribution machinery was less extensive, and determining the distribution of income directly via bargaining institutions seemed a straightforward attack on the problem. Furthermore, and contrary to many outsider interpretations of Sweden, the trade unions were traditionally no unconditional friends of a strong state.[20] The 1940s and 1950s were a period when an increased role of the state was widely seen as an inevitable trend, and the Swedish trade unions were in such circumstances keen to preserve their independence and autonomy. Finally, in the generally radicalized political atmosphere of the 1970s, there was in general much less awareness of the long-run constraints of the market which puts all collective arrangements to a test of incentive compatibility. Increasing the wages of low-paid workers seemed a reasonable political objective to many people, not only the social democrats.

At present, however, the state is by and large in retreat, so that maintaining and reinforcing its distributive functions should not present the trade unions with any ideological qualms. Furthermore, any attempt to re-establish a centralized determination of wage structure will arouse firm opposition from employers.

From an outsider's point of view, a rational political solution might be to moderate overall wage increases and let wage differentials widen while keeping the redistributive functions of the state strong at the same time — at least those functions which generate least welfare losses via the tax wedge and distortion of incentives. Similarly, if the objective of the unions is to generate an egalitarian structure of wages, a good long-term strategy is to influence the distribution of human capital by

---

[20] Nilsson (1993, p. 24) describes the spirit of mutual cooperation that prevailed between the labour-market parties at the time of the Basic Agreement: 'This cooperative spirit between the labour-market parties (the "Social Partners") was regarded as necessary to keep the wage negotiations system free from government intervention.'

subsidizing education and training. It is an open question whether such a political programme will turn out to be politically and technically feasible.

Seen from a strategic point of view, the social democratic dilemma can be put in the following way. It is clear that the political prestige of social democracy will suffer dramatically if full employment is not restored in a stable way. At present, Swedish trade unions have a very strong bargaining position, at the national level as well as in the various industries and firms. To restore full employment, the trade union movement must therefore contain its bargaining power and muster its internal strains, so that a coordinated wage moderation policy can be implemented.

If that strategy turns out to be infeasible, the only other way is to introduce legislation that weakens the bargaining hand of organized labour. That, in turn, can turn out politically difficult. It would involve cuts in the level and duration of unemployment benefits, new legislation on strike and lockout activities, and bargaining procedures and new legislation on workplace rules.[21] It is hard for social democracy to introduce legal reforms with the explicit aim of weakening the bargaining hand of wage-earners.

One way to implement coordinated wage moderation without weakening the unions would be to use vigorous tax-based incomes policy, so that the state would set clear incentives for the unions to keep their wage claims low. As emphasized above, this would require a new political opening in Sweden. Although tax-based incomes policy was debated in the early 1950s when Bent Hansen advocated such measures (Hansen, 1955), it has been part of the Swedish political consensus since then that the labour-market organizations assume the responsibility for wage setting. This has reflected the trade unions' aspiration for autonomy. In Swedish economic policy documents, this division of tasks is often characterized not by appealing to economic liberalism, nor by referring to trade union rights, but as a kind of *delegation* by the state.[22] One wonders whether this delegation is a consistent political solution in an economy in which there obviously exist strong collective preferences about the outcome for wages.

[21] One important example is the so-called 'last in, last out' rule for dismissals. According to present labour law, an employer needs the consent of the local trade union representatives to make exceptions to this rule.

[22] Thus, in his textbook on labour law, Schmidt (1989) writes: 'The freedom of contract and the trade unions' responsibility for labour-market settlements constitute the core of the Swedish model. One can consider this, inasmuch as it also implies responsibility for the country's economy, as a delegation of power prerogatives and responsibility by the state' (my translation).

Thus, the Social Democrats are at pains to act as a homogeneous and benevolent national political agent. These concerns have led to seminar reports and committee work the aim of which is to influence wage bargaining. For example, the LO has since 1996 operated a seminar project on wage formation.[23] More importantly, a government committee report on wage formation was published in 1998 (SOU, 1998). Building on a wide set of expert papers,[24] it adopted a compromise strategy by advocating institutional measures that favour coordination as well as legal reforms that put some limits to strike and lockout activity. At the time of writing, the fate of the reforms is unclear, but it seems likely that public intermediation of wage bargaining will be strengthened, possibly by establishing a function of a main intermediator backed by an institute that gathers labour market data. The task of the intermediator would be to enhance coordination in wage bargaining as well as to try to establish a common analysis of the labour-market situation.

Another legacy of the past, the role of which has not been appreciated in the academic literature, may be that the bold political ambitions of the Swedish trade union movement and their attempts to influence the overall distribution of wages in the economy have led to a situation where the *microeconomic structure* of collective wage agreements has remained less developed. Although European collective agreement systems differ in many ways, it is a characteristic of many modern collective agreements that they have at least partly internalized the requirements of wage flexibility and warranted relative wage differentials. Thus, many collective agreements in such corporatist countries as Germany and Finland contain recommendations on relative pay differentials at different levels of job complexity, plus systems of personal bonuses paid according to criteria agreed upon in the collective agreement. Such microeconomic features will probably be crucial in determining whether collective wage agreements will retain their central role in Northern Europe. To take the example of Finland — another neo-corporatist country in many ways similar to Sweden — Finnish social democracy never nurtured such ambitions of solidarism. This more docile attitude has led to a system of collective agreements which has not been as seriously questioned by the employers as has been the case

---

[23] The leader of LO, together with some influential trade union leaders, have, in principle, publicly endorsed the need for wage moderation in order to combat inflation (see Jonsson *et al.*, 1997).

[24] Expert papers published in the Annex to the main report were written by Steinar Holden, Karl Ove Moene, Nils Elvander, Niklas Bruun, A. T. J. M. Jacobs, David Metcalf, and Richard B. Freeman, *inter alia*.

in Sweden. Thus, the Finnish collective agreement system may well be able to internalize some of the requirements of flexibility and relative wage differentials that are characteristic of modern industrial relations.[25] It is difficult to obtain a comprehensive picture of the microeconomics of collective agreements in Europe, but similar sophisticated collective agreements have been used in many internal collective agreements of large US firms.

In Sweden, however, such collective agreements are relatively underdeveloped and trade union action has centred on the determination of overall pay increases and pay differentials across the board and between sectors. New kinds of incentive pay systems have been introduced, but mostly outside the scope of collective agreements.[26] This helps to explain the Swedish employers' hard attitudes towards collective agreements: they feel that collective agreements are an obstacle if they want to manage wage differentials at the workplace in order to create incentives and stimulate growth.[27] Thus, paradoxically, collective agreements might at the end of the day be pushed aside more easily in Sweden than in other comparable neo-corporatist countries, despite the fact the Swedish political values are extremely sympathetic to collectivistic political arrangements.

The contradictions of the Swedish labour-market model suggest that the management of the entire wage structure via a coordinated wage bargain between organized agents is a quasi-impossible task — even in such a culturally homogeneous country as Sweden, where social democracy has enjoyed an almost hegemonic political position. Again, with hindsight, this is perhaps no surprise, and it is not difficult to come up with convincing economic arguments that show that such a policy is bound to run into difficulties. A set of individual labour unions and employers' associations probably does not correspond to an organizational structure that can deliver an efficient and coordinated solution. Furthermore, any radical intervention into relative wages will run into economic difficulties, most obviously into the problem of diminished incentives to acquire skills and a shortage of skilled labour.

---

[25] For example, the collective agreement of the influential metal industry has a sophisticated microeconomic structure: tariff wage scales are established on the basis of job evaluation, and a system of personal bonuses is stipulated within the collective agreement, which specifies the criteria of the bonuses and their distribution within each firm and job level.

[26] Thus, for example, according to a survey carried out by the Metalworkers' Union in 1991, 55 per cent of its membership received some form of payment by results.

[27] See the employers' memoranda: SAF: Produktivitet och arbete, Stockholm 1990, and Verkstadsföreningen: Arbete, lön , effektivitet, Stockholm.

Thus, one tentative lesson is that coordination of wage policies should abstain from ambitious distributional objectives. Gösta Rehn and Rudolf Meidner had in their writings accepted wage differentials that were based on different job requirements and worker qualifications (Lindbeck, 1975, p. 53). Yet the Swedish experience also suggests that once the entire structure of wages is brought within the realm of collective intervention, it can be very difficult, at least in such an egalitarian and democratic political culture as Sweden's, *not* to burden the coordinating function with redistributive aims.[28] Thus, ironically, the present unsatisfactory state of affairs is a confirmation of Gösta Rehn's original scepticism (Rehn, 1988): a non-inflationary full employment equilibrium can hardly be sustained if there is no general feeling within the trade union movement that the existing distribution of income is acceptable. At present, most Swedish trade union leaders reject coordinated wage moderation and aim for wage increases that, together with drift, exceed the sum of productivity growth and the inflation target. Since the Swedish central bank is by now independent and probably able to implement its inflation target of 2 per cent, the likely outcome is a prolonged period of high unemployment. The irony is that coordination of wage bargains without ambitious distributional objectives could well be viable and useful in an economy with comprehensively organized agents, such as Sweden.[29] The experiences of such countries as Austria, Denmark, the Netherlands, and Finland show that it is in principle not an impossible task to moderate overall wage claims if the entire structure of relative wages is not on the bargaining agenda in each bargaining round.

Of course, positive scenarios are not ruled out for Sweden; one may imagine a gradual move towards German-type pay-bargaining in which different unions coordinate their wage increases while there is considerable room for local solutions (see also Pontusson, 1997). The considerable decrease in the pace of nominal wage increases after 1996 is somewhat encouraging in this respect.

Active labour-market policy, the other part of the Swedish labour-market model, is likely to persist in the long run, although in a leaner shape. The active labour-market policy of training, counselling, and

---

[28] Thus, it is a common idea in Sweden that solidaristic policies are an endogenous characteristic of coordination (see Calmfors, 1993), an idea that would appear alien in such neo-corporatist countries as Austria and Finland. In the latter countries, the trade unions have sought to control the average level of wages but have not challenged existing wage differentials to the same extent as their Swedish counterparts (see Pekkarinen *et al.*, 1992).

[29] See Soskice (1990) for a compact argument on the benefits of coordination.

subsidizing labour mobility has been an active part of Swedish labour-market policy since the 1950s. There has been a rising trend in expenditures for such programmes. Recent studies (see Calmfors, 1994, and Forslund and Krueger, 1997) indicate that some of these measures have been counterproductive, but that at least counselling and intensified placement activities have clearly contributed to employment (see also Layard, 1990).

4. Macroeconomic Management

As argued in the previous section, much of social democratic economic policy can be seen as a continuous struggle to reconcile the objective of full employment with price stability in an economy with a strong trade-union movement. How do fiscal and monetary policy fit into this picture? The social democrats' fiscal policy embraced at an early stage the Keynesian–Stockholmian ideas of active demand management. Already in the 1930s, a group of social democrats, led by Ernst Wigforss, worked out proposals for active fiscal expansion that had been inspired by the writings of Keynes. After the war, Keynesian orthodoxy became the dominant doctrine of fiscal policy and Swedish economists conducted vigorous policy debates on the proper formulation and execution of countercyclical fiscal policy.[30] As emphasized by Pekkarinen (1989), Swedish Keynesianism was from its beginnings concerned with problems of price stability and the supply side.

Together with the labour-market model, the adoption of Keynesian ideas was a central initiative of Swedish social democracy. It was thought to be and turned out to be extremely advantageous for social democracy, for three reasons. First, as a political project, it energized the labour movement around a reformist programme by offering a set of feasible policies that would replace the passive and fundamentalist attitude that had been typical of the Kautskian phase of social democracy. Waiting for the inevitable collapse of capitalism would thus give way to active policies. Second, it offered a way of keeping employment high, and thereby contributed to the social democrats' political success. In the eyes of the electorate, high employment would be a proof of the social democrats' capability of enhancing everybody's well-being.

There is even a third mechanism, more long-term and more implicit. The general acceptance of countercyclical fiscal policy would make it legitimate to let government expenditure stay high or even increase at

[30] See Tilton (1991), Lundberg (1985), Pekkarinen (1989), or, in Swedish, Lindbeck (1975).

times when other demand components grow slowly. Inasmuch as the political system would not cut expenditure in times of boom, fiscal activism would keep pushing for a higher structural GDP share of public income and expenditure. Of course, the social democrats could in any case count on broad political support for an expansion of public services and social security, but Keynesian policy could well provide an extra boost for these policies.[31] Indeed, it turned out to be the case that fiscal policy was almost always expansive in times of low activity, whereas subsequent tightening was often mild and lagged behind the restoration of rapid growth (Lindbeck, 1975, p. 89). Public demand grew consistently faster than the rest of the economy until the mid-1980s.

Thus, fiscal policy came to play a central political role in the social democrats' bid for power. Yet Keynesian ideas did not exhaust their political project. On the contrary, Swedish social democrats tended to see active fiscal policy in instrumental terms. They thought of aggregate demand management as a first-stage reform that would maintain full employment and thus enhance working-class power, building political resources for the development of economic democracy and social welfare (Pekkarinen, 1989).

The stabilization policy record of the 1950s and early 1960s confirmed social democratic optimism. That period is characterized by countercyclical fiscal policy reactions, high employment, and stable growth (Lindbeck, 1975). From the mid-1960s onwards, problems of inflation and external imbalances gradually grew more serious, and fiscal policy reactions became less clear-cut. Yet one can characterize the entire time period from the late 1940s to the early 1970s as one of relative stability, especially in comparison with later years and other countries during the same time period. Of course, it is more difficult to assess to what extent the good performance reflected discretionary economic policy choices. A comprehensive analysis of Swedish business cycles by Hassler et al. (1994) suggests that the Swedish economy has been more stable than most developed economies over a very long time span.

External imbalances and inflation were the main problems that challenged stabilization policy during these years. Although Swedish exports and imports have historically fluctuated in a rather synchronized way (Pekkarinen, 1989), balance-of-payments crises have arisen on several occasions, such as the end of the 1960s and the 1970s. At such stages, governments have tended to adopt traditional stop-go policies or to use the exchange rate as a safety valve. It was not until the mid-

---

[31] The effect of countercyclical fiscal policy on the gradual increase of the tax rate was pointed out by Lindbeck (1975).

1970s and the 1980s, however, that more serious problems of economic management emerged. At this stage, it is appropriate to bring monetary and exchange-rate policies into the picture.

The question of adequate monetary policy never acquired sharp political dimensions in the same way as fiscal policy and the labour-market model. Sweden's monetary institutions were, until the late 1970s, largely similar to those of other Nordic countries in the Bretton Woods era, with rationed credit markets, low interest rates, and fixed exchange rates.

It was understood in the 1970s that Swedish inflation would probably have to exceed the rate of increase of export prices regardless of wage-drift problems. This was due to the fact that the productivity growth in the sheltered sector was lower than in the open sector of the economy, and it was easier in the sheltered sector to pass increases in wage costs on to prices. The celebrated EFO model (Edgren *et al.*, 1970) was developed precisely to explain why the domestic inflation rate might have to differ from world inflation.

The 'main orientation' of the EFO model was to equate wage increases with world inflation and open-sector productivity growth.[32] Domestic inflation would then exceed world inflation by the sectoral productivity differential times the GDP share of the sheltered sector. Such a path would keep relative profitabilities unchanged. In practice, if and when wage increases exceeded that norm, a current account deficit emerged, and the authorities had to devalue the Swedish krona to restore competitiveness. Thus, external balance was the binding constraint that closed the model in practice. The experiences of the 1970s onwards show that the room for wage increases was often exceeded, which led to pressures for devaluation. The dramatic 1982 devaluation by Olof Palme's newly appointed cabinet can be seen as an attempt to correct a fundamental disequilibrium, the origins of which can be traced back to the high money-wage increases of 1974–6.

Thus, devaluations became the safety valve through which excessive wage inflation was corrected. They showed that the political control of wages had not worked in the desired way; on the other hand, they were in the 1970s and in the 1980s (and even in the recession of the 1990s) an extremely powerful short-term weapon, precisely because the wage-setting institutions were 'administrative' to such an extent that devaluations were not quickly eroded. Such a policy regime can be viable for

---

[32] This was understood by the EFO authors, but it went against the basic orientation of Gösta Rehn's writings, who had in 1957 thundered against inflation in his article 'Hate Inflation' (*Hata inflationen*) (see Rehn, 1988).

a long time if the devaluations are not incorporated into the agents' expectations. However, as it was the case that the 'system' had generated more wage inflation than the 'main orientation' would have stipulated, the agents who were, through their bargains, generating that extra inflation, would begin to incorporate expectations of devaluations into their wage claims. Such a suspicion is tentatively borne out by the fact that the magnitudes of Swedish devaluations seemed to increase from the 1970s onwards (Lybeck, 1985).

Swedish economic policy was generally expansive in the latter half of the 1970s; the currency was devalued several times in 1976–7, and fiscal policy loosened. There was a significant fiscal accommodation of the recessionary shock of the mid-1970s. This led to a weakening of the government budget position and a current account deficit. Fiscal policy was tightened in the 1980s, and monetary policy became the more important instrument of accommodation. The currency was again devalued in the years 1982 and 1983. Together with the earlier devaluations these measures meant a total depreciation of the effective exchange rate by about 35 per cent between 1976 and 1983 (Calmfors, 1993). This helped the wage bargaining system in keeping real wage increases low, and a substantial adjustment of Swedish real wages took place. The 1980s were consequently a decade of real wage restraint. Inflation slowed down in the mid-1980s (from 14 per cent p.a. around 1980 to about 5 per cent p.a. in 1985) but picked up again towards the end of the decade. Thus, disinflation took place later than in the rest of Europe. This probably contributed to the relatively good employment record during the 1980s.

In 1989 and 1990, inflation increased again and money wage costs for blue-collar workers grew by 11.2 per cent and 9.1 per cent, respectively. This happened in an already overheated economy, stimulated by both good export growth and the credit expansion fuelled by financial deregulation. As in neighbouring Finland and Norway, savings rates dropped to zero and a considerable external deficit arose. The late 1980s can perhaps best be interpreted as a time of outright policy mistakes: the unemployment rate was allowed to get extremely low — around 1.5 per cent — and probably below reasonable estimates of the NAIRU (non-accelerating inflation rate of unemployment). Such unemployment rates were not historically exceptional, but it is reasonable to think that structural unemployment had increased in Sweden as it had in most European countries. Fiscal policy and the public sector's impact on the economy can to some extent be blamed for these economic problems. True, fiscal policy became steadily more contractionary towards the end of the 1980s, but the restrictive effect could hardly match the general overheating of the economy.[33] As in neighbouring Finland, the Swedish economy entered a deep recession in the early 1990s. In the years 1991-3, GDP dropped by 5 per cent altogether and the rate of unemployment increased to about 8 per cent, a level unseen before in Sweden. Unemployment has not dropped significantly since then, although growth has resumed.

Thus, one 'nasty' interpretation of Swedish macroeconomic experiences since the late 1970s is that economic policy has had to change its strategy and institutions profoundly in order to get to grips with the problem of high and accelerating inflation.[34] The 'day of reckoning', i.e. disinflation, took place later than in other countries, but, once it had happened, unemployment rose to normal European levels. Coordinated wage bargains did contribute to the wage restraint of the 1980s, but a relatively high level of inflation was anyway essential in keeping employment up. Such a view suggests that the Rehn–Meidner model had been tried and failed: it had delivered wage restraint only because of high and accelerating inflation. By the end of the 1980s, the view that repeated devaluations would not work in an environment of deregulated financial markets gained general acceptance.

An alternative view would be that the problems were due to the fact that the Rehn–Meidner model was *abandoned*. It is true that Swedish inflation had from the early 1960s onwards increased steadily, but so had European inflation. Swedish inflation was not more explosive than that of Europe during that period, and real wage restraint was achieved, which partly explains the good employment performance. Would it have been possible to keep unemployment lower if disinflation had been less ambitious and the targeted (stable) inflation rate higher? Such an alternative interpretation would suggest that there was nothing fundamentally wrong with Swedish macroeconomic management, and the present difficulties can be traced back to the policy mistakes of the late 1980s, when the economy was allowed to overheat and unemployment was kept too low. The Swedish experience of the late 1980s resembles the textbook case of a political unemployment objective that is too ambitious *vis-à-vis* the NAIRU; as the authorities were unwilling to put brakes on the economy, inflation picked up again at the turn of the decade.

---

[33] The tax reform of the early 1990s makes it more difficult to assess the overall impact of the public sector. The reform by itself probably increased the structural budget deficit, but the short-run effect was to increase the incentive to save, and that deflationary effect was felt precisely when the savings rate was increasing again.

[34] Calmfors (1993) is an exposition of this interpretation.

Indeed, fiscal policy was at that time a subject of considerable divergence of opinion within Swedish social democracy. Kjell-Olof Feldt, the Minister of Finance in the years 1982–90, has described these internal conflicts in his political memoirs (Feldt, 1991). Feldt and most government ministers were in favour of a more restrictive stance, but the trade unions were opposed. Such an attitude was far from Rehn's prescriptions; thus, the insufficiently restrictive fiscal stance should be seen as a departure from the Rehn–Meidner model rather than a consequence of it. Whatever one's interpretation, the outcome was not satisfactory in the late 1980s and 1990s.

These mistakes notwithstanding, the originally social democratic idea of active fiscal policy is quite well established in Sweden, and the non-socialist Bildt government of 1992–5 did not deviate from this tradition during its time in office: the fiscal impact remained expansionary through the years of depression 1992–4,[35] as it had in the recession of the 1970s. It is interesting that non-socialist governments in Sweden have been no less eager than social democrats to increase the public deficit in order to sustain demand in times of recession. Thus, the commonplace political view of right-wing parties as austere and left-wing parties as spendthrift is hardly true of Sweden.

A fair overall assessment of Swedish fiscal-policy reactions is that they have by and large stabilized the economy.[36] This stabilizing influence rests partly on discretionary policy, partly on automatic stabilizers. The very size of the Swedish public sector, indeed, makes the impact of automatic stabilizing mechanisms larger than in any other comparable country.[37] This is an asset from the point of view of stabilization, but can become a burden when issues of solvency arise: with public debt at about 80 per cent of GDP, even cyclical deficits can appear very large in the eyes of investors. Such budget problems are

[35] OECD, *Economic Survey of Sweden* (1996).

[36] For example, that is the conclusion of Vredin and Ohlsson (1996), who have estimated a reaction function model of Swedish fiscal policy in years 1968–93. Any student of Swedish fiscal policy is tempted to think that there is really hardly much controversy in Swedish politics on the merits of countercyclical fiscal policy, and this belief is confirmed by the Vredin and Ohlsson study: they find hardly any election effects and even the partisan effects are weak and not in the 'conventional' direction.

[37] A fresh set of estimates by the Finnish team of experts on economic and monetary union (EMU) confirms this. The elasticity of the public-sector deficit as a share of GDP with respect to changes in the growth rate of GDP appears to be over unity in Sweden: when GDP growth slows down by 1 per cent, the public-sector deficit as a percentage of GDP increases by *more* than 1 per cent in Sweden. This elasticity appears to be twice as high as those of other OECD countries. This estimate is based on the years 1970–96 (Pekkarinen *et al.*, 1997).

largely a new phenomenon in Sweden. Before the 1980s, the Swedish state used to be an important net saver in the economy (Kosonen, 1992).

5. Taking Stock: Prospects for Swedish Social Democracy

What remains of Swedish social democracy? The success of a political movement needs many ingredients. First, it must generate short-run economic policies that work. Second, its package of policies and ideological mobilization must be able to sustain and reproduce the political constituency which supports the movement's power resources. Third, its policies and preferred institutions must work economically even in the long run. And, finally, whatever the success of specific policies, the ultimate test of a political movement is whether it can mould the preferences of the electorate and leave a lasting mark on society.

Whatever the economic failures, Swedish social democrats have been outstandingly successful according to the last criterion. Considering how difficult it is in general to impose lasting collectivist interventions on market-driven societies, Swedish social democrats have probably been as successful as can be. In a paradoxical way, they have been too successful. Many of the economic problems now blamed on social democracy are due to policies that were simply pushed too far. The Rehn model was sound, whereas its radicalized version and the fund project destroyed the compromise with employers. The welfare state can be equitable and efficient but can generate deadweight losses when it increases too much at the expense of the market-driven part of the economy. Yet, whatever one's ideological position, it is not surprising that Swedish social democrats undertook these initiatives: they were driven by strong political preferences, and it is natural for a hegemonic political movement to go to the limits of political and economic feasibility when trying to impose its values on society. Furthermore, the radical initiatives should be seen in their historical context. The Rehn–Meidner model, for example, was seen as an alternative to a more far-reaching command economy, at a time when socialism and planning was seriously discussed in many other European countries. The incentive problems of the welfare state are another case in point. They were hardly predicted in Sweden — but nor were they appreciated in general in the Western political and economic thought of the 1970s.

As to the future, the critical question is whether Swedish social democrats can modernize their economics while retaining their values. Many Swedish social democrats and Swedes in general are politically opposed to the liberal–neoclassical view of the world which tests the legitimacy and rationality of political initiatives by appealing to some measure of aggregated individual interests. Many Swedish politicians think that the state has the right to set political objectives and create institutions that need not be legitimated by appealing to such neoclassical calculus.

What about future prospects? The social democratic welfare state remains a robust institution to which a majority of the Swedish electorate seems to adhere. Although the Persson government that took office in 1995 has capped public expenditure across the board, this has been motivated mostly by budget considerations. After the tax reform of the early 1990s, the worst incentive problems due to the fiscal system were eliminated, and, after the rough austerity programme of 1995 and 1996 there is no reason to expect that a serious structural deficit problem would emerge. On the other hand, it seems clear that the expansion phase of the welfare state is over.

It is in stabilization, employment, and labour-market policy that Swedish social democracy appears more vulnerable. The Rehn model is not working and even other parts of the Swedish model are seriously questioned. Like those of many other countries, Swedish policy-makers have also committed themselves to the pursuit of low inflation. In many countries, institutional changes have been carried out to increase the independence of the central bank. The right-of-centre Bildt government introduced similar proposals in Sweden in 1993, but the social democrats' lukewarm attitude to central bank independence jeopardized the initiative at this stage. By and large, the Swedish social democrats' attitude to the new European tenets of monetary rectitude has been hesitant and uneasy. This has reflected a commitment to democracy, but, together with the uncertainties of the labour-market model, it has probably also contributed to the interest-rate differential between Sweden and the core European countries in the 1990s and thereby aggravated the problem of low employment growth of recent years. The Persson government's negative attitude towards Swedish participation to the single currency is cautious in the sense that the present uncertainties related to the rules of the game in the labour market make it risky for Sweden to bind itself irrevocably to a common currency and low inflation.

Estimates of the NAIRU suggest a structural unemployment rate of 4–7 per cent.[38] Actual unemployment, measured by the OECD standardized rate, has come down a bit and was at 8.2 per cent in 1998. According to 1999 OECD projections, it would have come down by an additional percentage point by 2000.[39] Thus, the unemployment situa-

---

[38] See Apel and Jansson (1997) for estimates.
[39] OECD Employment Outlook 1997 and 1999.

tion has clearly not improved in a way that should please Swedish social democrats.

Inasmuch as high structural unemployment is a result of high wage claims and generous transfers, reforming the wage-bargaining system and labour legislation can turn out to be difficult for a social democratic administration. As argued above, taking measures that induce the trade unions and trade unionists to do something that they would not do of their own accord is an idea inimical to Swedish social democracy. In that sense, Swedish social democracy is a workers' movement. It is that same attitude that generated many of the difficulties that the practical application of the Rehn model encountered: labour-market issues were left to the discretion of the trade unions, even when it was clear that some coordination with the government's macroeconomic management would have been welcome.

At present, many commentators see Swedish social democracy in deep crisis. Seen as a set of specific policies, many initiatives of the Swedish model, apart from the welfare state, have failed. The lasting characteristic of Swedish social democracy, however, is a vigorous pursuit of equality, even at the expense of efficiency. One can expect that this pursuit, in the course of time, will generate new political initiatives. Such political preferences can prevent the most efficient outcomes from happening, but a neoclassical economist can hardly criticize a nation for having inadequate preferences. There is no ethical imperative to grow faster than other nations, and, seen from the perspective of the least advantaged, Sweden is an extremely successful society.[40] There is an ethical imperative to be consistent, however, and this is where the Swedish social democrats are the most vulnerable at present: inasmuch as a return to full employment requires reforms opposed by the trade unions, it remains an open question as to whether such reforms are feasible under social democratic rule.

---

[40] Knowing that one would belong to the poorest decile, it would be wise to prefer Sweden to the USA: as pointed out by Freeman *et al.* (1997), the incomes of the poorest decile in Sweden are 63 per cent higher than those of bottom-decile Americans, although the US per-capita income is 28 per cent higher than Sweden's.

3

The Austrian Experience

ALOIS GUGER*

1. Introduction

In the post-Second World War period, the main political parties in Austria, the conservatives and the socialists, forming the Grand Coalition Government (1945–66) together with the social partners, agreed on the priority of a growth strategy. This would foster investment to rebuild the country and to catch up from a rather low level of productivity. In the 1960s, unemployment had not been a problem since growth had been constrained by labour shortages and Austria had to attract foreign labour. In 1970, after 4 years of a single-party conservative government, Bruno Kreisky formed the first socialist government in Austria. The country had a socialist as Federal Chancellor for 30 years; first, until 1983, a single-party government under Bruno Kreisky, then a socialist–liberal coalition, followed by a socialist–conservative coalition headed first by Franz Vranitzky (1986–97) and then from January 1997 to February 2000 by Viktor Klima.

In 1970, the new socialist government started off with a wide range of reform initiatives to expand and modernize the welfare state which ranged from a liberalization of civil and criminal law to an advancement of the educational and social security system. Thus, when in the early 1970s the first oil crisis started, a number of the new government's expansionary reform programmes were on their way in Austria. Furthermore, Bruno Kreisky gave full employment highest priority, even at a very early date, when professional forecasts still envisaged just a minor recession. Having studied some Marxian economics while imprisoned by the Fascists, he was convinced that a major crisis of

* Austrian Institute of Economic Research (WIFO).

capitalism was coming, and that unemployment would endanger democracy and nurture right-wing ideologies.[1]

Thus, in the aftermath of the first oil crisis, Austria pursued a rather exceptional policy; while most industrialized countries were mainly concerned about fighting inflation and followed restrictive monetarist recipes, Austria was first and foremost determined to maintain a high level of employment. Since inflation was seen as imported and cost-determined, the government pursued an expansionary fiscal policy to stabilize demand; and to reduce inflationary pressures from abroad, the Austrian National Bank tied the schilling to the appreciating Deutschmark.

This rather unusual assignment, control of inflation through the exchange rate and maintenance of international competitiveness by incomes policy, has probably only been possible owing to the corporatist institutional setting and the high degree of social consensus on which the Austrian social partnership is based. Together with the expansionary fiscal stance, this strategy was designed as a pragmatic short-term device to overcome the international recession caused by the supply shock of the first oil crisis. In the late 1970s, this strategy was proudly labelled as Austro-Keynesianism. But, in the more restrictive international environment of the 1980s, the expansionary part of this policy was gradually abandoned and fiscal consolidation was given priority over full employment, while the strong-currency option was never questioned, despite substantial structural problems in the exposed sectors of the economy in the aftermath of the continuous appreciation of the schilling.

2. Austria's Economic Performance from an International Comparative Perspective

After post-war inflation was brought under control, growth and full employment became the major policy concerns in Austria. According to these macroeconomic indicators, Austria's economic performance can stand comparison with most industrial countries.

[1] 'My experience of the terrible Great Depression of the 1930s had a profound effect on all my activities from the start, and I firmly believe in a causal link between the world economic crisis and the subsequent downfall of European democracies.' (pp. x–xi) 'The events of my youth having made a lasting experience on me, I, as a politician in office, consistently attempted to keep in mind the experiences of the Great Depression. Already in 1972 . . . I drew attention to the danger of unemployment . . . Quite early in my career I was intent on preventing an economic crisis . . . early in 1975 . . . I was advocating the prevention of a major crisis, while the economists were talking about stabilization.' (Kreisky, 1989, pp. xiv–v)

Starting from a low level of productivity after the war, Austria's rapid growth was the result of the reconstruction boom and of bridging the technological gap in the 1950s and 1960s. Although GDP per capita had reached almost the level of the EU average by 1970, Austria's economy continued the catching-up process, and in 1995 GDP per capita (in purchasing power parities) was about 12 per cent over and above the EU average (OECD, 1997d). And, while 25 years ago productivity levels in the Austrian goods-processing sectors were on average 25 per cent lower than in (West) Germany, they are about equal today (Guger, 1995).[2]

Austria's economic development compared particularly well in the stagflation period after the first oil crisis. When the world economy experienced a marked decline in growth and a substantial rise in inflation and unemployment, Austria responded with an expansionary strategy and gave full employment highest priority while abroad the fight against inflation became the main policy concern. Thus, in the 1970s, real per-capita growth was on average in Austria about one percentage point higher per year than in the EU or the OECD area (Table 1). But, after the second oil crisis, the policy response was much less expansionary; this was, on the one hand, due to a more restrictive international environment which was coupled with high interest rates and, on the other hand, due to the structural crisis in the nationalized iron and steel industries, which put heavy strains on the federal budget. On top of that, foreign demand was dampened by the rapid appreciation of the schilling in the mid-1980s. Nevertheless, growth achieved about the international average in the 1980s. At the beginning of the 1990s, demand had been boosted by the fall of the Iron Curtain and German reunification. However, first the restrictive policy of the German Bundesbank, coupled with a strong appreciation of the schilling along with the Deutschmark in autumn 1992, and then the measures to reduce public deficits in preparation for economic and monetary union

[2] This unbroken catching-up process of the Austrian economy *vis-à-vis* Germany is sometimes tentatively attributed to the in-flow of German capital into Austria. But German foreign direct investment in Austria has been rather low compared to its involvement elsewhere in Europe, e.g. Ireland, the Benelux countries, or the Netherlands (Egger *et al.*, 1998). A hypothesis based on Austria's high savings and investment rates seems to be more plausible. It goes like this: owing to higher levels of effective demand and capital utilization, capital accumulation was significantly higher in Austria than in Germany (Table 1). Consequently, the increase in both labour and total factor productivity was higher in Austria than in Germany; in Austria's industry, total factor productivity increased in the 1970s on average by 2.2 per cent per year, in the 1980s by 2.6 per cent; the figures for Germany are respectively 1.9 per cent and 1.1 per cent (Hahn, 1994).

Table 1
Growth and Capital Formation

Country	Real GDP per capita (average annual increase in %)				Gross fixed capital formation (% of GDP)			
	1960–73	1973–9	1979–89	1989–97	1960–73	1974–9	1980–9	1990–7
Austria	4.3	3.0	1.9	1.6	24.8	24.5	22.2	23.6
Belgium	4.4	2.2	1.9	1.4	21.6	21.7	17.2	18.2
Denmark	3.6	1.6	1.8	2.1	27.3	25.3	20.5	18.8
Finland	4.5	1.8	3.2	0.4	26.4	27.3	25.0	18.2
France	4.4	2.2	1.6	0.9	23.8	23.6	20.6	19.0
Germany	3.7	2.5	1.9	1.3	24.6	20.5	20.2	21.6
Italy	4.6	3.0	2.3	1.1	24.6	24.1	21.4	18.0
Netherlands	3.6	1.9	1.3	2.0	25.6	21.4	20.1	19.7
Sweden	3.4	1.5	1.8	0.3	23.3	20.5	19.4	16.1
Switzerland	3.0	-0.1	1.6	0.0	29.0	23.5	25.1	22.5
United Kingdom	2.6	1.5	2.2	1.2	18.3	19.4	17.5	16.1
USA	2.7	1.6	1.5	1.7	18.4	19.4	18.9	16.5
Total EU 15	4.0	2.1	2.0	1.3	23.3	22.4	20.3	19.4
Total OECD	3.7	1.9	1.7	1.5	22.1	22.5	21.2	20.2

Source: OECD (1999), *Historical Statistics, 1960–97.*

(EMU), dampened effective demand and thus growth, as elsewhere in Europe, in the first half of the 1990s.

Looking at the labour market, growth had been limited by labour shortages throughout the 1960s. Hence, a comprehensive system of investment promotion was introduced to foster capital accumulation and productivity growth, and the labour market was opened to foreign workers. The share of foreign workers in the labour force increased from about 1 per cent in the 1960s to about 9 per cent in 1995 (Figure 1).

Throughout the 1970s, Austria had been successful in maintaining full employment. Despite a considerable growth in labour supply, employment increased enough to keep unemployment below 2 per cent of the labour force. So in 1981, the unemployment rate exceeded the 2 per cent level for the first time since 1970. But, since the early 1980s, Austria has been more and more unable to uncouple its labour market from the European trend. First, in the recession after the second oil crisis, between 1981 and 1983, the numbers of registered unemployed doubled. Second, despite remarkable economic growth at the beginning of the 1990s, the Austrian labour market was not able to absorb the rapid increase in labour supply which was due to a sudden increase in

Figure 1
Labour-market Indicators

(a) Unemployment rates

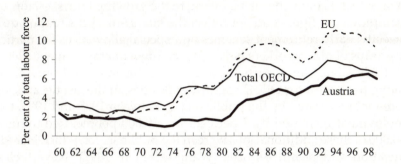

Source: OECD, WIFO.

(b) Unemployed and foreign workers

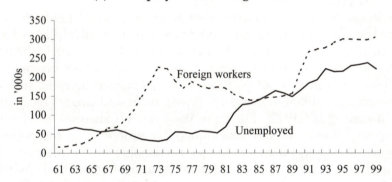

Source: Labour Market Service.

(c) Labour supply and employment

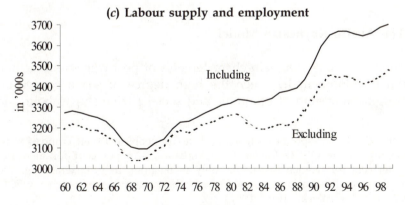

Source: Austrian Central Statistical Office, WIFO.

women's participation, as well as a large in-flow of foreign labour, and immigration (Figure 1).

By international standards, unemployment in Austria may seem moderate, in particular when we take into account seasonal unemployment, which is high and rising owing to the growing tourist sector. But unemployment figures do not reflect the labour-market situation quite correctly; early retirement schemes and special allowances for particular groups of older workers have reduced open unemployment. Hence, Austria's labour-force participation rates of people aged over 55 are among the lowest for OECD countries.[3] Besides, in the last decade, jobs were mainly created by the public sector. Between 1985 and 1995, total employment increased by 7 per cent or 210,000 people; two-thirds or 140,000 of these additional jobs were in the public sector, which includes education and health services (Walterskirchen, 1997). Nevertheless, taking things altogether, overall employment is relatively high in Austria, since Austria's employment–population ratio is well above European as well as OECD average, while part-time employment is still very low (Table 2).

The reasons why unemployment is, by European standards, still comparatively low in Austria and employment relatively high have primarily to be traced back to the policy of the 1970s. Hence, in the past 20 years, Austrian's economic record and policy have been noticed and analysed by a number of political scientists and economists, such as Flanagan *et al.* (1983), Katzenstein (1984), Blaas and Guger (1985), and Pekkarinen *et al.* (1992). But there has been no analysis of whether this policy was gradually abandoned for economic or for political reasons. Was this policy no longer sustainable in the international environment of the 1980s, or did the institutional or political environment change, when, for example, the social democrats had to form a coalition government after 1983? What are the prospects for the future?

3. The Austro-Keynesian Model

In Austria, one of the main characteristics of post-war economic and social development has been the high degree of social consensus. Through the system of economic and social partnership, labour and

---

[3] In 1995, the age-specific participation rates for people between 55 and 64 were, according to the OECD *Labour Force Statistics*, 42.6 per cent for men and 18.8 per cent for women in Austria; only in Belgium, Italy, Luxembourg, and Hungary were these rates lower and in the Netherlands marginally higher (OECD, *Employment Outlook*, July 1997).

Table 2
Employment and Unemployment

	Total employment (% of working-age population)				P-T*	Unemployment (% of total labour force)				
	1960–73	1974–9	1980–9	1990–7	1998	1960–73	1974–9	1980–9	1990–7	1998
Austria	67.8	63.9	63.8	67.5	11.5	1.7	1.6	3.7	5.7	6.5
Belgium	60.3	59.1	55.5	56.3	16.3	2.2	5.7	11.1	11.4	11.6
Denmark	72.7	73.1	75.0	74.9	17.0	1.3	6.1	8.1	10.2	6.4
Finland	72.5	71.1	73.5	64.7	9.7	2.0	4.4	4.9	12.1	11.4
France	66.6	65.1	60.3	58.8	14.8	2.0	4.5	8.9	11.1	11.8
Germany	69.4	66.1	63.6	65.7	16.6	0.8	3.4	6.7	7.6	9.3
Italy	58.4	55.6	54.5	53.9	11.8	5.3	6.6	9.9	10.4	11.9
Netherlands	59.4	54.0	54.8	64.3	30.0	1.1	4.9	9.8	6.3	4.2
Sweden	72.6	77.4	79.6	74.0	13.5	1.9	1.9	2.5	6.2	6.5
Switzerland	78.2	74.2	75.0	80.3	24.2	–	–	0.6	3.4	3.9
UK	71.1	70.7	67.1	69.1	23.0	1.9	4.2	9.5	8.4	6.2
USA	63.1	65.2	68.7	72.9	13.4	4.8	6.7	7.2	6.1	4.5
Total EU 15	65.3	63.2	60.1	61.0	16.0	2.3	4.6	9.2	9.9	10.1
Total OECD	66.1	65.2	64.8	66.0**	14.3	3.2	5.0	7.2	7.4	6.9

Note: *P-T is part-time employment as a percentage of total employment. **1991–7.
Sources: OECD, *Historical Statistics 1960–97*; *Economic Outlook*, 66; *Employment Outlook*, July 1999.

capital have, since the early 1950s, been integrated in the process of policy formulation. In addition, there was until the late 1980s the great importance of nationalization in industry and finance which influenced the balance of power between the social partners and the two large political parties, the socialists (SPÖ) and the conservatives (ÖVP). Hence, in the 1970s, when elsewhere high unemployment was tolerated to control inflation, the social democratic government was able to give full employment absolute priority and implement a new strategy to counteract stagflation.

The core elements of the new policy, *ex-post* labelled 'Austro-Keynesianism' (Seidel, 1982), were:

- absolute *priority for full employment and growth*;
- an *expansionary fiscal policy* to foster growth and employment through high built-in stabilizers in the social security system,

public investment programmes, accelerated depreciation schemes, and large-scale interest-rate subsidies to promote private investment;

- a *strong-currency policy* to fight imported inflation by tying the Austrian schilling to the Deutschmark and, therefore, appreciating the schilling against the currencies of most other trading partners; and
- a form of *voluntary and permanent incomes policy* based on the social partnership to control wages and prices and international competitiveness.

This Austro-Keynesian model differs from 'standard Keynesianism'; it is not confined to anti-cyclical demand management, but represents a long-term device to stabilize business expectations with the help of incomes and exchange-rate policies, thus fostering investment and growth; in fact, Austro-Keynesianism focuses extensively on stabilizing the private sector.[4]

Austro-Keynesianism is, on the one hand, based on rather fundamental Keynesian notions, such as uncertainty and volatile business expectations (Tichy, 1984), and on the other hand, on the corporatist institutions of the Austrian social partnership as an instrument to pursue incomes policy on a long-term basis. At least in societies with a strong labour movement, some form of such corporatist institutions may prove as necessary to the pursuit of long-run full-employment strategies as Keynes and Kalecki (1943) envisaged.

Furthermore, there is a specific assignment of instruments and goals that takes into account the openness of the country, its institutional situation, and the inflationary environment of the time. In the period of high imported inflation, the traditional assignment did not seem adequate for a small open economy. While the traditional fiscal policy of compensating for fluctuations in demand was extended to foster growth by investment promotion, exchange-rate policy was assigned to price stability, and incomes policy to external equilibrium by checking the price–wage spiral and preserving international competitiveness. Thus, moderate incomes policies had to soften the combined effects of hard-currency and expansionary fiscal policy on the balance of payments.

---

[4] In his discussions of the economic plans for the post-war period in the Treasury, Keynes stressed the importance of this point (Guger and Walterskirchen, 1988).

(a) *Institutional Preconditions: Social Partnership and Nationalized Industries*

(i) Social partnership

The Austrian economic and social partnership[5] has been widely considered as the centrepiece of Austria's post-war economic policy. Its scope is much wider than an institution of wage bargaining; it is a system of institutionalized cooperation between labour, business, and government, which is involved in all important aspects of economic and social policy. It was formed by the Austrian Trade Union Federation (ÖGB) and the Chambers of Agriculture, Commerce, and Labour in the 1950s to control post-war inflation and to overcome the shortcomings of public administration in the immediate post-war years. Both social partnership and the climate of consensus grew out of the institutional, political, and economic history of the country.

From an institutional perspective, there were the existing system of Chambers, as legal representatives with compulsory membership, and the formation of the Austrian Trade Union Federation in 1945; from a political perspective, there was the formation of a grand coalition between the conservatives and the socialists after 1945, with the aim of putting behind them the years of latent and open class struggle and civil war prior to 1938; and from an economic perspective, there was the need to rebuild the country and gain independence from the allied occupational forces, as well as to control post-war inflation (Guger, 1992).

The most important formal institution of social partnership is the Parity Commission for Wages and Prices, which was founded in 1957 and brings together the social partners represented by the Chambers and the Trade Union Federation, the Federal Chancellor, and the relevant ministers on a voluntary basis. Only the social partners have the right to vote and all decisions have to be unanimous. The Parity Commission has no legal authority nor means of applying direct sanctions. The threat to impose sanctions is left to the government, but has hardly ever been used.

The Parity Commission is the top-level bargaining institution of incomes policy in Austria; it was set up to control price and wage trends. Thanks to its tripartite structure, however, it has also become 'an instrument which gives the employers' and workers' organizations a voice in government economic policy in general and conversely enables the government to make sure of cooperation from these organizations in its economic policy measures' (Suppanz and Robinson, 1972, p. 17).

[5] Suppanz and Robinson (1972), Marin (1982), Gerlich *et al.* (1985).

But it is an instrument which has come under considerable strain in the last decade. The social partners can no longer be sure of having a sufficient voice in the policy formation process, nor, in any case, can the government rely any longer on the backing of these organizations.

The Parity Commission has formed sub-committees on prices and wages to handle its task of curbing prices and wages. The prices sub-committee authorized price increases which have to be justified by substantial cost increases and applied for by individual firms or branches. But, with the reduction of trade barriers in the process of European integration, foreign competition has intensified and many industries became price-takers. Thus, price regulation has more and more come to be considered outdated, and the prices sub-committee has been transformed into a sub-committee on competition.

The wages sub-committee exercises its control on wages by approving or refusing the opening of wage negotiations. Its task is to combine both wage-bargaining autonomy at the branch level and the introduction of macroeconomic considerations in the wage-formation process. To start wage negotiations, individual trade unions have to apply through the Trade Union Federation. Thus, although wage negotiations are conducted by the subordinate sectoral trade union bodies, the Federation has a voice in fixing the dates and coordinating the individual wage claims. There is a working party on wage policy at the trade union headquarters to formulate common objectives of wage policy. Although individual trade unions are autonomous in their actual wage negotiations, bargaining processes have to be authorized and are coordinated by the Trade Union Federation and the wages sub-committee.

It seems that the power of the Austrian Trade Union Federation *vis-à-vis* its subordinate sectoral trade unions is somewhat overestimated in international studies on wage bargaining and corporatism. For one thing, the high and growing wage differentials indicate that one needs to be careful not to put too much emphasis on the high degree of centralization of bargaining in Austria. By having control over finances, the Trade Union Federation is potentially very powerful, but it has given much autonomy to the individual unions.

In 1963, a third permanent sub-committee, the Economic and Social Advisory Board, was established to extend the activities of the Commission beyond incomes policies and to broaden the scientific basis of economic policy. The Advisory Board is composed of representatives of the social partners and ministries, as well as of academic experts. Its task is to prepare a scientific basis for policy recommendations to the government. Compared to similar institutions abroad, the Advisory Board has to be seen, on the one hand, as an instrument for finding consensus by providing a common assessment of important features of the economy. On the other hand, however, it has also served to suppress the discussion of crucial issues such as the problems of environmental protection.

In short, the Austrian social partnership, whose institutions and climate of consensus grew out of the history of the country, can be characterized by a rather high degree of centralization, a wide scope of policy involvement, a cooperative mode of industrial relations, the absence of direct government involvement, and by informality.

(ii) The role of nationalized industries in political exchange

In the aftermath of the Second World War, the largest industrial and financial companies were nationalized in Austria. Since most of them were so-called 'German property', nationalization was considered as a measure to keep these firms out of the reach of the Soviet Union and, therefore, not opposed by the conservative party, the ÖVP. On the contrary, the two main political parties considered the nationalized industries as their property and managed them with equal rights.

In the late 1970s, when the nationalized industries were still intact, firms in public ownership employed about 9 per cent of all employees, or 25 per cent of the employment in manufacturing. If employment in the railways and postal services as well as public employees are included, the employment share under public control rises to about 28 per cent (Pollan, 1997, p. 52).

There is a broad consensus on the importance of nationalization for Austria's economic and social structure (März and Weber, 1978; Pollan, 1997), which was concisely pointed out by Katzenstein (1984, pp. 136–7):

> The nationalization of most large industrial and financial corporations has shifted power away from Austria's business community toward a trade union eager to share in the exercise of power. This shift provides the economic foundation for a balance of power between the two major parties, the SPÖ and the ÖVP, as well as their ancillary organizations representing the interests of labour and business.

This close integration of labour in the governance structure of the country, stretching from policy-making within the social partnership to the management of industry and finance through nationalized firms, has enhanced a macroeconomic perspective in trade-union policy and facilitated both employment policy by hoarding labour (in the 1970s) and moderate wage claims to allow the strong-currency policy. In the mid-1980s, however, the structural crisis in the nationalized iron and steel works contributed to the problem of unemployment and the public deficit. In the process of restructuring and privatization, employment was reduced substantially to improve efficiency, while subsidies still had to be paid. Since, in the last couple of years, the three largest banks together with the large industrial corporations in their ownership have also been privatized, public employment is also in Austria more or less confined to the public and social services as well as gas, water, and electricity supply.

(b) Demand Management

After the Second World War, the promotion of economic growth had an absolute priority in Austria. Since growth was limited by labour shortages throughout the 1960s, both fiscal and monetary policy were committed to promoting investment and growth in labour productivity. Thus, when, after the first oil crisis, the maintenance of full employment became an issue, demand management was not confined to a short-run technique to mitigate cyclical fluctuations, but was a long-term instrument to stabilize business expectations and foster investment and growth.

Owing to the very size of the public sector, fiscal policy has been of great importance in Austria, and monetary policy has accommodated fiscal policy in accordance with the strong-currency option oriented at smoothing down financial speculation and stabilizing nominal interest rates.

From a short-run or cyclical point of view, Austria's federal budget shows a high degree of built-in flexibility. This implies that budget balances are highly sensitive to changes in output and employment through an extensive system of social security that brings about highly effective automatic stabilizers and ensures significant anti-cyclical effects of the federal budget. While these automatic stabilizers of the federal budget may have been of great importance,[6] there were also crucial discretionary fiscal actions in the 1970s; structural balances as well as full-employment budgets indicate a clear change to a more expansionary fiscal stance after 1975. When other countries turned to restrictive measures to combat inflation, Kreisky's government responded to the recession of 1975 with an expansionary strategy and gave full employment top priority.[7]

[6] Long-term comparisons by Hahn and Walterskirchen (1992) as well as by Elmeskov and Pichlmann (1993) show a rather low output variability in welfare states with a large public sector; see also Holzmann and Winckler (1983).

[7] The government's perception of unemployment in these years is best characterized by Chancellor Kreisky's often quoted remark that 'a few thousands more unemployed cause [him] more trouble than a billion more in public debt'.

Table 3
Fiscal Indicators

Country	Total government outlays (% of GDP)				Net government lending (% of GDP)			
	1960–73	1974–9	1980–9	1990–6	1960–73	1974–9	1980–9	1990–6
Austria	38.7	45.8	50.3	51.8	0.7	–2.0	–3.1	–3.5
Belgium	39.0	51.7	59.2	54.1	–2.8	–5.5	–9.3	–5.4
Denmark	33.8	49.1	59.0	61.3*	2.1	–0.2	–2.7	–2.6*
Finland	30.3	38.7	43.5	57.8	3.0	4.7	3.2	–3.6
France	38.0	43.3	50.2	53.1	0.5	–1.1	–2.1	–4.3
Germany	37.5	47.5	47.8	50.0	0.5	–3.0	–2.1	–4.0
Italy	33.7	42.9	49.2	54.3	–3.1	–9.2	–10.8	–9.2
Netherlands	40.1	53.6	61.2	57.1	–0.6	–2.0	–5.1	–4.3
Sweden	38.9	54.4	62.9	66.7	3.8	1.3	–1.6	–5.3
Switzerland	19.9	27.6	29.3	32.4	–	–	–	–2.1
UK	36.7	44.4	44.8	44.2	–0.8	–4.1	–2.5	–5.1
USA	29.1	32.2	35.3	36.4	–0.6	–1.5	–3.4	–3.8
Total EU 15	35.6	43.8	48.6	50.8	–0.3	–3.3	–4.2	–5.2
Total OECD	30.6	36.6	40.6	42.0	–0.2	–2.5	–3.4	–3.8

Note: * 1990–5.
Source: OECD (1999), *Historical Statistics 1960–97*.

From a long-run or growth perspective, there was an extensive system of tax incentives and subsidies, such as accelerated depreciation, tax credits, low-interest loans, and export guarantees, to promote private investment and export demand. All in all, the short-run fiscal demand policy, together with this long-run investment and export promotion, and the government's firm commitment to full employment gave business confidence and stabilized the private sector. Thus, on the one hand, Austria could maintain a high level of capital formation and growth throughout the 1970s, as illustrated in Table 1, while, on the other hand, the increase in net lending of the public sector did not exceed the European average (Table 3).

While 'fine tuning'[8] of the business cycle through the Federal Budget played an important role in the 1970s, this demand-side policy was also supported by supply-side measures on the labour market; these were:

---

[8] At this time, the Federal Budget included a stabilization fund, and the Minister of Finance was authorized to free the fund if the growth forecast of the Austrian Institute of Economic Research (WIFO) had signalled a recession. In other words, he could exceed the expenditure level of the budget by a stipulated amount to stimulate economic activity (Walterskirchen, 1991, p. 8f).

- a reduction of the legal working time in 1975;
- a more restrictive foreign labour policy; and
- some labour hoarding in the nationalized industries which contributed to the favourable employment performance.

But private firms were also rather cautious in their lay-off policies, since unemployment remained at a very low level and business expectations were fairly optimistic throughout the 1970s, as the rather high investment rates in Table 1 indicate. Since demand-management policies were coordinated with incomes and exchange-rate policies, business could count on the government not to over-tighten policies as soon as inflationary pressures arose; business could, actually, rely on the expansionary policy stance in the medium term which in itself promoted investment and stabilized demand.

However, in the aftermath of the second oil crisis, the policy response in Europe and in Germany in particular was much more restrictive; the political shift to conservative governments in the UK, the USA, and Germany, in addition to the implementation of monetarism made an isolated policy of 'diving through the recession' more difficult. While world-wide growth faltered, owing to the oil crisis and restrictive monetary policies, unemployment as well as public deficits jumped, and high interest rates made the costs of financing public debt very expensive. Moreover, in Austria the nationalized iron and steel industries experienced a structural crisis in the early 1980s which also put heavy strains on the federal budget. Thus, altogether, net borrowings of the federal budget as a percentage of GDP increased from 2.6 per cent in 1981 to 5.5 per cent in 1983.

In this environment, the anti-state and anti-activist ideologies of the time found ready acceptance, and when, in the election manifesto of 1983, Kreisky's government proposed a moderate tax at source on interest revenues[9] to divert parts of the high public interest payments back into the budget, to ease the finance of employment programmes, the SPÖ lost its majority in Parliament and had to form a coalition government.

---

[9] Two reasons were given: (i) interest revenues were, as income, taxable anyway, but were evaded on large scale owing to anonymous savings and capital accounts; (ii) in Austria, the savings rate has traditionally been very high and the propensity to save interest revenues is considered as significantly higher, hence the restrictive effects of taxes on interest revenues may be rather small. In 1984, a tax at source on interest revenue of 7.5 per cent was implemented and stepwise increased; today there is a general capital revenue tax of 25 per cent.

While the strong-currency option and moderate incomes policies have been maintained, the coalition governments which followed the majority rule of the SPÖ soon gave budget consolidation priority over full employment and pursued a less expansionary policy. Thus, primary balances (fiscal balance without interest payments on public debt), which amounted on average to –1.4 per cent of GDP in the second half of the 1970s (having a peak of –2.6 per cent in 1976), were, between 1980 and 1996, on average –0.4 per cent of GDP and never exceeded –1.7 per cent. Although in the 1980s and 1990s public deficits (in relation to GDP) have exceeded the levels of the 1970s (Table 3), their impact has been less expansionary; i.e. fiscal policy took a more discretionary stance in the 1970s, while, later, interest payments prevailed and deficits were more or less the results of endogenous processes.

This reorientation of economic policy from 'government-led growth to industrial adjustment' (Walterskirchen, 1991, p. 13) had negative implications for both employment and growth; unemployment figures more than doubled (Figure 1) in the early 1980s, and growth rates, which had been well above European average in the 1960s and 1970s, fell behind in the 1980s, until 1988.

But, when the restructuring and privatization process in national-ized industry got under way, the government managed to pursue its consolidation strategy. Enhanced by the world-wide boom in the late 1980s and the expansionary effects of the German unification process in the early 1990s, the public deficit fell from 4.4 per cent of GDP in 1987 to 1.8 per cent in 1992, despite a major tax reform in 1989, which reduced marginal tax rates and the average level of income taxation signifi-cantly, but increased progressivity (Guger, 1996). There were minor reductions in public benefits and slower increases in public pensions and public salaries, but also additional revenues from higher social security contributions and substantial revenues from privatizing na-tionalized industries.

At the beginning of the 1990s, Austria's relative growth perform-ance had recovered and public finances appeared sound, but owing to a large in-flow of foreign labour and rising labour-force participation rates for women, unemployment figures increased further. And when the currency crisis in the autumn of 1992 resulted in a trade-weighted revaluation of the schilling by 2½ per cent in 1993 and again in 1995, growth rates faltered and fell again below the European average. This was despite the fact that public deficits had in 1993 been sharply increased by discretionary measures — a major tax reform, which abol-ished asset taxation altogether and reduced income taxation, as well as substantially increasing public expenditures by introducing nursing care benefits, extending paid maternity leave to a second year, and increasing family tax credits.

At a time of high interest rates and a sharp revaluation of the schilling, all that resulted in an increase in public deficits to 5 per cent of GDP in 1995 and hardly any measurable improvement of the growth performance, but finally ended in two consolidation packages to fulfil the Maastricht Treaty. But, since interest rates have declined and the schilling devalued as a number of weak currencies recovered in the last 2 years, both growth rates and financial balances have improved and the net lending figure of the public sector amounted to 2.6 per cent of GDP in 1997.

(c) *The Strong Currency Policy*

Exchange-rate policy has traditionally been regarded as an instrument to balance the current account. Taking into account the conditions of a small open economy and the origin of inflation during the oil crisis, Austria has, since the 1970s, assigned price stability to the exchange rate and external equilibrium to incomes policy.

Since 1976, the Austrian schilling has been closely tied to the Deutschmark; the consequence has been a continuous effective appreciation of the schilling. This policy has been widely considered as a precondition for the expansionary demand policy in the face of high inflationary pressures from abroad.[10] It was, actually, suggested by the trade unions as an instrument to enhance incomes policy: on the one hand, because it would slow down the increase in import prices, but also because it may have made it easier for the trade unions to explain their moderate wage policy to their members as reflecting exchange-rate policy.

In the early 1970s, fiscal and monetary policy had been well coordinated in following a rather expansionary course. The National Bank aimed at stable nominal interest rates as well as a stable price level and exchange rate. Since the mid-1970s the Austrian schilling has been tied to the Deutschmark. Yet, mainly due to capital market imperfections, Austrian monetary policy managed to combine its policy of stable interest rates with a roughly constant exchange rate to the Deutschmark until 1979. Then, with growing capital market integration and rising German interest rates this policy became unsustainable and the National Bank gave up its interest policy. The decision to keep to the fixed

---

[10] The idea for this policy is based on the Scandinavian model of inflation (Frisch, 1976).

Figure 2
Relative Labour and Unit Labour Costs in Manufacturing
(Austria *vis-à-vis* trading partners on a schilling basis)

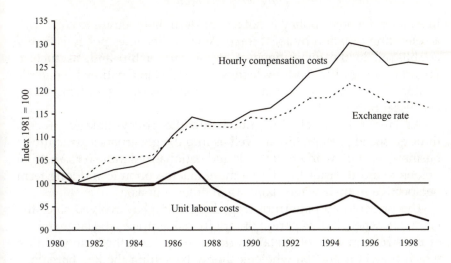

schilling–Deutschmark rate has since narrowed the room of manoeuvre for monetary policy and Austrian monetary policy has to a high degree been determined by both the Deutsche Bundesbank and the difference in inflation expectations between Austria and Germany.

There was also a widespread belief that a strong currency would increase competitive pressures from abroad and promote the restructuring of the economy. And, in fact, the increase in labour productivity in the highly exposed Austrian manufacturing sector has been exceptionally high compared to the main OECD trading partners (Guger, 1995). As Figure 2 illustrates, it has mainly been the appreciation of the schilling which caused the increase of hourly compensation in Austria's manufacturing relative to the main trading partners; but also that, most of the time, this increase in labour costs could be compensated for by improving labour productivity as the development of unit labour costs indicate.

This hard-currency option was certainly rather favourable in the period of inflationary pressures from abroad in the aftermath of the two oil shocks, but it has also been costly in terms of growth in periods of substantial overvaluation of the schilling. When Austria could improve its competitive position (measured by relative unit labour cost in common currency) compared to the EU, the Austrian growth performance outruns the EU average growth rate. Hence, it was often supposed that the unions would oppose the policy of exchange-rate appreciation when unemployment rose, but so far there has never been a move in this direction.

(d) *Incomes Policy from a Long-term Perspective*

In Austria, incomes policy is not a short-term manoeuvre to cope with accelerating inflation by legal force. Austrian incomes policy is firmly established in the institutions of social partnership and, as such, a voluntary long-term device which is embedded in a national economic strategy and coordinated with currency policy as well as with monetary and fiscal policy.

As labour is closely integrated into the policy-making process through social partnership, as well as into the governance structure of business through workers councils and nationalized industry, Austrian unions found it easier to adopt a more macroeconomic and long-term perspective in their wage claims than other unions.

The present-day pattern of wage bargaining has evolved since the late 1960s when, in this period of rapidly rising prices, the large unions of construction and of metal workers recognized the responsibility which they bore for the whole economy by setting the key bargains.

Without any formal agreement between the social partners, the unions themselves pursued a policy of wage restraint to ensure low inflation and international competitiveness. One of the instruments used by unions to moderate wage increases was to retard wage settlements for several months; two clear examples of this strategy were the wage bargains in the recession of 1967/68 and the slowdown of 1978 (Pollan, 1992, p. 4).

There is no 'national wage round' or official wage guideline in Austria because trade unions avoid such standards, which could be viewed as minimum increase and would foster unhealthy inter-union rivalry (Kienzl, 1973, p. 230-1). Although individual unions bargain their own settlements, wage bargains are informally coordinated through preparatory talks as well as through the wage leadership of certain unions. Thus, despite the absence of formal wage norms, the negotiated increases in the wage rates are remarkably uniform, but leave ample room for wage drift at the firm level. This means in industries with strong unions and high productivity growth, actual wage increases are higher than in low productivity/weak union branches. In consequence, wage differentials are rather high in Austria (Guger, 1990; Rowthorn, 1992).

Although collective wage bargaining takes place at the industry level, the bargaining process is highly concentrated. Grouping those units together which form a joint bargaining committee reveals that the three largest wage bargains (public services, white- and blue-collar workers in trade, and blue-collar workers in metal and engineering, including small-scale industries) cover about 45 per cent, and the 5 largest more than 60 per cent of the labour force in Austria. A mere 2 per cent are not covered by any collective agreements (domestic services, non-profit institutions) (Pollan, 1997, p. 50). Collective wage settlements are binding for all employees of the sector or the industry.

The Austrian trade unions have no explicit distributive goals: their policy has been based on a firm growth ideology. Trade union leaders argue that wage policy is not an effective redistributive instrument; it would be detrimental to growth and full employment by dampening investment and hence reducing long-term productivity and real wage growth. Distribution is considered as the sphere of the state, and progressive taxes and high public expenditures as more appropriate redistributive instruments than wage policy.[11] Hence, since the 1970s, trade union leaders and the politicians of the labour movement have emphasized uniformly that maintaining full employment is the most effective distributive policy.

Generally, the wage policy of the Trade Union Federation has been directed both at compensating for inflation and at long-run productivity growth. While during the period of full employment of the 1970s, real wage growth exceeded productivity increases by half a percentage point, distribution has changed in favour of capital in the 1980s and 1990s (Table 4).

In the 1960s, the unions pursued an explicit counter-cyclical wage policy, which implied rather moderate wage claims during business upswings and some pressure during a recession. Hence, wage policy had overall stabilizing effects. When, in the early 1970s, productivity growth ranged between 4 and 6 per cent, the trade unions aimed at promoting growth and full employment and formulated a new guideline, which aimed at a long-run real wage growth of 3 per cent, implying the acceptance of a shift in the functional distribution in favour of profits. But when, after the oil crisis, growth faltered and the current account slid into deficit, it soon became clear that a unilateral stimulation of demand would clash with external equilibrium. Thus, current account considerations were more and more taken into account in wage claims. According to wage equations for the period 1964–84, an increase of the ratio of the current account deficit to GDP of one percentage point dampened the growth of contractual wage rates by half a percentage

[11] In fact, because of low direct but high indirect taxation, the overall tax system is not progressive, but, rather, proportional in Austria. Redistribution by public expenditures, however, is effective (Guger, 1996).

Table 4
Wages, Labour Costs, Productivity, and Inflation
(average annual percentage change)

	1960–70	1970–80	1980–90	1990–9
Total economy				
Productivity	5.0	2.9	2.2	1.9
Real wages	4.8	3.4	1.4	1.0
Nominal wages	8.6	9.9	4.9	3.3
Inflation	3.6	6.2	3.5	2.3
Net real wages	4.2	2.7	1.3	0.1
Manufacturing				
Hourly compensation costs	8.9	11.2	5.6	4.2
Productivity	6.4	5.5	4.8	4.6
Unit labour costs	2.3	5.5	0.8	−0.4
Trade-weighted exchange rate*		2.3	1.3	0.2
Unit labour costs relative to weighted				
trading partners*	−0.8	0.6	−0.8	−0.3

Note: * A positive number means an appreciation of the exchange rate/a decline in cost competitiveness.
Sources: ÖSTAT, WIFO.

point; and by shortening the period by starting in 1970 the coefficient of the current balance as a percentage of GDP increases from 0.6 to 0.8–1.0. (Biffl *et al.*, 1987)

Actually, the wage explosion of 1975, which was mainly due to over-optimistic economic forecasts, was soon scaled back by moderate wage agreements in the following years. In fact, the development of wages was such that the international cost competitiveness of manufacturing improved significantly, despite a substantial revaluation of the Austrian schilling.

Since the early 1980s, a number of interrelated developments, such as the appreciation of the currency, the restructuring process in (nationalized) industry, and rising unemployment have led to a 'downward wage–price spiral', and real wage growth has fallen significantly behind the increase in productivity, meaning a substantial change in income distribution. As illustrated in Figure 2, in the 1980s the increase in relative labour costs was first and foremost due to the appreciation of the exchange rate. In common currency, the rise of hourly wage compensations in Austria's manufacturing outstripped the wage-cost increases of the trading partners by about 15 per cent. While in the first half of the decade this rise in relative wage costs could just about be compensated by higher productivity growth (except in 1986 and 1987),

Austria's manufacturing could significantly improve its competitive position between 1987 and 1991, when exchange rates were stable in the European Currency Union.

However, in the first half of the 1990s, when the so-called weak-currency countries managed to bring down price and wage inflation, Austria (like Germany), whose economy had more than proportionally benefited from the German unification boom, had problems in controlling inflation. Hence, wages in Austria rose much more than in its trading partners and when, in the autumn of 1992 and later on in 1995, important trading partners also devalued against the schilling, these wage-cost rises could no longer be compensated for, despite high productivity increases (Figure 2).

While corporatist institutions have often been considered as obstacles to flexible market adjustments, nominal and real wage flexibility in Austria is one of the highest among OECD countries.[12] Wage equations show that Austria is one of the few countries where the Phillips relation still holds, although there has been a remarkable shift in the 1980s. A comparison between the 1970s and 1980s also reveals that wage flexibility has risen in the 1980s, when unemployment started to rise significantly, which might be due to the fact that the Metal Workers Union, which acts as a quasi wage leader, was hit most severely by the crisis in the nationalized industries (Guger and Polt, 1994, p. 152). Recent tentative empirical studies suggest, however, that rising long-term unemployment may reduce the influence of unemployment on wage increases (Hofer and Pichlmann, 1996; OECD, *Economic Surveys: Austria*, 1997, p. 119).

4. Experiences: Limitations, Threats, and Changes in Policy

The outstanding performance of the Austrian economy in the 1970s has often been attributed to Austria's institutions and its specific policy model. In the 1980s, when the expansionary fiscal policy pillar was gradually abandoned, while the stabilizing elements, the hard-currency option and incomes policy, were maintained, the Austrian economy left the fast lane and the model lost its lustre, although the performance of the Austrian economy could still keep up with European or OECD average. Nevertheless, questions arise as to whether the Austro-Keynesian model has, in the long run, been unsustainable all

---

[12] OECD, *Employment Outlook*, 1997, referring to Layard *et al.* (1991); see also Pichlmann (1990) and Biffl *et al.* (1987).

along, or if the model has not been properly adjusted to new circumstances, and whether political and ideological changes were decisive.

(a) *Limitations and Flaws of the Model*

The Austro-Keynesian policy of the 1970s was essentially a macroeconomic strategy and suffered from both allocative inefficiencies and the absence of equity goals. In 1984, Tichy warned: 'If Austro-Keynesianism should fail in the longer term, it will probably be because of the fact that industrial policy is definitely conserving old and outdated structures' (p. 382). Industrial policy was more or less confined to indirect investment promotions affecting all industries across the board and favouring particularly capital-intensive industries. While this policy fitted in with the macroeconomic strategy to foster growth and a high level of employment, it ignored the long-run allocative effects and hampered the process of structural adjustment and technological progress (Landesmann, 1992). By lowering the costs for investment, this policy increased labour productivity to (West) German levels (Guger, 1995), but capital productivity remained rather low in international comparison. The catching-up process in labour productivity was achieved by a relative rise in capital intensity and not by the use of leading-edge technology; hence capital–output ratios in industry continued to increase in the 1980s, whereas they declined in most other countries (Hahn, 1994).

But there was another element of inefficiency in Austrian corporatism: there were numerous regulations protecting substantial parts of goods and services producers, in particular the professions, against new competitors. Hence, services are rather expensive by international standards. Actually, Austria seems to be a good example of 'defensive corporatism'. Landesmann (1992) has pointed to the fact that industrial policies are generally less conducive to centralized agreements and are therefore less often part of the tripartite negotiations of Austrian corporatism. Forward-looking measures, such as policies fostering structural change, the promotion of R&D, and the redirection of education and training, have only 'potential' advocates, while the protection of well-established interests is often pursued by coalitions between trade-unions and entrepreneurs.

Furthermore, nationalized industries were also an element of inefficiency, although they supported the overall employment strategy of the 1970s by hoarding redundant labour. But, since the mid-1980s, nationalized industry has been successfully restructured and privatized, counting today among the best performers on the stock exchange. Moreover, through the process of joining the Common Market, efficiency has in many respects significantly improved in the Austrian economy. Thus, while the macroeconomic force of the model faded, microeconomic efficiency has certainly improved since the mid-1980s.

As for equity, wage differentials are very high in Austria. According to total labour cost and earnings data for manual workers, Austria shows the highest inter-industry wage differentials in Europe (Guger, 1990; Rowthorn, 1992). Segmentation in the Austrian labour market is generally relatively high; and wage differentials according to social status and qualifications are much higher than in the Scandinavian countries, and higher than in Germany.

Since Austria's notion of 'solidaristic wage policy' was confined to the increase in contractual wages rates, and the actual development of effective earning were left to branch- or firm-specific negotiations, wage dispersion widened more or less continuously from 1970 to 1991 (Hofer and Pichlmann, 1996, p. 17). But, in the late 1980s, trade unions became aware of growing inequalities and enforced higher minimum wages in new wage contracts; hence wages dispersion has narrowed somewhat since 1991.

While wide wage differentials and a flexible wage structure have often been considered as instrumental to labour-market flexibility and productivity growth, the Austrian experience teaches rather the contrary. The large and widening inter-industrial wage differentials have rather hampered the process of structural adjustment — in the 1970s, by keeping labour and capital too long in marginal production, and later on by impeding the process of reallocating labour from high-wage but loss-making (nationalized) industries to profitable industries paying lower wages. A more solidaristic wage policy with higher wage increases in the low-wage sectors would probably have led to higher wage and labour-market rigidity, but certainly also to higher capital mobility and, thus, to faster structural adjustments in the period of high employment.

(b) *The System under Strain*

Since the early 1980s several factors have put heavy strain on the model. First, with regard to fiscal policy, high interest rates owing to restrictive monetary policies, in particular by the Bundesbank, made deficit-financed expansionary strategies rather costly. With public debt already high owing to the deficit spending policy of the 1970s and a cyclically highly sensitive budget, the interest burden of public debt increased sharply. Thus, fiscal policy changed from an expansionary course to budget consolidation. In the 1980s, budget consolidation was mainly accomplished by reducing public investment and privatization revenues from selling off minority stakes of nationalized industries and banks, but public consumption was hardly reduced (Marterbauer, 1993). In contrast, the latest consolidation packages of the mid-1990s were financed by the sale of majority stakes in nationalized industries and banks, as well as reductions in transfer payments and curbing outlays for personnel in the public sector by a 2-year wage-freeze for public employees and reductions in public employment; in addition, there was a 1-year freeze on public pensions. While the unions had by and large supported the policy of the 1980s, the latest consolidation strategy led to considerable tensions between the government and the ÖGB. But, enhanced by the recovery of the European economy, budget consolidation has been well under way and Austria will meet the net lending criterion of the Maastricht Treaty without problems.

Second, considering the power of speculative financial capital, sticking firmly to the hard-currency option may have been a right decision, but it has also been a costly strategy in real terms. While the Austrian schilling has appreciated against its trade partner by about 25 per cent since 1980, the exposed sectors of the economy have had to cope with sudden changes in their competitive position owing to speculative runs against the currencies of important trading partners.

Third, there has also been a significant change in the governance structure of the economy: corporatism and its institutions have generally been losing influence. On the one hand, the general process of globalization is internationalizing production and increasing competition in the markets of goods and services as well as in the factor markets ('Standortwettbewerb'). On the other hand, integration into the EU has limited the influence of the social partners on economic policy in general, as many areas of economic policy will be shifted to the central European level.

Concerning incomes policy, there have been tendencies which strain the governance capacity of social partnership in general and the power of unions in particular. First, owing to a number of factors, power has shifted away from labour to capital; there were structural causes, such as the changes in the employment structure, i.e. shifts from large-scale manufacturing production to services, and the virtual disappearance of the nationalized industries which had actually been the backbone of trade union power for a long time. Furthermore, the process of globalization in general, and the fall of the Iron Curtain in particular, have increased the relative mobility of capital *vis-à-vis* labour; i.e. the role of 'share-holder value' combined with the threat to relocate plants and thereby jobs has become an important argument in every bargaining process. Finally, the rise in unemployment and the influx of (cheap) labour from abroad have certainly, as everywhere in Europe, weakened labour's position significantly. But despite these tendencies, union density fell rather moderately in the 1980s (Traxler, 1992).

Second, enhanced by the process of deregulation and decentralization, the power of centralized bargaining institutions has declined over the years, while the power of individual bargaining units and of works councils rose. In fact, as Pollan (1997, p. 60) recently pointed out:

> Industrialists, ready to exploit the weakness and disarray of the unions, are pushing hard for an increase in labour market flexibility, for decentralized wage bargaining, and, alarmed by competition from Eastern Europe, for reductions in overall labour costs. On all fronts, unions and works councils are on the defensive.

The strength of trade union power wisely used in a long-term macroeconomic perspective was the main foundation of the Austrian social partnership. But, with the position of labour eroding, the imbalance in bargaining power has been growing, and it will be the responsibility of business leaders not to take too much advantage. To push labour too far into the background may destroy the still cooperative climate in the bargaining process.

(c) *Increasing Polarization in Politics*

In the 1960s and 1970s, both labour and capital and their political camps, the SPÖ and the ÖVP, shared by and large the same Keynesian paradigm and a state-interventionist ideology. Later on, with the rise of monetarism and the shift to conservative governments and firm anti-state ideologies in the UK and USA, the Austrian conservatives also adopted a view more critical of the state; first, in the early 1980s, in the institutions of social partnership and then, since 1987, also in the government. Furthermore, as the public deficit increased sharply while unemployment was still rising, voters also became more and more disenchanted. Thus, the coalition governments after 1983 have gradually given budget consolidation priority over full employment.

At the same time, an erosion of the main political camps in response to shifts in the occupational structure, particularly the growth of white-collar employment and the service sector, has also paved the way for an 'individualization' of values and gradually fading support for the corporate governance structure. With respect to incomes policy, on the business side, reservations about collective bargaining above the plant level are growing, and, on the labour side, the FPÖ, which has always been strongly opposed to social partnership, has recently founded a union to break up the monopoly of the ÖGB.

With the formation of the centre-right coalition between the ÖVP and the FPÖ in February 2000, the process of polarization in Austrian politics has entered a new stage. In contrast to the consensual strategy of the past, when the government tried to reach an agreement with the social partners in all relevant social and economic policy questions, the new government, under the motto 'speed kills', has hurried through its policy changes without regard to the interests of one social partner, namely the trade unions.

With the support of big industry the government has pursued a rather austere policy of budget consolidation (zero-deficit budgeting), coupled with re-distributive measures at the expense of employees, pensioners, low-income groups, and people living on welfare by increasing indirect taxation and reducing expenditures on social security; these measures have been fiercely opposed by the ÖGB. For entrepreneurs, on the other hand, the government holds out the prospect of reduced taxation and lower employers' contributions to social security with the aim of reducing labour costs at the end of the term.

This is not the end of Austrian social partnership, which had shown signs of erosion since the mid-1990s, though it is a significant institutional change: the new government has been attempting to confine social partnership to labour relations and incomes policy.

5. Conclusions and Prospects

In the aftermath of the first oil crisis, Austria's social democratic government pursued a distinct policy strategy which has been labelled 'Austro-Keynesianism'. The model had been formulated as a short-term device to overcome the period of stagflation and to maintain full employment in the second half of the 1970s. In the Keynesian tradition, the model assigned expansionary fiscal and monetary policy to stabilize effective demand and employment; but, taking into account the openness of the economy and the fast-rising import prices at that time, a strong currency was considered a proper instrument to curb inflation, while responsibility for the balance of trade was left to incomes policy moderation by the social partners.

In the 1970s, this strategy was successful; owing to the firm stand of Kreisky's government in favour of full employment and the support of the social partners, the policy was convincing and thus stabilized business expectations. In consequence, the macroeconomic performance of the Austrian economy was outstanding.

But, in the 1980s, the Austro-Keynesian model waned; the restrictive international environment, with enormously high interest rates, made an isolated expansionary fiscal policy more and more unsustainable. Thus, while maintaining the stabilizing elements of the model, i.e. the hard currency and moderate incomes policies, deficit spending as a discretionary strategy has been given up. At the same time, the economy has improved its microeconomic efficiency significantly; on the one hand, by restructuring the industrial sector, and, on the other hand, by joining the European Union so that services have been exposed to more competition from abroad. In fact, although the Austrian economy has been put under much competitive pressure owing to a continuous appreciation of the schilling along with the Deutschmark, its macroeconomic performance has been at least as good as the European or OECD average, but with lower unemployment.

Hence, while Austria has, on the one hand, been losing some of its distinctive features and has gradually been approaching a European standard, on the other hand, in the European Monetary Union, with more stable currency relations than in the past, its prospects look rather bright.

4

Social Democracy and Market Reform in Australia and New Zealand

JOHN QUIGGIN*

1. Introduction

The political and economic history of Australia and New Zealand over the past 25 years displays remarkable parallels. In 1972, both countries elected social democratic governments led by charismatic reformers, Gough Whitlam and Norman Kirk. Both governments seemed set to achieve long-held goals of the labour movement including the provision of free university education and medical care, more generous social welfare benefits, and public support for the arts and sciences. Labour (or, in the Australian spelling, Labor) appeared as the party of the future.

Twenty-five years later, these hopes are in ruins. Conservative governments pledged to radical free-market reforms hold office in both countries. Worse still, from the perspective of social democracy, the shift to the right is simply an extension of policies initiated by labour governments in the 1980s. The key components of the Thatcher revolution, including deregulation, privatization, competitive tendering, and contracting for public services, were implemented in Australia and New Zealand by labour governments. The only major task they left to their successors was that of breaking the (already greatly reduced) power of the union movement through labour-market reform.

* Australian National University and Queensland University of Technology.
This chapter would not have been possible without extensive discussions with Brian Easton and Andrew Glyn. I also thank an anonymous referee for helpful and perceptive comments.

2. The Fraser and Muldoon Governments

By 1975, the collapse of the long post-war boom had led to the downfall of labour governments in Australia and New Zealand. Particularly in Australia, reaction against the failures of the governments of 1972–5 was a major factor in Labor's subsequent shift to the right. The expansion of public spending and the rapid growth in real wages that took place under Whitlam were seen as major contributors to the recession of 1974 and to the emergence of sustained high unemployment. Subsequent Labor leaders were at pains to present themselves as responsible economic managers and to distance themselves, as much as possible, from Whitlam. There was also a reaction against Whitlam's style of government. The system of caucus democracy, in which Cabinet decisions were frequently rejected by the parliamentary party as a whole, was seen as symbolic of misgovernment. Whitlam's determination to implement the programme on which he had been elected, regardless of deteriorating economic circumstances, was seen as dogmatism.

The governments that replaced those of Whitlam and Kirk were led by conservative strong men: Malcolm Fraser in Australia and Robert Muldoon in New Zealand. When they took office, both men were seen as radical right-wingers, but from the vantage point of the 1990s, they are usually regarded as highly interventionist. This view is anachronistic, in that it projects policy concerns of the 1980s on to earlier periods (Kelly, 1992) and misleading, in that the trend of policy under the Fraser and Muldoon governments was towards deregulation, even if hesitantly and with frequent reversals. For example, the Fraser government laid the groundwork for much subsequent free-market reform, most notably through the establishment of the Campbell Committee of inquiry into the financial system, which recommended deregulation of financial markets and a freely floating exchange rate. Similarly, the Muldoon government liberalized foreign-exchange regulations, deregulated parts of the transport sector, and removed barriers to trade with Australia through the Closer Economic Relations agreement (Bollard and Buckle, 1987).

The conservatives initially assumed that the economic crisis of the early 1970s would be resolved by a combination of monetarist macro-economic policies and a cut in real wages. The second oil shock of 1979 made it clear that these assumptions were invalid, but provided a new hope, that of an export-led recovery based on minerals and energy. The most notable expression of this hope was Muldoon's 'Think Big' programme, a set of projects based on the exploitation of natural gas and other resources.

By the early 1980s, it was clear that hopes for an export-led recovery were misplaced. The booms never eventuated and the projects designed to exploit them resulted in growth in international debt, particularly in New Zealand. The contrast between apparently boundless resources and poor economic performance created a widespread sense of disillusionment with the economic policies of the past. Rising unemployment and slow growth were seen as the outcome of national economic failings rather than as a part of an economic crisis common to all developed countries. This view was supported by the assumption that international problems were primarily due to higher energy prices and should therefore not affect energy-rich countries.

In Australia, concern about poor economic performance was expressed in the growth of a literature focusing on the alleged decline of Australian living standards relative to those of other developed countries. Work in this literature began with the claim that, in 1870, Australians had enjoyed the highest standard of living in the world but that slow relative growth had led to Australia being overtaken by a dozen or more countries. Projecting this trend forward, it was suggested that Australians would soon be 'following the Argentinian path' (Duncan and Fogarty, 1985) or would become the 'poor white trash of the Pacific' (Scutt, 1985). Most Australian writers in the 'white trash' tradition blamed the 'Federation trifecta' of policies centred on tariff protection, the arbitration system of wage determination, and the White Australia policy for creating a backward-looking and inward-looking culture (Henderson, 1983).

A less dramatic version of the argument focused on below-average growth in income per capita in the period after 1950. The statistical basis of the literature on relative decline is weak (Quiggin, 1987), and most econometric studies conclude that, after taking account of convergence effects and differences in population growth rates, Australia's economic performance for the period 1950–80 was about average for the OECD (Gruen, 1986; Dowrick and Nguyen, 1989). Nevertheless, the steady decline in the terms of trade for exporters of primary products presented both countries with economic problems. Particular difficulties were created for New Zealand, which remained heavily reliant on British export markets over the post-war period and suffered economic losses when Britain entered the European Community in 1971. The extent to which New Zealand's poor economic performance over the 1970s can be explained by adverse trade shocks is open to debate. In any case, by the end of the decade, per-capita income in New Zealand was between 5 and 10 per cent lower than in Australia.

The claim that past policies have yielded poor outcomes implies support for radical change, but gives little guidance as to the appropriate direction of change. In the early 1980s, however, the debate in both countries was dominated by advocates of the ideas referred to in Australia as 'economic rationalism'. The term originated under the Whitlam government where it had the positive connotation of policy formulation on the basis of reasoned analysis, as opposed to tradition, emotion, and self-interest, but, with the exception of support for free trade, did not imply a presumption in favour of particular policy positions. Over time, however, most 'economic rationalists' came to assume that reasoned analysis would always lead to support for free-market policies. Hence, the analytical process could be dispensed with, and replaced by advocacy of a predetermined set of policies, those of market reform.

The example of the Industries Assistance Commission, set up by Whitlam to make recommendations on tariffs and agricultural support policies, was highly influential. After receiving a reference from the government to inquire into a policy area, the Committee held public hearings before producing a report, which almost invariably advocated a reduction in government intervention. The best of these reports achieved high standards in presenting a detailed consideration of the evidence and a tightly argued policy analysis, and even the worst were usually more impressive than the arguments put up by the Commission's opponents. Especially in its heyday in the 1970s and early 1980s, the Commission was seen as a model of rational policy-making by many economists. Critics who suggested that the Commission's conclusions were predetermined and that the inquiry procedures were little more than elaborate window-dressing (Quiggin, 1993; Toohey, 1994) had little influence before the 1990s.

Apart from the Commission's reports, the most important policy document produced by the economic rationalists was *Australia at the Crossroads* by Kasper *et al.* (1980), who proposed a radical free-market programme which, they predicted, would raise per-capita income by more than 70 per cent, relative to a no-change baseline. By the time of its defeat in 1996, the Hawke–Keating Labor government had implemented most of the programme proposed by Kasper *et al.* (1980), going well beyond it in many cases. However, growth in per-capita income was no higher than in the baseline scenario presented by Kasper *et al.*

In New Zealand, the future Finance Minister, Roger Douglas, had expressed his discontent with existing policies in his book *There's Got to Be a Better Way* (Douglas, 1980). As the title suggests, Douglas was looking for a radically new policy agenda. However, Douglas (1980) was still open to interventionist as well as free-market options. By 1983, drawing on advice from businessmen and Treasury officials, Douglas had developed a radical free-market programme (Easton, 1996a).

Parallel developments in the policy debate were unsurprising in view of the close linkage between the economies of Australia and New Zealand. Migration between Australia and New Zealand has always been unrestricted and the Closer Economic Relations agreement signed in 1983 removed most barriers to the flow of goods. The parallel economic performance of the two countries is therefore not surprising. The modest divergence in performance over the 1970s could reasonably be explained as a temporary shock, arising from New Zealand's greater reliance on the United Kingdom as an export market, and Australia's greater endowment of mineral resources, particularly coal and oil.

The surprise was the divergence that took place during the 1980s, when GDP per capita in New Zealand fell to a level 20 per cent below that prevailing in Australia, and remained there (Easton and Gerritsen, 1996). Even more surprisingly, most international commentary is based on the assumption that New Zealand's reforms have been highly successful, while Australia is seen to have suffered because of its less whole-hearted approach to free-market reform. In fact, as is shown in section 8, whereas Australia's economic performance has been very similar to the OECD average since 1983, New Zealand's has been considerably worse.

3. The Adoption of Free-market Reform

The term 'reform' is normally interpreted to mean 'change for the better'. This usage makes sense in a context where everyone agrees about the desirable direction of change, although there may be disagreements about the pace of change and the feasibility of particular reform strategies. For most of the present century, 'reform' has been broadly synonymous with 'social democratic reform'. The free-market policies introduced in Australia and New Zealand are described as reforms but involve repealing the reforms of the past. Rather than adopt a tendentious description of this process, such as 'reaction', I will use the term 'reform' to refer to policies promoting structural change, without any presumption that reforms are desirable. The Australian and New Zealand labour governments entered office as advocates of social democratic reform, but implemented policies of free-market reform.

In Australia, the Hawke Labor government was elected on the basis of a social democratic programme, embodied in its 1982 platform. This platform was the product of a thoroughgoing reassessment of the party's procedures and policies following the defeat of the Whitlam government. Although in some respects the platform marked a retreat from the ambitious goals of the Whitlam period, it maintained both a long-run commitment to social democratic ideals and a belief in the necessity for extensive intervention in the economy through active industry policy, public ownership of natural monopolies, and so on.

The platform also included innovative elements, of which the most important was the idea of a Prices and Incomes Accord. Shortly after its election, the government held a national economic summit conference in an attempt to extend the Accord relationship between the government and the unions to a tripartite process incorporating business. The summit, which reflected Hawke's personal commitment to consensus politics was a great political success. In the long term its greatest significance was that it served as a model for the Tax Summit of 1986, which prevented the introduction of a goods and service tax.

As well as establishing the Accord, the Hawke government took a number of steps towards implementing its social democratic pro-gramme, including raising social welfare benefits, introducing a na-tional health insurance scheme (Medibank), and maintaining the stimu-latory fiscal policy inherited from the outgoing Fraser government.

Nevertheless, the pressures for movement in a different direction were strong. The defining event for the Hawke government's economic policy came in December 1983. The dollar came under speculative pressure as foreign-exchange markets anticipated an appreciation. Instead of tightening controls on capital flows, as the Whitlam Labor government had done in similar circumstances, the government de-cided to float the currency and abolish exchange controls.

The float and, even more, the abolition of exchange controls, were significant steps in themselves. The effect of the float was to give financial markets greatly increased power over the government's economic policy, or, in the jargon of the day, to expose the government to 'market discipline'. On the other hand, the discipline on private-sector borrowings implicit in a fixed exchange rate was lost. Australia has always been a capital-importing country, but in the 1980s the inflow of capital, and the corresponding current-account deficits grew rapidly, exceeding 5 per cent of GDP in the late 1980s. At the same time, debt and portfolio holdings of equity replaced direct foreign investment. The results included an explosive growth in private overseas debt and an overvaluation of the currency leading to sustained current account deficits. Concern about debt and the current-account deficit eventually forced the government into the contractionary policies that precipi-tated the recession of 1989–91.

More fundamentally, the float marked the willingness of leading members of government to abandon traditional social democratic views in favour of free-market economic views. Rather than being seen as a regrettable necessity, the float was presented as a break with the dogmas of the past. For the first few years after 1983, the government prided itself on maintaining a 'clean' float, with minimal intervention from the Reserve Bank, though a more pragmatic stance emerged over time.

The enthusiastic reaction of the financial markets reinforced the government's change of direction. Keating was named Finance Minister of the Year by *Euromoney* magazine, and for a decade afterwards bore the (frequently ironic) nickname 'The World's Greatest Treasurer'. Roger Douglas won the same award the following year.

Although the business establishment maintained its historic links with the Liberal Party, Labor was closely linked with the rising 'entrepreneurs' of whom the archetypal example was Alan Bond.[1] Despite the name, the entrepreneurs were not noted for significant new undertakings, but focused on property speculation and takeover deals. They were initially embraced by the labour governments as proof of the dynamism generated by financial deregulation. However, the entrepreneurs were quickly disowned as their financial empires unravelled after the stock-market crash of 1987.

The enthusiastic reception of the float by financial markets, and the acquiescence of the Labor movement, emboldened the leaders of the government to move further away from traditional Labor views and further towards a thoroughgoing economic rationalism. Acceptance of more wide-ranging financial deregulation and the desirability of cutting back the public sector followed rapidly. The abandonment of Labor's belief in the public sector was formalized in the 'Trilogy' commitments of 1984. The commitments were:

- federal government tax revenue would not be permitted to grow as a proportion of GDP;
- federal government spending would not grow faster than the economy as a whole; and
- the Federal deficit would be reduced in money terms in 1985–6 and would not be permitted to grow as a proportion of GDP in the following 2 years.

The government was initially fairly successful in meeting these objectives, but the deficit and public expenditure grew rapidly after the economy went into recession in 1989. Nevertheless, after the Trilogy commitments, the direction of Labor's economic policy was set.

---

[1] As well as controlling assets worth billions of dollars, Bond was famous for owning the yacht which won the America's Cup, and for paying a world-record price for a Van Gogh painting, through a complex transaction which ended in a prison sentence.

Under Hawke's prime ministership (1983–91) and then Keating's (1992–6), the government's commitment to free-market policies became steadily stronger, and was embodied in a comprehensive programme of microeconomic reform.[2] In 1988, the government committed itself to a general reduction in tariffs, and to privatization of enterprises such as the Commonwealth Bank. In 1990 the two-airlines agreement came to an end, and the basis was laid for competition in telecommunications. During the early 1990s, policies of competitive tendering and contracting out and private provision of infrastructure led to a further contraction of the role of government.

In this respect, Labor's most significant legacy was the National Competition Policy Act, frequently referred to as the 'Hilmer reforms' after the report of Hilmer *et al.* (1993) on which the policy was based. This act bound both state and federal governments to implement comprehensive pro-market reforms, to be overseen by the unelected and unaccountable National Competition Council. The most noteworthy examples are the corporatization of government business enterprises and a comprehensive programme of competitive tendering and contracting for publicly provided services. As a result, although electors, and even the Howard Liberal government, have shown considerable 'reform fatigue', the policies of the free-market reformers who dominated the Labor government are still being implemented.

(a) *Explaining Australian Labor's Shift to the Right*

Throughout its shift to the right, the Australian Labor government followed, rather than led, the climate of opinion among the economic policy élite.[3] At least until the recession that commenced in 1990, this climate was one of increasingly unqualified economic rationalism.[4] It is, then, unsurprising that the Australian Labor Party moved to the right.

---

[2] More extensive discussion of microeconomic reform policies is given by Forsyth (1992), Gruen and Grattan (1993), and Quiggin (1996).

[3] The meaning and relevance of the term 'policy-making élite' has been debated. The policy-making élite included the Reserve Bank and the 'central' departments of the Federal government (Treasury, Finance, and Prime Minister's), and the Industry Commission. The economic rationalism of these institutions was supported and amplified by the majority of economic commentators, the Opposition Liberal Party, business organizations such as the Business Council of Australia and the National Farmers Federation, and a proliferation of private-sector think-tanks, which recruited many of their staff from institutions such as the Treasury. Some of these groups had little direct access to the government, but led opinion from outside.

[4] The pejorative use of the term 'economic rationalism' was first popularized in the early 1990s by a study of decision-making élites in the Commonwealth public service (Pusey, 1991).

In all of this, the experience of Australian Labor was broadly similar to that of European social democrats who, with greater or smaller degrees of reluctance, followed the prevailing trend towards free-market policies.

The fact that Australian Labor showed much less reluctance may be explained, in large measure, by the factional structure of the party. The dominant Right group, and to a lesser extent its Centre-Left allies, had a tradition of 'pragmatic' contempt for ideology, priding itself on its single-minded focus on obtaining and retaining office. This did not, of course, mean that the faction was free of ideology. Rather, the lack of any socialist ideological ballast left the Right open to capture by the newly dominant ideology of economic rationalism. Defence of traditional Labor policies was confined to the minority Left faction, which was largely ineffectual. After a few years in which the Left was successfully marginalized within the government, the main leaders of the Left, such as Brian Howe, were willing to accept the general policy of free-market reform in exchange for greater influence in areas such as social-security policy.

Hence, no serious attempt was made, within or outside the government, to put forward an alternative economic programme, except in some isolated areas of policy. During the period of opposition from 1975 to 1983, Labor's attention had been focused on macroeconomic issues and the development of an expansionary programme centred on the Accord. There had also been a vigorous debate on tariffs and industry policy, which led to support for a number of 'Industry Plans' adopted in the early years of the government.[5] With these exceptions, however, the terms of the policy debate were set by the economic rationalists. The question for the government was not which way to turn, but how fast to move in the free-market direction.

(b) *New Zealand*

The New Zealand Labour Party won office in 1984 on the basis of a fairly traditional, if vague, social democratic platform. However, the incoming Finance Minister, Roger Douglas, had already developed the policy

---

[5] The steel plan was generally viewed as highly successful, and adjustment plans for the motor vehicle and heavy engineering industry were qualified successes (Castles and Stewart, 1993). Attempts to smooth the contraction of the textile industry were less successful and policies aimed at stimulating 'sunrise' industries, such as biotechnology, had little impact. However, the abandonment of active industry policy was due far more to the advance of free-market ideology than to any empirical evaluation of its successes and failures.

programme that would be followed by the Labour government. As in Australia, the Labour government came to office as the result of a snap election, which was accompanied by a foreign-exchange crisis. The crisis atmosphere ensured that Douglas and his supporters could implement their policy programme without regard to community concerns or opposition within the Labour Party. The Prime Minister, David Lange initially left economic matters to Douglas, focusing attention on foreign-policy issues, such as the ban on nuclear ship visits.

Whereas Hawke's approach to politics was based on negotiation and consensus, Douglas favoured rapid implementation of reforms on a broad front, on the assumption that when the benefits of reform were evident, popular support would follow (Douglas, 1993). Douglas regarded consultative processes (New Zealand held its own economic summit in 1985) as little more than a device to confuse and neutralize opponents. Douglas's authoritarian approach was made easier by the fact that New Zealand is a unitary state with a unicameral Parliament. As Evans *et al.* (1996, pp. 1856–7) observe:

> The early pace of the reforms reflects in good part the deep-seated nature of the initial crisis, widespread recognition, particularly in the business community, of the need for change, strong intellectual and administrative support from key public sector advisers and New Zealand's constitutional arrangements. In New Zealand a governing party with a clear parliamentary majority can legislate its programme with few constitutional impediments. The major non-constitutional constraints on the executive are internal party unity, electoral support, and the disciplines imposed by external financial flows.

The electoral system until 1996 was one of single-member constituencies elected to a unicameral Parliament on a plurality basis, which permitted a government to achieve a substantial majority of seats while receiving a minority of votes cast. In Australia, by contrast, national governments have normally had the support of a reliable majority in the House of Representatives, elected by constituencies, but not in the Senate, which is elected by a system of proportional representation. In addition, power is divided between national and state governments and all governments are constrained by the constitutional limitations associated with a federal system. Finally, the links between the New Zealand Labour Party and the trade-union movement were weak, whereas those in Australia were strong and were made even stronger by the Accord.

It is important to consider whether the fact that reform was more radical in New Zealand than in Australia (or for that matter, anywhere else in the world) reflected broader discontent with the existing economic policy framework or whether it was simply the result of a set of institutions and personalities which made radical reform easier to implement. New Zealand's economic situation was objectively worse on most measures, though not with respect to unemployment. However, there was no shortage of discontent with Australia's economic performance, and the prophets of doom in the early 1980s were at least as prominent in Australia as in New Zealand (Duncan and Fogarty, 1985). The critical factor is that the New Zealand political system was open to the 'blitzkrieg' approach required to impose free-market reforms on an initially sceptical, and later actively hostile, public (Easton, 1997).

4. Financial Deregulation

The case for financial-market deregulation in Australia had been put forward in the report of the Campbell Committee of Inquiry, appointed by the Fraser government. In opposition, Labor had criticized the report, correctly predicting that,

> Total deregulation of financial markets, as advocated by the report, would bring about higher interest rates, increased government taxes and charges, less finance for housing, a more volatile exchange rate, greater foreign ownership and less control by government over the form or pace of development of the Australian economy. (quoted in Langmore, 1992)

However, as the Labor government moved towards acceptance of a freely floating exchange rate, commitment to a policy of regulation of domestic financial institutions became untenable. The government commissioned a new report which recommended the removal of all interest-rate controls and of restrictions on maturities on trading and savings bank interest-bearing deposits, and, most controversially, the admission of foreign banks. In the first major trial of strength with the Left of the party, the recommendation for the admission of foreign banks was pushed through the 1984 Annual Conference of the Australian Labor Party (Gruen and Grattan, 1993).

Financial deregulation in New Zealand commenced almost immediately after the government's election, and was even more rapid than in Australia. All controls on capital flows and on the asset portfolios of financial institutions were abolished. The abolition of exchange controls removed the main effective barrier to foreign investment and the majority of large companies became either partially or completely foreign-owned.

In both countries deregulation produced an explosion in financial speculation but did little to improve either the availability or the allocation of long-term investment capital. The most noticeable result was the rise and fall of paper financial empires of the 'entrepreneurs', such as Bond and Skase in Australia and Judge in New Zealand. However, the entrepreneurs were merely the most visible symbol of a boom in speculative lending and investment in which the major banks and well-established businesses were heavily involved.

The failure of deregulation may be traced to its one-sided nature. Although controls on banks and other financial institutions were removed, the government remained committed to maintaining the stability of the financial system, and therefore to protecting financial institutions from collapse. The advocates of deregulation accepted that prudential supervision of the banks aimed at controlling the risk of bank failures and financial panics, was required even in a deregulated setting, but failed to recognize that the effectiveness of prudential controls would be seriously compromised by the removal of the majority of existing regulations. Although some new controls, such as the prime asset ratio and capital adequacy controls, were introduced, they proved inadequate to the task.

Deregulation put the banks in a no-lose situation. They could and did adopt much more risky lending strategies. If their loans turned out well, the banks pocketed the profits. If they turned out badly, the government was there to pick up the tab. Examples abound, but the experience of Bond and Skase clearly demonstrated the inability or unwillingness of the banks rigorously to monitor their credit risks. A major outcome of deregulation was an increase in lending to marginal customers, many of whom borrowed to speculate. In the last 5 years of the 1980s, while personal credit grew at around 10 per cent a year and credit for housing by 15 per cent, business debt increased by 25 per cent a year. The boom in speculative lending was reflected in poor investment decisions. The Industry Commission (1997) estimates that capital productivity growth over the 1980s was negative.

In practice, the banks did not need to call on the Reserve Bank to act as lender of last resort. Publicly guaranteed banks are 'too big to fail'. That is, the cost of letting such banks become insolvent, and paying out the depositors, is greater than the cost of assisting them to carry on as going concerns. In addition, the effects of a major bank failure on international and domestic business confidence have been too serious to contemplate. As soon as it became apparent that banks were in serious difficulty, government began to tilt the 'level playing field' in their favour. Foreign ownership rules were bent to enable the banks to realize a better return on the assets in the media and other industries that they acquired as a result of the failure of the entrepreneurs to whom they had lent. The tax treatment of bank losses was made more

favourable. This pattern of rescuing failed institutions has been followed in other countries that have experienced a deregulation-led
boom and slump.

The New Zealand experience was slightly different. Most institutions were owned either by government or by foreign (largely Australian) financial institutions and were bailed out by their owners when
they ran into trouble. New Zealand has continued to maintain a *laissez-
faire* approach to financial regulation, effectively relying on the overseas
owners of its financial institutions, and their central banks, to maintain
the stability of the financial system.

It would have been difficult for any government to resist the
pressure for deregulation. The effectiveness of the controls which
existed at the beginning of the 1980s were being gradually eroded.
Financial institutions outside the controls had grown in influence and
the regulated financial institutions had created debt instruments that
were close substitutes for those which were controlled. However, there
were choices. Some countries, such as the Scandinavian countries, the
United Kingdom, New Zealand, and Australia, chose policies of radical
deregulation, while other European countries made only moderate
changes to their regulation policies. The results of radical deregulation
have been uniformly damaging and have followed a remarkably similar
pattern: an asset price boom followed by collapse and severe recession.

5. Tax Policy

The first major difference between Australia and New Zealand in the
process of free-market reform arose with respect to tax policy. The
advocates of free-market reform, led by the Treasurer, Paul Keating, in
Australia and the Finance Minister, Roger Douglas, in New Zealand,
were committed to the idea of a Goods and Services Tax (GST), that is,
a broad-based consumption tax using the value-added tax (VAT)
mechanism. Based on the experience of the introduction of a VAT in
Canada, the reformers favoured a flat-rate tax with no exemptions,
arguing that an exemption for say, food, would 'open the floodgates'
to demands for other exemptions and therefore defeat the purpose of
reform.

However, the inclusion of food in the tax base for the first time
ensured that the move to a GST would be regressive, especially when
combined with cuts in top marginal tax rates. This made the task of
securing a consensus in favour of such a tax-reform package virtually
impossible. Although a good deal of intellectual effort was expended
in attempts at squaring the circle, it was impossible to design a package

which compensated low-income earners and recipients of social security benefits for the regressive impact of the GST, while leaving enough net revenue to finance significant cuts in top marginal rates of income taxation.

In Australia, the cooperation of the unions was essential to the success of the government's wages policy, based on the Prices and Incomes Accord. Moreover, Hawke was philosophically committed to the idea of consensus. The government therefore organized a Tax Summit, at which it proposed a set of three tax options. The idea was that both the mildly radical Option A and the do-nothing Option B would prove unacceptable, leading to the formation of a consensus behind Option C, based on a GST. It was hoped that the unions and business groups would be attracted by the prospect of low marginal income tax rates and that the 'welfare lobby' would welcome the expansion of social welfare expenditure designed to offset the regressive impact of the GST.

In the event, however, the unions were sceptical about Option C, and welfare groups strongly opposed it. When business leaders, still hostile to Labor, refused to back the package, Hawke abandoned it, leading to the first major breach in his relationship with Keating. In the end, the government adopted tax reforms based on Option A, including taxes on fringe benefits and capital gains, offset by full dividend imputation and cuts in top marginal rates. As a result, the net impact of tax changes under Labor was broadly neutral, with the tax burden faced by different income groups changing very little over the period 1983–96

In New Zealand, the lack of popular support for a GST was not an obstacle to its implementation. The Labour government, with an outright majority in a unicameral Parliament, saw no need to seek national consensus before adopting a tax policy that had not been mentioned in its election campaign nor to worry about compensating low-income earners. The GST was introduced at a uniform rate of 10 per cent, later increased to 12.5 per cent, with food being taxed at the full rate, while the top marginal rate of income tax was reduced to 48 per cent and then to 33 per cent.

The case for cuts in the top marginal tax rate was based on the supposed disincentive effects of high marginal tax rates. This argument ignored the fact that in a tax-welfare system with targeted or means-tested welfare benefits, the highest effective marginal tax rates are usually those faced by low-income earners, many of whom are also likely to have more elastic labour supply than high-income earners.

The additional revenue from the GST was insufficient to fund the income tax cuts on a sustainable basis, and the resulting growth in the budget deficit put government spending under pressure. Hence, the limited measures introduced to compensate low-income earners were quickly eroded. The net impact of the tax policy changes was highly regressive.

From this point on, the development of economic policy in Australia and New Zealand diverged. Although the two countries followed much the same path towards free-market reforms, the Australian government was more cautious. It claimed to follow a pragmatic and realistic policy, a middle way between the irrelevance of adherence to traditional Labor shibboleths and the free-market dogmatism of the conservative parties.

The divergence is clearly apparent in the subsequent careers of Douglas and Keating. Douglas left the New Zealand Labour Party after the government fell in 1990, and became one of the founders of a new party, the Association of Consumers and Taxpayers, committed to an extreme free-market position, including the ultimate elimination of virtually all forms of government activity. By contrast, Keating, having replaced Hawke as Prime Minister at the end of 1991, won a seemingly impossible election victory in 1993 with an effective campaign against a package of free-market reforms centred on a GST. Although Keating left Parliament after the electoral disaster of 1996, he remains an influential figure in the Labor Party.

Following the 1993 victory, Labor adopted a stance of uncompromising opposition to any form of GST, in striking contrast to its pragmatic abandonment of policy positions with a much stronger basis in social democratic theory and Labor tradition. Partly as a result, the successful implementation of a broad-based GST continued to be regarded by advocates of free-market reform as a sort of holy grail. Following criticism of the slow pace of reform under his administration, Conservative Prime Minister, John Howard, reversed a previous position that a GST would 'never ever' be his policy, and put forward a new package of tax reforms, once again centred on a GST. The election of 1998, fought mainly on the question of tax policy, produced a narrow Conservative victory, although the two-party preferred vote marginally favoured Labor.

6. Health and Welfare

From a social democratic viewpoint, the Hawke–Keating government's greatest successes were in the area of health and welfare policy. The government reintroduced the national health insurance scheme, Medicare, which had been designed and introduced by the Whitlam government, but dismantled in a series of *ad hoc* steps by the Fraser government. Although subject to increasing stress as a result of the conflict between the government's desire to cut spending and growing demands for health services, Medicare provided universal access to high quality hospital and medical services at relatively low cost.

The conflict between the desire to constrain spending and growing demand for services was even more evident in the area of social welfare. The combination of an ageing population and unemployment well above the levels prevailing in the 1970s implied a rapid growth in the number of welfare beneficiaries. At the same time, it was evident that important welfare needs were not being met. Furthermore, the welfare system was characterized by 'poverty traps', that is, high effective marginal tax rates arising from the fact that benefits were reduced as the beneficiaries' income increased.

The government responded by targeting benefits more tightly and increasing benefits for the worst-off groups in the community, notably including welfare beneficiaries living in privately rented accommodation. Old-age pensions were subjected to means tests, and the government sought to make the payment of superannuation a standard condition of employment rather than one confined to managerial and professional employees. A further notable initiative was the Family Allowance Supplement, which was a payment made to low-income families, including those where parents were employed on low wages. The supplement reduced the problem of poverty traps, which arises when a family can derive a larger income from benefits than from employment. The net effect of policy changes in social welfare was progressive and at least partially offset the increase in inequality of pre-tax income associated with the government's free-market reforms.

The record of the Labor government on social welfare may be subject to two types of criticism. The first, expressed mainly by advocates of European-style universalist social welfare, is that targeting *per se* is undesirable. This view has had relatively little currency in Australia, where most participants in the policy debate agree that welfare benefits and taxes should be viewed as part of an integrated tax-welfare system. In such an integrated system, an income-tested welfare payment is logically equivalent to a progressive income tax. For any given amount of welfare spending, targeting achieves the maximum redistribution (Castles and Mitchell, 1994). Redistribution is constrained by the need to avoid excessive effective marginal tax rates, which in extreme cases lead to poverty traps.

The primary focus of the debate is therefore concerned with the aggregate volume of welfare spending, which is largely determined by standard benefit rates, most of which move in line with old-age pensions. The Hawke government raised the single old-age pension rate from 22.7 per cent of average weekly earnings when it took office, to 25 per cent in 1991 (Gruen and Grattan, 1993), a task which was admittedly made easier by restraint in real wages under the Accord. This achievement, which has survived the government's loss of office, must be viewed as a positive one in the economic circumstances.

In New Zealand, by contrast, the Labour government had few, if any, significant achievements in the area of social welfare. After initially raising some benefits, the government was faced with the problem of increasing demands for social-welfare expenditure associated with rising unemployment and the ageing of the population. A variety of *ad hoc* restrictions on benefits were introduced. An attempt at comprehensive reform was made in 1990, but Labour lost office before it could be implemented. The incoming National government cut welfare benefits in nominal terms, by more than 20 per cent in some cases, stopped inflation adjustments, and severely restricted eligibility.

The story in health care was similar. The free-market advocates within the government commissioned a report which recommended radical reforms based on the concept of a 'purchaser–provider' split. The government rejected this approach, but the general thrust towards commercialization undercut any movement in an alternative direction, such as the establishment of Area Health Boards. The incoming National government implemented the free-market reform proposals, replacing existing health services with Regional Health Authorities, which were supposed to purchase health services from hospitals, renamed as 'Crown Health Enterprises', and run by managers (named chief executive officers) on private-sector business lines. Health care was one of the biggest disaster areas of the New Zealand reforms, with most of the Crown Health Enterprises suffering heavy losses and the majority of chief executive officers resigning (Easton, 1997; Kelsey, 1997).

The widely accepted view of the New Zealand Labour government as the 'grave diggers' of social policy in contrast to the 'refurbishment' achieved in Australia is challenged by Castles and Shirley (1996), who suggest that the outcomes might have looked very different if the Australian Labor government had lost office in 1990 or 1993. Yet even Castles and Shirley observe that, 'in New Zealand, the record of the government was sufficiently lacking in purpose as to invite the question: "social policy: has there been one?" ', and state that policy developments such as targeting were part of 'a downward trajectory of welfare development'. It is hard to avoid the conclusion that the New Zealand Labour government dug the grave of social policy, even if the burial was left to its National successors.

7. Privatization

For a number of years, it appeared likely that privatization would represent the point at which the Australian Labor government would refuse to follow Thatcher's lead. The Labor Party's stated objective, reaffirmed after considerable debate in the late 1970s, was 'the socialization of the means of production, distribution, and exchange'. Labor won several state elections on the basis of energetic scare campaigns against conservative proposals for privatization.

By 1987, however, the situation had changed sufficiently to permit asset sales totalling $1 billion in the May Statement of that year. As Hawke (1994, p. 391) observes: 'Many of these were uncontentious – for example a partial sale of our embassy site in Tokyo and other land sales – but they presaged the broader privatisation debate ahead.'

Hawke assumed, like Thatcher, that the proceeds of asset sales could be treated like current income and used to finance current expenditure or reductions in taxes. Hawke (1994, p. 391) says:

> When it came to privatization, Brian [Howe] was able to argue that one dollar simply could not do two jobs. Putting a dollar of equity into the running of an airline was paid at the expense of programmes for the unemployed or the single mother.

A more sophisticated, though still ultimately fallacious, argument was that public-sector companies, such as Qantas, were starved of investment owing to constraints on public-sector borrowing (Walsh, 1995). The critical problem here is that the constraints themselves are determined by irrational objectives, such as the elimination of public-sector net financial debt. The relevant policy objective is to achieve an appropriate level of public-sector net worth, and net worth is increased when government business enterprises undertake profitable enterprises. It might be argued that reductions in net debt were 'demanded' by financial markets, and were therefore necessary regardless of the lack of any economic rationale. However, there is little evidence of this. In the period when Labor commenced privatization, the budget was in surplus even without privatization proceeds, so that the attitudes of financial markets had little direct significance for governments.

The commitment of the leading figures in the government to privatization was evident by late 1987, but it took some years before the opposition of the Labor Party membership and the public could be overcome, and large-scale privatization could be implemented. The Labor leadership attacked conservative proposals to privatize the Commonwealth Bank of Australia in the election campaign of early

1990, but made a decision in favour of partial privatization later the same year.

Privatization commenced on a large scale in 1991 with the sale of a tranche of shares in the Commonwealth Bank, the sale of Aussat to form the basis of Optus, preparations to merge and privatize Qantas and Australian Airlines, and the sale of Commonwealth Serum Laboratories, which was responsible for the preparation of blood products. In all of these cases, privatization reduced public-sector net worth, in that the interest savings attainable by using sale proceeds to repay public debt were less than the value of the earnings forgone (Hamilton and Quiggin, 1995; Quiggin, 1995)

As usual, New Zealand Labour moved earlier and faster on privatization, though, as in Australia, the government lied about its intentions until the last possible moment. Assets sold by the Labour government between 1984 and 1990 included New Zealand Telecom, Air New Zealand, and the Government Printing Office. As in Australia, the government treated the revenue from asset sales as current income.

The National government went much further, selling not only government business enterprises but cutting rights over state forests, mortgages held by the Housing Corporation, and so on. The loss of public wealth from privatization is illustrated by the case of New Zealand Telecom, which was sold for $4.25 billion to the American firms, Ameritech and Bell Atlantic, under conditions which guaranteed an effective monopoly. By 1996, the buyers had sold shares worth $3.1 billion, repatriated around $1 billion in dividends, and retained a majority shareholding valued at $7 billion (Kelsey, 1997).

Despite bipartisan support, privatization remained electorally unpopular, particularly in Australia. By the late 1990s, Labor drifted back towards support for public ownership, particularly with respect to high-profile proposals for privatization of the electricity and telecommunications industry. State elections in Tasmania and New South Wales, fought primarily on the issue of electricity privatization, resulted in landslide victories for Labor, even though the sincerity of the party's anti-privatization stance was highly questionable (in New South Wales, both the Premier and Treasurer had actively campaigned for privatization within the party).

8. Labour Markets and the Accord

The divergence between the Australian and New Zealand labour governments was most evident in the area of labour-market policy, although even here, the Australian Labor government drifted towards a free-market position over the course of its 13-year term. At least from 1983 to 1989, however, a highly interventionist labour-market policy played a central role in the Australian government's policy framework.

The Accord between the government and the Australian Council of Trade Unions was the most important policy innovation adopted by the Hawke government, and was conceived as part of a Keynesian expansionary strategy. The experience of the 1970s and early 1980s was seen as showing that the main constraint on expansion was the danger of rapid growth in nominal wages leading to an inflationary spiral. Under the Accord, it was intended that nominal wage increases should be agreed centrally in such a way as to allow modest growth in real wages and a gradual decline in the rate of inflation. Although no general programme of price controls was proposed, firms with substantial market power were subject to price surveillance.

The Keynesian analysis put forward by the designers of the Accord was criticized by those who argued that the primary economic problem was the 'real wage overhang', that is, the excessive level of real unit labour costs arising from the wages explosion of the mid-1970s and the resources boom of the early 1980s. Most advocates of the 'real wage overhang' model were sceptical of the value of incomes policies, but their views had a significant influence on the development of the Accord, beginning with the Labor Party's 1982 Conference at which the Accord's stated objective of 'maintaining and increasing real wages' was amended to read 'maintaining and increasing real wages over time'.

The 1982 amendment was the first step towards a reinterpretation of the Accord focusing on real wages and real unit labour costs. On this interpretation, the union movement accepted a sustained reduction in the labour share of national income (reversing the increase that took place in the 1970s) in return for government policies oriented towards employment growth and progressive social reforms. This version of the Accord was implemented as a series of special deals resulting in real wage reductions.

The first and most important was associated with the introduction of Medicare in early 1984, a health insurance system that involved indirect payment for services via an income tax surcharge. The consequent artificial reduction in the consumer price index was passed on to wages. The union movement's acceptance of such trade-offs indicated a willingness to make sacrifices in order to restore full employment. In return, the theory underlying the Accord proposed an expansion of the 'social wage' in the form of progressive expenditure on the provision of community services and welfare.

The first few years of the Accord were generally viewed as highly successful. The strong economic recovery which commenced in 1983 was accompanied by declining real wages and a gradual decline in the rate of inflation. Industrial disputes, which had previously been regarded as a major social and economic problem, became rare. Employment growth was strong, and the rate of unemployment declined steadily, reaching a minimum of 5.9 per cent in mid-1989. It has been argued that most of these developments would have taken place anyway, reflecting the worldwide decline in the power of unions (Moore, 1989). However, most analysts conclude that the Accord made a difference and was successful in achieving its main objectives (Beggs and Chapman, 1987; Chapman, 1997).

Over time, however, the Accord began to fall from favour. Concern with the aggregate level of real wages declined somewhat, and there was a widespread desire to achieve greater flexibility. Individual unions were concerned that a policy framework that delivered regular centralized wage increases rendered them irrelevant to their members, many of whom were discontented by the contrast between general wage constraint and the conspicuous consumption of upper-income earners, especially the 'entrepreneurs'. Employers were particularly concerned to secure higher levels of work intensity and greater control over work practices. In the end, the Industrial Relations Court (the body responsible for making decisions on wage increases under the centralized arbitration system) was left isolated as the sole defender of the system. The main disagreement was whether labour-market reform should be pursued through enterprise-level bargaining (the approach favoured by unions) or individual contracts (the approach favoured by advocates of microeconomic reform).

The recession of 1989 undermined the primary basis on which the Accord was premised, namely that it would deliver strong employment growth. The recession itself was induced by restrictive monetary policy based, in large measure, on the belief that the Accord would not be sufficient to control pressures for wage increases flowing from booming asset markets.

Although the Accord was formally renewed on seven occasions during the term of the Hawke–Keating government, it ceased to be a major factor in economic policy after 1989. The tightening of that monetary policy in that year, partly in response to a fear that the Accord was in danger of breaking down, induced a severe recession. The rate of unemployment rose to 11 per cent and has remained above 8 per cent ever since.

The attention of the government was briefly captured by the unemployment problem, as exemplified in the December 1993 Green

Paper, *Restoring Full Employment*, and the May 1994 White Paper, *Working Nation*, both of which argued that a growth rate of 4.5 per cent, complemented by job subsidies, training, and individual case management, was needed to bring long-term unemployment down. Evaluation of the Working Nation programmes is difficult in view of the fact that the programmes were only in operation for 2 years. Piggott and Chapman (1995) give an *ex-ante* evaluation, suggesting that the net budgetary cost per job created would be low, a view broadly supported by the *ex-post* studies of Junankar and Kapuscinski (1997) and Stromback *et al.* (1997). Official evaluations have varied from glowing (Crean, 1995) to circumspect (Department of Employment, Education, Training and Youth Affairs, 1996), to damning (unpublished research cited by the present Conservative government) according to the political demands of the occasion.

With the election of the Conservative Howard government in 1996, the Accord was abandoned in favour of labour-market reform aimed at pushing unions out of the bargaining process, rather than attempting to use the union movement as a force for wage restraint. Labour-market programmes were cut drastically, along with public-sector employment. Despite continued economic growth, the unemployment rose from around 8 per cent to 8.7 per cent.

Labour-market policy in New Zealand was largely one of drift. Although Douglas and others advocated radical labour-market reform, only modest changes were introduced. The Labour Relations Act of 1987 liberalized the private-sector labour market to some extent and sought to modernize the trade-union movement through mergers and enterprise bargaining. The 1988 State Sector Act extended these reforms to the public sector.

The real impact of the Labour government arose from the fact that it accepted rising unemployment as a necessary cost of reform. The weakened economic position of the unions, and their association with a generally discredited Labour Party, left them with little capacity to resist the radical labour-market reforms introduced by the Bolger National Party government in 1991, under which individual contracts became the primary basis for employment. These reforms were implemented through the Employment Contracts Act, which provides no union rights of any kind.

9. Economic Outcomes

Although free-market economists have contrasted the policy processes in Australia and New Zealand, rather less attention has been paid to

Table 1
Economic Performance in Australia and New Zealand
(average annual percentage change)

	1973–83	1983–90	1990–6
GDP per capita			
Australia	1.1	2.5	1.7
New Zealand	0.6	0.8 (1984–90= –0.2)	1.8
OECD	1.4	2.6	1.0
Excess of high (D9) over low (D1) pay, men			(1990–5)
Australia		–0.2	1.5
New Zealand		2.1 (1984–90)	0.7 (1990–4)
United States		1.6	1.9
United Kingdom		1.9	1.2
Consumer prices			
Australia	11.9	5.7	2.5
New Zealand	13.7	9.8	1.9
OECD	8.6	3.9	2.8
Employment			
Australia		3.2	0.8
New Zealand		0.2	2.2
OECD		1.6	0.6
Unemployment	1983	(% point change 1983–90)	(% point change 1990–6)
Australia	9.9	–3.0	1.6
New Zealand	5.6	+2.1	–1.6
OECD	8.5	–2.4	1.5
Labour productivity			
Australia		0.9	2.1
New Zealand		1.2	0.8
OECD		1.8	1.3

Note: Unemployment is a standardized measure except for New Zealand.
Sources: OECD, *Historical Statistics*, *Economic Outlook*, *Employment Outlook*.

differences in outcomes. New Zealand was consistently seen as the model of correct policy, yet economic outcomes in New Zealand have been consistently poorer than those in Australia. Table 1 presents information on a variety of economic indicators for Australia and New Zealand for the periods 1973–83, 1983–90, and 1990–6. The latter two periods cover the term of office of the Labor government in Australia and correspond fairly closely to the terms of the Labour and National governments in New Zealand. Although the cyclical experience of the two countries has not been identical, in both cases there was a cyclical peak just before 1990, followed by a severe recession and a recovery phase that is still under way.

The greatest divergence in economic performance took place while the Lange–Douglas government held office. The period from 1984 to 1990 was one of stagnation in New Zealand, whereas Australia enjoyed steady economic growth until the recession that commenced in 1989. As a result, the gap in per-capita incomes went from between 5 and 10 per cent in 1983 to around 20 per cent in 1991. As New Zealand's poor aggregate performance was accompanied by growing inequality in earnings and a more regressive tax system, whereas Australia experienced some wage compression owing to the Accord and tax reforms that were broadly neutral in their effect on income distribution, the divergence in outcomes for those on low incomes was even more dramatic.

As in most OECD countries, inflation rates in Australia and New Zealand generally declined from the early 1980s onwards. In Australia, the decline in the rate of inflation as measured by the GDP deflator was fairly uniform from the mid-1980s onwards. In New Zealand, the once-off effects of the introduction of the GST led to a temporary increase in inflation rates, but otherwise the process was similar. Nevertheless, fears of an inflationary upsurge were among the macroeconomic misjudgements that led to severe tightening of Australian monetary policy in late 1989 and the subsequent deep recession.

From 1984 to 1989, labour-market outcomes in Australia were clearly superior to those in New Zealand, and very good in absolute terms. Employment grew at an annual rate of 3.2 per cent from 1984–90, with unemployment falling to a low point of 5.9 per cent. However, employment contracted sharply during the recession, and strong employment growth in the initial stages of the subsequent recovery was not sustained. As a result, the rate of unemployment in Australia rose to 11 per cent during the 1989–91 recession, then fell back to 8 per cent, where it has remained. Average employment growth over the period 1990–6 was 0.8 per cent.

In New Zealand, Labour lost office in 1990 after a period during which labour-market performance deteriorated steadily. A detailed analysis of movements in unemployment is difficult as there are no official New Zealand unemployment figures for the period before 1986. The OECD estimates the unemployment rate in 1983 at 5.6 per cent, but this is not a standardized measure and other estimates are lower (Easton, personal communication). Unemployment rose steadily, reaching a peak of 11 per cent during the recession. Employment growth was close to zero, and labour-force participation rates declined. Large-scale labour-shedding resulted in relatively strong labour productivity growth over this period, a point which was emphasized by advocates of the New Zealand 'miracle'.

The incoming National Party government introduced both radical labour-market reforms and cuts of around 20 per cent in welfare benefits, with unemployment benefits being affected more than others. These changes, introduced just before the trough of the recession, had little immediate effect. However, the recovery produced fairly strong employment growth, a reduction in the unemployment rate, which fell to 5.9 per cent before rising to 6.7 per cent in 1997, and 2 years of very strong output growth in 1994 and 1995. From the viewpoint of advocates of the New Zealand 'miracle', these outcomes show that the only problem with the Labour government's approach was the failure to tackle labour-market reform.

The evidence presented in Table 1 suggests a far less optimistic account. In terms of GDP per capita, New Zealand did not regain any lost ground over the period 1990–6 and currently appears to be falling even further behind. Estimates produced by the New Zealand and Australian Reserve Banks suggest that, although the two countries have similar population growth rates, the sustainable growth rate for New Zealand is around 3 per cent (Brash, 1997), while the sustainable growth rate for Australia is around 3.5 per cent. The gap is generated primarily by weaker trend growth in employment in New Zealand and by slightly lower trend productivity growth. Even the achievement of the sustainable growth rate appears doubtful in view of the chronic current account deficit, currently above 5 per cent of GDP. It does not appear that the radical reforms undertaken by the Lange government had any long-term pay-off in terms of income growth, compared to the more cautious approach adopted in Australia.

A somewhat more favourable view of the outcome of the New Zealand reforms may be obtained from a comparison of performance over the reform period since 1984 with relatively poor performance prior to 1984. Evans et al. (1996) examine GDP per working-age adult, and conclude that growth since 1984 has been superior to that prevailing in the previous 17 years. The selection of this unusual performance measure, which happens to make the period before 1984 look particularly bad, entails the need to make arbitrary imputations, all of which are chosen in a way which yields low estimates of the pre-1984 growth rate. More generally, an analysis based on the hypothesis of convergence suggests that a low starting level of income resulting from prior weak growth makes the achievement of high growth easier, not harder. It is difficult to avoid the conclusion that the statistical evidence presented by Evans *et al.* was selected on the basis that it was the only available measure that gave any support to their highly favourable account of the reforms.

Growth in employment was somewhat more impressive, but only partially made up the ground lost over the period from 1984–90. Over the entire period since 1993, Australia had stronger growth in employment than New Zealand. Strong employment growth over the period 1990–6 was matched by weak labour productivity growth, more than wiping out New Zealand's slightly superior performance over the period 1984–90.[6] As with GDP, recent evidence suggests the gap in favour of Australia is widening further.

Finally, New Zealand's reduction in measured unemployment rates is overstated. As in other countries where income from unemployment benefit is less than that available from alternatives such as sickness and supporting parents benefit, the result was a shift from unemployment benefits to other benefits. Since eligibility for unemployment benefits is typically conditional on job search, while eligibility for other benefits is based on incapacity for work, such a shift in benefit category is typically reflected in a reduction in survey-based measures of the proportion of the population unemployed and actively seeking work.

Experience since 1996 is difficult to assess because the Australian and New Zealand business cycles have ceased to move in parallel. The New Zealand economy went into recession in 1997, while Australia maintained steady growth despite the impact of the Asian economic crisis. As a result, the gap in GDP per capita widened even further, and the measured unemployment rate in New Zealand exceeded that in Australia for the first time in several years. It remains to be seen whether New Zealand's further relative deterioration will be reversed when the Australian expansion comes to an end. Nevertheless, on the basis of experience since 1984, the New Zealand experiment has been an unambiguous failure.

(a) *The Erosion of Political Support*

In both Australia and New Zealand, the adoption of free-market policies was associated with a steady erosion of political support, particularly among working-class voters. Over the period since the Second World War, the Australian Labor Party had never received less than 40 per cent of the vote. Labor's strategists took this core of support

[6] In public discussion, many advocates of the New Zealand miracle cite both the strong productivity growth achieved in 1984–90 and the strong employment growth of 1990–6 to produce an impression of superior performance on both counts that is the exact opposite of the truth.

for granted, and concentrated on the need to win 'swinging voters'. The standard logic supporting 'middle of the road' policies was reinforced by features of the Australian electoral institutions, including compulsory voting and the preferential system, which required all voters to give a complete ranking of the alternatives. Under this system, it was suggested, disaffected Labor voters had 'nowhere else to go'. They could not abstain and, even if they cast a first-preference vote for a third party or independent candidate, it was the relative ranking of the major party candidates that was decisive.

The abandonment of traditional social democratic policies led to a steady decline in the number of committed Labor voters. As Labor moved steadily to the right, the Australian Democrats, originally a centrist group of former Liberals, became, by default, the main left-wing opposition party, along with a variety of green and anti-nuclear groups. Many former Labor supporters switched to these groups.

Nevertheless, the 'swinging voter' strategy was successful for a long time. Labor received 49.5 per cent of the first-preference vote in 1983, 47.5 per cent in 1984, 45.8 per cent in 1987, and 39.4 per cent in 1990, but retained office on the basis of second preferences and astute targeting of marginal seats. The adoption by the Liberals of a doctrinaire programme of free-market reforms, called *Fightback*, drove some traditional supporters back to the Labor Party in 1993, but the many commentators who interpreted this as evidence of solid support for Labor were mistaken.

The damaging long-term consequences of the swinging-voter strategy were felt in 1996, when Labor's primary vote fell to 38.8 per cent, the lowest since the Second World War, and one of the lowest since the Federation of Australia in 1901. Labor's primary vote recovered marginally in the 1998 election. More importantly, the conservative parties, once in office, disillusioned many of their supporters just as badly as Labor had done. Their primary vote fell sharply, particularly in rural areas, where voters turned to independents and to the One Nation Party which offered a mixture of anti-immigration rhetoric and opposition to free-market reform. As a result, Labor narrowly missed victory (and, on some estimates received a majority of the two-party preferred votes) despite receiving only 40 per cent of the primary vote.

In view of voter discontent with both major parties, it would be a mistake to write off Labor's electoral chances. The fundamental problem, however, is that it is difficult to identify either a policy programme that distinguishes the Labor Party from its opponents or a substantial social group for which the Labor Party speaks. The lack of distinctive policies is less damaging for the conservatives, since it reflects bipartisan support for a programme based on their own official ideology. The conservative parties may, therefore, be seen as the natural party of government and Labor as the 'B team', to be called upon when the electorate wearies of conservative governments that have become complacent and dogmatic after too long in office.

In New Zealand, the Lange Labour government was re-elected in 1987, in large measure because of the popularity of its anti-nuclear foreign policy, and related policy on human rights. The loss of traditional supporters was offset by Labour's capture of the votes (12.3 per cent of the total in 1984) that had formerly flowed to the New Zealand Party, which supported both free-market economics and an anti-nuclear foreign policy, with the result that Labour's share of the vote rose from 43 per cent in 1984 to 48 per cent in 1987. However, severe divisions over economic policy, both within the government and within the labour movement, led to a crushing defeat in 1990 from which the New Zealand Labour Party has never fully recovered. Labour received only 35 per cent of the vote. The party broke into fragments, with Douglas forming a radical free-market party and left activists combining with environmentalists to form the Alliance Party.

Many more Labour supporters, particularly Maori, were attracted to the New Zealand First Party, essentially a vehicle for its demagogic leader, Winston Peters, after he walked out of the National Party government. Labour received a little over 34.7 per cent of the vote in the 1993 and 28.2 per cent in the 1996 elections, falling at times to 20 per cent support in opinion polls. The party continues to represent an uneasy coalition of free-market reformers, Labour traditionalists, and those for whom Labour is the best of a bad lot.

The 1996 election in New Zealand was the first held under a system of multi-member proportional representation created as a response to discontent over the way the Lange and Bolger governments had used the disciplined majorities created by a constituency system to push unpopular reforms through Parliament. It left the balance of power with Peters, who eventually agreed to go into coalition with the National Party. The coalition subsequently broke down, but a minority National Party government remained in office at the time of writing. As in Australia, it is not impossible to imagine Labour regaining office, but it is hard to see what purpose the election of a Labour government would serve, except to remind the Conservatives that the electorate still has the capacity to punish them for poor performance.

10. An Assessment

Despite its abandonment of many traditional social democratic policies, the Australian Labor government continued to defend its claim to represent the values of the labour movement, and the current Labor Opposition has continued, at least until recently, to defend the record of the Hawke–Keating government. Until the recession that commenced in 1989, the government's claims were supported by strong employment growth and reductions in the rate of unemployment. A more durable claim is that, although total spending on social welfare was constrained, the government improved targeting through means tests and introduced other innovative welfare programmes such as family allowance supplements for low-income earners. This increased the redistributive impact of welfare spending and offset the rise in inequality in market incomes associated with policies of deregulation and privatization.

Arguably, the Australian Labor government may be seen as having done relatively well in an unfavourable environment. Given the breakdown of Keynesian macroeconomic policy, the increasing irrelevance of economic development strategies based on tariff protection, the rising influence of financial markets, and the fiscal demands created by increases in the demand for old age pensions, unemployment benefits, and publicly provided services such as health and education, any social democratic government would have faced a difficult task.

However, Labor's rhetoric did not convey this message. Rather than presenting itself as adapting to undeniable realities while doing its best to protect its core constituency against the worst impacts of globalization and competition, these two themes were embraced as the way of the future. In policy terms, the Labor government celebrated its successes in 'opening up' the Australian economy, and derided the policies of the 1950s and 1960s, a period remembered by most Australians as one of full employment and prosperity. At a personal level, the identification of leading Labor ministers with the wealthy beneficiaries of globalization was too obvious to be ignored. By both opponents and supporters, Hawke and Keating are remembered primarily for 'opening up the economy', and not for innovations in social policy.

It is hard to offer even a qualified defence of the New Zealand Labour government. In the few areas where the government did not follow anti-labour policies, it prepared the way for its National Party successors to do so. The government's leading figures, Douglas and Prebble, revealed themselves as extreme free-market ideologues after finally leaving the party. The abandonment of traditional policies was not rewarded by electoral or economic success. In *eight* years out of office, Labour has not succeeded in producing a coherent set of economic and social policies incorporating progressive elements of reform policies. Rather its current stance is one of accepting that previous governments have 'gone too far' without proposing a concrete alternative.

In summary, the experience of the Australian and New Zealand labour governments does not support the view that a combination of free-market economic policies and social democratic values represents a hopeful option for the labour movement. The tension between the two is evident, and tends to increase the longer a labour government remains in office. The tension would be reduced if free-market policies delivered the promised improvements in economic performance, but, so far, this has not been the case.

5

The Logic and Limits of *Désinflation Compétitive*

FRÉDÉRICK LORDON*

1. Introduction

In place for almost 15 years, maintained with an outstanding continuity over five changes of government, the French economic policy labelled *désinflation compétitive* (competitiveness through disinflation) involves such numerous and controversial aspects that it is impossible to cover it exhaustively in a limited contribution. The present chapter simply aims at presenting the most general features of *désinflation compétitive*. The task in itself is not simple since, unlike the old Keynesian economic policy model, *désinflation compétitive* has no canonic text where its doctrine is clearly set out and may easily be read. *Désinflation compétitive* has no IS-LM model—a lack which indicates its specific nature as an administrative and technocratic doctrine, rather than a properly academic construction. The main task is, thus, a conjectural synopsis of *désinflation compétitive*. However fuzzy, this synopsis exhibits, nevertheless, a kind of global coherence which will appear through the priority given to export-led growth. But coherence does not necessarily mean effectiveness. And scrutiny of the main mechanisms of *désinflation compétitive* will reveal major weaknesses which help us to understand the unfulfilled expectations of the 1990s. Effective insofar as the first requirement of economic policy was to wipe out inflation, *désinflation compétitive* became more and more irrelevant and counterproductive once inflation disappeared and unemployment remained the top priority on the economic policy agenda. Although it was well adapted to nominal targets, the real performance of *désinflation compétitive* has been dramatically poor. Growth and employment have been its blind spots. And this blindness is all the more paradoxical in that the Left, and especially the Socialist Party, has been the historical entrepreneur of *désinflation compétitive*. The paradox is even more challenging in the French case in that one should recall how far from social democratic was

* CNRS-CEPREMAP.

the bold initial programme upon which François Mitterrand was elected to the presidency of the Republic. How could it be that a Keynesian–Marxian programme advocating a boost in popular consumption and nationalizations eventually became an almost canonic conservative economic policy? Presenting *désinflation compétitive*, then, requires that light be shed on the historical sequence which has led to this unexpected conversion.

2. The *Programme Commun* of 1981: A Keynesian–Marxian Strategy

Viewed from 2000, *désinflation compétitive* is now so deeply rooted in the French economic landscape that one could be tempted to think that the main issue is not so much how the governments of the 1980s could so suddenly adopt a neo-liberal orientation, but how a strategy like the initial *programme commun* could ever have been envisaged! The early 1980s seem so far from us now, that recalling the economic logic of this programme seems to be a task for an historian.

The economic plan of the socialist party coming to power was merely the expression of the global political strategy of the union of the Left (socialists and communists) expressed in the *programme commun*,[1] and from which resulted the election of Mitterrand in 1981.[2] The economic flavour of the *programme commun* is clearly Keynesian and Marxian.

Keynesian first, because the crisis opened in the early 1970s was too recent to have led to a serious questioning of the inherited intellectual routines of the Keynesian period. Certainly, Raymond Barre's economic policy, especially between 1978 and 1981, can be viewed as the first steps towards the neo-liberal policies of the 1980s, but the Keynesian paradigm still remained very prominent in the politicians' minds, and particularly within the Left. The economic diagnosis of the crisis by the union of the Left was unsurprisingly Keynesian, therefore: the rise of unemployment was seen as an effect of a slow-down in final demand. The problem could be solved by a boost to both private consumption and public investments. Consumption could be fostered by a rise in the legal minimum wage, but also by a significant plan for recruitment of

[1] Even if the *programme commun* was born before the parliamentary elections of 1978, driving the union of the Left, at least formally, to breakdown, it remained more or less the doctrinal reference until the beginning of the 1980s.

[2] Rigorously speaking, one should distinguish between the *programme commun* negotiated in the early 1970s as the political basis of the union of the Left, and the '110 propositions' of Mitterrand, who in accordance with the personalization of the presidential election, aimed to depart from the party's programme.

civil servants—the two instruments at the disposal of the government. The socialist government was all the more inclined to apply such a strategy in that the economic experts consulted by the party during the electoral campaign were forecasting a world recovery, from which the French economic policy could benefit! The sequel shows us what to think of this prophesy by 'experts'.

However, it would be somehow misleading to take a purely 'Keynesian' view of the union of the Left's economic programme, which had two sides. If its demand side was certainly important, the supply side had not been completely neglected—and here comes what could be called the 'Marxian part' of the *programme commun*. Besides the analysis of the lack of demand, the *programme commun* also performs a diagnosis in terms of the structural weaknesses of the industrial system and of a trend loss of competitiveness. The nationalization plan made up the supply-side response of the *programme commun*. One cannot underestimate the breadth of this programme: 36 private banks, 2 investment banks, and 11 major industrial firms were nationalized in 1982, raising the public-sector share to 24 per cent in terms of total employment, 32 per cent in terms of business output, 30 per cent in terms of exports, and 60 per cent in terms of industrial and energy investment (Hall, 1988). The rationale of this programme was in fact threefold.

(i) Rescuing the largest firms that had been driven into bankruptcy by the failure of private shareholders. It is conceivable that without state intervention, major firms, such as Saint-Gobain and, especially, Rhône-Poulenc, could have disappeared.

(ii) Performing with political authority the restructuring of the industrial system, forming 'national champions' in order to increase competitiveness. The *fer de lance* policy was, in fact, a vertical integration strategy, aiming at building fully integrated industrial groups in the high technology sectors. In line with a long-standing French tradition, state intervention was viewed as a necessary substitute for a failing private entrepreneurship.

(iii) Finally, nationalized firms also had the task of providing privileged places for experimentation with 'new' social relationships. From this perspective, nationalizations could be interpreted as the attempt to develop a seed from which could arise a transformed system of 'wage–labour nexus' (Boyer, 1988), a new set of capital–labour relations.

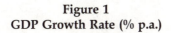

Figure 1
GDP Growth Rate (% p.a.)

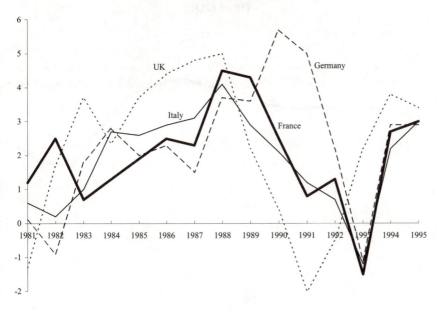

3. From the Failure of the *Programme Commun* to the Distress U-turn of *Désinflation Compétitive*

The expansionary economic policy was launched very rapidly after the election victory of 10 May 1981. The purchasing power of the SMIC (the minimum wage) increased by 10.6 per cent in 1981–2, compared to a rise of only 3.3 per cent in 1979–80 (Hall, 1988). The public recruitment programme created 110,000 jobs in the civil service. The whole set of measures resulted in a 2 per cent boost to GDP. But the experts were wrong, and there was nothing like a world recovery to support and reinforce the French economic policy. The expected growth rate upon which the 1982 budget was built was 3.3 per cent, whereas the actual rate ended up at 2.3 per cent (Figure 1). France was boosting its economy while almost all its partners were adopting restrictive policy stances. This isolated stimulation, taking place in a low-growth international context and upon a weak national industrial basis, logically led to a deterioration of the economic indicators. The public deficit reached 2.8 per cent of GDP in 1982 and 3.2 per cent in 1983 (Figure 2). It is worth recalling that, at that time, such an imbalance in public finances was considered a tremendous drama in France, most of the political commentators claiming that the whole country was driven into insolvency. Viewed from the 1990s, this catastrophic 3.2 per cent can seem quite

Figure 2
Budget Deficits
(% of GDP)

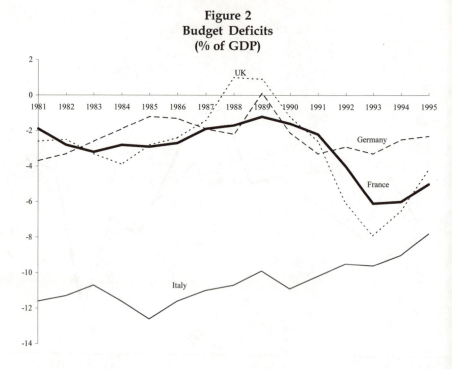

enviable! The external deficit, too, increased significantly, at 2.2 per cent of GDP in 1982. And despite the stimulation plan, unemployment was still rising (Figure 3). The extra public expenditure mainly benefited France's commercial partners. Moreover, faced with an increase in their costs, firms engaged in severe restructurings from which massive firings resulted. The Prime Minister, Pierre Mauroy, claimed to fight 'on the side of the 2 million unemployed', but this symbolic threshold was broken in 1983.

The deterioration of the macroeconomic situation was feeding a crisis with both monetary and political aspects.

(a) *Monetary Turmoil*

The beginning of the socialist policy had already brought two devaluations in 1981. The franc was all the more under scrutiny in that the French economic strategy was strongly diverging from the stance adopted in other countries — and because the left-wing government was suffering from prejudice against it in the international arena. As the Keynesian expansionary policy appeared to fail, French economic policy was once again driven into monetary turmoil. The franc, which had already been weak for several months, was fiercely attacked. A plan for a shift of the policy-mix had been studied by the government

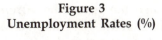

Figure 3
Unemployment Rates (%)

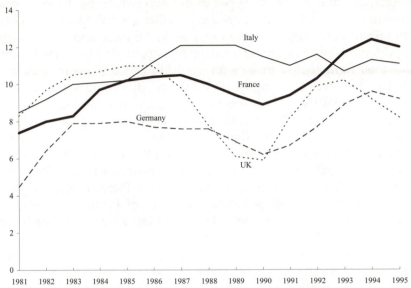

since 1982, but now the emergency escalated under the pressure of the foreign-exchange markets. After the devaluations of 1981 and 1982, a third exchange-rate adjustment would expose the French policy to general mistrust. The 1983 policy turnabout was thus negotiated in the feverish circumstances of a very severe monetary crisis. In the short run, it first appeared as a plan for restrictive policies to accompany the devaluation which, anyway, could not be avoided.

(b) *Political Crisis*

In fact, the threat did not only come from the financial markets. It also had political dimensions. Because of the deterioration of the budget and external trade deficits, and of the growth of the external debt, France was put under scrutiny by the IMF. The possibility of an adjustment plan imposed by the IMF was felt internally as an humiliation, and externally as an untenable weakening of France's position. It would recall the fate of the British Labour policy in the years 1974–6.

Memory of the Front Populaire fed the fear that once more the experiment of a left-wing government was unable to last. Since 1982, the socialist economic policy had been strongly criticized. In this context of high tension, the municipal elections of March 1983 acted as a catalyst. They were the first electoral test since the left-wing government had been in place. The first round was catastrophic for the Left, even though the second round rescued the government from a complete electoral wreck. Anyway, the shock to the reputation created by a succession of devaluations, the risk of being put under observation by the IMF, and generalized distrust all threatened a socialist government once more with failure in the field of economic policy. All these arguments were supported by the advocates of a radical turnabout. At a high level in the state, their fight against those who would be called *les visiteurs du soir* lasted a whole week, during which President Mitterrand seems to have hesitated and vacillated between two strategies: maintaining the initial political orientation of his mandate, or radically changing the economic policy. It is worth noting that among these *visiteurs du soir* who defended strict respect for the electoral commitments of 1981 and called for a severe restriction on capital flows to maintain nationalizations, expansive policy, and devaluation possibilities, Pierre Bérégovoy was very active. As soon as he became Minister of Finance in 1984, he suddenly became the most enthusiastic and intransigent proponent of *désinflation compétitive*. It would require more space to reproduce all the details of these crucial days (see, for instance, Favier and Martin-Roland, 1990) during which, in a monetary as well as cabinet crisis, one of the most important decisions of the 14 years of socialist rule was made. However, the general meaning of this decision is clear, and it is possible to interpret the economic choice of an orthodox policy as a political choice for the long run.

(c) *The Meaning of an Historical Bifurcation*

The radical turn of March 1983, which saw the withdrawal of an isolated national Keynesian policy and the adoption of the international standard economic policy, had thus a double nature. It was at the same time an emergency response to a feverish government crisis, and a structural choice grounded on a very long-term option.

As pointed out earlier, the context of the crisis was twofold: both macroeconomic and monetary. The deterioration of the fundamentals of the French economy is hardly disputable. The increase in unemployment continued, inflation remained at very high levels, the budgetary and trade deficits grew at a worrying pace, and, in the end, the national income distribution was very imbalanced, with low profits severely weakening firms. Costs—especially as regards their wage component—were rising, from which a loss of competitiveness resulted, as can be seen in the decrease in the French economy's share of the international markets. Among the nine world leading exporters (Figure 4), the French market share fell from 10.4 per cent in 1980 to 9 per cent in 1985 (Taddei and Coriat, 1992). Almost all economists retrospectively acknowledge that the 1981 economic policy was no longer sustainable and

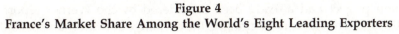

Figure 4
France's Market Share Among the World's Eight Leading Exporters

that a strong shift was required. Such a shift was all the more urgent in that foreign-exchange market speculation was inevitably leading to a third exchange-rate adjustment, calling for a plan for restriction to convince financial markets and break the series of uncontrolled devaluations. One can thus read the 1983 turnabout as reflecting a purely economic policy response to an urgent adjustment problem.

Beyond this emergency economic context, however, it is possible to see in the 1983 parting of the ways a much weightier structural shift pertaining to a more remote time-horizon. What the choice of *désinflation compétitive* fundamentally means is nothing other than the acceptance of the rules of the game of an opened-up and internationalized economy. The spectacular alignment with the international economic policy standard simultaneously indicated the renouncing of a heterodox policy in a single country, and full insertion in a world economy, the disciplines and the constraints of which were acknowledged and accepted.

In the French case, this acceptance was closely related to European integration which rapidly appeared as a guideline for a new global political project to be substituted for the *programme commun* of 1981. It is certainly possible to wonder about the exact degree of elaboration of a 'European strategy' at that time: the economic and monetary union (EMU) project was only to be formulated 6 years later, the integration of financial markets was not yet envisaged. Of course the idea of European economic integration was not totally unknown: a monetary union project had already been considered by the Werner report in 1970; and from its very beginning, the exchange-rate mechanism (ERM) had explicitly been conceived as a transitory device, supposedly leading to a single currency.

Anyway, Mitterrand is said to have been aware since 1982–3 of the sovereignty crisis confronting economic policy, and already to have viewed Europe as a way to overcome it. From the very first years of his 7-year term he would have had an inkling of the instrumental role of the ERM in European construction, and of the contradiction between this strategy and the unemployment reduction target. According to Attali (1993), Mitterrand felt torn between two ambitions: 'the European construction, and social justice'. The ERM was necessary to fulfil the former, but is seen as a limitation on the latter. One of his biographers suggests that Mitterrand soon realized that he had overestimated the power of the state in an open world: 'An original economic and social policy is inconsistent with European construction. But only Europe allows politics to restore its power' (Schneider, 1994, pp. 88–9). And if one wanted to identify symbolic dates in Mitterrand's conversion, one should pay special attention to the Versailles G7 summit of 1982 and to the Fontainebleau European summit of 1984. For the French government, the aim at Versailles was clearly to convince its partners to follow the French strategy and to cooperate in a coordinated Keynesian policy. But times had changed since the late 1970s. The USA and the UK were now led by a conservative president and prime minister who were not really strong Keynesian proponents! And Germany, which had already experienced the role of leading a failed international policy to boost the economy, was quite reluctant to give it another try. Versailles was, for the French, the discovery of their international isolation. And after having, first, overestimated their ability to conduct an expansion in a single country, and, then, discovered their inability to rally their partners to their own approach, there remained nothing to do but bury Keynesian illusions. Symmetrically, Fontainebleau in 1984 signalled the revival of European integration, taking a new leap forward which would lead to the Single Act and even to the EMU project. If Versailles was the end of the Keynesian socialist dream, Fontainebleau was the birth of a French socialism converted to the challenges of the world economy and to its neo-liberal requirements.

There is a risk in reading into the quotations about Mitterrand more than they can really bear, and it is possible to suspect that they contribute to an *ex-post* rewriting of the history, but it is also hard to deny that the 1983 decision was grounded on a strong—even if somewhat fuzzy—European commitment, based on an acceptance of the evolution of the world economy. The importance of this major strategic choice helps to explain the depth of the doctrinal *aggiornamento* performed by the socialist government at that time. *Désinflation compétitive* turnabout was not simply an ordinary adjustment to a local crisis situation. It stemmed from a kind of revolution in the principles underlying a whole vision of the world; a revolution the effects of which were to become perceptible far outside the narrow field of the policy-mix, in all aspects of economic life, and particularly in the new conceptions of profit and entrepreneurship which were paradoxically to be popularized mostly by the socialist power in these years. There is, thus, a global coherence in the various reorientations decided by the socialist governments about issues seemingly pertaining to independent fields, such as, for instance, the policy-mix on the one hand and the nationalizations on the other. And this coherence expresses the historical transformation of the *referential* (Jobert and Muller, 1987; Lordon, 1997), namely of the doctrinal corpus, the model of the world shared by the political and administrative élites. Crowding out the old Keynesian social democratic referential, the choice to play the game of the world economy leads to the adoption of a neo-liberal referential supposed to be in accordance with the new rules of the game.

4. *Désinflation Compétitive* as a New Model of Economic Policy

According to the line of argument developed above, *désinflation compétitive* appears as the outcome of a painful learning process imposed by external constraints. *Désinflation compétitive* may actually be viewed as the final step of a cognitive *tâtonnement* (trial and error), initiated by the exhaustion of the Keynesian–Fordian economic policy regime. The crisis is triggered by the opening of the economies with which national economic policy became increasingly at odds. It took almost 10 years for public power to acknowledge this contradiction and to envisage a radical transformation of the economic policy regime. Thus the first reactions of the governments of the 1970s are quite in line with the old routines of the Keynesian paradigm, as exemplified by the Chirac (1975) and Mauroy (1981) expansionary policies. The failure of the latter was so severe that it signalled the demise of the Keynesian model and gave way to a deep doctrinal revision from which *désinflation compétitive* would arise.

Reversing the former budgetary and monetary Keynesian regulation schemes, *désinflation compétitive* relied upon the three following principles: (i) it is impossible to conduct an isolated expansionary policy by stimulating consumption or public expenditures; (ii) growth must be

Figure 5
Inflation Rates (%)

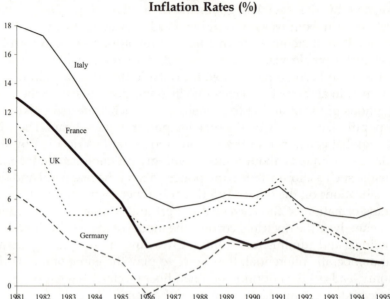

export-led; (iii) exporting requires competitiveness and having the lowest prices possible. The heart of the *désinflation compétitive* doctrine lies in the following sequence: disinflation→competitiveness→ exports→growth→employment.

This central logic is then diffracted into three main mechanisms: the *franc fort*, namely the pegging of the franc to the Deutschmark; wage discipline; and public-deficit reduction.

(a) *The* Franc Fort

In the early 1980s, inflation was considered the main problem of the French economy. Disinflation is viewed as the prerequisite for a reduction in unemployment. The 1981 inflation rate was 13 per cent, after a peak of 14.8 per cent in 1974, and an average rate around 9.5 per cent from 1976 to 1980 (OFCE, 1995) (Figure 5).

In its more compact form, *désinflation compétitive* may be identified with the pegging of the franc to the Deutschmark. The exchange-rate policy was conceived as the main instrument of disinflation. Refusing exchange-rate adjustment within the ERM aimed at importing German disinflation and, thus, reducing the inflation discrepancy with Germany, which is one of France's major trading partners.

Furthermore, the fixed exchange-rate strategy was aimed at a second target. From a credible commitment to give up devaluation, the monetary policy was expected to bring about a fall in the interest rate. This fall in the interest rate was, first, another contribution to the general slow-down of cost pressures. It was then supposed to foster investment, and through the embodiment of new technologies into capital, to improve structural competitiveness in the medium term.

(b) *Wage Discipline*

Wage discipline was also a prominent feature of *désinflation compétitive*. It was an obvious contribution to the target of low prices and improved competitiveness. Moreover, the diagnosis of the French economic situation in the early 1980s emphasizes a severe profitability problem. Actually the wage share in the national income reached its maximum in 1982 at 75 per cent (INSEE, 1996). From 1972 to 1982, almost 8 per cent of GDP was transferred from firms to households. The investment rate itself had been continuously decreasing since 1972 and reached its minimum at around 14 per cent in 1984 (INSEE, 1996). Influenced by supply-side economics, *désinflation compétitive* easily adopted the so-called 'Schmidt's theorem', according to which 'today's profits lead to tomorrow's investment'. Beyond its disinflation effects, wage discipline thus also aimed at restoring profitability and enhancing investment.

(c) *Public-deficit Reduction*

Finally, public-deficit reduction completed this general synopsis of *désinflation compétitive*. Here again, two mechanisms must be distinguished. According to the first, the reduction of the public deficit was supposed to weaken the crowding-out effect and thus to lower the interest rates. The second mechanism stemmed from a credibility effect. A restrictive budgetary orientation was expected to enhance the trust of financial markets and, at the same time, to lower the risk premium embodied in the interest rates and to strengthen the pegging of the franc to the Deutschmark.

(d) *A Renewed Vision of Structural Policy*

Even if, a priori, far from macroeconomic policy issues, the renewal of the structural policy conceptions was quite in line with the general orientations of the new referential. The interventionist state principles were abandoned to promote indirect incentive schemes. Three years after the socialist electoral success, the nationalization project was *de facto* driven into a dead-end when Prime Minister Laurent Fabius gave nationalized firms the instruction to operate according to private-sector management criteria—namely profitability. Two years was too short a period to harvest significant results in terms of improvement in global competitiveness. But, meanwhile, public-sector firms were incurring severe financial losses owing to the low growth context, to the general profit squeeze, but also to the specific constraints they faced as public firms. Even if they were previously top-level civil servants, even if they were in sympathy politically with the socialist government (which promoted them), some of the chairmen of the nationalized firms did not want their firms to bear any longer the burden of being 'social laboratories'. The most typical example of these public firms is Renault. The announcement of record losses in 1984–5 was a shock to public opinion. The recovery of profitability appeared as a necessity which justified putting aside any other target. The chairman, though promoted by the socialist government in 1982, was fired and replaced by a much more orthodox manager whose clear mission was drastically to improve productivity and financial results, whatever the consequences for employment.

In a very similar way to the radical turn of the economic policy itself, the public-sector industrial policy was thus reoriented towards meeting a short-term crisis, but also according to a major long-term policy shift. Restructurings would still be pursued, but in a defensive way. The emergency treatment of the bankruptcies replaced the forward-looking project of the 'national champions', which was to use nationalization as its main tool.

However, leaving aside the treatment of emergency situations, a new vision of restructuring seemed to arise. Restructurings were no longer envisaged as a strategic public intervention, but left to market adjustments or considered as a side-effect of the *franc fort* policy. One may at first sight wonder about the relationship between industrial restructurings and external monetary policy. In fact, the *franc fort* had early on been considered as a 'positive constraint', supposed to prompt firms to change their specialization. According to this doctrine, devaluations act as a moral hazard in preventing firms from improving price performance as long as they know that they can count on exchange-rate manipulation artificially to restore competitiveness. Faced with the immediate handicap of an overvalued currency, firms are obliged to pay attention to their costs and prices. But above all, they are given the incentive to abandon standardized products and to specialize in goods where qualitative non-price competitive advantage is relevant and may overcome the obstacle of a strong currency. The *franc fort* has thus been used as a macro incentive aiming at modifying the global specialization of the French economy and its position in the international division of labour (Aglietta and Baulant, 1993). One can easily appreciate the distance between this incentive scheme and the previous 'competitiveness through nationalization' project.

The failure of ambitions for nationalization and the turn to a completely different model of industrial policy, makes it easy to understand the doctrinal disarray of the socialists in the second half of the 1980s. Extending the public sector was impossible because of the previous failure, but also because of budgetary constraints. But accepting privatizations was also impossible, again from a symbolic point of view. The difficulty was amazingly solved by the doctrinal 'innovation' of the *'ni-ni'* (*ni nationalisation, ni privatisation*, neither nationalization nor privatization), first expressed in Mitterrand's re-election programme in 1988. Theorizing the *status quo*, the *ni-ni*, however, admitted some degrees of freedom: the 'public sector breathing' principle allowed the possibility of discretionary and very partial privatizations — as well as more or less discrete attempts at renationalizations.[3]

5. A Short Appraisal of the *Désinflation Compétitive* Results

Fifteen years surely provides a fair test of the results of an economic policy. The appraisal of *désinflation compétitive* is quite mixed. *Désinflation compétitive* certainly succeeded in wiping out inflation, but completely failed in the reduction of unemployment which was its ultimate target.

(a) *A Successful Disinflation*

French disinflation is indisputably a success. The inflation rate fell from 13 per cent in 1981 to 2.7 per cent in 1986 (Figure 5). How can it be explained that *désinflation compétitive* succeeded when the prices and wages freeze of the Plan Barre in 1976–8 had no effect on inflation? Two explanations, more complementary than really contradictory, compete to provide an answer to this question.

(i) A structural change in the wage- and price-setting mechanisms

According to the first explanation, the disinflation mainly stemmed from a twofold transformation in the wage- and price-setting mechanisms. First, the government decided in 1983 that wages would no longer be indexed to prices. The disindexation probably provides a significant part of the explanation of why the end of the wage and price freeze did not result in a rocketing of inflation, as frequently observed in the past. To this 'structural change' thesis should be added the fact that the monetary policy certainly played an unexpected role there. The

---

[3] As exemplified by the aborted takeover financed by public funds of the Société Générale, which was privatized by the right-wing *cohabitation* government in 1987.

credibility of the commitment to a fixed exchange rate had deeply altered the wage- and price-setting mechanisms: the agents were now informed that no devaluation would restore competitiveness if the wage–price spiral diverged. It is now common knowledge that a cumulative price discrepancy with France's main trade partners resulted in losses of competitiveness which were detrimental both to employers and employees. The publicly known restrictive orientations of the monetary policy, which ceased being accommodating, may have worked as a strong incentive on all social groups radically to change their price-setting behaviour.

(ii) High unemployment and 'reserve army' pressure

An alternative thesis emphasizes the loss of bargaining power owing to the higher and higher level of unemployment. The threat of being fired, added to the demise of the unions, certainly explains the weakness of wage pressure from the middle of the 1980s. Lecointe *et al.* (1989) and Confais and Muet (1994) found that the major part of the disinflation and of the competitiveness gains could be attributed to the pressure of unemployment on wages rather than to imported disinflation due to the *franc fort*.

The 'reserve army pressure' thesis also underlines what may be viewed as one of the major characteristics of the French disinflation process, as opposed to what could be observed in Germany, for example. Whereas German disinflation may be considered as the result of the functioning of a whole set of institutions—including the central bank, but also the rules of sectoral bargaining, and the values of social consensus and cooperative management—French disinflation mainly stems from market adjustments. Jobert and Théret (1994) have suggested that, in the absence of a strong enough neo-corporatism which could have driven a negotiated disinflation, wage discipline has been performed more brutally, by way of unemployment. Ideological and rhetorical auxiliaries, such as the European discourse, had to make it less bitter and to provide some legitimacy to the disinflation effort. Pointing at the European horizon was a way to give a meaning to the macroeconomic adjustment and to recreate consensus and consent that social institutions were too weak to provide. As the report of the *Xème Plan* acknowledged, 'Europe is a leverage which allowed us to control inflation in the freely accepted framework of the disciplines of the ERM' (CGP, 1989).

The lack of institutions, ruling out the possibility of a disinflation-by-agreement, allowed no solution other than a severe market-driven disinflation. And one may also see there the reason for the inability of the socialist government to imagine a non-liberal, social democratic alternative to the obsolete *programme commun*. France is characterized by a relative lack of these intermediary institutional forms, between state and agents, which make up the structure of a social democratic society. The absence of a 'bargaining and compromise' culture, a tradition of a non-cooperative capital–labour relationship, the recurrence of heated social crisis, calling for state intervention to solve the conflict: all these features suggest the discrepancy between France and a genuine social democracy. Moreover, the French Socialist Party never had a strong social democratic culture, but rather belongs to Jacobin tradition, pleading for a strongly centralized state. Even if the 1980s saw the ideological expansion of the *seconde gauche* of Michel Rocard, ideologically closer to the social democratic ideal than the more orthodox socialist stream of Mitterrand, the Socialist Party never built the network of contacts and relations with associations, unions, etc., which are the supports and the transmission belts for a social democratic policy within society (Bergounioux and Grunberg, 1992).

(b) *A Complete Failure on Unemployment*

If the slow-down of inflation has been a success, *désinflation compétitive* has dramatically failed on unemployment. Apart from the years of higher growth between 1988 and 1990, unemployment has continuously increased, from 8.3 per cent in 1983 to 12.6 per cent in 1997 (Figure 3). Scrutinizing the most important mechanisms of the general scheme of *désinflation compétitive* reveals that none of them provided the expected results.

(i) The profitability mistake

The correction in the national income distribution went too far and showed up the weakness of the argument of 'Schmidt's theorem'. Having declined to 24 per cent in 1982, the profit share grew to 32 per cent in 1990, to remain almost constant afterwards. A recovery of the investment rate (14 per cent in 1984, 18 per cent in 1990) seemed first to be correlated with the rise of the profit share, and thus to confirm Schmidt's theorem. But the investment rate slipped back in 1990 and declined to less than 16 per cent in 1993, while the profit share remained at its historical highest level. The theoretical argument is well known and hardly needs repeating. Wages are ambivalent insofar as they are at the same time a cost, with supply-side effects, and a key element of expenditure constituting the final demand. Malinvaud (1986) wondered early on whether the wage discipline had not gone too far. Artus (1989) addressed the issue of an optimal distribution, balancing the two contradictory effects, which means that wage restraint does not have to be pursued indefinitely and that investment does not monotonically vary with the profit share. These questions are all the more relevant in that the early 1990s simultaneously saw very high profitability indicators and depressed activity, as expressed in the capacity utilization rate (80 per cent in 1993, which was the lowest since the 1970s). The wage discipline of *désinflation compétitive* was maintained while the demand constraint was obviously becoming much tighter than the profitability constraint. And the 1990s probably give one of the most illuminating illustrations of a stagnationist under-consumption regime (Marglin and Badhuri, 1990). Keeping up the supply-side wage discipline in a typically Keynesian context of lack of demand will certainly appear as one of the major mistakes of *désinflation compétitive* during the 1990s.

(ii) The interest-rate mistake

Désinflation compétitive has also considerably overestimated what could be expected from the *franc fort* in terms of low interest rates. Because the French monetary policy never succeeded in becoming fully credible, the *franc fort* relied on the help of high interest rates — which was the exact opposite of the original strategy. Explaining this apparent paradox, of a continuously maintained orthodox economic policy failing to accumulate credibility, is impossible in the scope of the present chapter (see Lordon, 1997).[4, 5] But, even if the French economic policy had become credible, it cannot be concluded that the expected fall in the interest rate would have sufficed to foster investment and growth. The effects of the interest rates on activity are so numerous and contradictory that their

[4] The most recent years may give the impression that credibility has been accumulated by the French monetary policy, which almost succeeded in cancelling the risk premium with respect to German interest rates. Nevertheless, a twofold objection can be raised. First, one may note how long it took to get these credibility benefits: almost 15 years! Second, this credibility effect may be an optical illusion. It does not come from the virtue of *désinflation compétitive* itself, but rather from the fact that the French monetary policy 'imported' the credibility of the transition to the euro. If the euro were abandoned, the interest-rate discrepancy with Germany would probably increase again.

[5] Incidentally, one should not see a contradiction between this low credibility–high interest-rate diagnosis, and the statement above, according to which price- and wage-setting mechanisms have been radically transformed owing to the credibility of the no-devaluation monetary policy. Those two kinds of 'credibility effects' do not refer to the same groups of agents. The failure of *désinflation compétitive* to lower interest rates comes from a lack of credibility *vis-à-vis* the operators of international financial markets. National wage bargainers, however, have early on found credible the commitment to give up devaluing, and they have integrated in their strategies the fact that exchange-rate adjustment would no longer — or not frequently enough — erase the inflation drift of the wage–price spiral, and restore competitiveness.

net effect remains very ambiguous and, in the French case, seldom significant (Bordes *et al.*, 1995). Gambling on the interest-rate effects, as was done in the 1980s with the pegging of the franc, and as is done now with the public deficit adjustment programme, constitutes a very uncertain policy.

The interest-rate issue certainly gives the best illustration of the thesis according to which *désinflation compétitive*, though initially relevant, has been maintained after the end of the 1980s in a counterproductive way and regardless of its drawbacks. And the monetary crisis of 1992–3 acted to reveal the growing inefficiency as well as the rising political dimension of *désinflation compétitive*. The public decisions adopted during these speculative turmoils revealed the hard core of *désinflation compétitive*, which amounted merely to the pegging of the franc to the Deutschmark — the *franc fort*. More than just the axis of a macroeconomic strategy, the franc–Deutschmark link had above all a political meaning, as the basis of the ERM, and thus of the future EMU. Against all macroeconomic rationale, the pegging had to be defended at all costs, for political reasons, namely to avoid the wreck of the single currency. French monetary authorities decided to raise the interest rates to whatever level was necessary to thwart speculation. But these interest-rate rises were adopted regardless of the context, namely a slump. When the very low — and even negative — growth called for strong expansionary policies, monetary policy was tightened up again — which was all the more absurd in that the recession stemmed precisely from a credit-crunch mechanism (INSEE, 1994; Aglietta, 1995). Whereas the Federal Reserve has lowered its real interest rates to zero for more than a year, so as to foster the banking recovery (Le Cacheux, 1995), European central banks pushed up the real rates to historic levels at the very heart of the crisis! Nowhere has the dogma of the 'strong currency', associated with the political obsession with the EMU, exhibited more clearly its aberrations. Five years later, one can still feel its effects in terms of additional unemployment, and problems with public finance: the budgetary policy had to perform the adjustment monetary policy refused to do — and do it, moreover, in a high interest-rate context accelerating the cumulative dynamics of the public debt. Trapped into the *désinflation compétitive* doctrinal commandments, France has adopted a policy-mix diametrically opposed to what was required by the macroeconomic situation. Monetary policy must certainly account for a significant share of the unemployment of the 1990s.

(i) The competitiveness mistake

In the end, the competitiveness logic of *désinflation compétitive* must be directly questioned. It should first be noticed that, presented as the exact opposite of competitive devaluation, *désinflation compétitive* in fact fundamentally shares the same nominal logic. Both aim at increasing the competitiveness of the real exchange rate, the first through a devaluation of the nominal exchange rate, the second by a fall in the relative price of national goods. But foreign importers do not care at all about the means through which the price of French goods, expressed in their own currency, have decreased. In their eyes, devaluation and *désinflation compétitive* are strictly equivalent. And despite their claims that *désinflation compétitive* is completely contradictory to devaluation, the proponents of *désinflation compétitive* must be vaguely aware of this common logic. Why would have they been so horrified when the UK, Italy, and Spain carried out significant devaluations, if they were fully convinced of the inefficiency of devaluation?

But this is not yet the core criticism, which should, in fact, challenge directly the competitiveness vision of *désinflation compétitive*. Relying exclusively on price discipline, *désinflation compétitive* is probably based on a complete misunderstanding of the new logic of competitiveness. At the top reaches of the international division of labour, competitive advantage is not so much a matter of costs and prices, but stems from innovation, quality, specialization, and all the characteristics which enable firms to behave as price-makers. The new theories of growth and international trade (Krugman, 1990), as well as institutionalist approaches, such as the regulation school (Boyer, 1988), have long ago suggested that the high competitiveness and growth paths are associated with the capability of creating and exploiting monopolistic innovation rents. Keeping up with price competition *de facto* lowers a country within the international division of labour insofar as it implicitly identifies the middle-range new industrialized countries as relevant challengers. In such a category, competition is almost unsustainable for highly developed countries, the productivity of which cannot offset their high wage and social costs. *Désinflation compétitive* appears here particularly counterproductive because, in maintaining an exclusive focus on wage and price discipline, it precludes the transition towards a high-wage, high-qualification, and high-commitment capital–labour compromise, which is the sole route to structural competitiveness (Amable *et al.*, 1997). Trapped into the same nominal logic as competitive devaluation, *désinflation compétitive* seems to have especially misunderstood the real issues and challenges of competitiveness. Fifteen years of continuous application have shown that, under its particular set of constraints and 'incentives', the most likely behaviour of firms was to deepen the defensive strategies of firing, wage reduction, and productivity improvement. The main effect of *désinflation compétitive* has been to promote a non-cooperative capital–labour

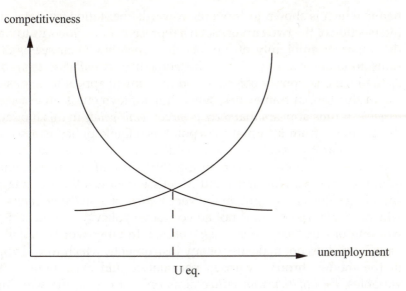

relationship which remains the most severe obstacle to high-quality competitiveness. After so many years, the competitive return on such hard work regarding wages appears to be very thin. The international market share of France in 1991 was still significantly lower than in the period 1975–80 (Figure 4)! *Désinflation compétitive,* which relied entirely upon an export-led growth strategy, has failed to turn round structural competitiveness.

To this brief analytical appraisal, one should also add the following comment, showing how little *désinflation compétitive* in fact felt concerned with the unemployment issue. This statement may appear at first sight quite paradoxical. Is not the reduction of unemployment the obvious purpose of any economic policy? In fact *désinflation compétitive* has progressively substituted its intermediary (disinflation) for its final objective. Using the inverse optimal control technique, within a neoclassical framework, Marti (1995) exhibits the implicit preferences of the French government over the years 1981–91. His analysis reveals that disinflation and external trade balance are tremendously dominant in the utility function of the French government(s). From another perspective, Blanchard and Muet (1993) try to formalize the main mechanism of *désinflation compétitive* as in the diagram above.

The first relationship between competitiveness and unemployment is increasing. Owing to the Phillips effect, the pressure of unemployment slows down wages and fosters competitiveness. The second relationship depicts the demand side and is decreasing. The improvement in competitiveness enhances exports, and then growth and employment. Blanchard and Muet specify an out-of-equilibrium dynamic which is shown to converge towards the stationary state, at the intersection of the two curves. Such a representation allows us to clarify the apparent ambiguity of the fact that unemployment seems at the same time an objective and an instrument of *désinflation compétitive*. Actually, the notions of objective and instrument appear to be misleading in this formal framework, where unemployment is an *endogenous variable*. It thus appears that *there is no economic policy* in this model. On the contrary, from a formal viewpoint, economic policy is associated with comparative static analysis, which tries to assess the effects of parameter variations (corresponding to the use of the instruments of economic policy). Blanchard and Muet's model has the advantage of shedding some crude light on the very nature of *désinflation compétitive* which, strictly speaking, is not an economic policy, but reduces to the working of *endogenous market adjustments*. In other words, *désinflation compétitive* does not make use of any instruments, which would appear in the model through various parameters and exogenous control variables. *Désinflation compétitive* aims only at easing the working of endogenous mechanisms which drive the convergence towards an equilibrium rate of unemployment. Furthermore, this equilibrium rate is very unlikely to correspond to full employment. It may even be very far from it—Sterdyniak *et al.* (1997) give the figure of 8.5 per cent for this rate for France during the period 1987–94. *Désinflation compétitive* then transfers to long-term 'structural policies' the task of lowering this equilibrium rate. Apart from statements by its advocates, *désinflation compétitive* appears thus to be little concerned with unemployment, so it is easier to understand why it had such poor results.

6. Conclusion: Has Jospin Broken with *Désinflation Compétitive*?

The metamorphosis of the *programme commun* into *désinflation compétitive* will probably remain one of the most striking and puzzling episodes of French political life of recent decades. In political terms, the U-turn could not be publicly presented as other than a 'pause' in the reforms. But the pause has lasted a long time. The real paradox to be explained is thus not so much the pause in itself but its permanence. And the paradox is all the more challenging in that, in addition to being ideologically diametrically opposed to the initial *programme commun*, *désinflation compétitive* appeared to be terribly ineffective as regards unemployment. Necessary from 1983 to, say, 1988, *désinflation compétitive* has become counterproductive since the late 1980s. Major imbalances in public deficits and distribution, too high a rate of inflation, and trend losses of competitiveness were surely calling for a significant correction in 1983. We can acknowledge that the objectives of *désinflation compétitive* were relevant for a time. But its continued relevance has to be questioned insofar as inflation has almost disappeared and unemployment keeps on growing.

Because they refused to criticize their own economic choices of the 1980s, and because they kept on claiming until the end that *désinflation compétitive* was the 'sole possible economic policy', the socialists were wiped out at the parliamentary elections of 1993, only to be returned to power in extraordinary circumstances in 1997. Lionel Jospin's whole electoral campaign aimed to emphasize that the lessons had been drawn from the mistakes of the 1980s. He particularly underlined the fact that he would refuse to accept a severe constraint on economic policy from European discipline, and that he would face a confrontation with Germany in order to negotiate a more growth-and-employment-oriented treatise in Amsterdam.

The break with the previous 'neo-liberal socialism' of the 1980s seemed to be credible and clearly appeared in Jospin's economic programme, which revolved more or less around the four following axes.

(i)   Distribution had to be reoriented in favour of wages. After the great reversal initiated in 1982, the share of profit was too high and detrimental to household consumption. Jospin thus unambiguously stated a Keynesian under-consumption diagnosis of the low growth of the 1990s, which significantly departed from the usual supply-side vision of *désinflation compétitive*.

(ii) The reduction in working hours was presented as the major economic reform of the future Left government.

(iii) The privatization programme would be stopped, especially in the utilities.

(iv) The transition to EMU had to be significantly reoriented:
      • the stability pact proposed by Germany would be refused as too deflationary a macroeconomic regulation framework; a growth pact, explicitly aiming at promoting employment, should be proposed in its place, which would mean relaxing the Maastricht criteria;
      • France would refuse to accept a 'strong euro' monetary policy from the European Central Bank;
      • the countries of the South — especially Italy and Spain — should participate from the very beginning in the euro;

- an 'economic government' should be constituted to counter-
  balance the excessive power of the non-elected European
  monetary authorities.

This set of propositions, exhibiting a clear break with the previous
logic of *désinflation compétitive*, certainly played a significant part in the
electoral victory of Jospin in May–June 1997. As usual, the problem was
knowing whether the campaign promises would be respected or not.
Two years later, one has a clearer idea, beyond the electoral rhetoric,
about the real orientations of Jospin's economic policy. This provisional
appraisal is quite mixed, but shows the strength of the *désinflation
compétitive* paradigm in the minds of the government, despite all the
speeches about a break with the past.

(i) The distribution issue

The under-consumption diagnosis and the subsequent commitment to
increase the wage share in the national income have found a mitigated
application. Actually, as soon as he arrived in power, Jospin was careful
enough to add two codicils to this commitment. First, a more balanced
distribution target must be pursued in the medium term. One should
not, therefore, expect a significant evolution in the very short run, the
point being to avoid a sudden rocketing of wages which could squeeze
profit and competitiveness and destabilize firms. Second, one must be
aware of the lack of instruments to implement a public-sector incomes
policy. The government has no say in private-sector wage negotiations.
Nevertheless, it can influence private-sector bargaining with the guidelines given to wages policy in the public sector (the administration and
nationalized firms). And it can also contribute to pushing upwards the
whole wage hierarchy by raising the minimum wage (the SMIC). The
very first months of the new socialist government have shown how
reluctant it was to use these two instruments. If not completely frozen,
civil-service wages have been kept under control for the sake of fiscal
adjustment, to meet the 3 per cent deficit target. And the SMIC has been
given the most symbolic and minimal push because of fears about the
excess labour cost of the less-qualified workers. However, Jospin's
government has not forgotten how to use taxation as an instrument of
incomes policy. In 1997, corporate taxes were increased and household
taxes lowered, thus operating a shift in distribution. In so doing, Jospin
avoided the mistake of Alain Juppé, in 1995, who did exactly the
opposite, leading to a breakdown of growth. Jospin has also modified
the social contributions regime, increasing the burden on financial
incomes and lowering it on direct wage incomes. All this resulted in a
rise in purchasing power and the consumption of households, which

certainly helped to boost growth. The decisions on fiscal and incomes policy which followed are not that straightforward. First, the increase in corporate taxes was deemed to be especially dedicated to the European fiscal convergence and was removed in 1999. Nevertheless the plan for the 35-hour week is intended to restore a special (and permanent) tax on the most highly profitable firms. On the other side nothing more has been done to enhance wage-earners' income: unlike in previous years, the SMIC for 1999 will receive no extra push beyond its automatic legal rise. This decision is clearly a side effect of the bargaining process between the government and employers around the reduction in working time. It certainly shows up how pervasive the wage-gap issue remains and, more generally, the ideas of *désinflation compétitive*, despite the Keynesian flavour of Jospin's speech on distribution.

The 1997 Wage and Employment Conference, involving employers, workers, and the government, was probably one of the most promising of Jospin's initiatives and raised high hopes. In fact, this conference could have been an important institutional creation: quite in line with the French tradition where state intervention is frequently required to overcome obstacles to the social bargain, this new institution could have had the advantage of setting wage bargaining at a highly centralized level, where Pareto-superior global compromises can be reached because of the possibility of taking account of externalities, macro coordination problems, and so on (Calmfors and Driffill, 1988). The conference could have been an important step in the transformation of a too weakly institutionalized capital–labour relationship from which resulted, for instance, the brutal market-driven disinflation of the 1980s, compared to the German disinflation-by-agreement. Unfortunately, 2 years later this institutional innovation appears as a one-off initiative with no long-run consequences, whereas one could have wished to see it expand and take its place permanently in the French mode of regulation.

(ii) The reduction in working time

After the aborted attempt of 1981–2, which was too weak (from 40 to 39 hours a week) to have any strong effect in one direction or the other, the reduction of working time has been promoted as one of the major targets of a left-wing government programme, precisely because of the extent to which it showed a significant divergence from the previous orthodoxy of *désinflation compétitive*. One may think that Jospin has tied his hands and that he is committed too strongly now to go back on the 35 hours without incurring a major, and probably final, political defeat. Of course, the government still has the flexibility to achieve the 35-hour week, but with so many concessions to firms that the reform would hardly cost them anything, and would have almost no effect on unemployment. Bargaining is in full swing and the making flexible and the annualization of working hours could be the counterparts to convince firms to cooperate. It is even possible to fear that the government would propose a project to develop pension funds as an element of this great transaction!

(iii) Stopping privatizations?

Jospin strongly claimed during the campaign that the privatization programme of the Juppé government would be stopped. In fact nothing has really changed in the socialists' doctrinal view of the nationalization issue: they are still as unable to redefine a positive project for the industrial public sector as they were in the second half of the 1980s. This lack of vision (added to the effects of time passing by!) has probably made it easier, despite the campaign speeches, to drop the *ni-ni* dogma (neither nationalization nor privatization) from which resulted the *status quo* in the frontiers of the public sector during Mitterrand's last years. It must then be said that this reticence has been rapidly overcome and that the present public-sector policy is diametrically opposed to what was promised before the elections. Actually, Jospin's privatization programme is very close to Juppé's: France Télécom, Thomson, Aérospatiale, Air France, Crédit Lyonnais, and CIC are or will soon be privatized, even if more partially and more progressively than under the previous right-wing government. In financial terms, Jospin's privatization programme already exceeds the sum of both the Balladur and Juppé privatizations (180 FF billion vs 123 FF billion). Privatization is certainly the issue over which the repudiation of campaign commitments is most visible. Especially in the cases of France Télécom and Thomson, privatization will have given an important signal to the financial markets, confirming the global orthodoxy of the socialist economic policy.

(iv) The EMU issue

The transition to the single currency was obviously the main criterion upon which to judge the extent to which current economic policy still remains in line with *désinflation compétitive*. On the European issue, appearances seem to fight with reality. Indeed, Jospin has opened the debate on growth and unemployment policies in Amsterdam and obtained a special annual European summit to be devoted to these questions. He has also obtained the creation of an embryonic 'economic government' which could help to coordinate national economic policies. And finally the recovery of the European business cycle helped Italy and Spain to qualify for the euro. So much for the appearances. But the reality is somewhat different. The main point upon which Jospin seemed to have built his economic programme was the denial of the Maastricht public finance criteria and of the German stability pact. Both have been accepted by France in Amsterdam. And whereas Jospin seemed to have been ready to accept conflict and to initiate crisis with Germany, a low-profile negotiation strategy has in fact prevailed. Jospin has only obtained from his European partners very soft commitments: an informal 'Euro council' as an economic government, with no well-defined tasks, and an annual summit on unemployment with no binding decisions. Meanwhile, the set of criteria actually binding the economic policies remains exactly the same, and has even been institutionalized as a permanent regime discipline by the stability pact validated in Amsterdam. The contradiction between the non-austerity programme announced by Jospin and European discipline has only apparently been solved, thanks to the unexpected higher growth of the second half of 1997 and 1998. But should the future growth rate be below government expectations and significantly decrease — which is not that unlikely in the general low-growth European context — the previous contradiction would rise up again. Respecting the 3 per cent GDP criterion for the deficit would require reducing public expenditure.

(v) What remains of *désinflation compétitive* since 1 January 1999?

One must pay special attention to the ambiguous relationship between *désinflation compétitive* and EMU. Was *désinflation compétitive* merely a radical turn towards neo-liberalism, or was it intended to be a neo-liberal route to a renewed European Keynesianism? What makes things difficult to disentangle is the fact that *désinflation compétitive* stemmed from various and contradictory projects. Some of its proponents, especially in the civil service, conceived it early on as the economic policy of a genuine neo-liberal project. In the political sphere, the socialists viewed *désinflation compétitive* as an instrument to perform a European integration aimed at recovering a Keynesian sovereignty (Lordon, 1997). But the instrument progressively appeared to leave irreversible effects, and it is now clear that nobody can believe any longer in this dialectic of Euro-Keynesianism through the transitory neo-liberalism of *désinflation compétitive*, except with a very remote time horizon and a very low discount rate — which is maybe still the case of Jospin's government! But how far can EMU be considered as *désinflation compétitive* extended to the European level? In fact the answer to this question is twofold.

Reduced to its core, *désinflation compétitive* is above all a policy to peg the exchange rate. From the viewpoint of intra-European monetary relationships it is quite obvious that under the single currency regime member states no longer suffer the previous constraints of the peg to Deutschmark in terms of subordinated monetary policy. However, the logic of the peg could still apply in the field of external monetary relationships and one might fear that the European Central Bank (ECB) would pursue a peg with respect to the dollar. The first decisions of the ECB suggest that this is not the case and, as far as we can judge in such a short period of time, Wim Duisenberg seems rather to push the ECB towards a US-type strategy, trying to promote the euro as a peg rather than as a pegged currency.

But *désinflation compétitive* is not simply a matter of the peg. *Désinflation compétitive* entails broader aspects of economic policy which will mainly remain unchanged now that the transition to the euro has been undertaken. One must first emphasize the permanence of an inflation-oriented monetary policy as stated by the statutes of the ECB. Budgetary discipline which was another key issue of *désinflation compétitive* at the national level is also strongly reaffirmed by the European stability pact. Even if, inside the Euro zone, the monetary constraints of the fixed exchange rates have disappeared, the macroeconomic constraints are still active. The fact that exchange-rate adjustments are ruled out implies a tighter monitoring of wages, production costs, and competitiveness. This deepening of the *désinflation compétitive* adjustments is all the more likely now that there are no other degrees of freedom to accommodate asymmetric shocks. As has been noted, not only are devaluations now impossible, but monetary policy is no longer available at the national level, national budgetary policies are tied by the stability pact, there is no significant federal budget which could provide automatic stabilization, and, finally, intra-European migration of the labour force will remain marginal for obvious linguistic and cultural reasons. The only way to accommodate a specific shock is the standard *désinflation compétitive* adjustment: rise of unemployment, wage restraint, rise in competitiveness, export boost, and recovery of demand. It is then not very surprising to hear Otmar Issing, the chief economist of the ECB, advising the governments to deregulate their labour markets so that the last remaining degree of freedom at least works properly!

The euro certainly allows the avoidance of the monetary implications of the peg in terms of high interest rates — which took a significant part in the rise of unemployment in the 1990s. But one must acknowledge that the main part of the macroeconomic logic of *désinflation compétitive* remains unchanged in the EMU regime. What was originally conceived — at least by the French socialists — as a transitional device to bring convergence towards the euro is in fact now established as a permanent economic policy regime.

The will of Jospin's government to escape from the old dogma of *désinflation compétitive* is — or was — certainly sincere. But, will has to be strong to escape the overwhelming influence of Europe on economic policy. Chirac, who gave to his 1995 campaign a somehow anti-*désinflation-compétitive*, anti-Maastricht flavour, became almost instantaneously after his election, the most active proponent of the European project. He has refused the referendum on EMU which he was demanding in 1995. Jospin is under the same pressures. The historical weight of the European project seems so great that nobody dares to risk being the one who will have to account for a major European crisis. Designed according to a neo-liberal plan, EMU then, unsurprisingly, obliges all governments to bring their economic policy into conformity with the neo-liberal guidelines written down in the Maastricht Treaty. It has been suggested above that the European project was the most powerful guarantor of the logic of *désinflation compétitive*. However disposed Jospin was to depart from *désinflation compétitive*, it seems that, as soon as he accepted the EMU horizon as the basis of his policy, he could no more escape than his predecessors.

6

The Political Economy of Social Democratic Economic Policies: The PASOK Experiment in Greece

EUCLID TSAKALOTOS*

In many ways, PASOK (the Panhellenic Socialist Movement) has been one of the most politically successful social democratic parties in Europe over the recent past. Since 1981, PASOK has only been out of power for 4 years. And yet, in the economic sphere, the subject of this paper, it cannot be labelled a success.

Like many other socialist experiments in government, PASOK started with a strategy of promoting two long-standing aspirations of social democracy. This was to promote redistribution and social justice and, at the same time, to extend democracy to the social and economic realms. As we shall see, these two planks were interdependent. For PASOK sought to distinguish itself from those social democratic currents that restricted themselves to social reform and redistribution, fearing that, in Przeworski's (1985, p. 41) words:

> mitigation does not become transformation: indeed, without transformation, the need to mitigate becomes eternal. Social democrats find themselves in the situation which Marx attributed to Louis Bonaparte: their policies seem contradictory since they are forced at the same time to strengthen the productive power of capital and counteract its effect.

That is to say, PASOK, as we shall see in section 1, sought to distinguish itself with regard not only to the ends of economic policy, but also to the means. Such policies, it was hoped, would help to restructure and modernize the Greek economy, while at the same time, by promoting institutional change and enhancing social control of the

* Athens University of Economics and Business.

Wlodzimierz Brus, Nikiforos Diamandouros, Heather Gibson, Torben Iversen, Theodore Lianos, Ken Mayhew, Dimitris Sotiropoulos, Panos Tsakloglou, Frank Vandenbroucke, and Juhana Vartiainen all made helpful comments on an earlier draft of this paper. I would like to express my gratitude to Andrew Glyn and a referee for insightful comments which have helped to improve the paper.

economy, would ensure that the social gains promoted by PASOK would be secure.

However, this strategy characterized, at the rhetorical level at least, only PASOK's first term of government (1981–5). As in other similar social democratic episodes, there was eventually to be a move in a rightwards direction with the adoption of a less distinctive set of economic priorities and policies. By 1993, when PASOK returned to government for its third main term of office, this turn to orthodoxy in economic policy-making was almost compete—although PASOK still sought to distinguish itself on the ends of economic policies.

PASOK's experiment is, however, interesting for a number of reasons. The argument of this paper is that PASOK's change in policy was not primarily the consequence of external pressures. Thus the focus here is on the internal causes that underlie the gradual abandonment of a distinctive set of economic policies. In particular, we argue that the Greek context was not propitious for introducing measures for extending democracy to the economic sphere. This argument is developed by looking at the political economy prerequisites for such social democratic strategies. Furthermore, by doing this, we can isolate a number of political economy factors which would constitute important obstacles to be overcome, not only in the Greek context, but elsewhere.

In section 1, we give a brief history of PASOK's rise to power as well as discussing its aspirations and programme. We focus on a set of economic initiatives—both supply-side and macroeconomic policies—that PASOK felt to be central to its whole strategy. We also briefly discuss their implementation. In section 2, we give an account of PASOK's economic record since 1981. In particular, we point to the growing macroeconomic imbalances and the absence of any notable supply-side response in the real economy throughout the 1980s. We also look briefly at the post-1993 economic record. In section 3, we look more closely at the political economy aspects which lie behind this economic record. Finally, in a concluding section, we try to give an overall assessment of PASOK's trajectory towards the adoption of more orthodox economic policies and we conclude with some general remarks on the wider relevance to social democratic economic policy-making of the PASOK experiment.

1. Evolution of PASOK's Economic Approach

PASOK was formed in 1974, immediately after the fall of the military dictatorship (1967–74), and it constituted a novel political formation within Greek politics. It was to become the first avowedly mass socialist party in Greece. In its first electoral confrontation in 1974, it won 13.6 per cent of the vote, thereby staking out the ground as the main left opposition, having overtaken the forces of the United Left (an alliance of Euro-communist and orthodox communist parties). By the second post-dictatorship election in 1977, when it won just over 25 per cent of the vote, it had become the main opposition party to the ruling New Democracy Party. In its third electoral confrontation in 1981, it won a massive 48 per cent of the vote (57 per cent of the seats in Parliament) and formed the first Greek socialist government. Since 1981, it has won a further three major election victories (1985, 1993, and 1996) and has only been out of power between 1989 and 1993. This constitutes an impressive political record by any standards, let alone those of the European Left in this period.

Not surprisingly, PASOK has undergone major changes in its ideology, aspirations, and policy programmes since 1974 and it is clearly beyond our scope here to give anything like a full account of all the twists and turns of this story.[1] Although a novel political formation within Greek politics, PASOK had its roots in the pre-1967 Centre Union (headed by Andreas Papandreou's father, George Papandreou) which itself had a significant undercurrent of socialist ideology (Catephores, 1983). In its first manifesto, the so-called Third of September Declaration, PASOK declared that its three main aspirations were national independence, popular sovereignty, and social liberation, and that it supported a third way to socialism lying somewhere between traditional social democracy and Leninism. Its early ideology was heavily based on the neo-Marxist and Dependency School traditions which had been popular in the USA in the 1960s and which had been adopted by Andreas Papandreou (a Professor of Economics at Berkeley before coming to Greece in the early 1960s). This approach, and especially the centre-periphery theoretical schema, was employed both to understand the nature of Greek society and the economy and, at the political level, to express the long-standing hostility of the Greek left to the USA, NATO, and, almost to the same extent, the then EEC. Whatever the merits of this tradition, it need not detain us since it became increasingly less influential, although its importance in mobilizing support for PASOK in the early years and, in particular, in outmanoeuvring the Euro-communist and orthodox left should not be underestimated.[2]

[1] On the political development of PASOK, see Lyrintzis (1987), Spourdalakis (1988), Featherstone (1987), and Morlino (1995).

[2] *Ex post*, some analysts have suggested that Papandreou's radicalism and Third-Worldism in this period was important in consolidating democracy by providing a cathartic outlet for Greece's historical resentments (Pridham, 1995, pp. 175–6). For details of PASOK's gradual shift to a more pro-European stance, see Featherstone (1986).

By the 1981 election, controlling for certain specificities of Greek history and Southern Europe in general, PASOK was recognizedly a social democratic party of the Left (Sassoon, 1996, p. 637). On the one hand, there was an increasingly moderate stand, not only on foreign relations issues, but also on matters of economic policy. This was associated with the decision to become a mass party which was to a great extent a catch-all party or in the words of PASOK itself, the party of 'non-privileged Greeks' (Gunther *et al.*, 1995, ch. 1). In many ways what united this broad coalition was not primarily a commitment to a specific set of policies, but the fact that it included many of those sections of society which had been marginalized and excluded from Greek political life since the Second World War and the ensuing civil war (Diamandouros, 1994). PASOK's ability to keep this alliance together and mediate between the myriad of different interests was to prove a key test to which we return later.

On the other hand, while increasingly moderate, PASOK in 1981 was still committed, at least at the rhetorical level, to a programme and a set of economic policies which were quintessentially social democratic. It can be located in the long-standing social democratic tradition of extending democracy from the political sphere to the social and economic spheres. Central to its manifesto and first government programme was a set of institutional and structural reforms. In the economics sphere, these included a set of supply-side initiatives which were based on a dual rationale. By extending participation and social control, they were seen to be a good in themselves: 'gradual reform of the economy so that the basic economic choices are made by the social whole' (Greek Government Programme, 1981, p. 28). By transforming the institutional framework, such policies would also further the modernization and development of the Greek economy.

Two points of interest can be made here. First, PASOK's approach can be termed left social democratic in its awareness of the fact that, without institutional and structural reforms to promote various forms of social control of the economy, distributional initiatives (a better welfare state, higher wages, etc.) are always insecure. Second, their approach is also reminiscent of left social democracy because PASOK sought to distinguish its approach by differentiating itself not just with respect to the ends of economic policy but also the means. This contrasts with right social democrats in Britain after the Second World War who believed that economics is about efficiency and socialist politics can be reformulated on the terrain of ethics and justice by such goals as income redistribution and the welfare state (Durbin, 1985). As many have pointed out, the decline of the social democratic consensus, somewhere between the late 1960s and early 1970s was based on the rejection of this approach (Goldthorpe, 1987). Monetarism was an ideology which challenged both the means and ends of post-war economic policy-making. Similarly, by the 1970s, social democratic parties (e.g. in Britain and France) were adopting a set of economic policies (national and local enterprise boards, planning agreements, etc.)[3] which transcended the traditional means of economic policy. PASOK's approach to economic policy can be seen in this light.

Interestingly enough, PASOK was aware of the limitations, in the Greek context, of both the private and public sectors with respect to carrying out some of the major goals of its alternative economic strategy. Thus, in 1983, Papandreou himself pointed to organizational limitations in the private sector and the short-term and speculative character of Greek capitalists who based their activities on maximizing the available subsidies and other forms of state assistance, rather than seeking to modernize and restructure their activities. He also pointed to the organizational limitations of the public sector, its bureaucratic nature and its creation on the basis of clientelistic relationships rather than as an instrument for rational intervention in the development process. It was for this reason that it was thought that PASOK could not rely exclusively on the existing public and private sectors but instead must intervene with a series of institutional and structural reforms (Tsakalotos, 1991a, pp. 129–30).

For the private sector, PASOK's policy relied on a number of such reforms. Originally, its strategy of socialization of the private sector entailed the nationalization of some of the 'commanding heights' of the economy — a conception bearing considerable similarity to that adopted by the Labour Party in Britain in the 1970s, which was influenced by the work of Stuart Holland. But by 1982, PASOK announced that it did not intend to nationalize well-operated profitable industries (as was done in France). Eventually, socialization of the private sector entailed the creation of supervisory councils which were to act as 'decentralized organs of social control'. Such councils would operate 'outside' the firms and their role was primarily advisory and one of supervision. They would consist of representatives of management, workers, local authorities, and the state. Their goal was to harness the private sector with the national plan and to rationalize state incentives to industry. However, much was left vague, perhaps to allow them to grow into something more substantial if economic planning proved successful (Catephores, 1983, pp. 55–9).

---

[3] For a full discussion of such policies and the extent to which PASOK's programme can be compared to that of the northern social democrats, see Tsakalotos (1991a, especially ch. 3).

Other initiatives for the private sector included planning agreements, sectoral industrial planning, and a policy for public procurements.[4] Additionally, the creation of a new state holding company was to help restructure a large number of so-called 'ailing' firms—firms which were essentially bankrupt and in debt, mainly to state banks. Here, too, the policy foresaw elements of social control in the restructuring of these firms. For the public sector, there was also a policy of socialization which is discussed in section 3.

There is little point in going to greater length concerning the implementation of these policies. It is not too much of an exaggeration to say that most of them hardly got off the ground. They were codified into laws and certain of the institutions and organs of social control envisaged were set up but in a most spasmodic and disorganized way. Thus only one supervisory council was ever established and no more than two or three planning agreements were ever signed with private-sector firms. Sectoral industrial planning experienced a tortuous history of being discussed, presented, and then forgotten, only to be rediscovered and the process begin again. The state holding company for 'ailing' firms was set up, but its experience in the 1980s was dismal, with the result that firms were neither privatized nor restructured, with the only consequence being that the economic cost of their debt continued to mount. Nearly all these institutions suffered from disorganization, *ad hoc* ministerial interventions at all levels, and were used for PASOK's wider social and electoral aspirations. It is not surprising, therefore, in this context that these initiatives led to little, or no, restructuring of the economy and, as we see in the next section, there was consequently little supply-side response.

The lack of a coherently implemented supply-side policy in PASOK's first term was also to be crucial for the evolution of its macroeconomic policy. This was particularly disappointing because, during this period, PASOK did manage to articulate a relatively sophisticated conception of how to integrate macroeconomic policy with other aspects of its alternative economic strategy. The strategy came to be known as 'stabilization through development' (STD) and 'gradual adjustment' (GA). As we have seen, PASOK's basic approach was to emphasize the importance of supply-side measures, believing that traditional macroeconomic instruments (deflation and/or devaluation), while perhaps improving imbalances in the short run, would not tackle the fundamental structural problems of the economy. At the same time, given the existence of these macroeconomic imbalances, PASOK recognized that appropriate macroeconomic policy would need to provide a frame-

---

[4] For a full account of all these policies, see Tsakalotos (1991a, chs 6 and 7).

work for the successful implementation of the supply-side measures. There was thus an awareness that, while the concerns of social justice (social expenditure, wages of public sector employees, etc.) could not be ignored, it was important that demand was kept tightly under control and was compatible with the other targets.[5]

Following the 1985 election, either the commitment to the supply-side initiatives described above remained at the level of pronouncements or they were promoted with little conviction and a narrower scope. Furthermore, at the ideological level, the emphasis was now more on modernization and efficiency and less on participation and transforming the balance of economic power within society. The new set of institutional/structural reforms increasingly emphasized the liberalization of the banking system, flexibility in the labour market, and the promotion of the stock market. It could be argued that, given the tradition of statist intervention in Greece, these new priorities did not necessarily contradict the old. However, a lack of a coherent industrial strategy and any further concern to extend democracy to the economic realm clearly signposts the change in direction.

On the macroeconomic front, the period immediately following the 1985 election can be characterized as the first attempt at macroeconomic stabilization. The level of macroeconomic control exerted during the first half of the 1980s was in no way compatible with the original intention as articulated by the STD and GA programme. As we shall see, given the virtual absence of the expected supply-side response, this was particularly serious. From 1985 to 1987, a fairly traditional stabilization programme was adopted. Devaluation in 1985, which provided an initial boost to the economy, was accompanied by a tight incomes policy and an attempt to control the public deficit.

In retrospect this period can be considered a 'test-run' of the policies undertaken with more conviction and more systematically after the return to power in 1993.[6] For by 1993 the turn to orthodox economic policies was more coherent and virtually complete.[7] Liberalization of the domestic financial sector, which continued throughout the late 1980s and into the 1990s and included the dismantling of administrative controls on credit allocation as well as allowing interest rates to be market determined, was to be completed along with external liberalization (including the removal of controls on capital movements). The

[5] For a full analysis of the policy of STD and GA, see Tsakalotos (1991*b*).

[6] The intermediate period, from 1987 to the election defeat of 1989, was characterized by PASOK's abandonment of both the stabilization programme and any commitment to the supply-side policies. It is generally recognized as PASOK's most 'populist' phase.

[7] On the post-1993 policies, see Bank of Greece *Annual Reports* and OECD *Economic Surveys*.

policy of privatization which had been begun by the New Democracy government of the early 1990s was to be continued, especially as a means of disposing of those 'ailing' firms which had been taken into the public sector by the state holding company set up after the 1981 election victory. Indeed, the policy was to be extended to include the partial privatization of the telecommunications company, OTE, something that New Democracy had failed to do.

The main objective of macroeconomic policy was to be disinflation and control of the public deficit. The former was to be achieved through a tight exchange-rate policy, involving a depreciation of the drachma against the European currency unit (ecu) by an amount less than the inflation differential between Greece and the other EU member states. Control of the public deficit was to rely on tax reform and, in particular, the introduction of the so-called 'objective criteria' as a means of assessing income[8] along with wealth taxes. The adoption of these policies occurred within the context of increasing integration between Greece and the EU and the desire by Greece to meet the Maastricht criteria and to be adjudged eligible for monetary union membership.[9] However, irrespective of Maastricht, the extent of economic imbalances created in the 1980s, as we shall see, meant that when PASOK returned to power in the 1990s, it had little choice but to implement a more or less orthodox stabilization plan, and there was little scope for experimenting with 'alternative' economic policies. Thus if there was some attempt by PASOK to distinguish itself with respect to the ends of economic policy (in so far as they sought to avoid the adverse social consequences of stabilization), this did not extend to the means of economic policy, and the transformation of PASOK to a centrist social democratic party was complete.

2. Economic Performance under PASOK

Table 1 presents some macroeconomic aggregates which provide an overview of the performance of the Greek economy. Annual data is presented after 1981 along with averages for the periods 1960–73, 1974–80, and 1981–9.

---

[8] The 'objective criteria' include, among others, the setting of lower limits for income declared by the self-employed as well as assessments of income based on the size and location of a firm's offices. More generally, lower limits for income declaration have also been set for all taxpayers depending on their ownership of items such as cars, yachts, etc.

[9] By 1993, PASOK's conversion to a pro-European party was complete and the Maastricht criteria were one of the central arguments used in defending its new strategy of stabilization and modernization.

Table 1
Selected Economic Aggregates

	1960–73	1974–80	1981–9	1981	1982	1983	1984	1985	1986	1987	1988	1989	1990	1991	1992	1993	1994	1995	1996	1997	1998
Real growth (GDP)	7.7	3.5	1.8	0.1	0.4	0.4	2.8	3.1	1.6	-0.5	4.5	3.8	0.0	3.1	0.7	-1.6	2.0	2.1	2.4	3.2	3.0
Catch-up vis-à-vis the EU 12[c]	46.9	56.1		57.9	57.4	56.5	56.6	56.9	56.2	54.3	54.4	54.5	52.9	52.5	52.1	52.5	52.4	51.6	—	—	—
Productivity growth*	—	1.8		-5.1	1.2	-0.7	2.4	2.1	1.2	-0.4	2.9	3.4	-1.3	5.4	-0.8	-2.5	0.1	1.2	1.1	3.7	1.6
Employment growth	-0.5	0.7		5.2	-0.8	1.1	0.4	1.0	0.4	-0.1	1.6	0.4	1.3	-2.3	1.5	0.9	1.9	0.9	1.3	-0.5	1.4
Investment/GDP[d]	24.6	25.3		27.4	24.6	25.0	22.8	23.5	22.7	21.1	21.4	22.5	23.0	22.5	21.2	20.2	18.6	18.5	19.3	20.0	—
Unemployment	4.6	1.9		4.0	5.8	7.9	8.1	7.8	7.4	7.4	7.7	7.5	7.0	7.7	8.7	9.7	9.6	10.0	10.3	10.3	10.0
Current account (% of GDP)	-2.9	-3.3		-5.4	-4.1	-4.4	-5.2	-8.1	-3.5	-2.2	-1.5	-3.8	-4.3	-1.7	-2.2	-0.8	-0.2	-2.5	-3.7	-4.1	-4.0
General government deficit (% of GDP)	—	-2.2[a]	-9.7	-8.3	-6.5	-7.1	-8.4	-11.5	-10.3	-9.5	-11.5	-14.4	-16.1	-11.5	-12.8	-13.8	-10.0	-10.6	-7.5	-4.0	-2.7
Gross government debt (% of GDP)	—	23.5[a]		27.1	29.8	34.0	40.9	47.8	48.4	53.3	63.5	66.6	90.1	92.4	98.8	111.6	109.4	110.1	112.2	109.5	108.7
Consumer price inflation	3.3	17.5	18.9	24.5	21.0	20.2	18.5	19.3	23.0	16.4	13.5	13.7	20.4	19.5	15.9	14.4	10.9	8.9	8.2	5.5	4.8
Election year[b]				P				P				C	ND			P			P		

Notes: [a] 1978–80. [b] P indicates that PASOK won the election of that year; ND indicates that New Democracy won; C denotes the formation of a coalition government following the elections. [c] Per-capita GDP relative to the average of the EU 12=100 in each period. Own calculations using OECD national accounts data. Purchasing power parity exchange rates from OECD are used. We use the old GDP series for Greece. The new series (which better incorporates the black economy) produces figures for the 1990s of around 65. However, the movements in the two series are qualitatively similar. [d] These figures are based on the new National Accounts series from 1981 (OECD and Greek National Statistical Service for 1996). Adjustments have been made for the averages for the 1960s and 1970s figures. Averages for 1960–73, 1974–80, and 1981–9 under the former system are 22.4, 23.0, and 19.1 respectively.
Source: OECD Economic Outlook, Paris. * Bank of Greece and Greek National Statistical Service.

There is very little evidence of stabilization or GA, either in PASOK's first or second terms (with the exception of the 1986–7 period). Rather, the picture is one of growing macroeconomic imbalances. Inflation remained in double figures throughout the 1980s and into the 1990s, the government deficit was well over 10 per cent by the end of the 1980s, and debt had risen sharply. With the adoption of the stabilization measures since 1993, however, the economy has experienced notable disinflation and a reduction in the general government deficit—CPI inflation in the 12 months to May 1999 stood at 2.4 per cent and the general government deficit by 1998 was within the Maastricht criterion.

The picture for the real economy is little better, reflecting the fact that few, if any, of the supply-side reforms were enacted. Growth was irregular throughout the decade, and there is no evidence of an improvement into the late 1980s when some of the supply-side measures might have been expected to start bearing fruit. The same is true of employment and productivity growth. Investment as a percentage of GDP has been declining fairly steadily, accompanied by significant periods of negative growth in gross fixed capital formation. Once again, the pattern shows some signs of altering post-1993. Growth has been positive and increasing since 1994 and investment has picked up. However, overall, the disappointing performance over the whole period and the failure of PASOK to place the economy on a new path of higher growth at an early stage is reflected in the index of per-capita GDP relative to the EU 12 average, which has stagnated since 1973 and by 1995 was just over 51 per cent having been almost 58 per cent in 1981.

A further consequence of the poor real performance has been a rise in unemployment to around 10 per cent. The initial rise from around 4 to 8 per cent in the early 1980s can be attributed, first, to an increased labour-force participation rate at a time when employment creation was limited (with the exception of 1981; see Lianos and Lazari, 1994) and, second, to large wage increases following democratization in 1974—both before and after PASOK came to power (OECD, 1996c). The more recent rise in unemployment stems from high levels of immigration from former communist countries (OECD, 1996c) and the effects of the various stabilization programmes of the 1990s.

At least some of the explanation for the particularly disappointing performance of the 1980s lies with exogenous factors. The two oil shocks and the deflationary policy implemented by many countries after the second oil shock were accompanied by EU entry and the required reduction in protection rates throughout the 1980s. At the same time, the economy experienced rapid structural change (including a decline in the importance of agriculture and a rise in service production) and the traditional safety value of emigration was lost as net immigration turned positive in the wake of persons of Greek origin returning from eastern European countries (OECD, 1996c). However, the poor performance of the economy cannot be attributed mainly to exogenous factors and, in order to examine the role of internal and external economic pressures on policy, we focus on three specific areas. This allows us to develop the themes of stagnation of the real economy, the worsening of macroeconomic imbalances of the 1980s and the failure of the STD and GA strategy in greater depth, before making some remarks about the more recent experience.

(a) Budget Deficits and Debt

One of the key features of the PASOK period during the 1980s has been the large accumulation of public debt (Table 1), with the result that it is now among the highest in the EU, exceeded only by Belgium and Italy. To examine the causes of the increase in the debt/GDP ratio in more detail, we use the familiar debt dynamics equation:

$$db/dt = -s + (r - y)b + d \qquad (1)$$

where b is the debt/income ratio and db/dt its rate of change; s is seigniorage; r is the real interest rate; y is real growth; and d is the primary deficit.

The key variables in equation (1) are shown in Figure 1, including the change in the debt/income ratio itself.[10] A number of interesting points can be gleaned. First, the basic cause of the rising debt/GDP ratio is the large primary deficit which persisted throughout the 1980s. It is notable that the deficit increased in election years (1981, 1985, 1989, 1993), suggesting the existence of political cycles.[11] Increased spending in election years (for example, on public works and the hiring of new employees in the public sector) is a significant feature of the political system in Greece, where clientelistic politics are prevalent (section 3). Table 2 supports this view, providing figures on public-sector employment for selected years.[12]

[10] Seigniorage is not shown, but on its declining importance in stabilizing the debt/GDP ratio, see Gros and Vandille (1995).

[11] Existing research supports more the existence of political cycles rather than partisan cycles in Greece (Andrikopoulos et al., 1997). It should be noted that the 1996 election is the first, since 1977, where an electoral cycle was largely absent.

[12] It should be noted that PASOK's social programme, including the creation of a national health service, required increases in public-sector employees. However, it is unlikely that this alone accounts for the expansion of government employment post-1981. It can also be argued that the figures underestimate recruitment because of the existence of generous early retirement conditions pre-1990. These are reflected in the fact that the ratio of civil-service pensioners to civil servants in 1995 was 1 compared with a ratio of 0.5 in the private sector (OECD, 1996c).

Figure 1
Debt Dynamics

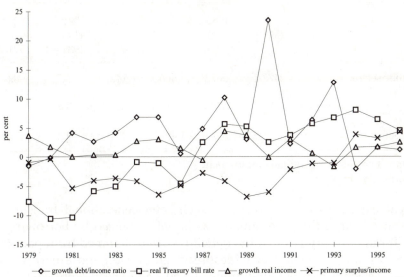

Source: OECD, *Economic Outlook*.

For a government like PASOK, one might expect rising deficits associated with its supply-side policies which implied increases in government capital expenditure. Indeed, it is often argued that increased deficits which result from increased investment expenditure should be treated differently from those that are a consequence of current consumption. However, there is little evidence that the increased deficits were associated with an investment drive. Throughout the 1980s, the deficit was over twice as large as government investment expenditure and there is no evidence of a substantial increase in government investment in the period 1981–4.

Of course, some increase in current expenditure was inevitable given PASOK's commitment to social justice. Between 1974 and 1982, there was a significant reduction in inequality, of which roughly half can be attributed to measures taken by PASOK (Tsakloglou, 1993, 1997). The most significant measures here were the increase in minimum pensions, a widening of their coverage, and an increase in minimum wages, as well as a number of social initiatives (e.g. the creation of a national health service and day-care centres for the elderly). Thus PASOK's record in the social sphere is a relatively positive one.[13] However, to a

[13] However, the level of inequality is still high by EU standards (Tsakloglou, 1997). For a number of interesting articles on more recent developments in the Greek welfare state, see Matsagannis (1999).

Table 2
Public-sector Employment

	1981 ('000)	1985 ('000)	1995 ('000)	1995 %[a]	% p.a. change 1981–91	% p.a. change 1991–5
Public sector of which:	477.1	567.9	566.1	14.6	1.7	–0.8
general government	283.3	373.7	385.1	2.8	2.8	0.0
Dependent private sector	1,221.9	1,362.6	1,494.0	39.8	1.1	3.4

Note: [a] Percentage of civilian employment.
Source: OECD (1996c).

great extent, this entailed an implicit inter-generational transfer of resources since the programme was largely financed by borrowing.

It might be argued that the deficit problem stemmed from poor tax receipts, a consequence of widespread tax evasion and a narrow tax base (agriculture was highly under-taxed and the self-employed were difficult to tax), rather than excessively high levels of expenditure (Stournaras, 1990). Indeed, government spending in Greece has long been lower than the EU average. Given that PASOK's programme involved increased social spending along with an increased public-sector wage bill, measures to increase revenues were of paramount importance. However, although recognized by PASOK, concrete policies to widen the tax base and reduce tax evasion were not forthcoming in the early 1980s and control was soon lost over the budget deficit (Tsakalotos, 1991b).

The second point which can be made from Figure 1 relates to real interest rates. Up until 1987, they were significantly negative.[14] Since then, a combination of lower inflation and rising nominal interest rates has contributed to rising and high real interest rates, which only recently have begun to fall. The rise in real interest rates can, at least in part, be attributed to the reform of the financial system, which began in the mid-1980s. While this reform was much-needed, it is clear that the subsequent rise in real interest rates was associated with a worsening debt/income ratio.[15]

[14] This was helped by an accommodating monetary policy for most of this period (Tsakalotos, 1991b).

[15] Between 1979 and 1987, the debt/income ratio grew at around an average of 4 per cent per annum; between 1987 and 1995, the average was 7.3 per cent. The experience of Greece with financial liberalization provides further evidence that macroeconomic stabilization should precede liberalization (McKinnon, 1989; Gibson and Tsakalotos, 1995).

Finally, real growth of GDP has been patchy, reflecting the lack of a supply-side response, and has contributed little to moderating the growth of the debt/income ratio. Moreover, growth has always been below real interest rates since they turned positive. As equation (1) shows, even in the presence of a balanced budget, a necessary condition for the debt/income ratio to be stabilized is that growth be higher than real interest rates. If the latter is not true, then continuous primary surpluses are required. Indeed, as Figure 1 shows, the decline in the debt/GDP ratio in 1997–8 is associated with increases in the primary deficit to over 6 per cent.

The consequences of the large debt are severe. Interest payments have increased enormously to over 40 per cent of total revenue by 1994. This has severely reduced the government's flexibility. It is difficult, therefore, in this context not to talk about a lack of macroeconomic control. Moreover, given the absence of a supply-side response and early measures to increase tax revenues, government imbalances worsened throughout the 1980s. The sustainability of the STD and GA strategy was quickly brought into question and it was not until PASOK's return to power in 1993 that sustained efforts at deficit reduction have been undertaken.

(b) *The Balance of Payments and the Current Account*

The 1985 turnaround in macroeconomic policy resembles similar U-turns by other socialist governments (most notably the French in 1983). Indeed, it has been argued that the deterioration of economic aggregates was precisely the reason behind the 15 per cent devaluation and the subsequent adoption of a tight incomes policy and stabilization programme (Simitis, 1989).[16] While the similarities are there, it would be difficult to argue that external pressures were the overwhelming cause of PASOK's U-Turn. Moreover, a careful examination of the figures suggests that PASOK had a unique opportunity to conduct policy in an environment not overly constrained by external pressures.

With respect to capital flows, controls were only finally removed in 1994, following successive liberalization from 1989 onwards. It is certainly true that in 1981, when PASOK was elected, and in the last quarter of 1985, when the devaluation occurred, capital outflows increased. However, in the intervening period, the capital account was

---

[16] There was some disagreement in the government about the underlying economic situation with Arsenis (1987) and Katseli (1985) claiming that the deterioration in the balance of payments was mainly the result of speculative activities. For a critique of this view, see Tsakalotos (1991*a*, ch. 5).

Figure 2
Current, Trade, and Invisibles Accounts (as percentage of GDP)

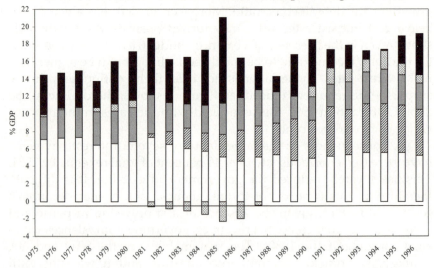

☐ remittances ▨ EU transfers ▧ net tourism receipts ▣ other invisibles ■ current account deficit

Source: Bank of Greece.

fairly calm and the 16 per cent devaluation of 1983 did not appear to cause any capital flight (Gibson and Tsakalotos, 1993).

Figure 2 illustrates the current account position of Greece since 1975. The main characteristic has been a large trade account (represented by the height of each column)[17] covered to a great extent by the invisible surplus (net tourist receipts, remittances, and, latterly, EU funds). Based in part on the information presented in Figure 2, two points can be made with respect to the external position of Greece. First, the large trade account deficit is indicative of the structural problems facing Greek industry that had been identified by PASOK before they came to power in 1981 and which the supply-side policies were designed to go some way to solving.[18] What is apparent from developments in the

[17] For 1975, for example, 7.1 percentage points (pp) of the trade deficit were covered by remittances; 2.6pp by tourism; 0.2pp by other invisibles; the current account deficit was 4.6pp. For the years 1981–7, when other invisibles were in deficit, the height of each column above the x-axis represents the combination of the trade and other invisibles accounts.

[18] Of course, it can always be argued that the trade deficit is a consequence of the comparative advantage that Greece has in shipping, tourism, and other services which keeps the exchange rate more appreciated than it would otherwise be. However, much analysis of Greek exports and imports pointed to the lack of non-price competitiveness of Greek goods, concentrated as they were in traditional areas, mainly agriculture and low value-added industrial sectors such as food, textiles, shoes, and clothing (Katseli, 1989; Leventakis, 1994).

trade account throughout the 1980s is that the supply-side reforms did little to improve the trade account, in spite of real depreciation over the whole period (Leventakis, 1994).

Moreover, a further conclusion can be drawn from a careful examination of the breakdown of the current account. Throughout the period, Greece has been fortunate to have benefited from large inflows in the form of remittances from Greeks living abroad (including Greek seamen) as well as, more recently, EU funds.[19] On average, during the 1980s, these amounted to around 8 per cent of GDP. These inflows offered PASOK a window of opportunity, since they severely loosened the external constraint which social democratic governments often face and provided them with the room to implement policies which could have facilitated restructuring. But this required a conscious decision to boost investment rather than to bolster consumption. In the event, PASOK followed the latter strategy (as the figures on investment in Table 1 indicate) and the inflows can be said to have provided them with a fairly soft external constraint which allowed them to postpone rather than promote structural adjustment.[20] Indeed, all too much of the EU funds available for structural change, necessary for Greece's integration with the EU, were used to shore up existing economic structures and to support the least competitive strata in society (Lyberaki, 1996; Diamandouros, 1994).

(c) Wages, Profits, and Productivity

Finally, we want to examine those factors which shed light on the relationship between wages, productivity, and profits. This also enables us to say something about investment and competitiveness. One of the traditional concerns of social democratic governments is a commitment to a redistribution of income from profits to wages. Figure 3 graphs the labour share in business-sector value-added since 1964.[21] The main feature in the post-dictatorship period is the rising wage share up until 1982, followed by a marked fall. In Figure 4, we illustrate recent trends in real wages and productivity. These allow us to interpret the changing wage share more systematically.

---

[19] On the inflows of EU funds and the prospects for the future, see Manassaki (1998).

[20] See Rodrik (1989) for a simple model which shows how EU subsidies can have a negative impact on an economy by loosening such constraints.

[21] We have chosen to use this OECD measure rather than the raw National Accounts figures. The large and changing number of self-employed persons in Greece makes the use of the national accounts data rather unreliable. The OECD has made some correction for self-employment and imputed to them a wage equal to the average compensation per employee.

Figure 3
Labour Share in Business-sector Value-added

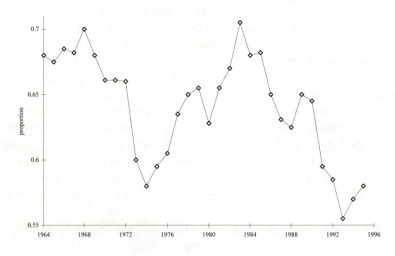

Source: OECD (1997*e*, p. 83).

Figure 4
Wages and Productivity

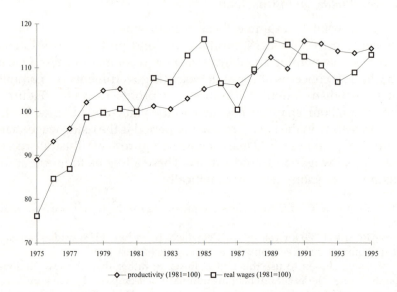

Source: Bank of Greece.

The rising wage share after 1974 reflects real wage increases of around 10 per cent per annum between 1975 and 1978. Following the election of PASOK in 1981, real wages were given a further boost in 1982 and again in 1983–4. Since 1983, the falling wage share can be attributed to real wage increases below productivity growth. The fall has not been continuous, with the pre-1989 election cycle clearly evident. It also appears that the wage share has fallen more sharply during New Democracy's stabilization attempts between 1990 and 1993 than it has during PASOK's (indeed, during the present programme, the wage share has actually been rising).

It seems appropriate, in view of the general rise in unemployment and the poor trade performance, to ask whether PASOK had too loose a wages policy. A number of observations can be made from Figure 4. First, since 1975, whereas productivity has increased by around 25 per cent in total, real wages have increased by around 48 per cent. However, most of the cumulative differential between real wages and productivity increases is the result of the pre-PASOK period. Since 1981, both productivity and real wages have risen by around 15 per cent.

Second, following increases in PASOK's first term, real wages have not risen further, fluctuating around the same level, with the large dips in 1987 and in the early 1990s reflecting PASOK's first stabilization attempt and that of New Democracy, respectively. Real wage gains above productivity growth were realized only in the first years following PASOK's election in 1981. The rest of the 1980s, it seems, were spent paying for this initial real wage boost.

These observations raise the question of the optimal timing of wage increases for social democratic governments. Pressures on these governments often take the form of demands for real wage increases immediately following their election. However, resisting such demands, while perhaps politically costly in the short run, may prove the best strategy over the longer term. For a strategy which allows for smaller increases initially, to allow space for the supply-side policies to work, may be more sustainable and indeed more favourable for the level of real wages and income distribution in the long run.

Indeed, such a conclusion is supported by the effect of the wage increases on both competitiveness and investment in the early 1980s. The rises in real unit labour costs were not offset through depreciation of the exchange rate with negative consequences for competitiveness. The real exchange rate appreciated from 1982 until the devaluation of October 1985 (Tsakalotos, 1991b; Leventakis, 1994), with the implication that any supply-side policies, which had been implemented, were not being supported by PASOK's macroeconomic strategy as had been envisaged in the STD programme.

Furthermore, private-sector investment was also badly affected by the initial wage increases of the early 1980s and the falling profit share up until 1983. Thus, the rate of growth of investment in manufacturing was negative in each of the years from 1981 to 1985 (Tsakalotos, 1991b). This was hardly an encouraging development, since it implied a lack of support from the private sector for the supply-side policies. However, it may not have been too serious if the planned expansion of public investment had gone ahead. As we have already seen, however, this did not occur, with the consequence that total investment as a share of national income fell throughout the period (Table 1).

(d) Post-1993 Developments

The results of the orthodox stabilization plan, which has been implemented by PASOK since its return to power in 1993, are shown in Table 1 and Figures 1–4. Inflation has fallen mainly as a result of the 'hard drachma' policy, with the rate of depreciation of the drachma against the ecu being less than the inflation differential between Greece and its EU trading partners in every year since 1994. In this respect, the government has been following a policy similar to that followed by other EU countries in the 1980s.

Initially, the policy was conducted outside the exchange-rate mechanism (ERM) and in May 1994, it came under pressure as expectations that the government would devalue at the same time as it was due to remove capital controls gathered momentum. High short-term interest rates, however, successfully maintained the exchange-rate policy with little cost to the real economy for two reasons. First, the household sector in Greece was, and indeed still is, a net creditor, since access to mortgage and consumer credit remains underdeveloped. Thus interest-rate rises do not affect households adversely. Second, the major commercial banks were able to maintain loan rates largely unchanged, because they do not rely enormously on the interbank market for raising funds but rather fund their loans from non-bank deposits. This insulated the business sector from the effect of the crisis.[22]

Further episodes of downward pressure were experienced at the end of 1997 and into 1998 with the turbulence on stock markets following the South-East Asian crisis. To reduce the pressure, the drachma joined the ERM on 16 March 1998 and since January 1999 has been participating (along with Denmark) in ERM II with the normal ±15

---

[22] See Flood and Kramer (1996) for an account of the May 1994 crisis. Following the removal of capital controls, the problem was one of capital inflows associated with the credibility of the exchange-rate target and high domestic interest rates (Brissimis and Gibson, 1997).

per cent fluctuation margins. Entry was accompanied by a devaluation of the drachma against the ecu of 12.3 per cent. Since entry, the drachma has been around 8 per cent appreciated relative to its central rate, maintaining the anti-inflationary effect of the exchange-rate policy.

At the same time as inflation has fallen, the general government budget deficit has also been brought under control, falling from 13.8 per cent of GDP in 1993 to an estimated 2.4 per cent for 1998, and it is expected to fall further to 1.9 per cent in 1999 (Ministry of National Economy estimates in the budget for 1999). A significant part of this reduction has come from the benefits of falling interest rates. However, it is also true that the government has been running a primary surplus which has risen from around 4 per cent in 1994 to 7 per cent in 1998, and such levels are projected to continue in the coming years. This is mainly a consequence of further tax reforms, along the lines discussed in section 1.[23]

What is interesting about these stabilization attempts is that they do not appear to have adversely affected the performance of the real economy. Real gross fixed capital formation has been increasing by around 10 per cent per annum since 1997, while growth has been positive and rising since 1994. The increase in investment comes both from the public sector (major infrastructural projects co-funded with the EU) and the private sector. Underlying the private-sector increase is the reduction in domestic interest rates which has accompanied the fall in inflation and budgetary consolidation. This has led to a significant reduction in firms' financing costs (OECD, 1997e). Additionally, the policy of using the exchange rate as a nominal anchor has allowed firms to borrow abroad at even lower interest rates. Finally, the exchange rate has also helped to stabilize raw material prices (in drachmas), leading to a reduction in costs since raw materials are an important input for Greek firms (Branson, 1986; Moschos and Stournaras, 1998). In total, this reduction in non-labour costs has significantly increased firm profitability and hence made funds available for investment.

Our concern in this paper, of course, is the extent to which the stabilization programme still contains elements which can be characterized as social democratic. As we noted in section 1, PASOK, even if it no longer sought to use different policies, was still committed, at least at the rhetorical level, to increased social justice and a reduction in

---

[23] On the recent macroeconomic performance of the economy in the framework of the Convergence Programme, see Bank of Greece (1999, especially ch. 2).

inequality. We can point to several characteristics of the stabilization programme which provide some support for this view.

First, stabilization has not been associated with a large increase in unemployment, suggesting a fairly steep Phillips curve. Positive real growth which has been accompanied by positive employment growth has helped here (Table 1). Additionally, privatization has not involved large job losses. The government has been willing to accept a lower price for companies sold off, provided some commitment to retaining employees is given.[24]

Second, real wages have increased in each year since 1993 (Figure 4). As we saw earlier, this implied a reversing of the downward trend in labour share in value-added (Figure 4). Moreover, the policy of allowing real wage increases has been concentrated more on the lower paid and has been accompanied by real pension increases. Both measures should help reduce inequality since a large number of pensioners are among the lowest income groups in Greece.

Finally, tax reforms have been aimed at increasing the contribution of the business and self-employed sectors and reducing that of wage earners and pensioners. Table 3 provides some figures which suggest some success in meeting that goal.[25]

Thus developments in the economy since 1993 point to some success at stabilization, with some attempt to minimize the cost to the real economy. The policies followed, however, have been fairly orthodox and show that PASOK has moved very far from the kind of social democratic policies which it was advocating in the early 1980s. The only distinguishing feature of the current policy is some attempt to share the burden of adjustment more fairly and to shelter, to some extent, the most vulnerable sections of society.

3. The Political Economy of Extending Democracy to the Economic Sphere

The social democratic argument has always been that economic performance relies as much on coordination of economic activity and cooperation between economic actors as it does on competition. Indeed, such a conceptualization has been given much support in recent economic thinking. While this cannot be anything but encouraging for the social democratic project of extending democracy to the economic

---

[24] On some occasions, responsibility for social security payments of employees of the privatized companies has been assumed by the government, or employees have been transferred to other areas in the private sector.

[25] Unfortunately, there are some indications that this improvement has not been sustained in 1998, nor, probably, in 1999.

Table 3
Contribution of Different Groups to Tax Revenues
(% of total direct tax revenues)

	Wage earners	Pensioners	Rentiers	Commercial/ industrial	Self- employed	Farmers and agricultural workers
1993	45.2	17.0	5.4	20.1	11.3	0.9
1994	44.1	16.3	5.9	20.5	12.2	0.9
1995	41.6	16.1	5.3	24.1	11.9	1.1
1996	40.1	14.9	5.2	25.4	13.2	1.0
1997	41.2	15.6	5.2	24.0	12.8	1.1

Source: Ministry of National Economy.

sphere, implementing strategies which promote such coordination and cooperation remain, as we shall see in this section, problematic.

The 'ideal' world of market liberals — or their metaphor for understanding the real world — is one of asocial atomistic individuals whose only relationship with each other is through exchange in the market. This is thought to be efficient in the sense that all mutually beneficial exchanges are made. Here, preferences of individuals are given, and achieving equilibrium is relatively straightforward, with the result that trade unions and other community groups or associations, the welfare state, and politics itself — not least if it results in state intervention in the economy — merely operate to inhibit the actions of market actors and distort the process of equilibrium formation. Recent economic thinking has explored the extent to which, in real economies, a lack of information and the potential for conflict can lead to uncertainty and insecurity in deregulated markets. As a result, it is difficult in market economies to achieve the necessary coordination and cooperation, with the consequence that many mutually beneficial agreements are costly or simply do not take place (Bowles and Gintis, 1993; Stiglitz, 1994; and Roemer, 1995).

Recognizing these problems, social scientists have recently been paying increasing attention to the idea that economic performance is not best understood merely by the role of markets and the state, or even by the appropriate balance between the two. Rather, they emphasize, albeit from different perspectives, that both the state and markets are socially embedded in a whole host of institutions, both formal, such as trade unions and production networks, and informal, such as social norms and wider cultural characteristics (Granovetter, 1985; Hodgson, 1988; Putnam, 1993; Bowles, 1998). These factors, which for convenience can collectively be seen as a form of social regulation, need to be added to state and market regulation if the economic performance of particular economies over time is to be understood. Furthermore, such an approach also sheds considerable light on the continuing, and significant, difference between advanced capitalist economies despite the impact of globalization.[26]

Two themes of this literature on social regulation are of particular significance for our purposes. First, forms of social regulation such as trust, norms (including reciprocity), and long-term strategies—collectively termed by Putnam (1993, p. 172) as social capital—are often best suited to confront the problems of information and conflict that characterize deregulated markets. Thus, for instance, trust—that is 'the belief that another party will continue to adhere to rules of reciprocity or 'fairness' even in circumstances in which it might be advantageous to defect' (Streeck, 1997, p. 202)—is important in confronting the type of opportunistic behaviour highlighted by game-theoretic approaches to social interaction.[27] The second theme is that social capital exists in, and is preserved by, communities, associations, networks, families, and clans (Polanyi, 1957; North, 1990; Putnam, 1993). While it cannot be assumed that the economic impact of the above is always, and everywhere, positive, it is equally true that they do not automatically constitute examples of market distortions and, indeed, it may often be the case that they actually improve the operation of the market. In this light, traditional social democratic concerns, such as social control and participation, can be seen once more in a favourable light, combining, potentially, both the concerns of social justice and economic efficiency.

However, this sanguine conclusion for the prospects of social democracy is tempered by the fact that it seems to be a testable hypothesis of this literature that social democratic strategies will be more successful to the extent that they rely on existing social formations, rich in the type of communities and networks that are associated with plentiful reserves of social capital. In the absence of such plentiful reserves, the success of social democratic strategies will depend on their ability to confront this absence.

What kind of social formation tends to be rich in social capital? Putnam (1993) has argued that it is *horizontal* networks of civil engagement (in horizontally ordered groups such as cooperatives, mutual aid societies, and sports clubs) that are important in solving the dilemmas of collective action.[28] Such horizontal networks—bringing together

---

[26] For a range of valuable articles on these themes, see Hollingsworth and Boyer (1997).

[27] On trust, see also Arrow (1972) and Fukuyama (1995).

[28] Putnam has a range of arguments which explain why horizontal linkages help cooperative behaviour. The basic point is that people who cooperate in one field are more likely to cooperate in others, and the more people cooperate, the easier and more beneficial it becomes (Putnam, 1993, ch. 6).

agents of equivalent power and status—are prevalent in north Italy, whereas the south is dominated by vertical networks. It is this difference, Putnam argues, that is crucial to understanding the diverging economic performance of north and south. Vertical networks, such as patron–client relations common in clientelistic politics, have long been recognized as asymmetric, involving significant inequality of power (Gellner, 1975). In this context, they are unlikely to be able to sustain trust and cooperation, since opportunism is more likely to characterize the patron's behaviour (exploitation) and the client's (shirking) (Putnam, 1993, pp. 174–5). Kinship ties, on the other hand, while horizontal, are also inimitable to fostering wider ties and merely sustain cooperation within a group (the extended family) and not between groups.

Putnam's conception that a social formation rich in horizontal networks is likely to be associated with better economic performance has not gone unchallenged.[29] However, this approach is instructive for our purposes for two reasons: first, because of certain similarities between Greece and southern Italy; and, second, because the prevalence of vertical networks and kinship relations may constitute problems not just for good economic performance in general, but for strategies which rely on promoting social control and forms of democracy in economic activity.

The existence of a strong state, and clientelistic relationships between politicians/political parties and the electorate, has been a dominant feature of Greek politics since the nineteenth century (Mouzelis, 1978; Mavrogordatos, 1983):

> Political life became characterized by strongly personalized links between patron-politician and client-voter, and by the exchange of *rousfeti* (political favours). Politics was a necessary evil, a self-defense mechanism used to uphold a traditional way of life, not an instrument of emancipation. (Sassoon, 1996, p. 628)

The other side of the coin is the weakness of civil society in the Greek social formation.[30] This affects all aspects of society. The state has, for instance, traditionally been involved in every part of economic activity.

---

[29] Putnam's work has been challenged on a number of fronts: that it misunderstands Italian history; that it is over-deterministic and relies too strongly on a path dependency in Italy since the Middle Ages, without specifying the mechanics of such path dependency; and that it under-theorizes and romanticizes horizontal linkages such as community groups. For a constructive engagement with Putnam's work, see Levi (1996), Goldberg (1996), and Sabetti (1996) in a special issue of *Politics and Society*.

[30] On the weakness of civil society and, in particular, the roots of the lack of intermediary institutions and structures, see Diamandouros (1994, especially pp. 14, 15, 28).

This has had important consequences for the nature of the private sector, which has concentrated its activities on expanding the degree of protection or level of subsidy, rather than relying on its own dynamism to improve its competitiveness or restructure its production.[31] It is not, however, only the private sector that seeks such a relationship with the state. Rather it extends to a wide range of social groups and classes whose activities are centred upon upholding a traditional way of life, and we have seen above examples of how this is, in part, responsible for the deficits of the PASOK era. The result is that the financial system and state subsidies have been used more as instruments of controlling income distribution than as development instruments. And, as we saw in the previous section, public-sector employment is central to clientelistic politics.[32] The well-known bureaucratic features of the Greek public administration, with its bewildering myriad of laws and regulations, are actually quite functional to the operation of the system — for clientelistic politics and relationships can ease access to state subsidies, licences, and other forms of protection.[33]

Of particular concern, given the interests of social democracy, is the lack of an independent labour movement. Schmitter (1995), in a comparison of organized interests and their capacity for class governance and convergence in Southern Europe, shows how far the Greek context is from that of Northern Europe. He argues that while class interests are represented by monopolistic institutions, such as the GSEE (Greek Trade Union Federation), this is the result of deliberate state policy and that this organizational unity 'is a political illusion. Parties, especially PASOK after it took over in 1981, have made concerted efforts to penetrate and capture leadership positions in GSEE' (Schmitter, 1995, p. 293). Moreover, Greece is further away from the Northern/Central European neocorporatist model than are Italy, Spain, and Portugal, and

[31] Katseli (1989) has used the notion of the soft budget constraint, where certain groups in society have easy access to government resources and hence do not face the traditional 'hard' budget constraint.

[32] The link to Putnam is strong here. For example, those who get a job in the public sector (in return for their vote) do not find it easy to engage in constructive dialogue with their employer which might involve criticism of, or disagreement with, the party to which they owe their job. But neither are they likely to abstain from shirking. The politician, to whom they owe their job, is less interested in how efficiently the particular office in which they are employed is working. And employees know their positions are safe because it is their 'contact' which matters, rather than their supervisors. Furthermore, employees are less likely to cooperate with each other since they are rivals for their patron's favour.

[33] Indeed, clientelistic politics often extends beyond simply getting access to state funds or protection. Relationships can also facilitate customers' access to services to which they are entitled (e.g. telephone line repair). The point is that in societies such as Greece *all* citizens are drawn into clientelistic behaviour and not just selected groups.

it still shares some characteristics of the 'older, predemocratic systems of state corporatism and has yet to be fully affected by the usual norms of associational freedom, voluntary contracts and collective bargaining'. This state of affairs has only begun to change gradually in the 1990s. The leaderships of both the trade union and employers' organizations have shown an increasing willingness to discuss reforms in the economic and political system. Indeed, in 1990, there was a significant move with the signing of a two-year collective-bargaining agreement, which included a reduction in the role played by the state in the administration of union funds (Diamandouros, 1994).

Such a context is not propitious for social democratic initiatives, either at the macroeconomic or supply-side levels. For instance, the failure of PASOK to institutionalize an incomes policy can be seen in this light. Throughout the 1980s, there was hardly any attempt to reach a 'social contract' with the unions. For all PASOK's repeated declarations of the need for consensus and dialogue as prerequisites for the success of its strategy, this never extended to discussion or negotiation over its macroeconomic strategy. In the context of a low-trust economy with few autonomous partners, there was little scope for forms of 'political exchange' (Pizzorno, 1978) which rely on both sides being able to make binding commitments. This allowed a more redistributive incomes policy than might otherwise have been the case — at least initially — and led, as we have seen, to short-term negative consequences for the supply side of the economy. But it did allow PASOK a freer hand, more autonomy, to adjust incomes according to specific considerations of the moment. The existence of electoral business cycles, discussed above, is hardly evidence of a consistent application of GA. Since 1993, PASOK has once more tried to renew 'social dialogue', in an attempt to broaden support for its stabilization policies, with some limited success.

The context was equally unpropitious for the supply-side measures. Consider, as an example, PASOK's approach towards existing nationalized industries, most evident in its policy of socialization (eventually codified in Law 1365/83). This constituted a relatively sophisticated approach which went beyond Morrisonian nationalization and self-management models (Tsakalotos, 1991a, ch. 6.3). Again, the rationale of the policy was two-fold. On the one hand, it was part of PASOK's ideological commitment to promote institutional and structural reforms in order to expand participation in economic decision-making and introduce elements of social control within the public sector. On the other hand, PASOK realized that for its new institutional measures to succeed, and thus achieve a greater legitimacy, they must work in favour of reconstructing the existing nationalized industries.[34]

---

[34] That is, the DEKO, especially OTE (telecommunications), DEH (electricity), and OSE (railways).

It is beyond our scope to give a full account of the new framework. In essence, though, there was a Management Council, and a General Manager, responsible for day-to-day management. This was to be supported by a body named ASKE (Representative Assembly of Social Control)[35] consisting of 27 representatives from the Greek state, employees, local government, consumer interests, etc. This body was responsible for medium- and long-term planning of the enterprise. The ASKE were also to provide an input to national planning with, for example, the ASKE of DEH (National Electricity Company) influencing the plan in the area of energy (Tsakalotos, 1991a, pp. 215–16). The state was still in a dominant position given the importance of these firms to the national economy, but the idea was that the ASKE could provide a form of social control that went far beyond the rather formal control of responsibility to Parliament through the relevant minister that characterizes Morrisonian nationalization. As we saw in section 1, this initiative, like so many, was never really fully implemented. Indeed, the numerous delays in implementation meant that the various institutions could not be fully working until PASOK's second administration. By then, though not without a certain amount of conflict, the PASOK government promoted the policy with little conviction and a narrower scope (Tsakalotos, 1991a, p. 267). As in all other areas, PASOK's initiatives were crucially weakened by the role of clientelistic practices in the appointment of officials, the use of the new institutions for social policy and its desire to build its electoral and social base, and ad hoc ministerial intervention at all levels. Instead of these new institutions developing new initiatives and administrative practices, they merely reproduced the practices and modes of operation of the existing public administration.

But the central point is that the responsibility for this state of affairs does not lie exclusively at PASOK's door. For the lack of autonomous trade unions,[36] local authorities, and consumer groups (all represented on the ASKE) meant that they were in no position to exploit the new legislation. Given society's organization with strong vertical linkages, the above lacked the knowledge, the resources, and the stock of 'social

---

[35] This conception can be usefully compared to modern discussions about the importance of stakeholders — that is, it is inefficient for a firm's policy to be determined solely by its shareholders and management (Block, 1990; Hutton, 1995; Roemer, 1995).

[36] For an account of the extent to which PASOK union policies were identified with that of the government, and also the extent to which PASOK union officials were dependent on the political wing of PASOK for their careers, see the article by T. Lianos, 'Telos kai afertiria gia ta syndicata', To Bima, 7 September 1997. Lianos also argues that these two effects had dire consequences for successive PASOK governments.

capital' to be able to enter into the type of long-term trust relations and cooperation entailed by the new legislation. Rather, mutual suspicions between groups, and between such groups and the government — whose ability to enter into long-term credible commitments was justifiably in severe doubt — made a focus on short-term gain the dominant strategy and entailed that the initiative was a dead letter before it started.[37]

A final consideration is worth discussing with respect to the failure of PASOK's economic strategy in the 1980s. This has to do with the nature of PASOK as a political organization. As we saw in section 1, as PASOK came closer to power, it became more of a coalition of disparate interests. There is nothing unusual in that, and one can envisage that any conceivable social democratic government would constitute a similar coalition. The issue is rather that PASOK, as a political party, was singularly ill-placed to deal with these conflicting interests (including intra-party factions, political networks supporting particular ministers, conflicting business circles influencing Papandreou himself, trade unions, and other organized interests) once it had achieved power. For a start, it lacked the basic democratic procedures of other social democratic parties. Although it had a similar organizational structure to other parties, such as congress and central committees,

> nevertheless, the control exercised by the party organisation has been almost exclusively bureaucratic and personal, rather than democratic, and the most eloquent testimony to this is the fact that the Party Congress met for the first time only in 1984, no less than a decade [!] after the party was first formed. (Hine, 1986, pp. 285–6)

The role of Andreas Papandreou in the first two administrations was paramount, with party officials drawing their legitimacy from the party leader rather than from party members and sympathizers (Spourdalakis, 1988). Furthermore, any opposition to the PASOK government was usually met with co-optation into the state apparatus, further weakening the autonomy of local party organizations (Morlino, 1995). Rather than a democratization of the state, what happened was a 'statization of the party', with almost all members of PASOK's central committee being co-opted into either the government administration or parallel advisory organizations (see Sotiropoulos, 1991, 1993; and Spourdalakis, 1988). This further strengthened the state and weakened civil society,

---

[37] We have concentrated here on PASOK's initiative with respect to the socialization of nationalized industries because it was an area where the policy initiative was most developed and the policy persevered with for longer. But similar considerations played a similar role with most other supply-side initiatives discussed in section 1.

since clientelism could now be mediated through a strong party machine (Mouzelis, 1987).

This was hardly a solid foundation on which to mediate conflicting interests in government. For instance, in opposition, PASOK had argued that it was important to get right the speed of introduction of the institutional/structural reforms—a very slow rate would risk their incorporation into the existing socio-economic system, while a too high rate would entail dislocation or disorganization of economic activities. However, in government, PASOK seems to have interpreted this sensible conception in a peculiarly populist[38] manner, which gave little operational guidance to what could and should be achieved. The conception was reinterpreted to mean that PASOK should not go further than the 'people' were willing to accept. The question arose of how the 'will' of the people could be ascertained. The resolution to this dilemma was that PASOK, because it lacked a framework for resolving differences and coordinating policy either at the level of party or government, responded, usually 'behind closed doors', depending on the strength of the organized expression of opinion hostile to individual measures. This also explains the delays and uncertainties on the nature and scope of various institutional interventions. The failure to present new and credible initiatives on tax evasion and the taxation of farmers, which may have limited the explosive fiscal situation, was the result of pressures on PASOK from elements within its political machine and its natural electoral constituency. For a new party in power does not act on a *tabula rasa*. Lacking a clear global strategy to mediate interests, or even a forum in which to develop such a strategy, to set priorities, and to provide ministries with operational plans, various social, economic, and political interests represented by PASOK had to find alternative means of expression.

In this context, it was difficult for PASOK to promote social capital within society, something which we have argued would greatly have helped its overall strategy, when the reserves of such capital were so meagre within PASOK itself.

4. Concluding Remarks

As we have seen, the PASOK social democratic experiment in economic policy-making was not a success. In particular, its distinctive supply-

[38] There is, in fact, a large body of opinion that believes that PASOK is in any case better understood as a populist party rather than a social democratic one. On PASOK and populism, see Sotiropoulos (1991, 1993), Diamandouros (1994), Featherstone (1986), and Mouzelis *et al.* (1989).

side economic initiatives hardly got off the ground throughout the 1980s. By 1985, the slow process of adaptation to a more orthodox set of economic policies had begun, with the adoption of a stabilization plan under the then chief economics minister, Kostas Simitis. This was brought to an abrupt halt in 1987, mainly because Papandreou took the decision that without a more 'populist' turn PASOK was unlikely to keep its hold on power. This was to prove a fateful decision that led to PASOK's least creditable period of government, associated with a lack of macroeconomic control, populist politics and a series of financial scandals, and a general loss of direction. It was also unsuccessful in its own terms since PASOK lost power in 1989. By 1993, when PASOK returned to power, the shift in policy to a more orthodox stance was clear and was confirmed with the election of Simitis to succeed Papandreou as leader in 1996.

On the other hand, with respect to promoting social justice, PASOK has been a little more successful. In the 1980s, we have seen, it took important steps with respect to pensions, minimum wages, the health service, and so on, which had a significant effect on reducing inequality and the level of poverty. To a certain extent this concern has survived the stabilization plans since 1993 with an attempt to preserve real wages, restructure the tax system, and minimize the employment costs of the strategy (see section 2). However, these initiatives were not bolstered, as was envisaged in PASOK's original programme, by institutional change (for instance to promote social control and thereby shift power relationships within society) or by significant restructuring of the economy. Whether this entails that the social gains are therefore insecure, as many social democrats and, in the past, PASOK itself have argued, remains to be seen.

How can we account for PASOK's trajectory outlined above? A popular argument is that radical strategies — such as PASOK's original conception — are no longer viable as a result of the increasing internationalization of production and financial liberalization. The 'globalization' thesis would suggest that PASOK's trajectory was in some sense an inevitable accommodation to reality which had to come sooner or later.[39] We have argued that PASOK did not, in fact, face an overwhelming external constraint in the 1980s. True, there was the current account crisis of 1985, but, on the whole, PASOK faced a window of opportunity and a rather soft current account constraint, as a result of the large

[39] Strictly speaking there are two issues here. First, how new and how significant is the process of globalization? For a sceptical account of globalization see, for instance, Hirst and Thompson (1996). Second, to what extent does globalization severely restrict economic strategies that are in some sense 'alternative'? For different perspectives on the latter issue see Glyn (1995a), Notermans (1993, 1994), and Moses (1994).

inflows in the form of remittances and EU funds. However, it is certainly true that, by the 1990s, influential policy-makers within PASOK did perceive, whether rightly or wrongly, the external constraint as binding.[40] This was strengthened by the process of European integration which entailed for Greece the liberalization of the financial system and the gradual removal of capital controls. The Maastricht criteria for participation in monetary union have also played a significant role, especially given Greece's reliance on EU funds and the perceived political benefits of membership (not least strengthening Greece's position with respect to Turkey). With respect to the above, the success of the government in staving off devaluation in the speculative crisis of May 1994, discussed earlier, was a decisive political landmark. It strengthened the position of the government with respect to international capital markets and expanded PASOK's popularity to centrist political forces impressed with its handling of the crisis. This political success was underlined by PASOK's 1996 election victory — this time under Kostas Simitis — by reinforcing the appeal of the more orthodox policy since it was shown that such a policy was not doomed at the polls.

However, for the 1980s, rather than the operation of an external constraint, we have emphasized PASOK's problems more in terms of its failure to control inflation and the budget deficits.[41] In part, this was a result of PASOK's inability, or unwillingness, to confront opposition to its strategy. As we have seen, the 1980s were characterized by what amounts to an investment strike on the part of capital — the rate of growth of gross fixed capital formation was negative in most of these years.[42] Furthermore, most of PASOK's supply-side measures, such as the supervisory councils and planning agreements, were bitterly opposed. That is to say, PASOK faced the problem of 'structural dependency' on capital that confronts all radical governments.[43] It cannot be

[40] See Wickham-Jones (1997) for how such a perception influenced the evolution of economic policy-making in the British Labour Party before 1997.

[41] For a similar argument with respect to Sweden and Norway and to France see Notermans (1994) and Glyn (1995a).

[42] It is true that this lack of investment predates the accession of PASOK to power in 1981, but on the other hand the hostility of capital to PASOK in its first period should not be underestimated.

[43] On the theory of structural dependency, see Offe and Ronge (1984) and Przeworski and Wallerstein (1988). For more empirical approaches which discuss how structural dependency affects social democratic parties in and out of power, see Przeworski (1985), Wickham-Jones (1995), and Hay (1997). Of course, it used to be the case that structural dependency was seen as a problem to be overcome. A major characteristic of New Labour or 'Third Way' politics is that this problem is either not recognized or is seen as a blessing in disguise which allows the 'modernization' of society.

said that PASOK developed any innovative response to this problem. More important still was the conflict that existed within the ranks of its own political constituency. We have argued implicitly in section 2 that, for the 1980s, both the budget deficits and inflation reflect the fact that PASOK did not exercise the necessary control over competing claims (see Tsakalotos, 1991*b*).

PASOK had won its first election victory as a broad coalition. This coalition had been brought together on a radical platform which promised both measures to promote social justice and institutional change. Thus measures to promote social control and democratic participation were not just economic policy proposals, but constituted central tenets of PASOK's political platform to outflank the Left. But, in power, PASOK would need not only to adjudicate between competing claims but also to ensure support for its institutional interventions and structural economic policies. However, PASOK was unable to manage a process of structural change in the economy in which there would have been clear winners and losers, especially since many of the losers were part of PASOK's natural political constituency. In this respect, many of PASOK's original measures even came to be seen as obstacles; for democratic planning, and in general the strategy of extending democracy to the economic sphere, almost by definition implies an increase in the transparency of economic decision-making in which clear winners and losers are indicated. Thus, in Diamandouros's (1994) conception, there was a movement from the 'moment of incorporation' — where previously excluded groups in society were incorporated, in part at least, into the political system — to the 'moment of consolidation' — where these new groups, and others, acted as an obstacle to structural change by seeking to preserve their traditional rights and newly found access to economic resources.

On the one hand, this course may have been a

> necessary price Greek society has had to pay for the long-overdue incorporation of these marginalized strata into the political system, for the dismantling of a post-civil war order based on the institutionalized inequality of citizens, in short, for the normalization of its politics following long and systematic derailment during the preceding quarter century. (Diamandouros, 1994, p. 54)

It might be argued that it is partly the wider recognition of PASOK's role in this process which lies behind its political success despite so many economic failures. On the other hand, these failures, the lack of structural change and continuing consumption, led to such macroeconomic imbalances that PASOK in the 1990s felt that it had little choice but to turn to orthodox stabilization measures to confront the mounting crisis and in order to keep alive the hope of continuing integration with the EU.

However, rather than the above considerations, PASOK's inability to promote its radical supply-side and institutional policies may reflect the fact that its original conception of such policies was in some way defective. That is to say that PASOK never had a clear conception of a coherent and implementable alternative. On the one hand, it is certainly the case that while PASOK at the programmatic level had a conception of instituting various planning and interventionist mechanisms and institutions, this did not, except perhaps in the example of the ASKE discussed in section 3, extend to fully worked-out operational plans of how these would function in practice. How comprehensive should planning be? In which areas, and on what rationale, should social ownership or planning agreements be promoted? What is the appropriate relationship between the state and the planners or between the planners and individual firms or sectors of industry? What role should workers participation play? To such questions, PASOK had, at best, a very hazy conception before coming to power, with the result that its initiatives once in power tended to be spasmodic and uncoordinated. On the other hand, PASOK's conception involved not only many of the elements that were common currency in social democratic political circles in the 1970s and early 1980s (planning agreements, national and local enterprise boards, and so on) but also many of its ideas (such as the ASKE) involved such concepts as stakeholding which are still central to modern social democratic thinking. The problem is that it is difficult to glean much from the PASOK experiment for the coherence and appropriateness of such social democratic initiatives, given that so many of its economic policies in this sphere were abandoned before they really had a chance to operate.[44]

It is for this reason that this paper has concentrated on the political economy aspects which lay behind PASOK's failure to implement the radical aspects of its policy and its gradual adoption of a more orthodox approach. We cannot restate the arguments here, but will merely point to some considerations of wider relevance to the potential for social democratic economic policies elsewhere.

We have argued that the Greek context constituted a peculiarly unfavourable one for a social democratic experiment. We have pointed, in this respect, to a number of factors: the statist tradition and the weakness of civil society; the lack of intermediary institutions and structures; the inability of social movements, such as trade unions, to act as an autonomous force within society; and so on. In such a context,

---

[44] For more discussion of these issues, see Tsakalotos (1991a).

trust and cooperation, important ingredients for the social democratic approach, are at a premium. Thus, in the Greek case, there was little scope for the type of politics which relies on various factions of a social democratic coalition showing solidarity with one another's concerns through, for instance, egalitarian payment for social measures and measures to compensate and reintegrate the losers of economic restructuring. Yet a number of authors (Esping-Andersen, 1985; Scharpf, 1991; Glyn, 1995a) have considered this sort of 'socialism in one class' a prerequisite for mobilizing support for, and consolidating the success of, social-democratic-type reforms.

However, it is important to point out that the political economy obstacles to such an approach, although acute in the case of Greece, would not be absent elsewhere. For neo-liberal economic policies since the 1980s, which have been most rigorously applied in the UK, but have also been an important force elsewhere in Europe, have, as many sociologists have been keen to point out, in many ways been aimed at reducing the 'capacity of social forces to organise in some sense "against the market" '(Goldthorpe, 1984, 1987). 'Flexibility' in labour markets, the lack of resources for governments' (including local government's) social and other expenditures, and in general the increased 'marketization' of the economy have all led to an increased individualism, a fragility in social networks, and more acute feelings of insecurity.[45] Elsewhere I have argued (Tsakalotos, 1999) that determining the appropriate scope of the market cannot be based solely on efficiency considerations, that is, the best possible satisfaction of existing preferences. Expanding the market domain entails also an expansion of the role of market norms (such as individualism and asociability) which influences the nature of individuals, including their preferences and their relationships with others (see also Bowles, 1998). There is something disingenuous in advocating more markets and flexibility, as supporters of New Labour and 'Third Way' politics are prone to do, and then bemoaning the fact that this sets limits on the degree of equity possible in society because of the efficiency consequences of egalitarian policies. In the context of the analysis of section 3, this suggests that policies that rely on trust and cooperation may be more difficult to promote, thereby limiting in many economies—and not just those which share the particular characteristics of Greece—the scope for the social democratic strategy of extending democracy to the economic sphere.

---

[45] For a discussion of the decline of social capital in the USA, see Putnam (1995a,b). Hall (1997) argues that a similar overall decline is not so much in evidence in Britain, although there is such a decline among the working and poorer classes.

A final consideration lies more in the domain of politics proper than of political economy. It was argued above that PASOK, especially in the 1970s and 1980s, found it difficult to adjudicate between competing claims and develop a coherent strategy balancing short-run and long-run priorities. Crucial to this phenomenon, it was argued, was the lack of democratic culture and institutions within the party itself. While European and other social democratic parties have a far greater tradition of democracy on which to draw, this factor may also be important in the future for other social democratic experiments. For the recent emphasis on style and presentation, and the media focus of politics, may leave social democratic parties in difficulties once in power. The weakening of internal democratic institutions, of which the marginalization of party conferences as policy-making institutions is but one example common to many social democratic parties, may increasingly undermine the ability of these parties to develop coherent and global programmes to which activists and supporters have some commitment. This may not be a crucial ingredient in winning elections, but may still be important in successful implementation of social democratic policies once in power.

7

The Spanish Socialists in Power:
Thirteen Years of Economic Policy

ALBERT RECIO AND JORDI ROCA*

1. Introduction

When the Spanish Socialist Party, the Partido Socialista Obrero Español (PSOE), came to power towards the end of 1982, the Spanish economy faced serious difficulties. The unemployment rate was more than 16 per cent, investment was decreasing, inflation was around 15 per cent, and there were important deficits both in the government budget and in the balance of payments (Segura, 1990).

From a more structural point of view, the Spanish economy also had considerable problems. Some of these had been inherited from the Franco era (Catalán, 1991, 1999). Too high a level of protection and an authoritarian model of industrial relations had allowed many small businesses to survive at a low level of technology on the basis of low salaries and paternalistic industrial relations. Despite protection and abundant export subsidies, the trade deficit was chronic and had traditionally been financed from other current account in-flows, such as tourism and remittances by emigrants in other European countries, and from the entry of foreign capital. Banking capital had enormous economic power, both because of its direct investment in companies and because of the low level of self-financing of the majority of firms. It was an oligopolistic sector which acted as a cartel, protected from foreign competition and with an enormous political influence.

The productive structure was also problematic. The agrarian sector was in a period of transformation which would intensify and lead to serious job losses.[1] The industrial sector was affected by a surplus of

* Autonomous University of Barcelona and University of Barcelona, respectively.

Thanks to Andrew Glyn, J. R. Sargent, Josep González Calvet, Jordi Catalán, Alfons Barceló, Agustí Colom, and two anonymous referees for their comments. We also acknowledge financial support from CICYT project SEC96-1011-CO2-02.

[1] In Spain, agrarian employment made up 18.5 per cent of the total in 1982, compared to 8.7 per cent for the countries which would comprise the 12-member European Union (EU) (Collado *et al.*, 1996, pp. 126–7).

productive capacity in many branches, and by its specialization in areas where international demand grew slowly and which were threatened by competition from newly industrializing countries (NICs) (Myro, 1988; Buesa and Molero, 1988). There was also a tradition of inefficient public administration, political clientelism, and low taxation. The 1978 tax reform, which had brought in a general, progressive income tax, was recent and tax evasion was still rife.

2. PSOE in 1982: The Party and the Electoral Programme

The PSOE was founded in 1879 and it secured a strong social base during the first third of this century. After the Civil War (1936–9) the organization was practically reduced to some groups in exile, progressively less connected to the Spanish situation. In the last years of the Franco dictatorship the support for PSOE was limited to a few groups, mainly of professional people. The resurgence of the party coincided with the political transition (1975–7) when it used very leftist propaganda in order to compete with the Communist Party and other radical left-wing groups. Good results in the first parliamentary elections (1977) stimulated the PSOE's growth and, at the same time, the leadership managed to transform the party, making it adopt a more centrist stance. In the PSOE's Congress of May 1979, 70.6 per cent of delegates had joined the party during the last 4 years (Caciagli, 1986, p. 211). During this Congress there was a sharp ideological confrontation and Felipe González resigned in order to force the abandonment of Marxism. After this crisis, González obtained great support in the extraordinary Congress of September 1979. The increasing expectations of forming the government and the effective control of local power in the most important villages encouraged the entry into the party of a new political class.

The 1982 electoral programme referred to a 'policy of expansion' within a strategy which focused on employment as the number one priority, to government investment as the 'motor' of the economy, and even to the idea of concerted planning (PSOE, 1982). However, it also contained orthodox references, such as to the prevalent role of the market and to anti-inflation policy. The failure of the Mitterrand experience had already occurred, and had an enormous impact on the PSOE, and economic policy was to be made by those with more 'market-oriented' positions, who did not believe in any expansionary programme, and who also mistrusted any other kind of employment policy apart from reform of labour-market institutions. Carlos Solchaga, Socialist Minister for Industry from 1982 to 1985 and Minister for the

Economy from 1985 to 1993, has explained the thinking of those who established economic policy:

> The problem of macroeconomic policy, and in particular monetary policy, was not unemployment, since this did not depend on the direction and content of economic policy, but inflation. Once this had been corrected, all the advantages which come from economic stability, including perhaps an increase in employment and reduction in unemployment, could be obtained. (Solchaga, 1997, p. 197)

They were also enormously concerned to show proof of their 'economic orthodoxy' to avoid capital flight and to earn international credibility. All these factors led the leadership into considering that the reduction of inflation, via wage moderation and restrictive monetary policies, was in practice the number one macroeconomic priority.

One of the socialist leaders of those years explains the situation: 'The priorities of the new socialist government were somewhat atypical in comparison with the social democracy of Northern Europe. These priorities were the "consolidation" of democracy and the "modernization" of the Spanish economy' (Maravall, 1991, p. 61). This modernization, of both the public and the business sectors, was identified with productive efficiency, economic growth, and social welfare, and was widely associated with the entry of Spain into the European Community.

3. Macroeconomic Trends, Monetary Policy, and Exchange-rate Policy

In the period analysed, the cyclical behaviour of the Spanish economy (Figure 1) was similar to that of the EU, although the fluctuations of GDP and, especially, employment, were larger.

During the first years of the socialist government, a period of economic and industrial adjustments, economic growth was low and the loss of jobs continued. A period of expansion began at the end of 1985, which brought the Spanish economy one of the highest growth rates in the OECD.

Strong growth of the GDP and of employment, and the fact that, at the same time, inflation decreased significantly, were considered by many, in Spain and abroad, to show that the Spanish economy had overcome its structural limitations. However, there were still important problems (Torrero, 1993; Naredo, 1996). The traditional trade deficit increased spectacularly. From 1988, the current account balance

Figure 1
Real GDP and Employment, 1982–95 (% annual change)

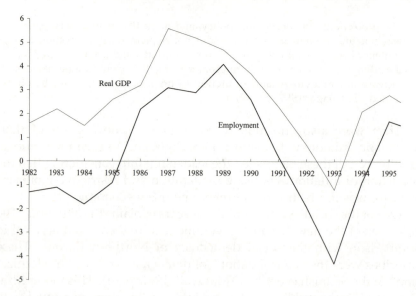

Source: OECD, *Economic Outlook*.

surpluses in other areas were incapable of covering this deficit, so the current account deficit became one of the largest in the OECD, more than 3 per cent of the GDP. Paradoxically, the current account deficits co-existed with an increase in foreign reserves which pushed the peseta exchange rate up.

This situation can only be understood if one takes into account that monetary and exchange-rate policies were dedicated almost exclusively to reducing inflation. During most of the period under study, monetary policy was quite restrictive, as seen in the high real interest rates. These, together with the deregulation of capital movements, stimulated the in-flow of foreign capital to acquire assets of all kinds, such as real estate and shares. Foreign in-flows were not only in search of speculative profits, but also had a longer-term investment perspective in an economy which was soon to become a full member of the EU.

After the large devaluation in December 1982 (one of the first economic measures of the first socialist government), the maintenance of the nominal exchange rate compared to the EU currencies was one of the mechanisms with which the socialists tried to 'anchor' the Spanish economy to reduce inflation. In 1989 this policy led to the entry into the European Monetary System (EMS) with a very overvalued exchange rate, as criticized at that time by various economists (Martín Seco, 1993;

Figure 2
Real Exchange Rate Based on CPI *Vis-à-vis* Developed Countries,
1982–95 (1982 = 100)

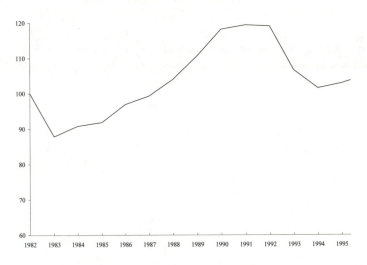

Source: Calculated from Banco de España, *Boletín Estadístico*.

De Velasco, 1996).[2] The appreciation in real terms of the peseta *vis-à-vis* developed countries was spectacular, with the real exchange rate peaking some 40 per cent above the level at the end of 1982 (Figure 2). Finally, in the context of the crisis of the EMS which began in the summer of 1992, the government could not avoid three successive devaluations of the peseta, which, however, helped to improve the current account.

The economic strategy of the government also created negative side effects. First, the large foreign capital in-flow was one of the factors which explains the significant increase in value of assets in this period,[3] which pushed up rents, and which encouraged a culture of quick profits through bold financial or property deals. The support of the government for this speculative 'boom' ended up making it appear as the accomplice in some of the fraudulent behaviour associated with this process.

Second, the appreciation of the peseta and the high cost of credit worsened the problems of many industrial companies. In many cases,

[2] It was not by chance that the decision to become part of the EMS was made in a context of a high level of union militancy, after the spectacular success of the general strike of 14 December 1988 (Solchaga, 1997, p. 108).

[3] It has been estimated that in some years the increase in value of assets exceeded annual GDP. Especially sharp was the increase in real estate values (Naredo, 1996).

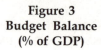

Figure 3
Budget Balance
(% of GDP)

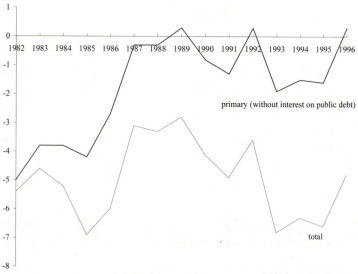

Source: OECD, *Economic Outlook*.

owners sold out to foreign capital, so as to invest in speculative activities which were highly profitable in the short term. This added to the increase in competition which resulted from Spain's integration into the European Community (which happened at a formal level in 1986).

Finally, from their first years in power, the socialists decided to finance the deficit in 'orthodox' ways, since liberalization of financial markets meant there was no escape from market interest rates. This decision formed part of their restrictive monetary policy, and was in line with the tendency to increase the autonomy of the Bank of Spain. (This accorded with the monetarist ideas inspiring the monetary policy designed in Maastricht and which the Spanish government not only accepted but also defended enthusiastically.) In a context of high interest rates, this meant the growing weight of interest payments, from 0.7 per cent of the GDP in 1982 to more than 5 per cent in the middle 1990s, so that the budget deficit fed on itself (Figure 3).

From the end of 1992, the economic crisis was particularly intense, with falls in GDP. A more expansionary period began in 1994, but growth rates were modest as compared to those experienced in the second half of the 1980s.

Figure 4
Unemployment Rate, 1982–95 (% of labour force)

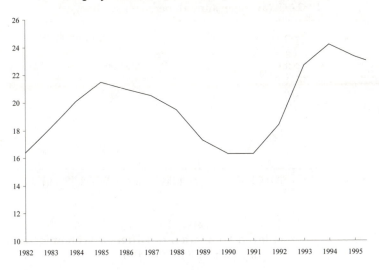

Source: OECD, *Economic Outlook*.

4. Employment and Unemployment

The objective of reducing unemployment, which was central to the PSOE's electoral programme, was a great failure. The annual unemployment rate never went below the 1982 level, 16 per cent, and when the socialists left the government it was over 22 per cent (Figure 4). The socialist failure in this area is very clear but it is necessary to add two qualifications.

The general trend in total employment in the period in Spain is similar to – or even a little better than – that in the whole EU (Table 1). Even so, a distinctive aspect was a special sensitivity of employment in Spain to the economic situation. The destruction of employment had begun in the middle 1970s – somewhat later than in other industrialized countries, but more intensely – and it continued until 1985. On the other hand, the growth of employment in the second half of the 1980s was spectacular, and between 1985 and 1990 it was the highest in the OECD countries, with the exception of Australia. Finally, for the period 1992–4, only a few OECD countries (such as Sweden and Finland) had a worse employment performance.

The worse outcome in terms of unemployment compared to the EU was due to a faster increase in the active population (Table 1). That can be explained partly because of the more rapid increase in the working-

Table 1

Changes in the Active and Employed Populations in Spain and in the EU, 1982–95 (average annual percentage changes)

	Active population		Employment	
	Spain	EU	Spain	EU
1982–5	+0.8	+0.7	−1.3	+0.1
1985–91	+1.5	+0.8	+2.5	+1.1
1991–5	+0.7	0.0	−1.4	−0.8
1982–95	+1.1	+0.5	+0.4	+0.3

Source: Calculated from OECD, *Economic Outlook*, Annex Tables 18 and 20.

Table 2

Changes in the Employed Population in Different Economic Sectors in Spain, 1982–95 ('000s)

Agrarian	−954.2
Non-agrarian	
industry	−333.0
construction	+177.9
services	+2,047.5
Total non-agrarian	+1,892.5
Total	+925.4

Source: Calculated from Instituto Nacional de Estadística, *Encuesta de Población Activa*.

age population. More importantly, the female participation rate was still very low when the PSOE came to power, and in the following years large numbers of women joined the labour market.[4]

A second qualification is that if we compare only the evolution of non-agrarian employment in Spain and in the EU for the whole period, the outcome in Spain is clearly better. Agrarian employment was, in 1982, higher only in Portugal and Greece among EU members (OECD, *Historical Statistics*, Table 2.9). The decrease of agrarian employment in the following years was particularly intense (Table 2). Some authors have even considered this as the main explanation for the fact that the unemployment rate was greatest in Spain (Marimon and Zilibotti, 1996). However, Portugal does not fit in with this explanation because

[4] According to the OECD, *Historical Statistics* (Table 2.8), the increase in the female participation rate in Spain during the period was greater only in the Netherlands and in New Zealand, among OECD countries.

there the unemployment rate was lower than in Spain, despite a larger decline in agrarian employment.

The expansion of the public sector created new jobs until 1992, and afterwards public employment remained more or less stable. Public employment generally followed a different pattern to that of the private sector: less job insecurity and a greater proportion of skilled jobs and of female workers. The net creation of public employment reflected contradictory trends, with a loss of jobs in industry and transport, and the creation of employment in administration, education, health, and social services. Thus the government has tended to increase the number of stable, relatively well-paid, white-collar jobs, and to decrease jobs for the industrial working class (Recio, 1996*b*; García *et al.*, 1997).

5. The Labour Market: Continual Reform

Throughout the period studied, the labour market has been one of the main areas of economic intervention, for several different reasons. First, there was the persistently high level of unemployment. Second, the dominant, neoclassical analysis of unemployment attributed it specifically to the malfunctioning of the labour market (Rojo, 1981; Viñals, 1983). In Spain, there was the added argument that there were special institutional rigidities resulting from the Franco era, such as the high cost of dismissal and elaborate regulations about working conditions. According to some authors, the legalization of the unions, and other institutional changes, had increased the already great inflexibility of the labour market and they argue that this was central to any explanation of the high unemployment in Spain (Malo de Molina, 1983; Bentolila and Blanchard, 1990). Third was the role given to wage control in achieving the main objective of reducing inflation. Fourth, there was the growing influence of new ideas about flexible production, which required a new model of management of the labour force.

As a result, the various socialist governments adopted a labour policy focused on two basic objectives: controlling wage costs and promoting job flexibility, seen as a high level of malleability of the labour force with respect to business needs. How these objectives were achieved varied according to the political and social balance of power in each situation.

With respect to wage increases, the PSOE generally managed to maintain, and accentuate, the moderation achieved at the end of the 1970s (Roca, 1991). The government was initially in favour of a policy of centralized, social agreements, but could only reach these in 1983

(Interconfederal Accord) and 1985–6 (Economic and Social Accord) (Espina, 1990; Roca, 1993a), taking advantage of the willingness of the unions at that time. When agreements were not reached (see section 6), the government continued to influence wage negotiations in various ways. Civil servants' salaries and the minimum wage were fixed unilaterally and the government instituted campaigns in the mass media, before the collective bargaining period, indicating the acceptable money-wage rises, and threatening to bring in more restrictive monetary policies if its advice was not followed.

Over the whole period, the share of wages decreased significantly in real terms (Figure 5)[5] (Roca, 1993b). Only in 1989–92 did average real labour costs grow more than productivity, which was largely due to a series of temporary circumstances, including the burst of economic growth which finally caused tightening in some particular labour markets (e.g. construction), and the constraint on industrial prices caused by the strong appreciation of the peseta. The moderation in labour costs was even more striking in terms of take-home pay, since there was a growth in social security contributions and income tax. In addition, the sharp rises in the cost of housing were not well reflected in the CPI and so increases in real wages were less than the CPI would indicate (Naredo, 1996, pp. 34–5).

The low increase in labour costs is explained not only by the moderation in collective bargaining, but also by changes in the structure of employment, which gave rise to an increase in the number of low-paid jobs (Recio, 1991). In this respect, the loss of purchasing power of the minimum wage is significant (Gutiérrez, 1994).

The objective of making labour conditions more flexible has been at the centre of different legislative measures which have introduced significant changes in the Spanish labour system. The most important changes have to do with temporary contracts, and there have also been significant changes in the system of unemployment benefits (analysed below in section 6). Although there were already some types of non-standard contracts, in 1984 an important modification in the labour laws was passed, which introduced a wide range of new kinds of temporary contract. When employment began to increase in 1985, almost all of the new jobs took one of these new forms, so the percentage of temporary jobs increased dramatically, especially in the private sector (Table 3). In

[5] The figure compares, for the whole economy, the evolution of real wages (in gross terms, including all types of social contribution), using the GDP deflator, with the evolution of productivity, measured as the ratio of real GDP to the employed population. In other words, it is the evolution of wage share in value-added, corrected to take into account the changes in the proportion of wage-earning people within the employed population.

Figure 5
Labour's Share, 1982–95 (1982 = 100)

Source: Calculated from Instituto Nacional de Estadística, *Contabilidad Nacional de España*.

1988 there was an attempt to introduce a new kind of temporary contract for young people, with even fewer rights than any of the already existing kinds of contract, and this was one of the main reasons for the 1988 general strike, which forced the withdrawal of the project (Aguilar and Roca, 1991).

The spectacular increase in temporary contracts has been explained as a reaction of employers to the high legal costs of firing permanent

Table 3
Temporary Work in Spain, 1987–95

	Permanent employment (millions of wage earners)	Temporary employment (millions of wage earners)
1987	6.52	1.61
1995	5.91	3.01

	Rate of temporary employment (as % of wage earners)		
	Public sector	Private sector	Whole economy
1987	9.9	22.6	19.8
1995	15.5	40.5	34.5

Note: There are no data for the years prior to 1987.
Source: Calculated from Instituto Nacional de Estadística, *Encuesta de Población Activa*.

employees, but there are facts that do not fit in with this explanation. First, in Spain there exist several ways to terminate employment and their associated monetary costs are very different. In the case of individual dismissal, the labour court can decide between four cases: 'according to law' by disciplinary causes; 'justified' by 'objective' (economic, technological, etc.) causes; 'unjustified', i.e. when the labour court considers there is not any cause; and 'null', only when there is sex discrimination, repression for union activity, or some such circumstance. The first case permits dismissal without any redundancy payment and the last is the only case in which the firm has to re-employ the worker. In the other cases, independently of the court decision, the firm can decide to maintain the dismissal, even though it has to pay different redundancy payments, depending on whether or not the court has declared that there are justified motives for the dismissal. The legal redundancy payment for justified collective dismissal is the same as for individual cases.[6] Several analysts have considered that the costs of justified dismissals are not especially high in the context of EU countries (Segura *et al.*, 1991; Toharia and Malo, 1997); when firms dismiss without any clear justification, the cost increases (CC.OO, 1992), and it is in this case that Spanish firing is very expensive in comparison with most European countries (Calviño and Lorente, 1996). Redundancy payment can be decided by a free agreement between the worker and the firm without the intervention of the labour court. In fact, this type of individual dismissal is the most usual (more than 60 per cent of total dismissals), with a cost to the employer of two to three times the average costs of the labour court dismissal. This suggests that monetary cost is only one aspect of the problem: firms accept paying more than the legal provision in order to avoid any kind of regulation.

Furthermore, if the high cost of dismissal was the most important determinant of employment decisions, then one would expect the cyclical fluctuations to affect permanent workers much less than temporary workers. However, in the last recession all the net destruction of jobs affected permanent employees (Alba-Ramírez and Alonso-Borrego, 1997; Recio, 1999), a fact that has been ignored by those who apply the 'insider–outsider' approach to the analysis of the Spanish labour market (Bentolila and Dolado, 1994). Some types of dismissal are expensive, but the 'flexibility' of legal provisions and the weakness of unions

[6] In the case of individual or collective justified dismissal, the minimum legal redundancy payment is of 20 days pay for each year of tenure (maximum 12 months); in the case of collective dismissal, the government pays 40 per cent of this cost (when the firm has only 25 or fewer workers). For individual 'unjustified' dismissal, the minimum legal redundancy payment was (before the last 1997 reform) of 45 days pay for each year of tenure (maximum 42 months).

(specially in small firms) have contributed to a massive destruction of permanent jobs (more than 600,000 jobs in the last economic recession of 1991–4). It appears that the proliferation of temporary jobs is not simply aimed at avoiding possible costs of dismissal but is a deliberate strategy based on the 'casualization' of employment and labour. In 1995 new labour contracts were equivalent to 82 per cent of the whole labour force and a large number of these contracts had a duration of only a month or less.[7] There are many studies, often ignored by orthodox economists, that demonstrate the proliferation, in many industries, of employers' policies centred on the search for cheap and non-unionized labour, authoritarian management, and casualization (Bilbao, 1991; Recio, 1996a; Cano, 1997), rather than 'high-wage' strategies oriented towards labour skills, worker cooperation, or industrial democratization (Jimeno and Toharia, 1993). This can be explained partly by the type of industrial specialization of the Spanish economy, which lacks high-tech activities, and partly by the tradition of paternalistic forms of management.

Faced with the growth in temporary jobs, the government only made a few timid attempts to balance the situation, bringing in union rights to information about the contracts signed (1990), and placing limits (1992) on the use of one of the most important types of temporary contracts, as had been suggested by a government-commissioned but independent report (Segura et al., 1991). These measures had practically no effect. In 1994, the government went further in its policy of strengthening the power of employers by introducing new contracts for young people and for part-time jobs with much reduced rights, by making dismissal easier in some cases, and by giving companies greater discretion in matters such as geographical mobility and the length of the working day (Martín and Santos, 1994). The legalization of temporary employment agencies has contributed to the dramatic growth of short-term labour contracts. In 1997, the number of new labour contracts exceeded the annual average of wage earners.

On the other hand, little attention has been given to active measures in the labour market, although after Spain's entry into the European Community the funds used for occupational training increased. Not only have few resources been allocated, but often a well-designed training programme has been lacking (Toharia, 1997).

---

[7] In 1997 the Conservative government introduced, simultaneously, a cut in firing payments and subsidies to permanent labour contracts. Despite this new reform, the rate of temporary employment was reduced only to 32.8 per cent in the first quarter of 1999.

6. The Conflict Between the Social Democratic Party and the Social Democratic Union

One of the striking aspects of the period is the strong conflict between the government (and the party) and the unions, and especially between the government and the Unión General de Trabajadores (UGT), which had traditionally been closely linked to the party (the main leaders of this trade union became PSOE members of parliament in 1982). The most intense moment of this conflict was the general strike that paralysed the country on 14 December 1988 (Aguilar and Roca, 1991).

The great success of the strike was due not only to the strength of unions (not very great, but underestimated by the small proportion of employees who were union members), but also to the dissatisfaction of a great part of the population with important aspects of economic and social development. The easy increase in wealth for some people and the triumphant government declarations in a context of high unemployment and increasing labour turnover explain in large measure the participation of a majority of the population in the general strike.

A very important element was the increasing perception of UGT leaders that the government was not seriously committed to a corporatist strategy of centralized agreements with the union. The union was basically invited to support measures previously decided by the government. If the support was effective, that was celebrated; but if not, the union was systematically accused of defending selfish interests, the interests of the employed against those of the unemployed.[8] This was in a context in which, on one hand, the labour-market situation (high unemployment and specially high labour turnover) made union activity more difficult and, on the other hand, influential economic sectors tended to think that centralized wage agreements were not necessary and could even be damaging by creating rigidity in relative wages.[9]

[8] According to some authors (Bentolila and Dolado, 1994), the coexistence in firms of two types of workers, permanent and temporary, reinforced the position of the former. In collective bargaining, unions would represent only (or at least mainly) the interests of the permanent workers and the unemployment risk associated with wage increases would decrease because the possible reduction of staff would only affect the temporary workers. We do not agree with this analysis at all. As we said in section 5, the loss of jobs has not only affected temporary workers, but also (sometimes even mostly) permanent workers, especially in the industrial sector, where, in the opinion of these authors, their analysis should work best. Furthermore, in general, unions at the big enterprises have tried to limit the use of temporary workers and have pressed for the temporary ones to be made into permanent workers, an attitude that, according to the analysis of Bentolila and Dolado, would prejudice the interests of permanent workers.

[9] As an example, in an enterprise's publication, we can read: 'The increase of wages has to become a variable interior to the firm . . . linked to the outcomes of each firm or each geographical area. . . . The system we favour is less inflationary than the centralised system' (Boletín del Círculo de Empresarios, **37**, 1987, p. 3).

Thus, there was a union reaction to a political and social evolution unfavourable to them and against anti-union ideologies. An additional factor has to do with the existence of two great union confederations with similar influence and in competition with each other. The UGT was an organization with a long historical tradition but relatively inactive during the Franco dictatorship and only revived at the end of the 1970s. Union activity during the 1960s and the 1970s was led by Comisiones Obreras (CC.OO), an organization that became very strong in spite of political repression and that was closely linked to the Partido Comunista, specially in the last years of Francoism. The initial identification between the UGT and the new socialist government probably lost this union some support in favour of CC.OO and this encouraged the confrontation between the leaders of UGT and the leaders of PSOE. The result was united action between UGT and CC.OO, which was a key factor in the success of the general strike.

There was no clear global alternative economic programme which differentiated the UGT and the PSOE. During the first years of socialist government, the UGT accepted the main priorities of macroeconomic policy, the wage freeze, and legal changes in order to favour temporary labour contracts (see section 5). The dissension concerned several areas. First, the UGT leaders opposed the reform of the public pension system in 1985. Second, the UGT felt cheated when the government did not carry out its promises about unemployment benefits, agreed to in the 1985 social accord.[10]

Finally, government and union positions on wage policy became sharply divergent. The UGT accepted the centralized agreements but, after 1986, demanded that real wages should not be frozen, but rather that money increases should exceed the expected rise in consumer prices, though it accepted that average real increases should not be greater than average productivity growth. These demands were defended with the argument that workers should share the benefits of periods of economic growth and not just the restraints in periods of recession. In our opinion, centralized agreements broke down more because of the inflexibility of the government than because of the radicalism of union leaders; there was a viable alternative if the government had been willing to trade support for workers' rights on the shop floor and further progressive changes in the tax system for continued wage restraint from the unions.

---

[10] According to this social pact, the government agreed that the coverage of unemployment benefits would be equal or greater than 48 per cent (i.e. nearly half the people registered in the public unemployment agencies were entitled to some benefit) at the end of 1986. At the time of the strike, this figure was about 30 per cent.

The UGT was also completely opposed to a new type of temporary labour contract for young people. This contract reduced wages and labour conditions without any specific requirement for training (Recio and Roca, 1989). In addition, the government decided on this policy without previous consultation with the union and in a context in which the different types of temporary contracts were used extensively and sometimes in a fraudulent way, with workers dismissed and then re-employed in order to preserve their temporary status or with training obligations flouted. The government was not prepared to control the situation and was not worried about its impact on the power of employers in the workplace.

One immediate cause of dissension related to the non-fulfilment of the government's inflation target for 1988. The objective was to reduce the CPI annual rate to 3 per cent from a previous value of around 5 per cent; in the event, the CPI rose by about 5 per cent. The unions demanded that the civil servant salaries, public pensions, and the minimum wage be revised in order to maintain their purchasing power. This demand was one of the most important in the general strike and became popular with the slogan that government had to pay its 'social debt'.

The conflict was revived in 1992 when government decreed a cut in unemployment benefits and in 1994 when labour law reform was approved in the Parliament with the votes of both the PSOE and the parties of the right. But the opposition was weaker than in 1988 because of the economic situation and because the unions changed their strategies. This change was partly due to their financial dependence on the state and their internal problems (conflicts among different factions both in the CC.OO and the UGT, important financial problems derived from UGT involvement in housing projects) and also because the government was successful in developing a policy of partial agreements with unions and employers' organizations in some specific areas (training, labour, health, and security) (Recio, 1998; Cachon y Palacio, 1999; Reina, 1999; Espina, 1999).

7. Government Intervention in the Economy

Those who directed the socialist economic policy were convinced that the modernization of the Spanish productive sectors had to come from the private sector. Their confidence in the correctness of this approach is explained first by their ideological orientation and, second, by their negative evaluation of the Spanish historical experience of high protectionism and 'socialization of losses', which had happened when bank-

rupt companies had been nationalized, generating productive inefficiency and costs which were higher than those of other competing
countries. Third, they were convinced that particular features of
Spanish companies meant that these were not a good base on which to
build autonomous productive development. The entry of multinationals was seen as a desirable alternative. Fourth, they lacked faith in the
public sector, which they saw as the paradigm of inefficiency (Segura,
1990). Because of all this, their political actions were focused on the
gradual liberalization, internally and externally, of the Spanish economy
(Etxezarreta, 1991).

In practice, the socialist government had to adapt its general
orientation to the difficult economic situation, especially in the first
phase, when it had to face up to the restructuring of sectors in crisis, not
only in manufacturing but also in the energy and banking sectors. The
financial rehabilitation of the sectors in crisis, the reduction of excess
productive capacity and of staff, required substantial financial aid
(unrepaid subsidies, the pardoning of fiscal debts and social security
payments, low interest loans, etc.) (González Calvet, 1991; Segura,
1992). This aid was devoted to the restructuring of 14 industrial areas
of activity in crisis, some of which were dominated by state-owned
companies (ship building, iron and steel making, aluminium, etc.), and
others by the private sector (textile, fertilizers, electrical parts, etc.),
including multinationals (Alcatel, Robert Bosch, etc.). The electrical
sector, which in 1982 was in a serious crisis owing to some unrealistic
plans for investment in nuclear power stations, and the financial sector
(both banks and insurance companies) were major beneficiaries of
public support. The banking sector also gained indirectly through the
restructuring of industrial or energy companies, in which the banks had
large holdings or to which they had made loans.

On the other hand, government activity has been quite sluggish in
helping the creation of new industries, being restricted to general
measures (e.g. the Innovation and Technological Development Plan),
and especially to the attraction of multinational companies via various
kinds of subsidies and assistance (the most important being those
carried out in the Urgent Reindustrialization Zones (Montes and
Carrasco, 1996)). The combination of macroeconomic and microeconomic policies carried out, the general tendency towards economic
globalization, and public assistance explain one of the most important
economic changes during this period: the large-scale entry of foreign
multinational groups, which came to control the majority of Spanish
industrial sectors, and which have tended to cause Spanish productive
capacity to be specialized in particular segments of the market (Recio,
1992; Montes, 1993; Martín and Velázquez, 1996; Castañer, 1998).

The PSOE government also instituted a policy of gradual privatization of public firms, including rehabilitated industrial companies (SEAT, Acenor, etc.) and, since 1987, this was extended to publicly owned utility companies (telephones, electricity, oil and gas distribution). Liberalization also includes the development of new activities regulated by means of operating licences (cellular telephones, waste management, and so forth). Many of these 'old' and 'new' public services are controlled by banking and construction companies and this has reinforced their core position in the Spanish economy (Martinez de Pablos, 1991) .

It is significant that, whereas in the industrial sector no large groupings have been created at an international level, the banking groups and utilities (with close connections with banks) have in fact gained important international positions. In the Spanish market, banking groups maintained substantial privileges (Pérez, 1999).

Construction has also expanded internationally with a few groups (in several cases, directly connected to banks) monopolizing most of the public works and maintaining a captive market which has also been central to one of the worst aspects of the experience of the socialist government: the corruption which in many cases has been part of the public tendering process. 'Transparency' and 'honesty' in the use of public money were promises in the 1982 electoral programme, and part of the socialist electoral success can be explained by the hopes that these promises awakened in many citizens. The proliferation of all kinds of cases of corruption, in some cases to finance the party and in others for personal gain, dashed these hopes. Of course, this phenomenon has not only been associated with the Socialist Party, as right-wing parties have been exposed as indulging in this kind of practice where they have been in power at a regional or municipal level. What stands out is that the widespread impression among citizens is that in this area the Socialist Party was no different at all from the other political groups.

8. Taxation and Welfare State

Table 4 shows the change in the share of taxation,[11] which increased significantly and continually until 1992 before declining. In 1982, the Spanish taxation schedule was not very progressive, given the great

---

[11] On the change in public spending and income since 1970, see González Calvet (1998). One should remember that growing proportions of income and, especially, of spending do not depend on the national government but on municipal and regional governments.

Table 4
Fiscal Pressure in Spain, 1982–95 (as % of GDP)

	Total	Direct taxes	Indirect taxes	Social security contributions
1982	27.9	6.9	7.7	13.2
1989	36.2	12.3	10.9	13.0
1992	38.5	12.6	11.3	14.6
1995	35.9	11.7	10.7	13.5
Changes (% GDP)				
1982/95	+8.0	+4.7	+3.0	+0.3

	As % of total taxes		
	Direct taxes	Indirect taxes	Social security contributions
1982	24.8	27.7	47.5
1989	33.9	30.1	36.0
1992	32.9	29.3	37.9
1995	33.2	28.4	38.4

Notes: Fiscal pressure includes taxes and social security contributions. It does not include other types of revenues.
Source: Calculated from Instituto Nacional de Estadística, *Contabilidad Nacional de España*.

weight of indirect taxes and social security contributions. Direct taxes made up less than a quarter of total taxes. The socialist governments increased the direct taxation burden, which grew until the end of the 1980s, both as a proportion of the GDP and also of total taxes (Table 4).

The main direct tax in Spain, the Personal Income Tax, grew the most. This is a tax with a highly progressive scale, although in practice this progressive nature is much reduced by the high level of tax evasion, especially by employers and self-employed professionals (Garde, 1995). The socialist governments fought tax evasion, which decreased, especially after a value-added tax was introduced in 1986, but it continued to be high because the resources allocated to this battle were limited, and because the matter was not always considered to be a political priority. Tax evasion and the various possible, and legal, ways of making deductions, used above all by high-income families, mean that taxes are paid disproportionately by wage earners (Sogo, 1994; Lagares, 1996).

The weight of the income tax increased, especially in the first few years of the PSOE government, largely as a result of fiscal drag which was probably especially severe for those on lower incomes (González Páramo, 1988). In 1985, 1988, and 1991, there were fiscal reforms which significantly altered the taxation scales. The first two clearly increased the progressive aspect of the taxation schedule, while the third acted slightly in the opposite way (Lasheras *et al.*, 1993). Furthermore, the 1991 fiscal reform considerably reduced the burden on certain property incomes. The overall balance is thus that the fiscal system became significantly more progressive during the 1980s,[12] although later there was a slight regression.

Table 5 shows the trend in public spending for the same period of 1982–95. The large increase in public spending, 9.5 per cent of GDP, is explained almost equally by two factors: the growing weight of interest payments on public debt (owing to the effects of the government deficit in a context of high interest rates as we saw in section 3), and the spending normally identified with the welfare state, i.e. payments to families and for basic services such as health and education.

'Social spending' expanded during the first few years of the socialist government, increased somewhat less than the GDP in the first period of growth from 1985 to 1988, and then increased more rapidly, partly owing to pressure from unions and other sections of society. The economic crisis of 1992–3 also contributed to the increase in social spending as a proportion of GDP. Finally, from 1993 to 1995, the reduction of social spending has been a fundamental element in the adjustments designed to allow the Spanish economy to come within the Maastricht limits.

The system of unemployment benefits has never had a universal coverage in Spain (Toharia, 1996). To receive the dole, one must have worked previously for a minimum period of time. It is a dual system, with two kinds of benefits: the first one (the contributory benefit) tied to the previous social security contributions, at a high proportion of the previous salary, but only for a limited period which depends on the number of years of contribution. The second (non-contributory welfare) allows some to receive 75 per cent of the minimum wage, but only for those workers whose family depends on them economically, whose

---

[12] According to our estimates, the average 1982 income-tax rates for a typical qualified worker with a university degree were 17.3 per cent (single, no children) and 15.6 per cent (married, two children, no other family income). In 1992, these rates had risen to 22.6 per cent and 18.6 per cent respectively. For an unskilled worker, the rates had gone down over the same period from 10.9 per cent (single) and 4.9 per cent (married, two children) to 8.1 per cent and 1.4 per cent.

Table 5
Government Spending in Spain, 1982–95 (as % of GDP)

	Total	Interest on public debt	Total without interest	Main social expenses	Other expenses
1982	37.6	1.0	36.6	19.8	16.8
1985	42.4	3.4	39.0	21.8	17.1
1988	41.1	3.4	37.7	21.4	16.3
1991	45.3	3.9	41.4	23.2	18.2
1993	49.6	5.2	44.4	26.0	18.5
1995	47.1	5.4	41.7	24.7	17.0
Variation (% GDP)					
1982/95	+9.5	+4.4	+5.1	+4.9	+0.2

Social expenses (as % of GDP)

	Pensions	Unemployment	Health	Education	Other
1982	8.2	2.6	4.3	3.0	1.7
1985	9.1	2.8	4.7	3.8	1.5
1988	8.8	2.7	4.7	3.9	1.3
1991	9.2	3.2	5.1	4.1	1.6
1993	10.4	3.7	5.9	4.5	1.5
1995	10.5	2.6	5.9	4.3	1.4
Variation (% GDP)					
1982/95	+2.3	+0.0	+1.6	+1.3	–0.3

Notes: The 'other expenses' column includes a wide variety of spending categories, among which are: defence, government investments, transfers to public and private companies, etc. 'Pensions' includes all kinds of old-age, widows', and disability pensions.
Source: Calculated from Instituto Nacional de Estadística, *Contabilidad Nacional de España*. The estimates of health and education public spending are those of the FIES Foundation (see Departamento de Estadística y Coyuntura de la Fundación FIES, 1996, p. 16).

normal unemployment benefits have run out, and who can demonstrate a situation of need with all that this implies in terms of social stigma.[13]

When the socialist government came to power, less than one-third of the unemployed received some kind of benefit. In 1984, a reform was introduced which increased the period during which benefits based on contributions could be received , extended the coverage of the means-

[13] The socialists also created a special benefit for temporary agricultural workers in Andalucia and Extremadura (regions with strong socialist majorities), which required the local authorities to certify that the beneficiary had worked a minimum number of days. In the opinion of many, this created a great deal of political clientelism.

tested safety-net for those whose entitlements had run out, and reduced the differential between the maximum and minimum contributory benefits. However, the reform did not change things drastically, and the majority of the unemployed continued without any kind of benefit. Subsequently the government's policy was guided by the idea that unemployment benefits were too generous and were one of the fundamental causes of the high unemployment rate. However, in 1989 it was obliged to give in to union pressure and extend the system to many other groups, especially those unemployed who were close to retiring age.[14] These measures and increased job turnover meant that many more workers had the right to receive unemployment benefits, and thus spending on unemployment rose.

In 1992, and to a lesser extent in 1994, there were important changes which restricted the period, the amounts, and the conditions of unemployment benefits. It should be noted that these reforms, challenged by the unions, were justified not only as a means of slowing the growth in public spending, but also as a means of improving the efficiency of the labour market and reducing unemployment, because of the dole's supposedly negative effect on labour supply. This was despite the fact that there was no clear evidence that the probability of getting a job was affected by the greater or lesser period to which a worker was entitled to receive unemployment benefits (Cebrián *et al.*, 1996). It is striking that spending on unemployment was the same proportion of GDP in 1995 as it had been in 1982, yet unemployment had increased from 16.4 per cent to 22.3 per cent of the active population.

The figures for public spending on pensions show an overall increase of 2.3 per cent of GDP, although in the final years of this period spending stabilized. The ageing population is obviously one of the factors which explain this increase, but there are also other factors which made spending grow in the early years of the socialist government, such as the use of early retirement as the main way of avoiding simple lay-offs in companies in crisis, and the lack of control over disability pensions, which were sometimes granted when they were not deserved.

During the socialist governments, the overall situation of the majority of pensioners, who also benefited from various social programmes, improved significantly. Most contributory pension minima increased significantly until the beginning of the 1990s, although later this tendency ceased completely. Average pensions increased continually in

---

[14] Carlos Solchaga explains this extension as an agreement between the Ministry of Labour and the unions, to which he was always opposed (Solchaga, 1997, pp. 291–4).

real terms, especially as a result of workers on higher salaries retiring. The very low old-age and disability pensions, for those without sufficient contributions and in need, increased sharply in 1990 in response to union demands.

In 1985 the socialist government brought in an important reform of the pension system, and later promoted an agreement between almost all the political forces on future lines of reform (Pactos de Toledo, in 1995). The first objective was to reduce public pensions for future pensioners in general in order to prevent the ageing of the population from significantly increasing the proportion of the GDP spent on pensions. It was made more difficult to receive contributory pensions. This may have helped to avoid some pension fraud, but it excluded many of those workers who have not worked continuously throughout their working life, which has become very relevant in the context of the increase in temporary contracts, and especially for women who retire from the labour market many years before reaching the retirement age. Pensions were made more actuarial, by making the benefits depend more on the contributions paid throughout one's working life. Finally, the policy of reduction in state benefits has been accompanied by the promotion of complementary private pension plans. The representatives of finance capital, who have had excellent relations with the socialist governments in many cases, have pressed hard for a more congenial environment for private pension funds. So the private funds have been favoured by tax deductions for private pension payments which especially benefit middle and high income taxpayers.

There were important improvements in spending on education and on health. Health spending had highly progressive, redistributive effects (Bandrés, 1995; Calonge and Manresa, 1997), and the government managed to ensure that practically the entire population had access to the public health system, although it is significant that this was not considered an automatic right for the whole population.[15] Public spending on primary education not only financed state schools, but also the private ones to which mostly the middle classes send their children. In practice, this dual system of primary schools contributes to social stratification. Spending on health and education have both been strongly affected by the policy of cuts in public spending, and this has been despite the fact that such spending as a proportion of GDP is lower than that of the majority of EU countries, especially as regards spending on education.

[15] Although these criteria are not always strictly applied, in theory free access to public health services happens via social security contributions (for workers, pensioners, and family dependants), or via social services for the 'poor'.

Table 6
Distribution of Available Monetary Income, 1980 and 1990
(% of income in each decile)

Decile	1980/1	1990/1
First	2.7	3.1
Second	4.6	5.0
Third	5.7	6.1
Fourth	6.8	7.0
Fifth	7.9	8.1
Sixth	9.0	9.2
Seventh	10.4	10.5
Eighth	12.2	12.2
Ninth	15.2	14.9
Tenth	25.4	23.9
Gini index	0.330	0.305

Note: To go from family income to individual income, household income is equivalized using the OECD scale.
Source: Data from Family Budget Surveys (see Alvárez Aledo *et al.*, 1996, pp. 167–8).

Government spending on housing, for which the figures do not appear in the table, is very low. Housing policy has basically consisted of tax deductions for housing mortgages, which benefits those with middle and higher incomes, rather than families on low incomes. For years, one could have deductions for buying a dwelling that was not even one's normal place of residence. The deductions did not have a redistributive aim, but rather created an incentive for construction activity.

9. Income and Wealth Distribution

Unfortunately, we do not have reliable data on the changes in personal income distribution which would allow us to measure this change over all the period of the Socialist Party government.

The only reasonably reliable data we have are from the Family Budget Surveys of 1980–1 and 1990–1, which show a clear improvement in the distribution of income (and of spending) (Table 6). However, these data should be assessed critically, for several reasons (Naredo, 1994). This kind of survey does not reflect the two extremes very well, and these could have grown further apart. That is, the incomes of the very rich are significantly undervalued, and those of people in situations of extreme poverty, such as the homeless, are not included.

Moreover, the economic growth period of the second half of the 1980s generated very large increases in the value of assets. This increased the difference between rich and poor, although the importance of this factor cannot be grasped from the information provided by the Family Budget Surveys (Naredo, 1996).

In any case, the apparent improvement in income distribution of the 1980s should be viewed in the context of the analysis above as resulting from the coincidence of a series of favourable factors. The 1980s saw the consolidation of the recently created Personal Income Tax. Furthermore, in 1985 and 1988, there were tax changes which were advantageous for the lower-income families. Inequalities in gross salaries became worse in the private sector, but this was partially compensated for by taxation changes (Roca and Gonzalez Calvet, 1999). Also, there was an increase in public employment, with its characteristically smaller wage differentials (Ayala *et al.*, 1995). There were also significant improvements in the majority of basic pensions. The economic situation in 1990–1 was one of growth, and there had just been an extension in the coverage of unemployment benefits. However, one should take into account that a very great part of the unemployed in Spain are young people living with their parents (Garcia Serrano *et al.*, 1999)

During the 1990s, the improvements in old-age and disability non-contributory pensions[16] probably reduced the risk of absolute poverty. However, the majority of favourable factors which are apparent when we compare the beginning and the end of the 1980s did not continue after this decade. Taxation did not become more progressive, unemployment benefits were cut, minimum pensions were frozen in real terms, and government employment was affected by public spending cuts. So it is quite possible that in the first half of the 1990s there was an increase in income inequality, or at least that it did not continue to decrease, although we have no reliable data to test this hypothesis.[17]

[16] Together with other social programmes for those in situations of extreme poverty, which depend on regional governments and thus not on decisions of the national government.

[17] The only unsatisfactory source we have is the *Encuesta Continua de Presupuestos Familiares*. Using this source, the Banco Bilbao-Vizcaya (*Informe Económico 1995*, p. 165) has published the annual income Gini index figures for 1986–94. This index decreases from 1986 (0.356) until 1988 (0.345), but then has no clear tendency, and its value in 1994 (0.343) is practically the same as in 1988.

10. A Sceptical Assessment

Can we consider the economic policy put into practice by the PSOE government to be a social democratic alternative to the wave of neo-liberal policies? In general terms, we consider that the answer to this question must be negative, although some important qualifications must be made.

Among the data which suggest an affirmative answer are the slight improvement in income distribution during the period of expansion of the pension system, the consolidation of the new progressive income tax, and the strong increase in spending on public services. But one must bear in mind that these advances started from a situation of greater inequality in comparison with other European countries, and very low levels of social protection. Furthermore, some of the advances in the areas of redistributive policies and welfare spending came about because of the pressure of social movements (trade unions, neighbour-hood associations, etc.) which forced the government to adopt some measures that had not been part of its plans. And then, at the end of its period in office, and in the context of the integration into the EU, even some of these social advances were beginning to be challenged, as can be seen from the projects to reform the system of state pensions. Another achievement was the great creation of non-agrarian employ-ment since 1985, even though it remained highly vulnerable to the economic situation, as the last economic recession showed.

The most negative element was probably the push to change the labour market, which in many areas conceded a disproportionate power to employers, and converted the working life of many people into an experience dominated by insecurity and lack of autonomy, eroding the already limited strength of the trade unions. The organi-zation of the workers has not been seen at all as balancing asymmetrical power relations between labour and capital, but as an obstacle to the efficient functioning of the labour market.

Nor in the productive sectors have the socialist policies departed from the dominant model. Although it is true that opening up the economy to foreign competition has produced improvements in pro-ductivity, the modernization project has ended up being basically a rearrangement of the large Spanish oligopolistic groups, which have rehabilitated and reoriented their activities, and permission for multi-national groups to control Spanish industry. The Spanish economy largely depends on the ups and downs of the world economy and is disproportionately vulnerable to its cyclical crises.

It also seems necessary to emphasize that the priorities of public investment and economic policy in general have not taken into account one of the main challenges today, the integration of environmental policy into economic decision-making as a whole. An alternative economic policy ought to include other instruments for measuring economic success, different from the traditional indicators, in order to take into account factors such as environmental degradation and resource depletion. The left should be concerned not only about intragenerational equity but also about intergenerational equity.

The coming to power of a new, right-wing government in Spain has not meant a radical break with the economic policy of the PSOE. The labour and pension reforms passed recently continued the earlier trend and have had the parliamentary backing of the socialists. The conservatives have also continued a policy of partial agreements with employers and unions. This does not mean that there are no important differences, such as a lesser commitment to a progressive taxation system (already there have been important regressive decisions in this respect), much less concern for the access of the whole of the population to quality essential services, whose management is beginning to be privatized in some cases, and greater deregulation in some sectors, such as the energy sector.

Thus, in our view, the experience of Spain cannot be seen as a successful example of putting into practice an alternative model to the dominant neo-liberal one. On the contrary, it demonstrates the cultural success of this model, and just how difficult it is to find ways of carrying out economic policy that directs economic activity towards an overall improvement in equality, towards greater personal autonomy, and towards greater ecological sustainability. The commitment of many socialist leaders to such values was very weak, or even non-existent, but one must recognize the objective difficulties which must be faced by any left-wing alternative which tries to introduce important changes. These difficulties come from international economic institutions and the concentration of economic power, and in the case of Spain there was also a series of specific problems connected with the economic and political legacy which made a left-wing economic policy even more difficult.

8

New Labour's Economic Policy

ANDREW GLYN AND STEWART WOOD*

1. Introduction

Social democratic parties have returned to power across Western Europe in the 1990s. However, as the contributions to this volume show, the rediscovery of electoral success has been accompanied by a marked ideological and policy shift away from the traditional terrain of social democracy. Nowhere has this shift been espoused with more enthusiasm, or coincided with a more spectacular victory at the polls, than in the case of the British Labour Party under the leadership of Tony Blair, cloaked in the embryonic ideology of the 'Third Way'. Since taking over from John Smith in 1994, Blair has continually stressed the need to 'modernize' traditional social democratic policy platforms, advocating an 'adherence to our values but also a willingness to change our old approaches and traditional policy instruments' (Blair and Schröder, 1999). To many, the rapid policy movement that Blair has initiated seems more like an ideological retreat than modernization. For example, Labour's 1992 election manifesto contained commitments to raise the top rate of income tax from 40 per cent to 50 per cent, to restore the link between the state pension and average earnings, and to increase welfare spending significantly. By the time Labour returned to power in a landslide electoral victory in May 1997, 'New Labour' (as the leadership renamed the party) had abandoned these commitments, pledging instead to retain the existing top rate of income tax and to abide by Tory spending plans for the first 2 years of government.

But to what extent has the New Labour government abandoned social democratic ambitions and policies? Two-thirds through one term

*Corpus Christi College, University of Oxford, and Magdalen College, University of Oxford, respectively. Our thanks to Perry Anderson, Wendy Carlin, Esra Erdem, Des King, Bob Rowthorn, and Stuart White for helpful comments and to Carl Emmerson, Holly Sutherland, and Jayne Taylor for valuable information.

in office the contours of Labour's economic policy seem clear enough. This chapter examines the main economic policies of the Blair government, and provides an assessment of their content and likely consequences. It covers macroeconomic and spending policies, where 'prudence' rules and where control over interest rates has been delegated to the Bank of England, before proceeding to aspects of welfare policy and implications for income distribution. The focus then shifts to education and training, which Blair has stressed as central to economic policy, and finally to broader issues of industrial and industrial relations policy. Preoccupation with the supply side is the most distinctive aspect of Labour policy, combining a wholesale reorientation of the welfare state towards encouraging work with abandonment of both the interventionist policies towards industry and the collaboration with trade unions so characteristic of social democracy in the 1960s and 1970s.

2. Macroeconomic Policy

Labour's macroeconomic policy places overriding importance on devising a framework for economic stability. This has both political and economic origins. Economic mismanagement was widely blamed for Labour's loss of power in 1979 in the aftermath of the collapse of its pay policy in the 'winter of discontent'. Thirteen years later the Tory government suffered an irretrievable collapse of support after sterling's ignominious exit from the European Exchange Rate Mechanism (see King, 1998). Avoidance of such macroeconomic debacles has accordingly been a political priority. In narrower economic terms the UK suffered extremely severe recessions in both the early 1980s and early 1990s, punctuated by the unsustainable Lawson boom. The government's 1999 budget statement noted: 'Over the past three decades, the UK economy has exhibited high volatility in output and inflation. . . . The Government has reformed the framework for macroeconomic policy to promote economic stability. . . . Stability is essential for high levels of growth and employment' (HM Treasury, 1999, Economic and Fiscal Strategy Report, paras 2.1, 2.3, 2.4). Securing steady growth at the long-term sustainable rate is hardly controversial as an objective. The question is how to achieve it?

Monetary policy has been placed in the hands of the Monetary Policy Committee (MPC), with Bank of England officials in the majority and the remainder economists appointed by the government. The MPC is charged with hitting the government's inflation target of 2.5 per cent per year. The idea is that interest rates would be changed in a timely manner to offset inflationary or deflationary pressures. Removing monetary policy from short-term political manipulation is supposed to enhance its 'credibility' in the eyes of the financial markets and the government claims the reduction in the differential between German and UK bond yields (from more than 1 per cent in the months before the election to around 0.25 per cent in the autumn of 1999) as a significant achievement. The MPC is charged with hitting the inflation target, not staying beneath it, and this is supposed to prevent over-zealous central bankers focusing solely on minimizing inflation without regard to the consequences for employment.

Labour's pursuit of longer-term goals has extended to fiscal policy as well. The government has 'set two strict fiscal rules to deliver sound public finances': first, the *golden rule* decrees that on average over the economic cycle, the government will borrow only to invest and not to fund current spending; second the government pledges that its (net) debt 'will be held over the economic cycle at a stable and prudent level' (HM Treasury, 1999, para 2.16). With government (net) investment forecast to average only 1 per cent of GDP per year up to 2003–4, the public sector's net debt should gently decline to less than 40 per cent of GDP. Reaching this trajectory has involved a severe fiscal squeeze. Between 1996–7 and 1998–9 the government estimates that the cyclically adjusted deficit will have fallen by almost 4 per cent of GDP.

This policy framework does not necessarily constrain macroeconomic policy from acting to support demand and employment. If unemployment was rising and inflation was below the target, the Bank of England would be expected to cut interest rates and the government could allow the automatic fiscal stabilizers to work and even engage in some discretionary fiscal expansion as well. The real test of the policy will come if unemployment was rising and inflation was above the target; only then would the claim that the Bank of England can 'respond where necessary with discretion' and 'without paying a high price in terms of lost output' (Balls, 1998) be put to the test. Under such circumstances it would obviously be convenient for the government to deflect criticism by blaming the Bank of England for high or rising interest rates.

Unemployment declined steadily over the government's first two and a half years, but before attributing this to successful macroeconomic policy it is important to remember that no previous Labour government had inherited such a favourable economic conjuncture. When Labour took office, unemployment had been falling for 4 years as the sharp depreciation in 1992 set in train a strong export recovery; inflation was about 2 per cent per year and the world economy was delivering steadily growing export markets and stable commodity prices. Even the government deficit, which had reached an alarming 7.9 per cent of GDP in 1993/4, had been halved. This favourable pattern has been maintained under Labour and by the middle of 1999 unemployment had fallen to 5.8 per cent (not much more than one half the level in France, Germany, and Italy) without serious signs of resurgent inflation. Thus the government's macroeconomic framework consolidated the expansion which was launched by the monetary policy implemented by the Tory Chancellor, Kenneth Clarke, after 1992. However, this expansion was more fragile than appeared at first sight.

The weak point has been the chronic overvaluation of sterling, to which higher interest rates than elsewhere in Europe have contributed. Sterling's effective rate rose 24 per cent between the middle of 1996 and 1998. Worse still, this appreciation has occurred while unit wage costs grew faster in the UK than elsewhere. This has led to terrific pressure on UK industry, with relative unit labour costs rising by 41 per cent between 1993 and 1998. As a consequence, cost competitiveness has been dragged down to the level reached in 1981 in the depths of Thatcher's monetary squeeze. The result of the high exchange rate is that the expansion has been severely biased away from manufacturing. Manufacturing output in the middle of 1999 was only 3 per cent higher than a decade before. This has contributed to the maintenance of large regional differentials in joblessness (discussed below). However, the high exchange rate contributed to holding down inflation; a fall in sterling to more competitive levels would have pushed up import prices and reduced the competitive pressure on UK firms selling in the domestic market. It is probable that it was the overvalued pound which allowed unemployment to fall so low without compromising the inflation target. If sterling were to fall sharply to a more realistic long-run level, then the MPC would feel obliged to slam on the brakes, and the implication for jobs of privileging the inflation target would become clear.

Further falls in unemployment, while staying within the inflation target, depend on policies to reduce the unemployment rate at which inflation would begin to rise (the non-accelerating inflation rate of unemployment—NAIRU). The more optimistic of the government's longer-term projections assume that 'improved labour market performance leads to a ½ percentage point decline in the sustainable rate of unemployment (or NAIRU) in both 1999 and 2000 and a further ¼ percentage point reduction in 2001' (HM Treasury, 1999, p. 128). Policies to achieve this 'supply-side' improvement are the core of Labour's economic programme.

3. Employment, Welfare to Work, and the New Deal

Keynesians regard unemployment as being largely 'involuntary', in that the unemployed would work for the going level of wages if jobs were available. Expanding aggregate demand allows them to find work. However, it is the involuntarily unemployed who constitute the reserve army of labour and thus hold in check wage bargaining (see Carlin and Soskice, 1990, ch. 6). So the possibilities of reducing unemployment by a durable macroeconomic expansion are limited to situations where the economy has 'surplus' unemployment (that is, more than the NAIRU). But is it really the case that all types of unemployed worker are equally 'effective' as members of the reserve army? Richard Layard, now economic adviser at the Department for Education and Employment (DfEE,) has argued forcefully that the long-term unemployed in particular exert little downward pressure on wage bargaining as they are semi-detached from the labour market (e.g. Layard, 1997). They are too demoralized or stigmatized by employers to be actively or realistically seeking work. If they can be enticed or cajoled back into searching for work (or if employers can be persuaded that they are in fact employable) then the extra competition they inject into the labour market will bring downward pressure on wages. This would allow a more expansionary demand-management policy to generate extra jobs, without the inflationary pressure which would otherwise result. The NAIRU would be reduced and the sustainable level of employment increased.

If successful, such a policy leads not only to lower unemployment but also to higher tax receipts (from the incomes of the additional people at work) and reduced social security benefits (to those previously unemployed). Even quite expensive policies (in terms of employment subsidies or in-work benefits) could pay for themselves if they brought many more earners and thus tax-payers. Moreover, this approach can be extended from the long-term unemployed to other groups who are not working. Lone parents with small children, people claiming disability benefits, those in early retirement because of lack of work, and partners of unemployed people caught in the benefit system's 'unemployment trap' may all be targets for persuasion, by an appropriate mixture of incentives and sanctions, to re-enter the labour force. The downward pressure on wages which these additional recruits to the reserve army would bring would allow faster growth. Sustainable employment would rise and non-employment would fall.[1]

[1] Labour-force participation by people not previously counted as unemployed would not reduce the NAIRU, but would raise the sustainable level of employment. The principles behind the New Deal are summarized in paras 4.9 and 4.10 of the Economic and Fiscal Strategy Report (HM Treasury, 1999).

The standard bearer for the New Deal programmes is that relating to the young long-term unemployed (18–24-year-olds unemployed for more than 6 months). They enter a 'gateway' period of intensive career counselling; if they do not move into education or a job they choose one of four 'options': a 6-month job, with the employer subsidized by £60 per week (or help with becoming self-employed); work with a voluntary organization; work with an environmental task-force (where they receive a little more than benefit); or, if their educational level is considered a serious hindrance to their finding work, a period of formal education of up to 12 months (Undy, 1999). There is no 'fifth option' of simply remaining on unemployment benefit. Similar schemes, either on a pilot or economy-wide basis, but so far usually voluntary, have been introduced for other age groups of the long-term unemployed, lone parents, the partners of unemployed people, and the disabled.

In addition to making people on benefits more 'employable' the government has reformed the system of in-work benefits for families with children and disabled people, to help 'make work pay'. The biggest change has been the Working Families Tax Credit (WFTC), aimed at guaranteeing any family with a full-time worker £214 per week (by spring 2001). It was set at a considerably more generous level than the Family Credit programme which it replaced, and was boosted by an additional subsidy to cover child-care expenses for the low paid. Those on low earnings will also benefit from adjustments to the bottom end of the tax and national insurance schedules. The 1999 Budget (HM Treasury, 1999, Table 4.2) claimed that the number of those at work who face effective marginal tax (and withdrawal of benefit) rates of more than 70 per cent has fallen from 715,000 to 230,000.[2] Single-earner families with two children will be £30–40 per week better off over quite a range of weekly earnings (£120–280 per week).[3]

The *Financial Times* (23 March 1999) reported, under the headline 'Brown plans tax credit for all in employment', that:

> The government wants to give a guaranteed minimum income to all people in work as part of a comprehensive plan to integrate the tax and benefit

[2] However, the inevitable effect of greater generosity and slower withdrawal of benefits is that many more people receive (and lose) them so that numbers on marginal rates of more than 60 per cent *rise* from 730,000 to 915,000.

[3] By transforming a range of benefits into tax credits the government also contrived to reduce measures of the social security bill (with tax credits not included) and the average burden of taxation (tax credits counting as negative taxation). By 2001–2 tax credits will be cutting the tax bill by 0.6 per cent of GDP—shades of Mrs Thatcher's massaging of the public-sector deficit by subtracting receipts from privatization!

systems. . . . The absorption of benefits in the new employment tax credit, as the Treasury has christened it, would be the culmination of Gordon Brown's ambition to provide subsidized jobs for those fit for work. Only the chronically disabled and lone parents with very young children would be expected to live on benefits.

The implication is that the element of compulsion in the New Deal, so far most apparent in the 'no fifth option' for the young long-term unemployed, will be applied much more generally. This represents a radical redefinition of the functions of the welfare state, and raises a number of questions about the tension between compulsion and individual rights in social democratic thinking (King, 1999; White, 2000). Although welfare rights in Britain since 1945 have been predominantly 'unconditional', the widely praised 'welfare to work' model in Sweden has always relied upon pressures from withdrawal of unemployment benefits after a fixed period (Esping-Andersen, 1990). Of course, such compulsion to take up an employment or training alternative to benefits depends very much on what these alternatives really offer.

In assessing the economic impact of the British version of 'welfare to work', three issues are particularly important.

- How big will the effect be on labour supply, i.e. on the number actively seeking work?
- Will jobs be available?
- What will be the effect on the pattern of wages?

If the New Deal for the young long-term unemployed really increases their 'employability', then substantially more of those who enter the 'gateway' should be employed after leaving the New Deal than would otherwise be the case. This would then cumulate into a substantial impact on the stock of people in or actively seeking work. Even if a subsidized job had no longer-term effects on the job prospect of the person concerned, and was simply used by employers as a substitute for another worker, there would be some effect on wage pressure if those 'displaced' by the New Dealers were more 'effective' in job search.

Numbers who have passed through the New Deal into unsubsidized jobs can provide impressive sound bites for politicians, but convey little information about the true impact of the programme since many would have found work anyway. Analysis by the National Institute (reported in the *Financial Times*, 12 July 2000) suggests that the New Deal may have increased employment of young people by a very modest 13,000 by the spring of 2000. Youth unemployment was estimated to be reduced by

41,000, with the difference accounted for by some of those who would have been unemployed moving into education or one of the other options.

Blundell and Reed (1999) report a number of studies which modelled the effects of WFTC and which agree that those actively seeking work may increase by some 30,000 (with increased participation by lone mothers and people with non-working partners offsetting reduced participation by people whose partner was already working and who would receive more benefits under the proposals). Somewhat similar effects result from the reductions in national insurance and from the introduction of the new 10p income tax rate (Gregg *et al.*, 1999) and the minimum wage would further tend to increase labour-force participation (especially of women). Combined with the impact of other measures to increase job search, it is quite possible that the whole New Deal/ Making Work Pay programme could increase the effective labour supply by around 100,000. If these estimates are roughly accurate, they suggest a distinctly modest effect (perhaps ½ per cent rise in the labour force or ¾ on the Treasury's more optimistic forecast).

In simulations, the impacts on the labour supply are often reported as 'employment effects'. This begs the very important question of whether Say's Law (supply creates its own demand) really applies in the labour market. It is important to reiterate that the mechanism proposed is fundamentally macroeconomic, with the extra competition in the labour market reducing inflationary pressure. As a result, the MPC can take a more relaxed attitude to interest rates and allow demand to expand. While not all those joining the labour supply would necessarily get jobs themselves, additional jobs would be created by the macro-economy until the unemployment rate as a whole falls to the new lower NAIRU. The most problematic part of this story is whether the posited additions to the labour supply would really bring the expected easing of wage pressure.

The emphasis in the economic analysis underlying the strategy is on the impact of employment status on wage pressure—the short-term unemployed look actively for work and constitute effective labour-market competition; the long-term unemployed search less effectively and on average bring much less downward pressure on wages; those out of the labour force (e.g. lone parents) have no effect whatsoever. Transforming the position of the long-term unemployed, or lone parents, so that they are both involuntarily unemployed and employable in the eyes of employers, will swell the reserve army and ease wage pressure. But if the long-term unemployed, lone parents, people taking early retirement, and those on sickness benefit disproportionately have low qualifications and live in areas of mass unemployment, then will their moving into active job search have much effect on the overall degree of wage pressure in the economy generally?

There is a huge jobs deficit in the old industrial areas, especially for jobs for the less qualified. In Merseyside, for example, a minority of men of working age without qualifications are working (though many fewer are categorized as unemployed). If the least qualified one-quarter of the population were to have as many jobs in the rest of the country as they do in the prosperous south-east, then there would have to be an additional 850,000 extra jobs for them (calculated from Labour Force Survey for 1998 — see Erdem and Glyn, 2000, for fuller discussion). Many of those brought into the labour force by the Welfare to Work measures will have relatively poor qualifications and will live in an area where labour demand is already weak, especially for the unskilled. Increasing the reserve army of labour in these areas is unlikely signifi-cantly to hold down wages in the economy as a whole and thus allow macroeconomic expansion. Conversely, macroeconomic expansion, to the extent that it really was facilitated, will definitely not create jobs *disproportionately* in the areas where Welfare to Work has most clients.

For the policy to work, either the less qualified would have to be encouraged to move to the high-employment southern parts of the UK or jobs would have to be created deliberately in the areas where labour supply is most expanded, reversing the process of job destruction which caused their unemployment and labour-force non-participation rates to be so high in the first place (see Turok and Webster, 1998, for trenchant criticism along these lines). However, the government has fought hard against the idea of a 'North–South divide' in employment, emphasizing instead the problem of localized employment blackspots (see Webster, 2000). Thus there is a New Deal for Communities aimed at the 'intensive regeneration of some of our poorest neighbourhoods' and Employ-ment Zones have been set up. But again most of the focus is on quality of life in the area and on special measures to make individuals there more employable, rather than on deliberate creation of work through public spending, introducing incentives for employers to locate in these areas, and so forth.

If substantial numbers of less-qualified people seeking work were to find jobs, what would be the implication for their wages? 'Making work pay' applies to employers as well as employees and they would only offer less-qualified people more jobs if the relative cost of less-qualified labour declined. There is a real danger that getting a large number of less-qualified people into the labour force by one means or another will drive down wages at the bottom of the pay scale. This could bring conflict with the minimum-wage regulations and would raise the cost of in-work benefits for those who have low-paid jobs already. To the extent that the New Deal really does improve skill levels, this problem would be reduced, but it is notoriously difficult substantially to raise the skill levels of many of those targeted by these schemes.

To summarize, the government's macroeconomic strategy puts great weight on increasing labour supply, though existing estimates suggest relatively modest effects. Moreover, the belief that raising labour supply will allow sustainable higher employment without inflationary pressure ignores the regional concentration of the workless. Ensuring that work is available for such people, without further substantial increases in pay dispersion, requires much more deliberate action to target increases in demand for labour on the areas and skill-groups most affected by joblessness.

One glaring absence in this whole approach concerns wage bargaining. Blair has repeatedly made it clear that New Labour's return to power after 18 years of Conservative government will not usher in the return of 'beer and sandwiches' at 10 Downing Street. Addressing the TUC Annual Congress in September 1999, Blair asserted that 'in many ways we have a better, clearer relationship than ever before between trade unions and Labour. . . . You run the unions. We run the government. We will never confuse the two again.' This renunciation by New Labour of Old Labour's corporatism has left the government without any means to encourage the kind of coordination of wage bargaining which appears to have played a significant part in a number of recent 'employment miracles', the Netherlands and Ireland, for example (Visser and Hemerijck, 1997).

Whenever wage increases appeared to be moving up, Gordon Brown has been reduced to urging employers and unions to show restraint in their wage bargaining. However, such appeals from the sidelines will fall on deaf ears unless there is a serious attempt to solve the coordination problem — why should any union in a strong bargaining position or employer with a shortage of skilled labour show restraint while there is no mechanism for ensuring that others will follow suit? Given the weakness of unions in wide sections of the private sector (Brown, 1994) and the employers' hostility towards constraints on their freedom of manoeuvre, attempting to steer them towards coordinated bargaining would be very difficult. But it seems that political considerations — fear of appearing to favour union power and corporatism — have dictated a prohibition even on discussion of the issue. In the event that the UK joins the euro, with no possibility of depreciation to offset faster cost increases, the issue of wage coordination will become, if anything, more important.

4. Income Distribution

Labour inherited a Britain with rapidly growing inequality. Between 1978 and 1990 household income inequality in the UK rose much more than in any other OECD country for which data are available (Gottschalk and Smeeding, 1997), more or less overturning all the reduction in household income inequality in the UK achieved since 1938. Tony Blair said in 1996, 'I believe in greater equality. If the next Labour Government has not raised the living standards of the poorest by the end of its time in office it will have failed' (*Guardian*, 16 December 1998). Blair has also committed himself to the very bold target of eliminating child poverty over 20 years (currently 30 per cent of UK children live in households with less than half average income, which appears to be the criterion of poverty he is using). Nevertheless his government clearly prefers to talk of social inclusion and equality of opportunity than to espouse the goal of equality of outcome.

The fundamental constraint which New Labour has set for itself is its commitment not to raise the tax burden.[4] It should be emphasized that the UK has a very low share of government expenditure by EU standards (in 1999 general government spending was some 40.8 per cent of UK GDP, compared with the EU average of 47.6 per cent, 47.1 per cent per cent in Germany, 54.1 per cent in France, and 60.2 per cent in Sweden, for example). A major contribution to the rise in inequality was Mrs Thatcher's decision to index benefits to prices rather than earnings. Since the poorest households receive most of their incomes from benefits, this inevitably drags down the share of the poorest groups whenever real incomes rise. New Labour steadfastly refused to reverse this general policy, arguing that benefits compensate for poverty rather than eliminate its causes.[5] The main thrust has been to concentrate support on 'work as the best way out of poverty' (HM Treasury, 1999, p. 65), as discussed in the previous section; quite consistent with this approach is to refuse to reinstate the link between benefits, especially for the unemployed. Aside from the increases in in-work benefits, the introduction of a minimum wage in April 1999, albeit at a level well below the proposal of trade unions, represents an

---

[4] Controversy abounds over precisely what measure is relevant here. The 1999 Budget shows the share of taxes in GDP (the broadest and most sensible measure) rising from 35.4 per cent in 1996/7 to 36.7 per cent in 2000/1, which will give plenty of scope for arguments about how much of the tax increases in New Labour's first year were 'Tory taxes' that Labour inherited.

[5] The 1999 Budget represented some retreat on this with its commitment to up-rate the Minimum Income Guarantee for pensioners (in effect a renamed and slightly more generous version of Income Support) by *earnings* in April 2000.

important policy initiative. Although its impact on the very bottom of the income distribution is limited because most of the poorest households have nobody working, it is still the case that the bottom decile gains most from the minimum wage; moreover, 70 per cent of those who benefit from the minimum wage live in the poorest 40 per cent of working households (Dickens, 1999).

The most comprehensive estimates of the impact of Labour's changes to the tax and benefit system up to the spring of 2000 show the worst-off 20 per cent of households gaining by around 8.5 per cent on average whereas the best-off 20 per cent lost around 0.5 per cent.[6] The worst-off 20 per cent of households with children, are estimated by the Treasury to be going to benefit by 30 per cent, which must make some inroads into the child poverty which Blair promised to reduce by 700,000 by the next election.

In one respect these figures underestimate the effect of Labour's measures for they are based on the present pattern of behaviour of households. If large numbers respond to the incentives provided by the WFTC, for example, and take a job, then the extra income they receive will constitute an additional gain for low-income groups over and above the extra benefits received by people already working. However, the analyses discussed earlier suggest that these effects will be relatively small and so the main effect on inequality of these measures comes via the boost to incomes of existing low-income workers.

Moreover, the estimates quoted earlier of the redistributive impact of Labour's measures give an over-optimistic impression of what is happening to inequality. The benchmark against which budget changes are measured is the up-rating of benefits in line with prices. With earnings tending to grow faster than prices, the incomes of those mainly dependent on benefits tend to fall systematically behind average incomes as a whole (the bottom 20 per cent are dependent on benefits for more than 80 per cent of their incomes). If the government does nothing (beyond increasing benefits in line with the cost of living) then the benefit system itself implies rising inequality.

In the first 2 years of the Labour government the measures implemented were not large enough to offset this 'benefit drag' and household income inequality increased. Institute for Fiscal Studies (IFS) calculations suggest incomes rose by less than 2 per cent for the typical household in the bottom 20 per cent, while the increase was 7 per cent for a typical household in the top 20 per cent. In real terms income per head rose about £2 per week at the bottom and £47 a week at the top.[7] Numbers in poverty (less than half average incomes) rose.

[6] IFS calculations available at www.ifs.org\budget. The figures would be a little larger if the impact of the minimum wage were included (see Immervoll et al., 1999).

[7] Information kindly supplied by Jayne Taylor of IFS.

Table 1
Government Spending
(average per cent per year increases of real spending)

	Blair government 1997–2002	Major government 1992–7	Thatcher and Major 1979–97
Health	4.7	2.6	3.1
Education	3.8	1.6	1.5
Defence	–0.6	–3.1	–0.2
Social security	1.5	3.8	3.5
Total spending	1.8	2.0	1.6

Note: Social security includes tax credits as spending (for comparability); when excluded (as they are in the total figure), the growth rate for social security spending is projected at 0.4 per cent per year.
Source: Chennells *et al.* (2000) plus updating and detail kindly supplied by Carl Emmerson (IFS) to include impact of the Comprehensive Spending Review of July 2000.

Now it is true that important measures, such as the WFTC and the minimum wage, had not come into effect in the period covered by these calculations. Overall the measures announced for Labour's first 4 years should bring some reduction in household income inequality if nothing else changes.[8] However, other factors may be pushing in the opposite direction. Over Labour's first 2 years the pay distribution widened only marginally, and interest payments, which benefit mainly the better off, stagnated. However, if shortages of skilled labour push up wages faster at the top end of the pay distribution, and if interest rates were to rise, then all Labour's measures would be absorbed simply in preventing inequality rising further. So it is quite possible that inequality will be only slightly, if at all, lower at the end of the government's first term in office than at the beginning. Of course this is better than the previous upward trend, but there is no chance of a substantial reversal of the unprecedented rise in inequality since 1979. This would require a major increase in the general level of benefits.

Although not included in the conventional figures on income distribution, spending programmes on the welfare state have an important egalitarian effect because the benefits are spread relatively evenly. The combination of reducing the budget deficit and holding the share of taxation (roughly) constant have inevitably constrained spending programmes. IFS calculations (Table 1) provide comparisons of real spend-

---

[8] Calculations carried out by Holly Sutherland with the Cambridge microsimulation model suggest that about one-half of the 'redistribution' from Labour's measures would be absorbed in preventing inequality from rising as a result of benefit drag.

ing increases planned by Labour, compared to both the preceding Major government and the whole 18 years of Tory rule.

The government is delivering distinctly faster increases in health and education spending than its Conservative predecessors, and, especially in the case of health, a definite rise in the share of GDP. Overall, however, government expenditure as a percentage of GDP is expected to fall from 41.2 per cent in 1996/7 to 39.7 per cent in 2001/2, essentially stabilizing after the cut inherited from the Tories during the first year of government.[9] Over a 5-year period the Blair government would raise total public spending at a slower rate than the Major government and only slightly faster than Conservative governments over the previous 18 years—an extraordinary outcome. The big increases in health and education are to be achieved by squeezing some other parts of public spending, notably defence spending and interest payments.[10] However, the most important diversion is to come from social security spending which Labour plans to raise by 2 per cent per year less than under the Tories (even excluding the reduction in spending resulting from the switch from benefits, which do count as spending, to tax credits, which do not). Even if substantial numbers come off benefits, such a target could never be met if benefits were generally and consistently indexed to wages rather than prices, let alone if their relative value was pushed back towards 1979 levels. Given the government's reluctance to raise taxation the only way that substantial increases in spending on government services can be financed is by squeezing social security.

The pressures emerging from the tight rein on spending of the first 2 years of the Blair government were dramatically revealed by a crisis in the health service at the end of 1999. This pushed Tony Blair into appearing to promise to raise UK health spending to the EU average. Increases of 6.2 per cent per year in real terms are now planned between 1999 and 2004. The extent to which these welcome increases are being financed by the squeeze on social security is not widely appreciated.

[9] These data refer to the fairly comprehensive definition of total managed expenditure as a percentage of GDP

[10] The figures for the increases in 'real spending' have to be handled with care. They overstate the real volume of inputs because low productivity growth in the sectors providing these labour-intensive services pushes up their costs faster than in the economy as a whole (around 0.5 per cent per year between 1990 and 1996, for example). See also footnote 3 above.

5. Education and Training Policy

Under Blair education policy has assumed primary importance as a tool of economic policy. In part this is the result of Labour's self-imposed constraints on conventional macroeconomic policy levers discussed earlier. Yet it also arises from a belief in the centrality of educational attainment to improving individuals' labour-market prospects. Education, in other words, is regarded primarily from an economic point of view. The government's first policy proposal on educational policy began, 'Learning is the key to prosperity' (DfEE, 1998).

Labour's main initiative in adult education has been to spread the gospel of 'lifelong learning'. The government's aim is to break the exclusive association of learning with schooling by emphasizing the variety of formats in which learning can take place, and by stressing that education continues *throughout* working lives rather than exclusively prior to them. Though this campaign has so far been largely a rhetorical one, there have been some innovations. In 1998 the University for Industry (UfI) scheme was launched – in essence, an internet-based brokering service which will offer information on a range of education and training courses in different regions. The UfI was accompanied by 'Learning Direct', a new freephone national advice and information service about learning and career options. The main financial instrument for boosting lifelong learning has been the introduction of Individual Learning Accounts (ILAs). ILAs are intended to enable individuals to invest in up-skilling and re-skilling throughout their careers. The Chancellor announced in his March 1999 Budget that a million ILAs will be created this year, with an initial government contribution of £150 per person. Both employers and employees will be able to contribute tax-free to these accounts. In addition any adult with an Individual Learning Account will be able to claim a discount of 20 per cent, or an additional grant of up to £100, on the cost of the training they choose. Adults signing up to improve their basic education – including computer literacy – will receive a discount of 80 per cent on course fees.

In other respects, New Labour's approach to learning in the workplace is a mixture of exhortations to train more, calls for partnership between government and business, and a continuation of structures and schemes developed under the previous government. Government training programmes, for example, continue to be administered by regional employer-led Training and Enterprise Councils (TECs). In the summer of 1999 an umbrella body – the Learning and Skills Council – was created to coordinate the various educational programmes targeted at those over 16 who do not stay in formal education, including in-firm training offered through the New Deal employment programme. Nevertheless, although the emphasis on training has become more prominent under New Labour, the structures responsible for delivering it have not been reformed in any significant way. This contrasts strongly with the proposals developed by the party in the late 1980s. By 1990 Labour had committed itself to a National Training Fund financed by a levy of 0.5 per cent on companies' payrolls, and involving the participation of trade union representatives. Prompted by the opposition of business, and under the influence of Blair—first as employment spokesman, later as leader—the party gradually abandoned this corporatist approach in favour of one stressing the responsibility of individuals and employers for training, and seeking to involve business in the delivery of training rather than relying on tripartite consultation (King and Wickham-Jones, 1999). In training as in other policy areas, trade unions remain firmly outside the decision-making process.

There remains considerable doubt about the impact these educational policies will make on the distribution of opportunities in the UK. The British educational system, like those of other Anglo Saxon countries, delivers a very inegalitarian pattern of educational outcomes. Standardized tests reveal a distance between the literacy skills of the least able 5 per cent of the labour force and the average that is more than half as big again as in Germany, for example (OECD, 1997c, Table 1.1). A major attempt to raise educational standards targeted especially at the bottom end of the distribution would help to reduce earnings inequality. It would also represent an unambiguous increase in economic efficiency as there is ample evidence of appalling wastage of talent in a system where educational achievement is so closely tied to the social and economic background of pupils (see Edwards and Whitty, 1994). Some of New Labour's flagship educational policies could, indeed, be interpreted as part of a radical agenda to improve the opportunities available to those at the 'bottom end'. Currently in a pilot phase, educational maintenance allowances have been introduced as means-tested financial incentives for 16-year-olds to stay in full-time education. Meanwhile the DfEE has demonstrated its willingness to intervene directly in the management of schools—over the heads of local education authorities—in order to improve standards and eliminate poor teaching. This interventionist approach is being combined with an effort to involve business more directly in education activities in their localities, mainly through the newly created Education Action Zones in areas of poor educational performance. In one case a private-sector company took over direct responsibility for the management of a school. These and other policies testify to Labour's commitment to use the arm of central government to redress failure of local governments to carry out their educational responsibilities.

However, leaving aside the question of whether the educational reforms are well conceived in themselves, a further question concerns the economic context in which they are introduced. Educational achievements are lowest precisely in the areas where poverty and joblessness is most prevalent (Bradley and Taylor, 1996). There are a number of reasons for this. Children (and parents) are less likely to take hard work at school seriously when there is a widespread perception that effort and job prospects are only weakly related. And learning will be difficult in schools which have high concentrations of children from low-literacy and low-numeracy backgrounds. Sustained improvements in educational outcomes in such areas probably depend on bringing employment to these areas, thereby increasing the 'point' of gaining qualifications and reducing household poverty. The weakness of the welfare-to-work policies in the face of joblessness in these areas noted earlier is likely to jeopardize the government's hopes for a radical extension of equality of opportunity through educational reform.

6. Labour and the Trade Unions

Between his accession to the Labour Party leadership in 1994 and the general election 3 years later, Tony Blair spent considerable energy undermining the party's links to the trade union movement. The somewhat surprising electoral defeat in 1992 was attributed in part to the continuing identification of Labour as a party representing the special interests of organized labour. In April 1995 the Labour leadership succeeded in ditching Labour's symbolic commitment to nationalization after party members voted 9:1 to delete the famous Clause 4 from the party's constitution. Union influence within the party was further diminished when the unions' block vote at the annual conference was lowered from 70 per cent to 50 per cent. A month later Blair told the TUC Conference that the unions would have no more influence than employers over a Labour government's policy agenda, promising to 'govern for the whole nation, not any vested interest within it'.

In two areas, however, Labour did bow to union pressure before coming to power in 1997. First, it maintained its pledge to introduce a minimum wage; second, it promised that firms would be compelled to recognize and negotiate with unions where they are supported by a majority of the work-force. In both cases, however, the government insisted on important caveats that continued to generate tense relations with the unions after the 1997 election. Despite continued pressure the Labour leadership refused to commit itself to a stated minimum wage, arguing instead that a specially convened independent Low Pay Commission would set the figure. The Commission's recommendations, adopted by the government in late 1998, disappointed the union movement hugely. First, the government set a minimum wage of £3.60 per hour, whereas the TUC had called for £4, and some unions (such as the public-sector workers' union, Unison, and the Trade and General Workers Union) for £5. Second, it added a lower minimum of £3 per hour for workers aged 18–21, a figure which will remain unchanged until 2001 (as does the adult rate). Once in power, the Labour government also infuriated unions by demanding extra conditions on the procedure for union recognition in the workplace. After a year of heated tripartite negotiations, the TUC conceded to government demands that a majority of those voting *and* at least 40 per cent of those eligible to vote would be required before a union would be recognized. In addition, firms with fewer than 21 employees are exempted from recognition procedures, and a derecognition provision has been included 'if employee support for recognition arrangements reduces significantly'.

These bitter rows between Labour and the unions have been tempered somewhat by the package of measures concerning employee rights contained within the *Fairness at Work* proposals (now the Employment Relations Act). The mandatory recognition procedures are accompanied by a range of increases in statutory minima that the TUC has hailed as the 'biggest advance in workers' rights for a generation'. First, the proposals include a raft of family-friendly regulations for employed parents. Maternity leave will be increased for all employees from 14 to 18 weeks, notice arrangements for leave will be simplified, and leave entitlement will apply after less than a year of employment. A statutory right of 3 months' parental leave for all employees is to be introduced. Contracts of employment will continue to be in force during parental leave and additional maternity leave unless expressly terminated by dismissal or resignation. Second, the individual employee's rights in the event of dismissal have been strengthened. The period of employment before an employee can qualify for protection against unfair dismissal is to be reduced from 2 years to 1, and maximum amounts of compensation awards will be raised from £12,000 to £50,000. Employees will also be given a right to be accompanied by a trade union representative in disciplinary or grievance procedures. Third, trade unions have secured moderate but important gains from the bill. Blacklisting and workplace discrimination against workers because of union membership will no longer be allowed, and public funds are to be provided for training union representatives.

These measures may well constitute 'the most comprehensive package of legislative proposals to extend employee and trade union rights . . . for more than a quarter of a century' (Taylor, 1998). That this is the case, however, is more a testament to the neo-liberal revolution in industrial relations law under the Conservatives than to the radical content of these proposals. The Employment Relations Act is fundamentally concerned with individual employment rights rather than those of trade unions. Though the bill expands union powers and protection, it is far from clear that their bargaining strength in the workplace will be any greater than before. Even when union recognition has been secured, for example, there is nothing in the bill that forces the employer to bargain in good faith. Nor will the law prevent individual employees from agreeing different terms with their employer to those agreed between the company and the recognized trade union. Second, the significance of the catalogue of employment protections proposed should not be overstated. Workers' rights in Britain continue to lag far behind those of their EU counterparts in Germany, France, and elsewhere. Finally, but most importantly of all, Labour's most significant decision remains that of not reversing the most important inroads into statutory protection for unions and employees that the Conservatives introduced in the 1980s, such as restrictions on strike activity and enforced liabilities for the economic consequences of strikes at firm level.

Despite this reluctance to restore union rights, individual workers' prospects may improve considerably as a result of Labour's decision to sign the Social Chapter of the Maastricht Treaty. In itself, the Social Chapter constitutes little more than broad areas of priority for social policy, such as affirming equal treatment for men and women, the protection of the rights of workers who move within the EU, and the improvement of conditions of employment. Signing up to the Chapter, however, binds Britain to implementation of European Commission directives regulating specific aspects of working life. In December 1997 Britain become subject to the terms of the Parental Leave Directive, later incorporated into the Employment Relations Act. At the same time the European Works Council Directive came into force in the UK, requiring companies with at least 1,000 employees in total, and at least 150 workers in each of two EU member states, to establish consultative structures with the work-force on issues affecting them.

Most controversial has been the adoption of the Working Time Directive, which stipulates that EU workers must not be required to work over 48 hours per week. The politics surrounding the implementation of this Directive capture many of the dilemmas confronting New Labour. Britain's average working hours are considerably longer than those of other nations (in 1997 average annual hours worked were 1,731 in the UK compared to 1,656 in France, 1,574 in Germany, and 1,552 in Sweden).[11] The relative effect of the Directive in the UK's highly deregulated labour market would thus be sizeable. Yet the restriction of working hours by legislative fiat is something that the Blair government would almost certainly not have chosen to introduce, anxious as it is to reassure business of its commitment to the neo-liberal conditions for competitiveness. New Labour's response to the inescapability of implementing the undesirable has been to introduce amendments to the legislative version of the Directive which would exempt millions of workers from coverage by the 48-hour rule. The government proposes to exempt voluntary work hours above the contractual maximum from the 48-hour limit, as well as exempting employers from maintaining detailed records on employees' overtime. Blanket restrictions apply to a number of categories of employment, particularly in the public sector.

In other areas of social and industrial relations policy the Labour government is fighting within the European Commission and the Council of Ministers to amend and/or veto additional directives—for example, requiring employee consultation within companies solely operating at the national level. The government's opposition to creeping regulation from Brussels has predictably earned it strong support from employers' organizations and hostility from the TUC. Labour is therefore able to claim credit for the social welfare improvements forced upon it by EU membership, while simultaneously fighting to dilute their impact.

7. Competitiveness

Labour's competitiveness strategy is classic Third Way politics: 'Old-fashioned state intervention did not and cannot work. But neither does naïve reliance on markets' (Tony Blair, Foreword to *Our Competitive Future* (DTI, 1998)). The government's Competitiveness White Paper conceives of a division of labour between companies and government— the state's job is to establish and police competitive markets to allow entrepreneurs to innovate, but also to invest in companies' 'capabilities' when they cannot do so alone (for example, investment in a work-force with good basic skills). The government stresses repeatedly the need for companies to adapt their competitive strategies to the realities of the

---

[11] OECD, *Employment Outlook* (1998, Table F, p. 207).

new 'knowledge-driven economy', and to that end has introduced measures designed to promote links between educational and research institutions and industry (Education Action Zones, and an extra investment of £2 billion in science and engineering research, for example).

Primarily, however, New Labour endorses the view that the best approach to improving competitiveness is for governments to keep intervention and regulatory burdens to a minimum. This approach to state–industry relations reflects one of the most significant policy continuities with the Conservative governments under Thatcher and Major that preceded it. New Labour has not only rejected calls for the re-nationalization of industries privatized under the Tories, most spectacularly after the Paddington rail disaster when opinion polls suggested huge public support for re-nationalizing Railtrack. It is also actively pursuing *further* privatizations, most notably of the air traffic control system. Labour is also initiating a restructuring of the ownership structure of the Post Office, proposing its conversion into a public limited company with all shares owned by the government. In a similar vein, New Labour has taken up the Tory policy of introducing private-sector capital into the public sector through private finance initiatives (PFIs). By 2004 the UK government will be paying out £3.5 billion per year under PFI contracts, much of which will involve purchase of current services (such as hospital maintenance) as well as interest payments which, as Chennells *et al.* (2000) note, 'will always cost more under the PFI than under conventional finance, since the government is able to borrow more cheaply than the private sector' (p. 37). British business is now heavily involved not only in investment in infrastructure in education, health, and other areas of the public sector, but is also extending beachheads into public-sector management—for example, in the management of educational authorities, schools, and urban regeneration zones.

8. Conclusion

Although New Labour's policies share little with those classically identified with social democracy, it would be wrong to characterize them as devoid of any overall objective or coherence. Clearly Labour has prioritized macroeconomic stability—partly in response to the anxieties about a return to the economic tribulations of the 1970s. From this perspective, joining the ERM, thereby ensuring much greater stability for the exchange rate, seems an entirely logical next step (provided it occurred at a reasonable exchange rate for sterling). Gordon Brown's five economic tests for judging whether the time is right for entry are pitched at an extraordinary level of generality (for example, 'If problems emerge, is there sufficient flexibility to deal with them?') and give ample latitude for justifying whatever decision on entry is felt to be politically expedient.

In its quest for economic stability and the political centre ground, Labour has imposed upon itself stringent constraints on its tax and spending capacities, and this rules out many of the redistributive policies that left parties have traditionally pursued. Yet this is not a source of regret for Blair's New Labour, as the pursuit of greater equality by active redistribution of income is rejected *in principle*, for a mixture of political, economic, and moral reasons. Redistribution implies a zero-sum trade-off between the interests of rich and poor that New Labour considers misguided. New Labour's egalitarianism lies in its various attempts to construct incentive structures for individuals on low incomes to increase their earnings potential through their own efforts. These and other policies reflect an approach to poverty which focuses solely on the absolute position of the least advantaged, one which would accept greater inequality if this was a necessary by-product of raising standards at the bottom end via supposed 'trickle-down' effects resulting from improved incentives for entrepreneurs at the top end. So this concern for improving the position of the most disadvantaged coexists with policies that reflect a tolerance for (and even actively encourage) the further acquisition of wealth by the most advantaged. The result of this combination is one which may well be *more* inegalitarian, though arguably more meritocratic and with a higher floor than before. In this respect New Labour has disentangled the traditional social democratic aims of promoting equality and eliminating poverty in ways that many on the left find both unaccept-able (in respect of greater inequality in the top half of the distribution) and unconvincing (in respect of the near exclusive emphasis on the labour market).

The central feature in New Labour's strategy for addressing pov-erty, disadvantage, and social exclusion is the reliance on *work*, and government policies are being tailored to encourage, and in some cases compel, individuals to enter and remain in employment. These have had positive effects on the distribution of income but fall far short of a comprehensive assault on the trend towards greater inequality and increased poverty. A radical improvement in educational performance, especially in areas of low educational achievement, would be an important component of a more thorough strategy to tackle these problems. But it needs to be complemented by:

- deliberate policies for job creation in the areas of highest joblessness, currently missing from New Labour's supply-side approach;
- a comprehensive attempt to improve conditions of employment at the bottom of the labour market (where the minimum wage stands in contrast to the government's stress on flexibility);
- acceptance of greater redistribution towards those at the lower end of the income distribution for whom education and the labour market does not provide an escape route.

The broader point for comparative social democracy is that the policies introduced by Blair's government so far imply a significant redrawing of the boundaries of state activity. Rather than provide a generous safety net for the unemployed, for example, New Labour sees the state's role as stimulating their re-entry into the labour market. As the welfare state evolves from a generous and comprehensive safety net for multiple categories of individuals into a series of employment programmes with lower levels of long-term 'dependency', the rationale for increasing the state's share of GNP will diminish further. In macroeconomic policy the fiscal ambition of social democracy is rejected, and control of interest-rate policy is seen as better exercised by an (almost) independent central bank (whether in London or Frankfurt), than by the government.

Responsibility for training and re-training, meanwhile, must rest with individuals and employers, not with the state. Neither should the state involve itself in private-sector industrial relations or wage bargaining. And with regard to ownership and investment in industry and services — even those in the public sector — the private solution is instinctively preferred to one relying on the state. The difficulties with a strategy of combining an improvement in the position of the worst-off with a diminishing role for the state has been the theme of this chapter. If New Labour could square this particular circle it would be the envy of many a social democrat abroad.

9

Why the Social Democratic Option Failed: Poland's Experience of Systemic Change

TADEUSZ KOWALIK*

1. Introduction: The Political Winners as the Economic Losers

'To our misfortune, we have won!' exclaimed Lech Wałęsa after the first relatively free election, on 4 June 1989.[1] No doubt he failed to realize quite what this exclamation conveyed. At that time, his words were still those of a manual worker and trade union leader. But now even the liberal journal, *Polityka*, enthusiastically supporting Leszek Balcerowicz's shock therapy, confirms that this victory was indeed a misfortune for the working class (Janicki and Władyka, 1997). The winners were very quickly to become the losers. The new social order was to signify, above all, the emergence of an extremely high level of a permanent mass unemployment, a more than doubling of the number of people living below the poverty line, and a dramatic redistribution from the poor to the rich (called, by one specialist, 'a real revolution in incomes').

Of course, while paradoxical, this is nothing new. It is a banal historical truth that the working class several times played a crucial role in the bourgeois revolutions of continental Europe. Oskar Lange, an eminent Polish socialist thinker and economist, commented especially perceptively:

> After the war, when the remnants of the ancient regime collapsed in all the countries of Central Europe—in Germany, Austria, Hungary, in the Czech lands, and in Poland—the bourgeois democratic republics that emerged from the ruins of the Hohenzollern, Habsburg, and Romanov monarchies were created by the labour movement. Lacking sufficient power to give the republics it had created a proletarian class character, the labour movement

---

* Warsaw. I would like to thank Andrew Glyn for his comments and editorial advice.

[1] A chronology of the main political developments in Poland over the 1980s and 1990s is given on p. 251.

was unable to prevent them becoming bourgeois class states . . . a tragicomic situation. (Lange, 1931, p. 93)

The novelty of the situation in Poland is that the labour movement did not confront a stronger, better-organized force. A fully fledged capitalist revolution took place under conditions where a bourgeois class and its organized representation were non-existent. Thus the new rulers were anticipating the future in creating the foundations of a new system favourable to the middle-class-to-be.

Among the communist countries, Poland, before 1989, unquestionably had the strongest opposition movement, the most conscious working class, the largest trade union organization in Europe (in 1980/81 9.5m members), and the longest tradition of militant workers with the record of several insurrections (workers' revolts in 1956, 1970, 1976, and 1980). Moreover, Poland has also had the strongest (after Yugoslavia) self-management (or, better, participatory) movement, composed of employee councils in almost all state firms, an association of self-management activists, even journals. Moreover, among the countries of the Soviet bloc, Poland was undoubtedly the best prepared intellectually for complex reforms. The first 'Solidarity' ratified in 1981 a radical programme of reforms, entitled 'A Self-Governing Republic', based on social pluralism, pluralism of ownership forms, combining planning with an extended market. Later, its continuing radicalism was reflected in the agreement reached at the Round Table negotiations between the opposition and the old communist élite. Until late summer 1989, however, all these reforms were kept within the limits of the former socio-economic mega-system. Systemic transformation was then led by the government which emerged from the ranks of this victorious trade union and shared political power with the representatives of the old communist regime.

Usually regimes created as an outcome of a social agreement between the representatives of great social groups bring benefits to both sides. And yet, the most surprising outcome of the post-1989 development was that Poland became the most élitist, anti-egalitarian country in Central Europe (Milic-Czerniak, 1998; Borkowska, 1998). Employees' and peasants' living standards, working conditions, and social status were diminished to a greater extent by the transformation than was the case in the Czech Republic, Slovakia, Slovenia, and Hungary, though in all these countries the opposition was many times weaker than in Poland.

How can this unexpected development be explained?

First, what happened to that unprecedented mass movement, Solidarity, and its programme? Why did this syndicalist, semi-socialist movement tolerate, without visible resistance, a neo-liberal free-market programme which was such a far cry from the 1981 Programme, the Round Table agreement, and the 1989 election declaration launched only a couple of months before the creation of the first non-communist government?

In order to understand the depth of the defeat of the Polish workers and of the original Solidarity, let us recall that even the above mentioned post-1918 bourgeois revolutions in Central Europe were lost by the workers' parties at the political, but not the social level. On the contrary, these revolutions ushered in the first major breakthrough in labour legislation. Polish workers, for example, won or were granted an 8-hour working day and other rights. This time, however, workers lost in social as well as political terms. Was this because, as some argue, workers had had to be bought off at a time when the socialist revolution was knocking at the door, whereas 70 years later it was a period of counter-revolution? Obviously, there is something in this, but as an explanation it is too general. Also too simplistic, though not without a grain of truth, is the belief of many rank-and-file trade unionists that they were betrayed by the intellectuals.

Let us consider some more concrete factors. The first is the transformation of Solidarity between 1981 and 1989. After 8 years of illegality it never re-emerged as a mass movement. The frequently noted excess of democracy had been transformed into an organizational structure ruled by co-optation and nomination. Decisions taken by individuals and small groups have to be arbitrary, with no room for critical or independent evaluation. Loyalty and discipline were required to hold the organization together and the narrow groups of activists (revolutionists) lost touch with their social base and mostly became absorbed in purely political issues. Some trade-union functions were taken over, almost naturally, by councils of employees, revived and tolerated by the authorities.

From this phase of illegality a new élite emerged, which later on was transformed into a 'republic of buddies' (Modzelewski, 1993, p. 9). Even though the revolution was peaceful, combatants came to treat the state as their trophy, as Wałęsa noticed. After the 'explosion' of Poland's independence in 1918, governmental, parliamentary, diplomatic, and administrative posts were up for grabs. This time, however, the administrative apparatus was several times larger and in addition national wealth (state ownership) was to be distributed, many market niches were there to be filled, and a financial system had to be built, almost from scratch. Thus it was really difficult not to be seduced either by money, or by political power, or by both. The creation of a new government under the banner of Solidarity justified an exodus of thousands of activists into the administration, including almost all the intellectuals, ending their historical alliance with the workers. In this way the workers' Solidarity was, in a sense, decapitated.

However, the workers' attitudes and expectations, and consequently their role, changed substantially as well. They suffered not only a sudden reduction in living standards (discussed later), but also a shocking psychological earthquake influencing their social attitudes. In response, three groups of employees emerged. Engineers and managers with university degrees accepted neo-liberal economic policy and became an influential part of the new ruling class. At the other extreme, unskilled workers maintained their traditional egalitarian and pro-statist vision, but became marginalized as an underclass, not involved in social organizations or elections. The third group, the bulk of employees, play no visible role on the political scene because their orientation and attitudes are ambivalent, isolating and disarming them. They expected a 'friendly market economy' (Gardawski, 1996, p. 117), accepting competition but not unemployment, the introduction of greater efficiency, but not lay-offs. They combined a general acceptance of privatization, with an opposition to privatization of the firm in which they worked, believing that it should remain in state hands or become the property of all its employees. Their main worry was to defend their firm from outside systemic interference. The main consequence of this double thinking was 'cracks in the traditional sense of solidarity and the disappearance of the climate of support for collective action on a national scale' (ibid., p. 119). The new mentality of the workers was the main factor enabling the implementation of the Balcerowicz Plan. In the years of the first Solidarity Cabinets 1989–93, the number of strikes, demonstrations, and even hunger marches grew rapidly.[2] But they were mostly spontaneous, wild-cat actions, seldom directed by the main trade unions.

This new mentality not only weakened the Solidarity Trade Union and unions generally, but also undermined the social basis for an alternative political movement. Employees' ambivalence created a confused environment for the formation of the post-communist Social Democratic Party, and afterwards the Left-Democratic Alliance (which included the post-communist party and union, SdRP and OPZZ, as well as some 25 smaller political parties and organizations). When finally the Solidarity parliamentary faction defeated its own government, bringing an unexpected election victory for the post-communist parties, a change in the direction of economic policy seemed a possibility.

[2] Between 1990 and 1993 the number of strikes grew from 250 to almost 7,500 (Główny, 1994, p. 125).

The new coalition government was expected by its predecessors to signal a return to the communist past and to bring economic chaos. No such thing happened. The post-communists exerted great effort to gain acceptance by the West and by the anti-communists as well. The US Ambassador summed up the position clearly:

> When, for example, the post-communist forces won the parliamentary elections in 1993, they were not sure of themselves. Though they were reluctant to implement structural reforms . . . they continued with the macroeconomic policy in order to gain acceptance by the West and to ensure favourable external conditions for growth, and to have good prospects for the next elections. (Simons, 1999)[3]

In some cases they were *plus catholique que le pape même*: the post-communists ratified exceptionally harsh tenancy regulations, legally making homeless many impoverished tenants. Thus the improvement of the political climate with the new government was due to the slow-down or halting of reforms and delays to privatization rather than to a shift in social priorities. The government's left-wing label further increased ambivalence and confusion among employees, with the number of strikes falling from 429 in 1994 to 21 in 1996.

2. The Dark Side of the Polish Success

Western public opinion is systematically fed on the great success of the Polish economy, while the ugly side is frequently ignored. It is true that over the past 6 years the economy has been expanding rather rapidly (a rate of GDP growth of over 5 per cent per annum), and the official propaganda celebrates such 'growthmanship' as though it was more or less beneficial to all social groups. However, this 'trickle down' theory is far from the reality and this decisively shapes both the growth experience and the main features of the socio-economic system that has emerged over the past 10 years. Certainly, the system will continue to change. The public sector will contract in favour of the private sector, and there will be further marketization of the state sector including in social services. But it is almost certain that the foundations of the new system, as one of the variants and components of the mega-system called capitalism, have already been laid. If one assumes that strong

---

[3] According to Simons, the sharp polarization of the political scene in Poland and the attacks of the anti-communists helped the reform process by compelling the post-communists to behave themselves.

social movements will not come into the reckoning, then this new system is not threatened by reverses or radical change.

The most important features of the present economic system and economic situation in Poland are, in my opinion, the following:[4]

(a) Massive and Permanent Unemployment

Unemployment grew from almost zero in 1989 to more then 16 per cent in 1994, and by the spring of 2000 was about 14 per cent and rising. However, the decline in numbers of registered unemployed is reflected only to a limited extent in employment growth. Quite a number of the unemployed went back to the village, augmenting disguised unemployment in agriculture. Second, in the space of only 1 year, the proportion of the unemployed entitled to benefit dropped from 50 per cent to less than 25 per cent. The rapid change in benefit entitlement may have caused many of the unemployed to see no advantage in being registered — as many as one-third according to the Statistical Office (Łagodziński, 1999). Moreover, Poland is facing an exceptionally rapid growth of young entrants to the labour market, so joblessness will surely continue to be a great and painful problem unless deliberate and broadly programmed action is taken. Unfortunately, the present government theoretically justifies its inaction with the Minister of Labour (formerly a top official of the Solidarity trade union), publicly asserting that the 'natural rate of unemployment is in present Poland between 8 and 10 per cent' (Komołowski, 1999)!

(b) Widespread Poverty

Researchers employ different criteria for poverty, but numerous domestic studies (Beskid, 1998; Deniszczuk, 1995; Golinowska, 1996a, b), together with the World Bank (1994), and finally the Statistical Office, all agree that in the course of the last 8–10 years the number of people living in poverty more than doubled. According to the Vienna Institute of Human Studies (Rada, 1998, p. 24), the number of people receiving

---

[4] I shall not analyse here organization and methods of resource allocation, and co-ordination, and, moreover, I will not try to distinguish the results of the stabilization programme itself, as implemented in 1990, from systemic changes as such, or (using the terminology of German Ordo-liberals) what was the result of Processpolitik from what was an effect of Ordnungspolitik (current as opposed to systemic policy), and of the intended from unintended changes. I should perhaps only express my opinion, that the widely seen as mistaken 'overshooting' of the Balcerowicz stabilization plan was highly instrumental in creating the socio-economic system that emerged, particularly in shifting incomes from the poor to the rich.

half average disposable income or less (on an equivalent basis) amounted in 1995 to 18.3 per cent in Poland, 9.3 per cent in Hungary, 6.7 per cent in Slovakia, 6.1 per cent in the Czech Republic, and 6.6 per cent in East Germany. The subsequent years of high growth brought only an insignificant improvement. Although comparisons are more difficult here, the proportion of people in poverty in Poland is one of the highest in Europe, west of the Ukraine. That high rate of poverty was prompted by high unemployment, a sharp fall in real wages, and the large proportion on minimum wages.

(c) *Exceptionally Large Disparities of Wages and Incomes*

These are associated with the mass unemployment and large sector of population affected by poverty. As several researchers (Milanovic, 1995; Atkinson, 1996; Borkowska, 1998) show, Polish disparities of income are the highest among Central European countries and are among the highest of the Western Europeans. Inequality measured in 1996 by a Gini coefficient (34 for household incomes, 30 for wages) outstripped the majority of countries in Europe, not just the Scandinavian ones: 'In 1999 Poland entered the group of the most inegalitarian countries such as Italy and the USA. . . . Higher "non-civilized" disparities are only in Albania and Russia' (Golinowska, 1999).

The greed of managers, or rather their lack of restraint in increasing their benefits, merits particular attention. Their earnings are already more than 60 times the average wage, a rate similar to that displayed in the United States a dozen or so years ago. Moreover, managers' salaries are still rising rapidly, led recently by the heads of state-owned firms. This could not have happened without the quiet acquiescence of a government with a left-wing label. Poland also comes out very badly in comparative studies of wage discrimination against women.[5]

Before our eyes then, with our silent or active complicity, what Roy Harrod described as an oligarchy of wealth (Harrod, 1958, cited by Hirsh, 1977, p. 23) has emerged, bringing with it an oligarchic democracy. However, policies designed to assist the poor, which are attracting increasing popular support, are likely to perpetuate the inegalitarian system rather than destroy it. This is the 'paradox of redistribution' (Korpi and Palme, 1997) which confronts social democratic governments.

---

[5] According to comparative research by the Vienna Institute of Human Studies, an average of the total (main job and additional) earnings of women was 56.7 per cent of men's earnings, lower than not only Bulgaria, the Czech Republic, Slovakia, and Hungary, but also Russia (Domanski, 1997, p. 124).

(d) *Nineteenth-century Working Conditions in the Private Sector*

Private firms generally do not respect health and safety regulations at work and do not comply with the conditions laid down in legally binding written contracts of employment. In regions of high unemployment and/or immigration from the east and the south, wages are often below the statutory minimum. Trade-union activity is not allowed, which is why 'in the new private firms trade unions are practically absent, and in privatized firms are disappearing' (Gardawski, 1999b). At the outset, this could be explained by the inexperience of the new owners, the exceptional situation, reorganization, and, therefore, a temporary breakdown in monitoring. We should, however, be deeply perturbed that the annual report of the State Labour Inspectorate (PIP) indicates that working conditions are far from improving, and actually are getting worse. Hopes that this private sector will become more civilized are receding dangerously.

(e) *The Catastrophic Situation with Regard to Housing*

The number of apartments we are building now is about one-third of the number we built 10 years ago, despite waiting lists for a municipal flat of 5–8 years. This coincides not only with mass unemployment, but also a huge excess of production capacity in steel mills and the cement industry.

(f) *Uncertainty of Social and Employee Entitlements*

In order to finance transfers to growing numbers of poor people, including the unemployed and pensioners, the authorities felt compelled to cut pensions and other benefit levels. This is understandable, perhaps, but ultimately must be attributed to failure to combat unemployment. However, the authorities have many times repeated that the Polish economy is over-socialized and declared their intention of reducing the share of state expenditure to one-third of GDP, from the present level of nearly a half. So far they have only succeeded in reducing the share by a couple of per cent, but the threat remains (Ministerstwo Finansów, 1998a, b). Also under consideration is a parliamentary bill on 'flexibilization' of the labour market, making it possible, for example, to fire employees on sick-leave.

(g) *The Privatization Process Contrary to Distributive Justice Requirement*

This issue deserves separate consideration and is discussed in the next section.

3. The Struggle Over Ownership

In contemporary societies, ownership of means of production or of equities constitutes owners' power over other people.

> Ownership and control contribute to the creation of great differences among citizens in wealth, income, status, skill, information, control over information and propaganda, access to political leaders, and, on the average, predictable life chances, not only for mature adults but also for the unborn, infants, and children. After all due qualifications have been made, differences like these help in turn to generate significant inequalities among citizens in their capacities and opportunities for participating as political equals in governing the state. (Dahl,1985, p. 55)

The battle for ownership and property rights is being played out in Poland as in all post-communist countries and its result has considerable importance in shaping the new system. This was clearly expressed by one of the politicians of the Conservative Liberal Party and sociologist, Jacek Kurczewski (1995):

> Poland again finds itself at the initial point of departure, when ownership titles must be handed out among the participants of the social game.... Absolutely everybody is taking part in the battle for power, ownership and property, although at the start the opportunities were not equal and this inequality is obvious at every step—the feeling of injustice on the one hand and of arrogance on the other.

Thus, the analysis of privatization should not limit itself to the problem of the efficiency of different paths and forms, but should consider questions of its social content, such as material working conditions (environment, safety network, etc.), employees' interrelations, participation in decision-making, and income disparities. We turn next to these problems, focusing on only three forms of property: the 'new private sector' of small firms, employee companies, and National Investment Funds. The last two are widely regarded as the most distinctive components of Poland's programme of privatization.

(a) *The Old and New Private Sector of Small Firms*

Owing to limitations on space I touch only briefly on that part of the private sector that has developed outside the privatization process of state-owned firms, focusing only on the most important characteristics of how the new firms developed.

The years 1989–93 saw a doubling in the number of firms belonging to individuals and small commercial companies, from over 800,000 to 1.6m. This path proved the basic method for privatizing the national economy. Thus, the private sector (excluding individual farmers) currently employs approximately 5m people, of whom private firms resulting from the transformation of state-owned firms—privatized by direct purchase ('the capital method'), through National Investment Funds (NIFs), or as employee-owned companies—jointly employ no more than 0.75m people. Moreover, the state still has a considerable ownership share in the majority of these privatized firms.

The speed of expansion among private firms outside the state-owned sector was helped by the following circumstances:

- the legal ease of establishing private firms;
- the existence of many market niches, particularly in trade and services that in the earlier system had been either neglected or even prohibited;
- the extreme liberalization of foreign trade;
- the takeover by private firms of some of the state-owned production equipment (this particularly relates to so-called wild or *nomenklatura* privatization); and, finally,
- taxes on private firms several times lower than on state-owned firms and payments to pension funds made by the owners of private firms, about half those by wage earners. In this sense the state-owned sector worked for the benefit of privatization and financed it through the budget.

The doubling of the number of individual owners of private firms meant material and social advance for hundreds of thousands of people—particularly because as many as three-quarters of these new owners were former unskilled or skilled labourers, with only one-quarter originating from the intelligentsia or white-collar workers (Domański, 1997, p. 56). These new owners have not brought progress for the workers employed by them. Quite the opposite—workers employed here are experiencing nineteenth-century employment conditions. Infringement of elementary Labour Code regulations with regard to safety, as well as the legal requirement to conclude written work contracts, is extremely common in these firms. What is worse, reports by the state's Labour Inspectors (the PIP) raised the alarm on several occasions and suggest that 'the Labour Code is being more and more frequently infringed in the more dangerous jobs' (Olczyk and Pilczyński, 1996). For instance, we read in one PIP report that in 1995, the number of (work-related) accidents rose by 20 per cent compared to the preceding year, while the number of criminal verdicts rose by 12 per cent. In as many as 70 per cent of the firms inspected, infringements of wage regulations were discovered, including payment of wages below the legal minimum. In the last few years the number of accidents and infringements has grown more rapidly than the number of firms, refuting any idea that this was just a transitional problem.

(b) *Employee Companies*

The development in Poland of 'employee companies' (called sometimes leasing companies, because this was an overwhelming method through which payment for state property was arranged) was a great surprise to many politicians and economists. First, they became the most frequent form of privatization of state firms, despite open hostility from the first Solidarity government and lack of support from the Cabinets which followed. Leszek Balcerowicz, himself, denounced employee companies as creeping (or non-statist form of) socialism (abo, 1992). One of the top officials in the Ministry of Privatization and later of the Treasury openly said that 'the so-called worker companies are either managerial from the outset or rapidly transforming into entities whose ownership is dominated by the management staff' (Bukowski, 1995, p. 146). One may be sure that this was more wish than description.[6]

Second, contrary to the strongly held prejudices of many politicians and economists, they have performed so far surprisingly efficiently: their rate of gross return and net profitability was on average considerably higher than those seen on other privatization paths, and, in 1996, even exceeded returns to companies transformed by sale to outsiders (see Kowalik, 1998).[7] Their current problem is indeed a relatively low rate of investment. One may presume, however, that after having paid all leasing instalments and received full ownership rights, they will get access to external funds, and at least a majority of these companies may display a capacity for growth not worse than the rest of the private sector.

It is true that the rate of new starts of employee companies has recently been low. However, Mario Nuti greatly exaggerates when he writes that the list of potential candidates and takers for them has been virtually exhausted. This should be seen in the light of more general tendencies. The rate of new starts on all other privatization paths is even slower. For example, in the last 2 years, only 13 state enterprises

[6] In his opinion the American ESOPS (Employee Stock Ownership Plans) are based on 'the doctrinal collectivist concept', which was in 1990 rightly rejected by a Polish parliament (Bukowski, 1995, p. 148). The idea of using the employee companies as a purely transitional tool leading to normal joint stock companies was first presented by the representative of the American Heritage Foundation (Krawczyk, 1990, p. 152).

[7] Główny Urząd Statystyczny (1997a, b).

were privatized by the Privatization Agency, even though one of the principal slogans of the present right-wing coalition called for accelerated privatization.[8] It is precisely employee companies that have been the only form of privatization clearly to win favour with employees up till now.

Employee companies also brought another surprise for the economists nourished by a neoclassical presumption of the necessarily lower efficiency of cooperative firms than purely private firms and also suspicious of all types of social movements, such as trade unions and participatory schemes, as undermining market mechanisms. In this case, a social movement fathered not only the most popular form of ownership transformation,[9] but also the most, or one of the most, efficient types of firm. Our employee companies grew out of an adjustment to new conditions by the activists of the self-management movement — perhaps the strongest and most spontaneous movement of this kind in the whole of the Soviet bloc, developed under the umbrella of Solidarity. From the West came only a ready-made model, chiefly in the form of American (but also British)[10] ESOPs. The Pope also spoke up for worker shareholder groups (particularly in *Laborem Exercens* and *Solicitudo rei Socialis*). And yet, the political power regards them with ill-disguised disfavour or even enmity.

Let us remember that in the early days of the system's transformation the self-management movement had in Poland its own association, a weekly journal, and even an institute. It tried to take advantage of advice from foreign experts. In the years 1989–91, one could admire how quickly the movement's activists adjusted to the new circumstances. When it was publicly declared that a private market economy was being created, these activists abandoned the old concept of worker councils and stepped forward with a whole range of initiatives and concepts that fitted within the new framework, but at the same time maintained certain values of employee participation in the enterprises.

---

[8] The slowing down of the privatization has much deeper causes that I am not able to discuss here. One is society's loss of faith, particularly of wage-earning employees, in the beneficial effects of privatization; something to which a considerable section of the power élite has also succumbed.

[9] Gardawski (1999a, p. 85) writes that, according to his investigation of the industrial élites, 82 per cent of respondents were in favour of this form of ownership.

[10] In the first months of systemic changes some British experts (financed by the Know-How Fund) were helping Polish activists to create ESOP-type firms. This was stopped after the minister responsible for privatization wrote to the British Embassy that this sort of assistance was against Polish government policy. He favoured at that time a British model of privatization (case-by-case transformation of state enterprises into joint stock companies).

When the first Solidarity government was created, they were met, however, with hostility from the ruling establishment. This was a shock for them, since only a couple of months earlier (spring 1989), one of the principal agreements of the Round Table, to be protected in the constitution, was the principle of equal treatment of different forms of ownership which was to be extended to include employee participation.[11]

The power élites' initial hostility towards, and then unfriendly tolerance of, employee companies has greatly contributed not only to a declining number of newly created ones, but also to the widely shared characterization of them as a 'transitional form permitting the attainment of proper capital privatization in the least conflictual way' (Pańkow and Gąciarz, 1999, p. 142). Indeed, the evolution of property rights inside these companies seems to confirm this prognosis. There is a substantial shift of shares from the rank-and-file employees to the managers.

The unfriendly attitude of the ruling establishment to the employee companies would be difficult to explain by motives other than the ideological ones.[12] In the first years of transformation it may have seemed clear to the politicians that this form of transformation would ('dangerously') dominate the Polish economy, or at least the sector that was hitherto state controlled. Today such a fear is unfounded. Despite being numerous (more than 1,200 firms), their share in the economy is modest—they employ merely a few per cent of the country's workforce (approximately 200,000 persons), and their share in fixed-asset ownership is even smaller.

[11] Academic historians (Kochanowicz, 1997) direct our attention to the fact that the difference between the well-developed welfare state in Europe and its modest scope in the United States (and Australia) has historical origins. In Europe, capitalism arose as a negation, but in a certain respect also a continuation of the patriarchal tradition, rural communities, and guilds, whereas in the United States emphasis was from the beginning laid on the independence and responsibility of the individual. This in my opinion also shapes differences in the development of ownership forms. In Europe, we have a considerably greater degree of mixed or non-private forms of ownership. In Europe there is a much greater tradition of cooperatives, worker participation, municipal ownership, and a state-owned sector both in services and industry.

[12] Similar was its attitude towards cooperatives and their organizations. In a country with a more than one century long and rich tradition of a cooperative movement, the majority of them were at the start of systemic transformation liquidated in a purely administrative way, instead of being helped in de-bureaucratization or de-statization. Only recently, after big peasants' demonstrations and road blockades as a protest against low prices for their products, a deputy prime minister advised farmers to create cooperatives instead in order to reduce trade profits in favour of primary food prices.

Thus, anxious anticipation of the day when they will finally cease to be employee companies is entirely unjustified. True, employee companies have and should have the ability to transform themselves into 'normal companies' and several of them did already take advantage of this opportunity. But they should also be aware that they do not constitute some interim anomaly, tarred with the 'odium' of collectivism. However, first and foremost, they should be aware of the full palette of varied solutions available. In the Western world there exists a wide variety of ownership and/or participatory firms with varying degrees of both individualism and collectivism. There is also a wealth of experience in protecting the worker-based nature of these companies. This is true even in the United States, a country that, in contrast to Europe, has no common property traditions from a pre-capitalist period. In the light of this, either hanging on for grim death to this one home-grown variety or, conversely, treating it as necessarily potentially managerial is precisely ideological doctrinairism.

How should Polish employee companies be seen from the point of view of distributive justice? In theory they are created just because they promise equal distribution of property rights (shares) and thus participation in the decision-making process. In the context of Polish privatization they are more or less distanced from theory. Even with equal distribution of shares, they may be controlled by managers. At the beginning of the 1990s managers managed to hold on to quite a substantial part of shares (38.6 per cent). By 1996 they owned more shares than the rank-and file employees: 39.7 per cent and 37.5 per cent respectively. Managers gained slightly, but the rank-and-file employees lost more than one-fifth of their holdings (Gardawski, 1999a, p. 94, Table 5).

Two kinds of emerging companies can be distinguished. The first is characterized by a two-tiered owner group—the owner élite and a handful of shareholders with middle-sized stakes on the one side, and a dwindling group of small rank-and-file shareholders on the other. We may call these manager-owned companies. The second is a more egalitarian, or cooperative type of firm (Gardawski, 1999a, p. 95). But share ownership does not automatically mean that, even in the second type of company, the small owners have a say in the decision-making process. Managers may monopolize knowledge and information, which permits them to manipulate and dominate decision-making, as several studies confirm. A sociologist concludes:

> even if employee shareholders do not have a large say in the management of the companies they own, they are convinced of their responsibility for it, and they themselves feel like co-owners. This is certainly one of their reasons

for wage restraint in these firms. In general the respondents agree that labour relations are good. Nevertheless, the conditions in the firms do not indicate a significant degree of employee participation, and labour relations can be described as paternalistic rather than democratic. (Szostkiewicz, 1996, p. 85)

Existing literature does not clearly differentiate employee from manager companies from the point of view of wage disparities. From fragmentary data (Gardawski, 1995, p. 64; Szostkiewicz, 1994, p. 87) one may conclude disparities are quite high, are growing, and are only insignificantly smaller than in the rest of the private sector.

In these conditions, one may be puzzled as to why not only those companies which are dominated by small shareholders, but also those dominated by managers are regarded by researchers and politicians as 'oases of social peace' and, moreover, treated by employees as belonging to them. This can only be partially explained by the way they have been created as an outcome of involvement of (agreement with) the whole work-force, and very often after a struggle against bureaucracy.

(c) National Investment Funds (NIFs)

The first proposals for putting state ownership in the hands of all adult citizens described it as a democratization of ownership or the creation of a 'democratic' or 'people's' capitalism. The most recent models were provided for the initiators by Margaret Thatcher, who carried out privatization in England under this banner. The Chilean government of General Pinochet announced and to a modest degree carried through a similar privatization in the second half of the 1980s. However, there also were quite clear socio-technical reasons for mass privatization as representing an indirect route to concentrating ownership in private hands, although only a few admitted this openly.

In promoting the idea of mass privatization and perhaps even more in building up unrealistic expectations, a considerable role was played by Lech Wałęsa. Both during the presidential election campaign in 1990 and later as president, he promised citizens a substantial share in the nation's assets. He mentioned sums of 100m and even 300m old złoty, or 10,000 US dollars.

On the other hand the Gdansk conservative Liberals, particularly J. Lewandowski and J. Szomburg, sought in a similar way a rapid and socially acceptable privatization path. Their preliminary concept was similar to the Czech coupon-based privatization. This, however, quickly became linked with the idea of NIFs as management bodies that would draw widely on foreign management institutions. Following some legislative delays the final result was the inclusion of 512 state enterprises (Treasury-owned companies) in a programme divided among and managed by 15 NIFs. They were generally weak, small or medium-sized enterprises, together representing only a small proportion of the nation's assets. Currently less than 500 NIF companies employ only around 250,000 people, approximately 2 per cent of the country's work-force, and hold a similar share of the Treasury's assets (Korona, 1999, p. 11).

The contrast between the early promises of society's enfranchise-ment in the form of distributing ownership among all adult citizens, democratizing capitalism, and the real size of the NIF programme, entirely justifies the conclusion that 'a mountain has given birth to a mouse' — a mouse that has consumed so much legislative, organiza-tional, and financial effort. In addition, the long-lasting general slump on the financial market has further marginalized this programme. This slump affected the NIFs the most: by autumn 1999 their share price had fallen by 69.3 per cent since their initial quotation. Most recently the market price facing owners of one or just a few certificates was only double the original 20 złoty purchase price. Thus if we take into account the inflation of the last few years, the citizen who did not sell his share certificates during their initial price rise has received a present from the state with an equivalent value of just a couple of US dollars, i.e. more than a thousand times less than the promise made by Wałęsa.

Thus we may be justified in saying that the PPP privatization programme, so loudly proclaimed at the outset and popularized as an act of social justice, has ended up as a complete fiasco, if not a large-scale manipulation of the populace. In the opinion of Premier H. Suchocka: general privatization 'will give everyone a part of the national wealth and enable them to directly feel the advantage of reforms' (Wujec, 1993). The programme's true creator, Minister J. Lewandowski, has repeatedly claimed that the purpose of the PPP programme is to distribute national ownership (for example, A.K.K., 1992). This refutes statements that 'no one ever claimed that the individual citizen may get any substantial share in national wealth' (Bochniarz and Wiœniewski, 1999). What really happened suggests that the citizenry was taken in by a popular slogan, subsequently deepening its suspicion of the govern-ment's reform efforts.

The NIF programme was often compared with the Czech coupon-based privatization, a many times more ambitious programme. How-ever, if we leave aside the question of scale, we see that in the construction of the Polish programme, the degree of risk incurred by the original, generally only temporary, share certificate owners was lower than in the Czech programme (as we know, the differences in the real value of Czech coupons could have been as big as 1: 1,000). It is also possible that the Polish programme created to a lesser degree opportunities for corruption and favouritism. The differences, however, end there, for the ownership concentration processes are similar and are far from the ideals of democratic ownership proclaimed earlier.

Incomplete information suggests a far-reaching process of concentrating shares in the hands of domestic and, first and foremost, foreign institutional investors:

> foreign shareholders — chiefly in the form of hedge type funds, planning short-term, up to 2–3 year, investments . . . have already gained a dominant position among NIF shareholders. They are now in a position to create shareholder groups jointly owning 20–30 per cent of capital and . . . acquire 50 per cent of votes at general shareholders meetings, elect supervisory boards and in consequence take over full control of the Funds. (Bochniarz and Wiœniewski, 1999)

In the opinion of the authors quoted, domination of the NIFs by foreign capital, mainly hedge funds, will have serious consequences in the future. Aiming at as large and rapid a return on capital as possible, control over several NIFs may be given to a single management firm in order to reduce the wage bill for Fund managers. Such managers may concentrate on selling off companies rather than restructuring.

> Following the sale of the few best companies from each NIF it will then be possible to achieve a satisfactorily large shareholder profit, while the remaining, weaker companies would be sold at any price, without duly securing the interests of either the firms themselves or their employees. Fund authorities or their management firms may then be forced to conduct liquidation proceedings and float fund assets at any price. The property not liquidated (companies in poor economic shape that cannot be sold) may thus become a serious problem for the State Treasury. (Bochniarz and Wiœniewski, 1999)

The situation is made worse by the fact that 'domestic investors are allying themselves with or giving capital support to foreign investors'.[13]

To summarize: this form of privatization achieved neither egalitarian ownership objectives nor effective restructuring in the interests of productive efficiency. While promoted as egalitarian, its real purpose was to concentrate ownership with a view to restructuring, but its effect was enrichment of certain individuals.

---

[13] Ms H. Bochniarz is a former Minister for Industry and is currently the Chair of NICOM Consulting Ltd, the company that carried out the preliminary selection of enterprises destined for the PPP privatization programme. Thus, in a certain sense, she was co-author of the PPP programme. Her present testimony is for that reason all the more valuable.

4. Public Sector—In a Deadlock

In Poland, contrary to all other communist countries, the state sector never had a monopolistic position. Dominant in industry and trade, but not in agriculture (about 80 per cent of which was in the hands of individual farmers), state firms (SFs) coexisted with small and medium private enterprises (SMPEs). Already in the 1980s SMPEs were growing in number and strength. The 1982 reforms limited state planning and enlarged the autonomy of SFs operating in (still regulated) markets. All this gave Poland's SFs a greater ability to adjust to a market economy than those in other post-communist countries. That is why many state firms have shown, at least at the beginning of the systemic changes, quite a remarkable vigour. Two facts illustrate this.

Before 1990 Polish foreign trade was overwhelmingly oriented towards the East, mainly the USSR. The collapse of the Soviet Union and of COMECON meant a sharp decline in these markets. Unexpectedly, given the widely held opinion that they were inflexible and hopelessly bureaucratic, Polish enterprises, particularly foreign trade companies, at that time mostly state-owned, were able immediately to re-direct their activity towards the West and fully made up for the losses of trade in the East.

Moreover, quite a lot of them demonstrated a remarkable flexibility in adjusting themselves to a market economy with its sudden openness to foreign competition. This has been noticed in a study by the World Bank:

> Evidence is presented that shows state-owned enterprises in much more favourable light than the stereotype of miyopic, decapitalizing companies that dominates discussion of the state sector. Success stories are emerging and the state sector is far from a write-off. Further, these are drawn from all manufacturing sectors, attesting to the potential for a diversified manufacturing base. In view of the largely autonomous operations of state owned enterprises, the positive adjustments indicate that decentralized approaches to transformation adjustments could work if bolstered by managerial incentive. (Pinto *et al.*, 1993)

This evidence seems to confirm the opinion of Joe Berliner (1993) that gains from privatization of state firms depend on many environmental and historical circumstances[14] and are usually much

---

[14] He aptly remarked: 'The fact that it would be better to have had private enterprises rather than state enterprises in the first place is not an argument for rapid privatization, or for slow privatization, or even for any privatization at all. It all depends on what funny things might happen on the way to the Forum.' (Berliner, 1993, p. 3)

Table 1
Gross and Net Profitability of State and Private Sectors (% of turnover)

Sectors	State sector			Private sector		
Years	1995	1996	1997	1995	1996	1997
Gross	4.3	2.9	3.4	3.2	3.5	3.1
Net	1.7	0.8	1.4	1.7	2.0	1.7

Source: Central Statistical Office, 1998.

smaller than those from the decentralization and marketization of the economy.

Unfortunately, however, the whole thrust of economic policy was in a different direction—fiscal discrimination, if not outright hostility towards the state sector and an obsession with privatization (Kowalik, 1994). During the first stage of transformation, SFs were sacrificed on the altar of a doctrinaire belief that their rapid privatization was a condition *sine qua non* of an efficient market economy. In a process of transformation, at least three other factors started to co-determine governments' and managers' drive for rapid privatization. First, governments treated privatization as a rich and permanent source of budget revenue, needed, for example, for financing a transition from a pay-as-you-go pension system to a very costly partially funded system. Second, many reports by the Supreme Chamber of Control (SCC) show that privatization is the most vulnerable sphere for corruption (this is the opinion openly expressed by the SCC chairman). The third factor is the pressure for re-privatization of nationalized enterprises and premises, or for compensation for former owners of nationalized firms. In the near future also a fourth factor, the necessity to repay foreign debts, may play an important role. In these circumstances the efficiency of the present SFs and future privatized firms is not the decisive issue for economic policy.

Despite the obsession with privatization, the openly discriminatory policy towards SFs, together with the great uncertainty they operate under, their performance is not radically different from private firms. In the first years of transformation (till 1994), statistical data of financial conditions have shown higher profitability (gross and net) of SFs than of private ones. The usual explanation was that private firms hide profits in undeclared activities or by artificially raising costs (treating privately used cars, computers, tourist trips, etc. as costs). Data for recent years show better performance of the private than state sector (Table 1).

Of course, these are very rough data on a limited dimension of efficiency.[15] However, much other research also shows no great differences in profitability of these two sectors. Particularly when we exclude from the state sector the so-called 'socialist dinosaurs', such as railways, tractors, mining, military equipment, which bring great losses and which traditionally are highly politicized, the performance of these two sectors is rather similar.

This outcome is quite surprising, because there were several factors putting the state firms at a disadvantage. Some of them are historical, some created by government policies. First, the rapid transition from a centrally planned to market economy, together with the 'revolution in incomes distribution', led to a sharp decline of production with a radically changed structure of demand. The old and particularly newly private small trade and manufacturing firms could easily have met this demand, whereas state firms, especially bigger ones, were overburdened by old, usually inflexible, and often redundant production equipment.

Second, this equipment was in many cases depleted by the phenomenon widely known as enfranchisement of the *nomenklatura*. Managers of state firms succeeded in transferring over some of the best pieces of state firms into newly created private firms. Unfortunately, we do not know the scope of this grey form of privatization. Some researchers (Krajewski and Piasecki, 1999) regard it as one of the most important factors determining the dynamics of SMPEs. In such cases, those managers who wanted to participate in the insider's privatization were 'preparing' their firms for privatization, deliberately making them less and less efficient in order to reduce their price. In cases of application for transforming SFs into leasing employee companies, both managers and work-force had a common interest in this way of reducing the leased firm's value.

The third factor is probably the most important. According to a unique study of tax burden in 1993 (Krajewska, 1994),[16] SFs paid on average at least three times more income tax than private ones, and this even excludes private firms' participation in the untaxed grey economy. Even after VAT was introduced, this type of discrimination still exists,

[15] The picture is different when we compare efficiency of SFs with *privatized* firms only. We have to remember, however, that for privatization by direct sale, and particularly sale to foreigners, the most efficient or promising firms were selected. Now being privatized, Telekomunikacja Polska and petrol holding, both worth more than US$20 billion, are regarded as among the last 'silver jewels'.

[16] It is shameful that this study is the only serious research of tax burdens and liabilities of the two sectors. At present it is very difficult to get data, because the way the statistics are arranged makes such studies almost impossible.

though to a lesser extent. This is partially due to special taxes paid by SFs and partially to an inefficient or currupt fiscal administration. Some state companies have to compete with foreign corporations profiting from long-lasting tax holidays. Sectoral differences in contributions to social security are also unfavourable to SFs.

By and large, then, in spite of many attempts to speed up the privatization of SFs, they still contributed almost half of production in 1996. In such branches as mining, supply of energy, gas, and water, only 2–2.5 per cent was in the hands of private firms. In transport, chemicals, textiles, metallurgy, and machinery, SFs still dominate. As we have seen, the private sector became dominant in the Polish economy as a whole, due to newly created firms, and not to privatization of SFs. As far as the number of employees and value of assets is concerned, we are still in the initial stage of SF privatization. Since their performance is not bad, despite many disadvantages, the basis of economic policy should be to put state and private firms on an equal footing, paying much more attention to the state sector as such rather than treating it simply as a target for privatization only. Instead of this, many Solidarity trade unionists and MPs are obsessed by the illusion of mass enfranchisement. However, why should public ownership, when combined with political democracy (or with liberal corporatism), demonopolized, socially controlled, and efficiently managed, not be seen as society's enfranchisement?

5. Mass Enfranchisement

The present conflict between the Union of Freedom and Solidarity Action for the Election (AWS) over proposals for mass citizens enfranchisement is a continuation of an old Wałęsa and Solidarity struggle to align privatization closer to social justice and equality.

The issue of mass enfranchisement has been again and again brought up in public debates. In 1991 Wałęsa's programme in its most mature form proposed highly preferential credits, the equivalent of US$10,000, provided in the form of coupons and repayable over a period of 20 years. This credit was to be interest free for the first 10 years, after which interest would be paid at a rate of 10 per cent, secured against the assets acquired. These coupons would enable acquisition of: state-owned enterprises or shares in privatized enterprises, state or co-operative apartments, municipal property, and even the products of enterprises. The programme was eventually rejected by the government as utopian (and disavowed by Wałęsa's own advisors, as the fantasy of an ignoramus).

The project for a 300 million złoty credit for each adult Pole, presented by the 'Network' of Solidarity Plant Committees fared no better. It was put forward as an alternative to National Investment Funds during the final phase of legislative work on the latter. This project also foresaw the purchase of apartments, shops, shares, etc. on even more favourable terms than in Wałęsa's proposals (Suwalski, 1997).

Citizen enfranchisement has always been popular in the 'Solidarity' union. At the 6th NSZZ 'Solidarity' Congress in June 1995 the Union demanded a national referendum on this issue, which took place in February 1996 but did not achieve a sufficient majority.[17] The idea took the shape of a draft act submitted by Parliament only in 1997, after AWS came to power. Since May 1997, the bill on general enfranchisement, signed by 111 AWS parliamentarians, has been in parliament along with competing proposals (Semprich, 1998). The government has also promised its own draft act in an attempt to keep one of its most important election promises.

The author of the most radical draft is a professor of the Catholic University in Lublin, Adam Biela, and his support is strongest in the Regional Enfranchisement Societies connected with some chapters of the Solidarity union and particularly with the populist and nationalistic Radio Maria. The authors declare their desire to cancel out the injustice resulting from the fact that employees of privatized state firms have the right to get free of charge 15 per cent of the shares of their enterprise (according to the first Privatization Act of 1990, this right amounted to 20 per cent of shares purchased for a price equal to half the market price). So it is a question of 'enfranchising' those citizens who were unable to take advantage of this right.

The bill provides for two types of enfranchisement: direct and indirect. In the first of these, participation will be by the residents of co-operative apartments, perpetual leaseholders of land, and the lease-holders of recreational plots. They are to become their fully lawful owners. Those, on the other hand, who do not belong to this group of leaseholders would receive bonds constituting the equivalent in value

---

[17] Regardless of the defeat suffered by the project's authors, this idea, as Lewandowski has written (1999), played 'an important role in mobilizing and consolidating the AWS electorate. The enfranchisement campaign in 1996 was the first battle won by the solidarity camp since Lech Wałęsa's election defeat. . . . The intensity of enfranchisement hysteria was comparable to that surrounding the constitutional campaign.'

of an average annual wage! They would be entitled to exchange these bonds for shares or stocks in companies, properties of the Agricultural Ownership Agency or shares in pension funds. An alternative submitted by the 21 AWS parliamentarians is slightly less radical and the government programme that has been announced will doubtless be even more realistic.

Critics of the enfranchisement programme, particularly Lewandowski (1999), quite justifiably point out that first, this programme is extremely delayed because in the meantime the State Treasury's assets have been seriously diminished, and second, that the financial needs and obligations of the state are now enormous. Just recently the government passed over to the parliament a bill on property restitution. This is a gigantic programme, burdening the budget for many years, since the government proposes to abolish the Agrarian Reform Act of 1944 and the Nationalization Act of 1946 and to hand over the assets to or compensate the old owners and their inheritors. Thus we may easily foresee another defeat being suffered by the enfranchisement idea. The point, however, is that there is not only a debate, but open and as yet unresolved conflicts over equitable privatization also within the present coalition.

One may, however, look upon the stubborn renewal of the enfranchisement idea from a more general point of view: as society's lack of acceptance of the privatization policy conducted by each new government. In Władysław Adamski's opinion:

> Blue-collar workers today are the only influential social class which has not yet come to terms with the status which the newly-emerging economic system has to offer. What distinguishes this class from the remaining ones is: (a) strong and still rising aspirations to 'start a business of their own' along with even stronger and even more rapidly increasing rejection of the ongoing privatization of state owned firms; (b) aversion towards hired work in private firms and consistent clinging to the public employer whose only acceptable alternative is the model of employee-owned enterprise or some other form of ownership with significant employee participation. (Adamski, 1999, p. 181)

The answers given by peasant respondents involve even sharper criticisms:

> Peasants as a group are relatively least interested in market solutions and most approving of egalitarian ones if we compare them with urban categories of industrial workers.... They view the process of structural change ... as something predominantly evil.... If we consider that the peasants as a social group have always been struggling for private ownership, the resentment with which they view privatization comes as something of a surprise ... they are more attached than any other segment of Polish society to socialist ideas and the social reality of the past. Farmers, as a social group, are also the most pronounced critics of capitalism.... Even the unemployed differ from the

peasants—their appraisals of socialism are less lenient and they are less resentful of capitalism. (Szafraniec and Adamski, 1999, pp. 143-4)

Up to now, these two social groups have acted independently. The new phenomenon of mass demonstrations by peasants early in 1999 were the first indications of joint worker–peasant action. A potential threat for the entire socio-economic order, a threat of rebellion, or at least destabilizing class struggles stem from the fact that the systemic transformations, including ownership transformations, are being carried out against the will of the two basic social classes—workers and peasants. Jacek Kuroń (1997) justifiably warned recently that:

> when large social groups feel that they have been pushed outside the framework of society, that they have been deprived of the chance to share in a normal life and that the opportunity to fulfil their aspirations has been taken from them, they begin to rebel against such order and may destroy it.

All the above described phenomena prevent me from accepting the opinion which has been particularly popular in the West, that in the past years 'Poland experienced an unprecedented boom and social progress' (*Time*, 3 May 1999). The transformation to date has created a system fraught with social conflicts. Even if the revival of our economy during the last 6 years is characterized as a boom, I would not see it as bringing 'social progress'. This boom went hand in hand, rather, with social regress, as expressed in mass unemployment, rapidly increased poverty and inequalities, reduced real wages of the majority of employees, a catastrophic situation in housing, and the flouting of social justice in the privatization of the national economy. There are, of course, some winners. How many? Some say about 15 per cent, some even one-third of the population. Even if it is so, they do not, and cannot balance the sufferings of the losers, who are much more numerous.

During periods of cyclical boom, unemployment may decline slightly, and the number of those who have been marginalized may fall somewhat. But income inequality, unemployment, and marginalization of a large part of the population will probably remain for years as the most characteristic features of the new social order (at least, until the next great upheaval).

6. The First in the Classroom

Karol Modzelewski writes that 'the ease with which the élites, called to life by the workers' movement, were able to make a turn about 180 degrees and discard the values, hitherto considered essential' was for him 'a great surprise' (Modzelewski, 1993). This observation by a veteran of left-wing opposition to the communist regime and one of a very few Solidarity activists who maintained a consistent position was fully confirmed by the investigation of two political sociologists surveying the new parliamentary élite (Białecki and Mach, 1992, pp. 129-30). Respondents on the street considered the three most important issues for the government to be limitation of unemployment, reduction of inflation, and agricultural protection. Next on the list were: struggle against poverty, criminality, and chaos and, finally, construction of housing. For the Solidarity MPs, on the other hand, the most important issues were privatization, struggle against chaos, and the moral renewal of society. Only one Solidarity MP regarded unemployment as the most important issue. None chose poverty (remember that during the first year of 'shock therapy' real wages dropped for more than one-third).

We observe the same 180-degree turn in the mass media. The most glaring example was the daily newspaper, *Gazeta Wyborcza*,[18] founded and led for a long time by the internationally known[19] leftist, Adam Michnik, and other members of the famous Kommittee of Workers Defence (KOR), or the illegal journal, *Robotnik* (*The Worker*). The daily is an adamant defender of the liberal conservative party 'Union of Freedom' (together with the Polish Big Bang). On the other hand it fiercely condemned workers' and peasants' demonstrations, highway blockades, and hunger strikes as compromising the social order, violating the law, and destabilizing the state. It has also been highly critical of all forms of collective property — state, cooperative, or employee companies.

The main mission (if not obsession) of this new élite was Poland's modernization of the economy by 'jumping into the West' as shown by a sample of views of the most eminent new rulers. One of the architects of our present political system, Professor Bronisław Geremek, was justifying *post-factum* Polish 'shock therapy':

[I] knew that it, in fact, was the only possibility which would allow Poland the chance to attain a place in the European economic order . . . I also knew that we had to move very quickly because Europe had no intention of waiting for us. (Geremek, 1990, p. 365)

[18] Operating as a form of joint stock company, recently accepted by Warsaw Stock Exchange. It was revealed that among the shareholders there are more than one hundred of *Gazeta* journalists millionaires (some of them multi-millionaires).

[19] Michnik was nominated Doctor Honoris Causa by the new School of Social Research, the unique left-wing American university. The initiator of this act, Ira Katznelson (1995), who delivered it to Michnik half legally in the 1980s, expressed his surprise in a book: *Liberalism's Crooked Circle. Letters to Adam Michnik*. A couple of years ago he tried to convince Michnik that he would be open at least to *social* liberalism's arguments.

Hall (1993) comments: 'We should carry out the process quickly because a particular economic chance never lasts long.' When Wałęsa was accused by his colleagues of not working for the restoration of a strong Solidarity trade union, he answered that, with a strong union, radical economic reform would be impossible (Ławiński, 1989). Already as a president, he used to talk about 'instant, lightning speed privatization'. Integration with Western Europe was widely believed to be the quickest way to obtain the Western standard of life.

In 1989 Poland's economy was suffering a 'debt trap'. Thus it was rather self-evident that it could have come under strong pressure from the creditors, mainly the USA, IMF, and the World Bank. This pressure, however, did not need to be applied because the new élite accepted the IMF proposals without any resistance. The IMF expert (Bruno, 1992)[20] reports that when the IMF team presented three different options for a stabilization programme, the Polish government unanimously chose the most radical one, apparently believing that this would be the quickest route to necessary modernization. Most probably they believed that the more radical the stabilization programme the greater would be the level of Western financial assistance.

Perhaps one of the most influential elements of 'sociological and economic imagination' of the Polish ruling élite is a deeply rooted belief that Poland has to go through a process of 'primitive capital accumulation'. Many politicians and economists believe that Poland has to follow the old experience of the United States, Great Britain, or even of Germany. In accordance with this opinion, the rich and their wealth are the main source of investment and development. Some even repeat an old saying that the legendary first million dollars from speculation or fraud should be tolerated. One Solidarity activist wrote,

> In Poland's return to Europe the economic and psychological revolution has to take place first and this means nineteenth century capitalism with its primitive accumulation of capital, exploitation and inequalities; then we can talk of the more modern forms of state and economic organization. (Surdykowski, 1990)

One of the top government advisors believed that, 'The pre-condition of rapid economic growth is the emergence of a financial, intellectual and professional élite which will, through the accumulation of resources and knowledge guarantee the engines of development (invest-

---

[20] Bruno was surprised at how easy it was to reach an agreement with the Polish negotiators, and compares it with very tough negotiations with governments of the Third World countries.

ments, know-how, science)' (Zienkowski, 1996). For former Finance Minister Kołodko, transition to a market economy presupposes 'a substantial shift in income from the poorest to the wealthiest', simply because there cannot be capitalism without capital or capitalists. This shift is always risky and 'more difficult than similar historical processes of primitive accumulation because of the current severe contraction and even economic depression' (Kołodko, 1999, p. 202). Believing in it, even well-known leftists (such as Jacek Kuroń) suspended their social democratic views 'while the foundations of a market economy were being built'. All of them ignore the fact that, in this century, several private market economies (for example, Austria, Finland, and, more recently, Spain), have been modernized without mass impoverishment, as well as the fact that Poland has already been industrialized (in some branches even over-industrialized) and can finance additional accumulation from retained profits.

One more question should be touched here. Namely, why among the countries of Central Europe, Poland is in the lead in so many negative phenomena: highest unemployment, largest increase of families living below the line of poverty, highest (Gini) coefficients of income and wage inequalities, the largest gap between men and women's incomes and salaries (Domański, 1996).

This itself raises many questions. Does a high rate of economic growth have its source, as some say, exactly in these negative phenomena. Joseph Stiglitz regards as one of the main experiences of the Asian 'tigers' the fact that they proved exactly the opposite, that 'the high saving rate [that is, savings that guarantee high share of investments in GDP – TK] *can be assured in an egalitarian surrounding and that accumulation of human capital is equally important – if not more important than the increase of physical capital'* (Stiglitz, 1997, p. 13, emphasis by TK).

On the other hand, one can give numerous examples, indicating that, not only in 1989, Poland was the pioneer in overturning communism and shaping a model of peaceful transition from a monocentric political system to political pluralism and also in starting the 'great operation', as it was called at that time, of a jump to a private market economy. Its final form was the result of a conscious choice. The unswerving commitment of Balcerowicz in introducing this reform, combined with the attractiveness of the political model, caused the Polish transformation process to be followed by other post-communist countries right up to the present, more or less successfully, though usually in a milder form.

Removing the customs barriers in 1990 made Poland one of the most *laissez-faire*-ist countries in the world (just behind Hong Kong). The urge to make Poland 'the first in the classroom' persists up to the present, as the following examples suggest.

In many Western countries the pension system is under pressure, because of the ageing of society and also because of the decline of the average rate of economic growth. But still a public pension (pay-as-you-go) system is dominant. Poland, as advised by the World Bank, is introducing a reform that has a very high — perhaps the highest in Europe — funded element, dependent on the situation in the financial markets, including the stock market. This further enlarges the area of uncertainty in social life.

At this very moment Poland has one of the highest shares of the private sector in the health-care services, perhaps the highest if we include the grey economy (Tymowska, 1999). Nevertheless, the reform introduced on 1 January 1999 emphasizes the continued rapid privatization of the health-care services.

In agriculture Poland has one of the most free-trade regimes in Europe, west of the Ukraine. Agricultural production is hardly subsidized and this creates a striking asymmetry in competition between Polish agricultural products and those from highly subsidized Western Europe. That is why the income of farmers is persistently more than one-third lower than 10 years ago.

Two more current government initiatives in economic policy are worth mentioning. The finance minister has attempted to introduce a linear income tax, which up till now has only been experimented with in Estonia. In all other countries there are more or less progressive taxation systems. But lately this idea has been revived and among the ruling élite there is the view that the initial defeat was caused not by the substance of the proposal, but by tactical defections (lack of proper negotiation within the coalition). And finally Poland may prove to be a pioneer in the field of educational vouchers, originally proposed by Milton Friedman.

In the light of all these reforms and proposals it is necessary to reconsider Poland's pioneering role. The events of 1989 obliged the Polish political élite to become pioneers in the reforms required to introduce a market economy. But already the 1989 programme of stabilization and systemic changes contained many elements of deliberate pioneering. This programme and its definite 'overshooting' may be considered as instrumental in creating a new system according to models promoted by the IMF, the World Bank, and many American advisors. The 'revolution in income distribution' and the emergence of the new social structure were shaped mainly by: the drastic inflationary reduction of and never compensated personal savings; the equally drastic, and also up until now not compensated for, drop in real wages and salaries;[21] almost total abolition of customs barriers; and near to symbolic tax for private firms.

By and large then, Polish authorities behave as if they wanted to pay the high 'penalty of being in the lead' (as Veblen famously put it). But one must also consider the very frequent criticism by the main architect of the Polish transformation model, Leszek Balcerowicz, directed at the 'oversocialization' of Western economies, particularly of the German economy. From this one may conclude that Poland wants to 'spring into Europe' based not on the continental European economic model, but rather on the highly anti-egalitarian North American one.

Chronology

August–September 1980 – worker's mass strikes in Gdańsk and Szczecin shipyards, the railways, Silesian coal mines, etc. ended with several agreements between the political authorities (Communist Party and government) and the strikers, legalizing the independent and self-governing trade union, 'Solidarnoœeæ' (Solidarity). This mass social movement soon counted almost 10m members.

October 1981 – ratification of the Solidarity Programme entitled The Self-Governing Republic, pro-market and pro-syndicalist.

13 December 1981–Summer 1993 – Marshall Law de-legalizing Solidarity and limiting several human and citizens' rights.

January 1982 – an economic reform sharply reducing central planning, but preserving rationing of assets and funds (creating a system often called 'neither plan nor market').

February-April 1989 – the Round Table negotiations between the political authorities and the representatives of a broad opposition circle (dominated by Solidarity) accomplished an agreement on some liberalization of parliamentary elections (one-third of seats in Sejm and free election to a newly created Senat), legalization of Solidarity, and radical economic reforms.

4 June 1989 – unintended by the political authorities and unexpected by the opposition, spectacular victory of Solidarity in parliamentary election.

September 1989 – formation of a non-communist government led by a Catholic, Tadeusz Mazowiecki. It was dominated by the Solidarity activists, but some communists were included. Leszek Balcerowicz was nominated as a deputy prime minister and finance minister.

---

[21] At the end of 1996 they were about one-fifth lower than in 1989 (Zienkowski, 1998), or in 1981 (Jacukowicz, 1997), though GDP was already slightly higher.

End of December 1989 — parliamentary ratification of government's 11 bills containing the so-called Balcerowicza Plan (called by opponents 'shock without therapy' or 'Big Bang'). These laws came into force on 1 January 1990.

January 1990 — dissolution of the Polish Workers United Party and a creation of a much smaller Social-Democracy of Polish Republic (SDPR). Soon the Alliance of the Democratic Left (ADL) was formed, a non-Solidarity federation of trade unions and some two dozen other political and social units, clearly dominated by SDPR.

13 July 1990 — law on privatization was ratified (subsequently amended many times).

January 1991 (after Wałęsa's victory in presidential elections) — creation of a new Cabinet of Jan K. Bielecki. Balcerowicz preserves his posts.

Autumn 1991 — the first free parliamentary elections. Twenty-nine mostly newly created parties had a seat in Sejm. Main parties: ADL, Polish Peasant Party (PPP), The Union of Labour — on the left; and Union of National Christians, Alliance of the Centre, Liberal Democratic Congress, Democratic Union chaired by T. Mazowiecki (later both unified into Union of Freedom chaired by L. Balcerowicz) — on the right. In 1991-3 there were several Cabinets led by parties stemming from a split in Solidarity.

Spring 1993 — Hanna Suchocka's Cabinet lost Parliament's vote of confidence and new elections were called.

September 1993 — at the elections the ADL and other parties in opposition got a majority in parliament. Several post-Solidarity and right-wing parties did not get a newly fixed minimum of 5 per cent of the votes and remained outside the parliament. Between 1993 and 1997 a coalition of the ADF and the PPP was in government. Surprisingly, the IMF-supported 'market friendly policy' (with some minor changes) was continued.

25 May 1997 — the Constitution of the Polish Republic was ratified in a referendum. The constitution states that the foundation of the economic system is 'social market economy based on freedom of economic activity, private property, solidarity, dialog and cooperation of social partners' (art. 22) and that The Republic realizes 'principles of social justice' (art. 2). The Constitution was an outcome of a great compromise between four main parliamentary factions, but furiously attacked by Solidarity and the right-wing parties which were outside parliament.

September 1997 — an electoral victory for Solidarity Action for the Election (AWS), which was an alliance of the Solidarity trade union and many Christian, right-wing parties. A coalition of AWS and Union of Freedom formed a government headed by Jerzy Buzek (prime minister, former Solidarity activist) and Leszek Balcerowicz as his deputy and minister of finance.

10

The Choices for Scandinavian Social Democracy in Comparative Perspective

TORBEN IVERSEN*

1. Introduction

The purpose of this chapter is threefold. First, it seeks to describe the rise, maturation, and eventual decline of two of the most systematic attempts to implement a social democratic economic model: Denmark and Sweden. Focusing on the 1980s and 1990s, I devote particular attention to the breakdown of peak-level coordination of macroeconomic policies and wage bargaining, which in the past had facilitated full employment and exceptional levels of wage equality. Second, through a comparison of the Danish and Swedish experiences with those of other Northern European democracies, I attempt to provide a more general understanding of the interaction between economic policies and macro institutions, and how this interaction is conditioned by internationalization of financial markets, the rise of the service economy, and the introduction of new technology. Third, I try to draw general lessons from the Scandinavian experiences by outlining some of the main choices that face social democracy in the 1990s. In particular, I argue that social democracy faces a difficult 'trilemma' where fiscal responsibility in the sense of tight constraints on spending engenders a steeper trade-off between social democracy's traditional goals of equality and full employment.

The rest of the chapter is divided into three parts. Section 2 is a very brief history of the rise of the Scandinavian model, focusing on some of its main institutional characteristics and the role of social democracy. Section 3 discusses the challenges to the model in the 1980s and 1990s, and how social democratic governments have sought to address these, emphasizing changes in the wage bargaining system, in the macroeco-

* Department of Government, Harvard University.

I wish to thank Andrew Glyn and two anonymous reviewers for many helpful comments and suggestions on a previous version of this paper.

nomic regime, and in the employment structure. The final section discusses the economic policy trade-offs facing social democracy, and how these trade-offs may be alleviated.

2. The Rise of the Scandinavian Model

In the decade after the Second World War, Denmark was a relatively stagnant society with low growth, high unemployment, and an under-developed industrial base (Hansen, 1983, ch. 18). Unlike in the other Scandinavian countries, there was little state regulation of industrial development, and credit markets were comparatively open and left to the oversight of an independent central bank (Mjøset, 1986, p. 137; Uusitalo, 1984). By contrast, the Swedish economy in the 1950s had reached a high level of industrialization (greatly facilitated by a large raw material base), and the state was actively engaged in promoting industrial growth—partly through investment funds and active labour-market policies, and partly through comprehensive credit and currency market controls. The central bank wielded considerable power over credit formation in the economy, and the government used its strong influence over the bank to pursue counter-cyclical monetary policies and to steer investments by means of credit rationing (Mjøset, 1986, p. 131; Scharpf, 1991, p. 205).

During the 1960s, however, the economic and political-institutional infrastructures of the two economies began to converge. Along with a liberalization of manufacturing trade (through the European Free Trade Association (EFTA)), small and medium-sized firms in the Danish industrial sector went through a dynamic phase of expansion (especially in the machine tool industry), causing agriculture to lose its position as the main export sector, and generating high levels of real growth accompanied by virtually full employment. New credit institutions also emerged to provide low-cost capital for the booming industrial sector, and labour-market policies became notably more active.

The industrial-relations systems in the two countries also grew more similar during the 1960s. The combination of a building boom and a rapid expansion of public-service production prompted the main union confederation (LO) and employer association (DA) in Denmark to assume direct bargaining competence over all general negotiation issues; and since agreements had to be approved by a collective vote, after which a strict peace clause would kick in, the autonomy of individual unions was strictly limited (Due et al., 1994). In Sweden the centralization of wage bargaining initiated by the Saltsjöbaden Agreement of 1938 was furthered by yielding greater authority to the LO executive committee over bargaining and the use of strike funds, and at the 1951 LO congress a decisive step towards centralization was taken with the adoption of the Rehn–Meidner model of solidaristic wage policies.

The basic idea behind the Rehn–Meidner model was that by demanding 'equal wages for equal work' across industries and sectors, it was possible for LO not only to promote the egalitarian ideals of the union movement, but also to ensure a dynamic modernization of the economy by forcing inefficient companies either to rationalize or close down, while simultaneously assisting the expansion of efficient firms. Profit–wage spirals would be prevented through restrained fiscal policies, while local and industry-specific unemployment was to be alleviated through active labour-market policies (Martin, 1979; Elvander, 1988, pp. 32–3; Swenson, 1989, pp. 130–3).

By the beginning of the 1960s, both countries were dominated by highly centralized bargaining systems, and with social democratic parties whose electoral support reached all-time highs of 42 per cent in Denmark and 47 per cent in Sweden, the stage was set for a 'golden period' of social democratic welfare capitalism. The government was increasing employment and educational opportunities for everyone (mainly through public services), while wages and prices were successfully held back through consensual wage agreements between peak associations of labour and capital. The public economy in Denmark almost doubled in size during the decade of the 1960s, catching up to Sweden in the mid-1970s when total public spending in both countries reached about half of the GDP. Moreover, rapid economic growth made income redistribution through solidaristic wage policies and increases in the 'social wage' (i.e. transfer payments and social services) both a politically viable strategy, as well as a means to facilitate rapid sectoral transformation and high labour mobility.

A prominent example of the Danish politics of class compromise was the 1963 Danish 'package solution' (*Helhedsløsningen*). One of the first of its kind in Western Europe, this comprehensive agreement between a social-democratic-led government and the main labour-market organizations provided for moderate wage increases and low-wage supplements, combined with legislation that increased various social benefits and instituted a new pension scheme (ATP) whose funds were earmarked for investment in Danish industry. The agreement thus contained all the core elements of the corporatist bargain: wage restraint (to be self-administered by LO and DA), wage solidarity (low-wage supplements), an increase in the social wage, and provisions to reassure workers about their future welfare (the ATP fund) (Esping-Andersen, 1990, pp. 171–2).

It is a testimony to the entrenchment of this 'bridge-building' policy in Denmark that it was continued and even expanded during the centre-right majority government from 1968 to 1971. Although the economy was getting 'overheated' as a result of expansionary macroeconomic policies (Nannestad, 1991, p. 137), the bourgeois government embarked on an ambitious 'spend-and-tax' programme that dwarfed anything the social democrats had done in the past (taxes increased from 33 to 44 per cent of GNP between 1968 and 1971). This was the background for the (in many ways quite reasonable) claim by Mogens Glistrup — the flamboyant founder of the right-wing Progress Party — that Denmark had four social democratic parties (the Social Democrats, the Conservatives, the Liberals, and the Radical Liberals) and only one liberal one (his own).

In Sweden the economic policies of the social democratic government also led to a rapid expansion of public consumption, although 'supply-side' policies continued to play a greater role than in Denmark (Stephens *et al.*, 1999, p. 180). In particular, the active labour-market policy (administered by the Labor Market Board with representatives from both LO and the employers' federation, SAF) funnelled large resources into training and relocation programmes to re-employ those made redundant by the solidaristic wage policy (Erixon, 1984; Scharpf, 1991, pp. 90–4). The policy had the effect of relieving some of the pressure on fiscal policies because it facilitated job growth in the dynamic sectors of the economy without the need for fiscal expansionism (Rehn, 1985). Although fiscal policies were never restrictive in the sense envisaged by the Rehn–Meidner model, Swedish full employment policies were thus not subject to the same 'overheating' problems as the Danish. Swings in the Swedish business cycle were also counteracted through investment policies that hoarded business surpluses during economic upswings and released them during downturns (Mjøset, 1986, p. 130). Tax and interest-rate policies supported this strategy through a combination of high profit taxes and low interest rates which strongly favoured investments over consumption (Pontusson, 1992*a*).[1]

3. The Scandinavian Model in Transition

During the 1970s and 1980s a number of both domestic and international economic developments started to produce cracks in the veneer

[1] Although, as mentioned above, it became more difficult during the 1960s to maintain interest rates significantly below the international level as a result of growing internationalization of capital markets.

of the social democratic project. Two of its core components — centralized, solidaristic wage bargaining and the commitment to full employment — came under particularly intense pressure. I discuss each in turn.

(a) *Centralized and Solidaristic Bargaining*

In both countries, centralized bargaining had facilitated negotiated wage restraint, but it had also produced a notable compression of wages by giving low-wage unions considerable organizational influence over the distribution of wages. In Denmark the central negotiation committee of the LO was composed of the chairpersons of LO and the major national unions — with the Metalworkers' Union (Metal), the General Workers' Union (SID), and later the Union of Commercial and Clerical Employees (HK) in the role of veto-players. Consequently, 'no agreement could be reached without granting rises to low-paid groups', creating a 'vigorous element of solidarity' (Due *et al.*, 1994, p. 189). The Swedish LO's solidaristic wage policy had a more articulated intellectual and ideological justification, but the logic of bargaining power being equalized between high- and low-wage workers through centralization was similar. Although the industrial union structure in Sweden is less polarized between high- and low-wage unions than in Denmark, unions with predominantly low-paid members formed a majority in LO's collegiate council which determines the collective bargaining strategy (Swenson, 1989, p. 59).

Using a variety of statistical sources, wage dispersion for Danish manual workers diminished by about 54 per cent between 1963 and 1977, while in the period from 1970 to 1982 the decline for salaried private employees in Denmark was 26 per cent. In Sweden, wage dispersion in the LO–SAF area decreased by about 54 per cent between 1970 and 1980, while the decline for the PTK–SAF area was 26 per cent between 1972 and 1980.[2] As a result, Denmark and Sweden (along with Norway) have some of the most compressed wage structures in the OECD, and compression is closely related to bargaining centralization (see Figure 1). In quantitative terms, a Swedish worker in the lowest decile of the earnings distribution earns about 80 per cent of the earnings of the median worker ('d1/d5 ratios'), while in Canada the comparable figure is 45 per cent.

---

[2] These figures are my own calculations from various data sources (mostly from national statistical offices, but also from the main employers associations' wage statistics and data provided in Hibbs and Locking, 1991). It should be noted that because the data are based on different methodologies, the relative sizes of the figures must be taken with a grain of salt.

Figure 1
Earnings Equality and Centralization of Wage Bargaining

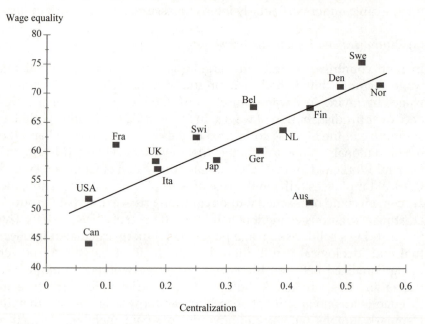

Notes: Wage equality is measured as the ratio of gross earnings (including all employer contributions for pensions, social security, etc.) of a worker at the bottom decile of the earnings distribution relative to the worker at the median (d1/d5 ratios). Figures are averages for the period 1977–93 computed from the OECD's *Employment Outlook* (1991, 1996). Centralization is an index based on the number of unions and the importance of different bargaining levels (see Iversen, 1998).

Solidaristic wage policies ran into difficulties in the 1980s for a variety of reasons. One problem was that the market position of the high-skilled/well-educated segment of the labour force grew out of line with relative wages. While standardized and skill-extensive modes of production in the past had facilitated compression of wages, and made overall wage restraint the most important component of competitiveness, the introduction of more knowledge-intensive and flexible technologies ('diversified quality production') placed greater emphasis on employee qualifications and commitment, and less on the level of their wages (Pontusson and Swenson, 1996; Iversen, 1996). This gave skilled workers opportunities for additional wage increases at the firm level, and simultaneously exposed low-skilled workers to greater risk of unemployment.

For employers, especially in the engineering sector, solidaristic wage policies were seen as an obstacle to achieving greater production flexibility and international competitiveness (see Pontusson and Swenson, 1996, for Sweden, and Ibsen and Stamhus, 1993, pp. 74–92, for Denmark). As technology became more skill-intensive, and as more decision-making power was delegated to the shop-floor, many employers (especially in the engineering sector) found it imperative to improve the wage and employment conditions for their skilled employees, and to encourage their continued acquisition of firm-specific skills through appropriately designed incentive systems. But the introduction of more flexible remuneration systems created problems in the centralized bargaining structure because non-standard forms of payment broke the upper limits of centrally negotiated wage norms and registered as wage drift (see Ibsen and Stamhus, 1993, pp. 53–8; Pontusson and Swenson, 1996). In turn, such drift triggered payments of compensation to other employees, either directly via formal compensation mechanisms ('earnings-development guarantees' in Sweden, and wage-indexation schemes in Denmark), or indirectly, via solidaristic wage demands in subsequent bargaining rounds.

This type of wage 'contagion' from high- to low-productivity groups extended across economic sectors through a dense network of formal and informal coordination mechanisms, themselves created to ensure centralized control over wages, and came to pose a particularly acute problem in the context of rapidly declining industrial employment.[3] High and increasing wages for the low-paid meant that labour-intensive and low-productivity private-service-sector jobs — especially in retail trade, restaurants, and hotels, and in social and personal services — would be priced out of the market.[4] The problem was exacerbated by the tendency, evident across all OECD countries, for growth in service-sector productivity significantly to lag that in manufacturing. Thus, OECD's estimates of total factor productivity indicate a persistent gap in productivity growth between private services and manufacturing, averaging about 2.5 per cent on an annual basis between 1970 and 1994.[5] If wages in services relative to wages in manufacturing had

[3] Some of these linkages were direct since portions of public employees were organized in LO member unions (the large Swedish and Danish municipal workers' unions, SKAF and DKA, are the primary examples). Equally important were more informal coordination efforts between private-sector organizations and governments, where the latter used agreements concluded in the private sector as the norm for reaching public-sector wage settlements. The consequence was that public-sector unions were subjected to private-sector wage discipline.

[4] This argument was first introduced by Baumol and Bowen (1966) and by Baumol (1967). See Gordon (1987) for carefully constructed data on productivity.

[5] This figure is calculated as an average for 14 OECD countries based on data published in the OECD's *International Sectoral Data Base* (1996).

Figure 2
Wage Equality and Expansion of Private-service-sector Employment,
1970–92

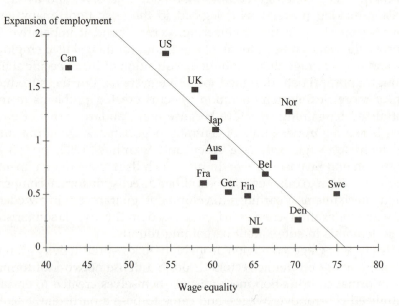

Notes: Equality of earnings is defined as d1/d5 ratios as in Figure 1. Private-service-sector expansion is the average annual increase in employment in all private services as a percentage of the working-age population.
Sources: OECD, *Employment Outlook* (1991, 1996); OECD, *International Sectoral Data Base* (1997).

to remain stable, therefore, relative prices would necessarily have to be rising. Except for very price-inelastic types of services, primarily those requiring highly educated workers, this dampened the expansion of jobs in the private-service sector.

Figure 2 illustrates this logic nicely. It shows the relationship between earnings equality – measured again as d1/d5 ratios – and the average annual increase in private-services employment as a percentage of the working-age population. The association is strong and holds across time for a variety of definitions of the dependent variable, and after control for a number of potentially confounding factors (see Glyn, 1997b, and Iversen and Wren, 1998). Norway is an outlier in Figure 2 primarily because of the rapid growth in gross incomes, which is in turn related to the expansionary macroeconomic effects of the booming oil and petrochemical sectors.

The dynamics of employment expansion in the rising service economy turns the Rehn–Meidner model on its head. While solidaristic wage policies were compatible with, and possibly even facilitating, private-sector employment growth when the potential for such growth was concentrated in the most dynamic branches of the industrial economy, such policies served as a brake on employment expansion from the mid-1960s when the greatest potential for job expansion was in low-productivity services. Barring very high levels of wage restraint (which Rehn and Meidner never believed possible) the Rehn–Meidner model therefore cannot ensure full employment in the post-industrializing economy *except* if the government steps in and employs increasingly large numbers of low-skilled workers in public services (Esping-Andersen, 1990; Appelbaum and Schettkat, 1994; Iversen and Wren, 1998).[6]

This was precisely the route followed by social democratic governments in Scandinavia as illustrated by the comparative data in Table 1. For all countries in the table, and indeed across the entire OECD, there has been a marked decline in manufacturing employment, but the magnitudes and composition of service-sector employment growth differ sharply between countries. In the social-democratic-dominated Scandinavian countries, employment in private services has been stagnant or declining throughout the 1970–92 period, whereas public-sector employment rose rapidly during the 1970s and early 1980s. By contrast, in countries such as the USA and Britain, where neo-liberal policies for privatization and deregulation held sway during the 1980s and early 1990s, employment in private services rose at a very fast pace, while public-sector employment was stagnant. Not surprisingly, these are also the countries with relatively *in*egalitarian wage structures (refer back to Figure 1), and unlike the other countries in the table, Britain and the USA grew notably more inegalitarian during the 1980s.[7]

But there is clearly an alternative to the social democratic and neo-liberal models as exemplified by Germany and the Netherlands. In these cases services employment has been stagnant in *both* the public sector (as in the neo-liberal cases) *and* in the private sector (as in the social democratic cases). Governments in these countries have been able to maintain a relatively egalitarian wage structure, while successfully controlling public consumption and taxes (before unification, in

[6] The alternative to public-sector employment expansion, while pursuing full employment and wage equality, is to discourage labour-market entry (especially of women) and encourage labour-market exit (especially of older workers). As discussed below, this is a strategy that has been followed in Austria, Germany, and some other countries dominated by Christian democracy. It is not a strategy that has been pursued consistently by either social democratic governments or liberal governments (although this may be changing).

[7] According to the OECD wage data the d1/d5 ratios went from 60 to 55 in Britain, and from 55 to 48 in the USA during the 1980s (OECD, 1996a).

Table 1
Public- and Private-service-sector Employment in Six OECD Countries,
1970–92
(% of adult population)

	Denmark	Sweden	UK	USA	Germany	Netherlands
1970–3	14 20	17 19	13 20	10 26	8 17	7 21
1974–7	17 20	20 20	15 22	10 26	9 17	7 21
1978–81	20 20	24 20	15 23	11 29	10 18	8 21
1982–5	22 20	26 20	14 24	10 31	10 18	8 20
1986–9	22 21	26 22	14 28	11 35	10 19	7 22
1990–2	22 21	26 23	14 31	11 36	10 17	7 24
Change	8 1	9 3	0 11	1 11	2 0	0 3

Note: First column is total government employment as a percentage of the adult population; second column is total private-service-sector employment as a percentage of the adult population (excluding transport and communication).
Source: OECD, International Sectoral Data Base (1996).

the case of Germany). This combination is at least partly a result of the strong influence over government policies of Christian democratic parties. In the case of the Netherlands a 'consociational' political system has accorded equal weight to the Christian democratic concern for keeping the state in a subordinate role and the social democratic concern for class solidarity and equality (van Kersbergen, 1995, ch. 4). Correspondingly, wage equality in this country is close to Scandinavian levels, but government consumption has remained almost constant at around 10–12 per cent of GDP, whereas in Scandinavia it has more than doubled from a similar starting point in the early 1960s. The 'cost' of these policies has instead come in the form of much lower labour-market participation rates, especially among women and older workers.

The Dutch model has been undergoing significant change over the past decade. Although female participation rates are still considerably lower than in either Scandinavia or North America, the gap has been narrowing somewhat in the 1980s and early 1990s. At the same time, unemployment has been almost halved from its peak in the early 1980s. Both trends are at least partly attributable to reforms aimed at making the labour market more flexible and encouraging the expansion of private-sector employment. But there has been no wholesale attempt at neo-liberal deregulation, as suggested by some observers. Wage dispersion has only increased moderately — partly as a result of the continued role of national unions in collective bargaining — and labour-market participation rates have remained close to the bottom among

OECD countries. The Dutch 'employment miracle' is rather due to an effective macroeconomic adjustment (more on this below) combined with a substantial rise in part-time female employment, early retirement, and in the number of people on disability pensions or other public assistance (Schmid, 1997).[8] The Dutch solution to employment problems is thus distinctly Christian democratic. It combines job-sharing and labour-market exit with restrictive macroeconomic policies — *neither* wholesale deregulation as in Britain or the USA, *nor* large-scale public-sector service expansion, as in Scandinavia.

In one respect, however, the Netherlands has followed a similar path as in Denmark and Sweden. Starting in the early 1980s, authority over wage-setting has shifted from the peak-level to the industry and local levels. Although tripartite bargaining continues to play a coordinating role in the Netherlands, it does not have the same compulsory character as in the 1960s and 1970s, and the solidaristic profile of wage policies has weakened (Visser, 1990). In Denmark, the practice of decentralized bargaining was initiated in 1981 (the first truly decentralized round since the early 1930s), and, as in the Netherlands, it was prompted by pressure from engineering employers and skilled workers. Despite a partial return to centralized bargaining in 1983 and in 1985, the bargaining functions of the Danish employers' association have been eclipsed by sectoral associations (especially the powerful Association of Danish Industry) that are opposed to a resumption of peak-level bargaining (Iversen, 1996). In Sweden, the metalworking sector started to conclude separate agreements in 1983 and, although decentralized industry-level bargaining has since then been interspersed with more centralized forms of bargaining (prompted by government pressure), deeper institutional changes suggest an irreversible process. SAF has shut down its central bargaining unit, and has since the mid-1980s been withdrawing from virtually all government bodies, including the previously all-important Labor Market Board (Kjellberg, 1992, p. 100). But this 'making more flexible' of the bargaining system and the wage structure is no more neo-liberal in nature than the labour-market reforms in the Netherlands. Wage dispersion has been on the rise, but it is nowhere near the levels in liberal countries such as the UK or USA, and generous unemployment replacement rates coupled with an egalitarian transfer payment system have guaranteed a continuously high 'social wage'.

---

[8] Seventy-five per cent of the increase in service-sector employment between 1985 and 1990 was part-time, and by 1989 an astonishing 13 per cent of the total labour force was listed as worker-disabled (Jones, 1998).

(b) *Macroeconomic Policies*

Until recently, Sweden was one of the small European countries that most adamantly defended its macroeconomic policy autonomy. Central to this autonomy was the choice of a 'soft' currency that enabled *ad hoc* 'technical' adjustments to exchange rates, and gave the government the capacity for occasionally large 'surprise' devaluations. The flexible exchange-rate policy undoubtedly facilitated the Swedish full-employment strategy during the 1970s and 1980s, but it clearly depended on the centralized bargaining system because devaluations only worked if followed by across-the-board wage restraint (Martin, 1985; Gylfason, 1990). For example, the social democratic government's 'Third Way' strategy of devaluation-led reflation after the election in 1982 was based on an advance agreement by LO *not* to demand compensation for the cost of living increases expected from higher prices on imports (Elvander, 1988, p. 291; Pontusson, 1992*b*, pp. 116–17).

But the economic success of centralized bargaining also came to depend crucially on monetary policy flexibility. Because collective wage bargains were inevitably followed by some wage drift, and because drift undermined the redistributive terms of the centralized bargain, it was very difficult for low-wage unions during periods of low growth to agree to bargained wage increases that would leave competitiveness unchanged without currency devaluations. LO negotiators knew that the higher the level of bargained wage increases, the lower the proportional size of wage drift, and the higher the increase in wage compression and total wage increases. Because the wage demands by LO were the result of a delicate compromise between different groups of wage earners groups, it was therefore difficult for LO to accept wage restraint at a level necessary to maintain competitiveness with fixed exchange rates during the severe recessions in the mid-1970s and early 1980s. Instead, the restoration of Swedish competitiveness was achieved through infrequent but large currency devaluations followed by negotiated wage restraint. This strategy allowed Swedish nominal wage costs to grow at a rate compatible with the LO's solidaristic wage strategy (and generally at a faster rate than in most of its competitor countries),[9] while simultaneously achieving a real wage adjustment sufficient to restore competitiveness.

Of course, this does not tell us what would have happened if centralized bargaining was *not* accompanied by flexible monetary

[9] Swedish unit labour costs in manufacturing grew by an average annual rate of 11.3 per cent during 1973–9 compared to 9.4 per cent in Denmark, 5.3 per cent in Austria, 5 per cent in Germany, and 8.8 per cent in the entire OECD.

policies, but the Danish experience in the mid- to late 1970s can throw some light on this. Denmark had joined the Snake when it was formed in 1973, and it subsequently became a member of the European Monetary System (EMS) in 1979.[10] Participation in these organizations was strongly favoured by the central bank, by the financial community, and by the Radical Party, whose support consecutive social democratic governments depended on for legislative majorities.[11] The main problem with membership in the European exchange-rate mechanisms was that the negotiated devaluations they permitted were too small to accommodate *nominal* wage increases in the Danish labour market. As a result, the Danish real effective exchange rate appreciated by 18 per cent in the first 3 years of membership of the Snake, and even when exchange-rate adjustment policies became more permissive during the 1976–8 period, Danish price competitiveness remained unchanged, while Sweden achieved a significant 12 per cent improvement (Gros and Thygesen, 1992, p. 19).

To make matters worse, because Danish inflation was above the German level, Danish interest rates incorporated a substantial 'risk premium' (real long-term interest rates in Denmark in the 1973–82 period were an average of 2.7 per cent above those in Germany). Notwithstanding the political and ideological commitments of the government, Danish economic institutions were therefore not well suited to maintain full employment during a severe recession, and unemployment soared from about 2 per cent in 1974 to over 9 per cent in 1981. At that point, real interest rates were so high that housing construction had come to an almost complete halt, and the public debt (domestic and foreign) was rising exponentially. The impasse came to a pitiful conclusion in 1982 when the social democrats, without calling for an election, simply handed the reins to a centre-right coalition government—a political and moral low point for Danish social democracy.

The Danish experience is also instructive because of what happened to the economy after the new government instituted a fundamental reorientation of economic policies. The anchor for the new low-inflation policy was a pegging of the currency to the Deutschmark,

[10] Sweden briefly joined the European currency Snake in 1973, but when the soft currency policy came into conflict with the aim of maintaining exchange-rate stability in the system, Sweden resolutely withdrew (in 1977).

[11] Representing farmer interests, the Radicals were anxious to maintain an alignment between the value of the 'Green Krone' — which was used by the European Community to compensate Danish agricultural producers for goods sold under the auspices of the Common Agricultural Policy—and the main exchange rate.

while credibility was achieved by liberalizing capital markets, eliminating the fiscal budget deficit, and suspending all cost-of-living indexation.[12] The policies enabled a gradual downward convergence of Danish interest rates to German rates with real rates falling from 10.9 to 5.5 per cent.[13] The expansionary effect of this decline, leading to massive wealth gains in securities and one-family houses, was stronger than the contractionary effects of the government's freeze on public consumption and tax increases. Simultaneously, unions' wage policies became much more restrained, and this enabled a substantial improvement in Danish competitiveness.

If the Danish case thus shows that non-accommodation in a sector-based bargaining system is compatible with wage restraint and good economic performance, the Swedish experience in the 1980s shows what happens when accommodating policies are not supported by a centralized wage-setting system. In the absence of effective peak-level control, and in the context of tight labour markets, it proved impossible for the Swedish government to prevent unions in sheltered and booming sectors from exploiting their bargaining power and 'leapfrogging' other unions.[14] The result was a rapid deterioration of Swedish competitiveness.[15] Although this could have been an argument for renewed centralization, the largest Swedish companies were opposed, and the krona was now so vulnerable to international currency speculations that the continuation of accommodating policies proved impractical. Most capital controls had been lifted during the 1980s in response to the expansion of world capital markets and the liberalization of capital controls in most other OECD countries, and this now came to haunt the social democrats (Moses, 1994, pp. 140–2). Without these controls it was difficult, if not impossible, for the government to manage a devaluation strategy, and

[12] The hard-currency policy was singled out as the centrepiece in the new government's economic strategy: 'The new government is firmly determined to recreate the balance in the Danish economy. The government has no intentions of devaluing the krone. Confidence in the value of the Danish krone at home and abroad is a good start for a new economic policy.' (Inauguration speech, 10 September 1982)

[13] Using rates on 10-year government bonds and the GDP deflator.

[14] A perverse example is the 1988 bargaining round, where an agreement was first reached in the baking [sic] sector which awarded wage increases that were totally unacceptable to the exposed industries. Another example is the decentralized 1984 bargaining round when public-sector wages broke the proposed 6 per cent pay norm.

[15] Unit labour costs rose much faster than in the rest of OECD, and in 8 of the 10 years since 1980 hourly earnings in manufacturing increased faster in Sweden than in Denmark.

since employers knew this, they had few incentives to agree to centralized coordination.[16]

Like the Danish policy reversal in 1982, the pegging of the value of the krona to the ecu in May 1991 was arguably the most important change in Swedish macroeconomic policies since the 1950s. It signalled a *de facto* abandonment of the social democratic commitment to full employment. Once the government had tied itself to a fixed exchange-rate policy, it had also committed itself to bringing other economic policy goals into line with the pursuit of this strategy, including unemployment. Fiscal policies were tightened, interest rates increased, and EC membership and participation in the EMS became government policy.

But the timing of the hard currency policy could hardly have been worse. Unlike the Danish situation prior to the 1982 Deutschmark-peg, the Swedish currency was considerably over-valued,[17] and in a poor position so it could not withstand the 1992 EMS crisis and the subsequent floating of the Finnish markka. The abandonment of the peg created some uncertainty about the commitment of the government to a non-accommodating policy, and this uncertainty was fuelled for some time by the social democratic government's close consultation with the unions and its call for a resumption of centralized bargaining. Undoubtedly this hurt the Swedish economy and worsened the unemployment situation. Gradually, however, the new restrictive macroeconomic policy has been solidified through tight fiscal policies and a *de facto* as well as *de jure* increase in the independence of the central bank. According to one analysis, the Swedish central bank has gone from being one of the most politically dependent in the 1980s to being independent on a par with the US Federal Reserve (Kilponen, 1999).

[16] An interesting question is whether the Swedish government could have gone against the tide of international capital market liberalization in the 1980s. Moses (1994), reflecting the views of most observers, argues that rapidly expanding grey markets would have made this very difficult. Notermans (1993), on the other hand, contends that new policy instruments would have made it fairly unproblematic. Be this as it may, once liberalization had been implemented it would have been very costly (in political as well as economic terms) for the government to reinstate controls when the need arose in the 1990s.

[17] It would have made sense to have devalued before instituting the peg, but the government was probably concerned that this would have looked too much like business as usual and thus have undermined the credibility of the new policy. By contrast, in Denmark the centre-right government in 1982 was in the fortunate situation that the devaluation of the currency had occurred under the previous (social democratic) government, and therefore did not signal anything about the current government's policy preferences. I wish to thank one of the anonymous reviewers for suggesting this to me.

Table 2
Unemployment Rates (%) by Monetary Regime and Centralization of
Wage Bargaining in 15 OECD Countries, 1973–93
(number of observations in parenthesis)

		Centralization of wage bargaining			
		Low	Intermediate	High	Low–High
Monetary regime	Accommodation	8.0 (12)	6.9 (12)	3.8 (13)	4.2
	Non-accommodation	7.9 (10)	3.6 (25)	7.1 (3)	0.8
	Row differences	0.1	3.3	−3.3	

Note: Data were grouped into five 4-year intervals for each country. Unemployment refers to standardized rates; the measurement of the independent variables is described in the text. The figures have been corrected for period differences in unemployment.
Sources: For dependent variable, OECD, *Economic Outlook* (various years); for independent variables, Iversen (1998).

Correspondingly, wage demands by the unions have become much more restrained, and competitiveness and unemployment have improved considerably in recent years. In many respects the macroeconomic situation in Sweden can thus be likened to the situation following the policy turnaround in Denmark in the 1980s.

The interaction between monetary regimes, bargaining institutions, and economic performance can be usefully illustrated with some comparative data (see Table 2). The monetary regime is here measured as an average of an institutional variable, central bank independence, and a more policy-sensitive variable based on relative exchange-rate movements.[18] The data are for the same 15 OECD countries as listed in Figure 1, but have been grouped into five 4-year intervals starting in 1973 (for a total of 75 observations). The centralization variable was divided into three classes: a decentralized category where firm and plant-level bargaining dominate; an intermediately centralized category with most bargaining taking place at the industry or sectoral level; and a centralized category with an important role for peak-level bargaining between encompassing organizations of labour and capital

---

[18] The index of central bank independence is an average (after standardization) of three widely used indices by Bade and Parkin (1982), Grilli *et al.* (1991), and Cukierman (1992). The exchange-rate index is based on OECD data for relative growth in nominal effective exchange rates.

(the monetary regime variable was simply divided into two categories with an equal number of cases).

The most interesting part of the table is the bottom row which shows the difference in performance between cases with 'accommodating' and 'non-accommodating' monetary regimes. Note that for highly centralized systems, there appears to be an employment loss from having a restrictive regime, while for intermediately centralized systems the opposite holds true. For decentralized systems—where wage-setters are atomistic and therefore do not interact strategically with the central bank—there are no apparent employment effects from the monetary regime. These patterns resonate well with the Scandinavian experience since, in centralized systems, where monetary authorities have been prepared to facilitate intra-confederal distributive compromises through accommodating policies—Norway and Sweden are exemplary cases until recently—employment performance has been very good. By contrast, the restrictive monetary policy regime in Denmark in the mid- to late 1970s created intense distributional conflicts and high unemployment.

In a similar vein, the table suggests why the breakdown of centralized bargaining in Denmark and Sweden placed governments, left as well as right, under considerable pressure to reform the monetary regime in a non-accommodating direction. With accommodating policies it is difficult to contain wage militancy, and unemployment and inflation are correspondingly high. Conversely, industry- and sector-level bargaining is clearly not incompatible with low unemployment if accompanied by a non-accommodating monetary regime. The reasons, which have been developed in Hall and Franzese (1998), Iversen (1998, 1999), and Soskice and Iversen (1998a), have to do with the capacity of the monetary authority to *deter* wage militancy. When unions are sufficiently large for their agreements to affect the general price level, and when monetary policy responses are predictable, a non-accommodating monetary policy rule gives bargainers an incentive to moderate demands because they know that such moderation will raise the real money supply, and hence demand and employment. This linkage between wage demands and the real money supply is missing when monetary policies are accommodating or difficult to predict.

The logic may be exemplified by Germany before unification and the Netherlands since the early 1980s. According to Hall (1994), the German central bank is not only committed to a non-accommodating strategy, but its constitution permits it to send credible signals to unions and employers about its policy intentions. Because wage bargaining is conducted at the industry level by well-organized strategic players, it is in the interest of unions and employers to adjust their behaviour to the anticipated non-accommodating reaction of the central bank. And since the central bank is politically independent, 'pronouncements by the Bundesbank about the kind of monetary stance a projected set of wage settlements might engender are especially credible' (Hall, 1994, p. 12).

In the case of the Netherlands, there are interesting parallels to the Danish experience. As in Denmark, Dutch wage-setting underwent a transition away from a highly centralized incomes-policy-based system in the 1970s and early 1980s to a system dominated by industry-level bargaining, and this transition was followed by a shift to a more non-accommodating monetary regime anchored to a Deutschmark currency peg. As in Denmark, this macroeconomic regime shift was initiated by a centre-right government, and it appears to have assisted in the restoration of Dutch competitiveness. Thus, unions accepted a substantial downward real wage adjustment, and unemployment rates were gradually cut in half.

In terms of the coupling of monetary policies and wage-bargaining institutions, the Netherlands thus seems to have joined Denmark and Sweden in a movement towards a German-type system. Indeed, as a result of new technology, internationalization of capital markets, and the rise of services, it may no longer be feasible for countries to combine centralized bargaining with an accommodating monetary regime (the upper right-hand corner in Table 2). If correct, this poses a severe challenge to a very influential line of scholarship during the 1970s and 1980s, neo-corporatism, which maintained that centralized wage bargaining combined with flexible neo-Keynesian economic policy was a politically attractive, and economically superior, political–institutional system (see, for example, Cameron, 1984, and Lange and Garrett, 1985).

It is still possible to point to cases, Austria and Norway in particular, which seem to conform to a neo-corporatist pattern (e.g. Wallerstein *et al.*, 1997). But I do not think these lend strong support to the neo-corporatist thesis. In Austria, the corporatist Parity Commission, the Federal Economic Chamber (representing employers), and the ÖGB (the union confederation) certainly continue to form a highly centralized setting for the bargaining of wages (not unlike tripartism in the Netherlands). However, the wage-setting process in Austria differs in one important respect from that which used to characterize Scandinavia: the distribution of wage increases has never been subject to centralized bargaining. Instead, adjustment of relative wages in response to changes in labour demand and supply is achieved through a complex system of plant- and sector-level negotiations, where wage increases for particular groups of employees are approved by the Parity

Commission if they can be justified in terms of changes in relative labour scarcities (note that Austria is an outlier in Figure 1).

This is a crucial point because it helps us to understand why Austria has been able to combine a non-accommodating policy regime with a relatively centralized bargaining system. Thus, without solidaristic wage policies, it is possible in a centralized system to negotiate downward real wage adjustments without currency devaluations during recessions and without rises in unemployment. To my knowledge Austria is the *only* OECD country that satisfies these conditions, and they may be very difficult to replicate elsewhere. Unlike the Scandinavian labour confederations, individual unions have little democratic influence over the formulation of ÖGB wage strategies (Katzenstein, 1984, pp. 47, 61; Visser, 1990), and Austrian social democracy has a very different history and character than Scandinavian (see Katzenstein, 1984, pp. 181–90; Scharpf, 1991, pp. 178–80, 188–90, 193–4). The commitment to wage equality, in particular, is much weaker. To cite just one piece of evidence, when Austrian socialist party voters were asked whether they thought it was fair or unfair for two secretaries with similar jobs to be paid differently based on productivity, only 5 per cent thought that it was unfair, while in Scandinavia the corresponding figure was between 30 per cent in Denmark and 60 per cent in Norway.[19]

Norway, which retained a relatively centralized bargaining system with an accommodating macroeconomic regime well into the 1990s, also turns out to be a rather exceptional case because of the role of oil. The oil boom from the early to mid-1970s generated huge capital investments, drove up demand for labour, and permitted governments to pursue very expansionist fiscal policies (including a 40 per cent increase in public employment between 1973 and 1989) (Calmfors, 1993, pp. 26–8; Dølvik and Stokland, 1992, p. 155). When oil prices suddenly dropped in 1986, the cushion effect of oil revenues on the Norwegian economy was removed, and the long decline in the competitiveness of Norwegian industry was manifested in a rapid deterioration of the external current account. Against this background, the social democratic government (which came to power in 1986) declared 1987 a year of 'emergency incomes policies' and agreed with LO and NAF that centrally negotiated limits on wage increases were absolutely essential for restoring the competitiveness of Norwegian industry (Mjøset, 1989, p. 334; Calmfors, 1993, p. 33).

The re-centralization of Norwegian bargaining institutions was a natural consequence of the rapid growth of the oil industry, expansionary fiscal and monetary policies, and the wage-push inflation that this

[19] The data are taken from the 1990/1 World Values Survey.

economic expansion generated. The relative success of centralization in the late 1980s and early 1990s should therefore not blind us to underlying pressures for decentralization. As in Denmark and Sweden, credit market liberalization during the 1980s has reduced the degrees of freedom in economic policies (Dølvik and Stokland, 1992; Moses, 1994). Likewise, the making more flexible of production and work organization has created pressures for greater wage dispersion (reflected in the introduction of new pay systems) that run up against the solidaristic wage policy (Dølvik and Stokland, 1992, p. 161). In fact, the bargaining system has exhibited subtle signs of decentralization throughout the early 1990s, with an increasing portion of total increases (between 55 and 85 per cent) coming in the form of wage drift, and with bargaining cartels forming at the sectoral level to take over responsibilities from LO in a more decentralized bargaining system.

4. The Social Democratic Trilemma

Decentralization of wage bargaining and the linking of economic policies to a non-accommodating monetary policy rule remove two of the most important pillars of social democratic corporatism: solidaristic wage policies and full employment. Without these supports, other elements of the system, in particular the universalistic welfare state, come under strain. Since much of the political–economic rationale behind the Scandinavian welfare state in the centralized-flexible institutional context was to support income solidarity and to 'socialize' the threat of unemployment, these elements lose their *raison d'être* and even work at cross-purposes in a decentralized system that is premised on greater wage dispersion and 'privatization' of the risk of unemployment. Moreover, along with the internationalization and the making more flexible of the private-sector economy, and given the tighter fiscal constraints on government spending, the class solidarity that served as a seal for public–private-sector collaboration starts to fall apart. No longer are solidaristic wages and public-sector expansion likely to be viewed by either employers or better-paid, better-educated groups (especially in the private sector) as a necessary *quid pro quo* for 'well-behaved' low-wage unions (especially in the public sector). Rather, decentralization of wage bargaining removes the rationale underpinning redistributive welfare policies, and points to a potential break-up of, or at least a redefinition of the terms of, the electoral coalition supporting a continuation of the social democratic welfare state and full employment policies.

In the context of the transition towards a service economy, and in the absence of labour-market institutions which facilitate wage restraint and equality, the government will find it both politically and economically harder to combine egalitarian wage policies with full employment. It is not that the promotion of pay equality through public policies is impossible. Equal pay and minimum wage legislation, cost-of-living indexation, mandatory extension laws, as well as a whole range of welfare and regulatory provisions (including unemployment compensation and competition policy) can significantly influence the relative pay and bargaining power of low-wage unions. But because the government cannot depend on centralized bargaining institutions to sponsor and 'subsidize' such policies through wage restraint among the better paid, it has to rely more heavily on expansion of public-sector employment to accomplish its full employment goal. And such an expansion runs counter not only to a non-accommodating macroeconomic strategy which uses the threat of unemployment to deter militant union behaviour, it may also be politically unpalatable.

During the 1970s and 1980s, soaring levels of taxation met with increasing opposition from business and private-sector unions, and the electoral success of the Danish Progress Party and the Swedish Conservatives in the 1970s — both running on a neo-liberal, anti-tax political platform — sent a clear message to politicians that there can be electoral costs associated with public-sector expansion.[20] Indeed, both left and right governments have found it imperative to bring public consumption under control by taking tougher stands against the demands of public-sector unions, and by reforming the budgetary process. As a result, the relative wages of public-sector workers have been declining, and a series of budgetary and administrative reforms have been aimed at bringing public expenditures under control (see Elvander, 1988, pp. 314–16; Due and Madsen, 1988; Kjellberg, 1992; Pontusson, 1992b, p. 119; Schwartz, 1994a). As is evident from the data presented in Table 1, public-sector employment also seems to have reached a maximum in the early to mid-1980s. Perhaps most tellingly, public-sector employment has remained unchanged from the early 1980s and has even started to decline in recent years.

As Anne Wren and I have argued elsewhere (Iversen and Wren, 1998), the choices facing social democracy at the turn of the century may be characterized (borrowing a term from Peter Swenson) as a 'trilemma' where the pursuit of the traditional goals of social democracy — earnings equality and employment for all — is prone to run into an upper

[20] For an analysis of the growing polarization of public- and private-sector interests in Sweden, see Swenson (1991, pp. 379–99).

budgetary ceiling. Conversely, if social democracy wants to exercise budgetary restraint it cannot simultaneously achieve its employment and equality goals. Instead, it faces a hard choice between a more 'neo-liberal' strategy where private service-sector employment is promoted through deregulation and a more flexible (inegalitarian) wage structure, and a more 'Christian democratic' strategy, where employment is sacrificed for equality and fiscal responsibility. Judging from the experience over the past decade, Danish and Swedish social democrats appear to have chosen to sacrifice employment. Unemployment in both countries is above the OECD average, and early retirement schemes have been introduced in both countries to encourage exit from the labour market.[21] The result is that the number of people in employment as a percentage of the working-age population has dropped from its peak of over 76 per cent in 1986 to about 70 per cent in 1994 in the case of Denmark, and from over 82 per cent in 1989 to less than 72 per cent in 1994 in the case of Sweden.[22] Employment rates are still much higher than in Germany and the Netherlands, but the direction of change nevertheless indicates a clear departure from the past.

Some changes *have* been made to loosen the egalitarian effects of the welfare state, most notably in the area of unemployment compensation. Denmark and, later, Sweden have implemented a notable reduction in the average replacement rate, and although this reduction was initiated under centre-right governments—in Denmark in the early 1980s, in Sweden in the early 1990s—it has not been reversed by succeeding social democratic governments. Likewise, the progressivity of the tax systems has been notably reduced. Still, the reforms in the unemployment benefit system have only marginally affected replacement rates for the lowest paid, and since low-paid workers tend to be semi-skilled with the highest incidence of unemployment, the wage-disciplining effects of a less generous benefit system have been the weakest where they are most 'needed'.

It is difficult to see how social democracy can transcend the trilemma in the future in the way that the Rehn–Meidner model did in the past. A return to the centralized coordination of wages and macroeconomic

---

[21] Of course, unemployment in Sweden is also a result of short-term forces that are outside the immediate control of the government. Only time will provide clearer indicators of policy choices. In Denmark, however, where unemployment among low-skilled workers has been very high for decades, it seems appropriate to talk about a conscious political choice.

[22] The magnitudes of the figures are slightly reduced by subtracting cyclical unemployment, defined as the difference between the actual unemployment rate and OECD's estimate of the NAIRU (non-accelerating inflation rate of unemployment) (OECD, 1996b).

policies is probably impractical in the foreseeable future, and monetarism (in the sense of non-accommodating macroeconomic policy regimes) seems to have become a necessary evil for social democracy. Although this does not rule out full employment—as perhaps the Austrian and Dutch experiences show—it does seem to preclude highly egalitarian wage policies unless there is a radical break with the social democratic commitment to employment for all. To put it in the starkest terms possible, the question for Scandinavian social democracy is whether it wants to deepen class divisions by accepting greater inequalities, or whether it wants to create a marginalized group of people, excluded from full participation in the economy.

If the first option is chosen there are clearly policies that can cushion the unequalizing effects of a more market-conforming wage structure, such as negative income taxes, wage subsidies, and the conversion of universal benefits into need-tested ones. As exemplified by the Danish social democratic government's policy of the right to sabbaticals, more emphasis can also be placed on ensuring that people have access to further education, and thus to participation in the stream of wealth creation in the post-Fordist economy. In an institutional and technological environment where production of goods and services is becoming more knowledge-intensive and more decentralized, it may prove very costly for social democratic governments to try to ensure equality of outcomes, but they can greatly facilitate educational opportunities while simultaneously promoting economic growth. The negative effects of the second option can also be lessened by emphasizing voluntary early retirement schemes, and by encouraging work-sharing through part-time employment and fixed-term contracts. This will not please unions—traditionally opposed to temporary and part-time employment—and it challenges social democratic notions of equality between the sexes since it is mainly women who end up in part-time employment. However, in the post-industrial economy, and constrained by a monetarist international monetary system, social democracy appears compelled to make hard choices between different forms of labour-market inequalities.

11

The Social Democratic Welfare State

EVELYNE HUBER AND JOHN D. STEPHENS*

1. Introduction

The social democratic welfare state, along with all other welfare states, has been under considerable pressure for the past two decades. The key questions are whether the pressures are more intense on the social democratic welfare state than on other types, whether these pressures are eroding the distinctive features of the social democratic welfare state, and whether there are ways to adapt the social democratic welfare state to new international and national economic conditions while preserving its central achievements. To answer these questions, we must begin with an analysis of the basic characteristics of the social democratic compared to other welfare-state regimes, and its impact on poverty and inequality. Since welfare-state regimes are embedded in capitalist economies with distinctive forms of organization which we call production regimes, we also need to understand the characteristics of different production regimes and the ways in which they are related to welfare-state regimes. Then, we must identify the major changes in the international economy over the past two decades and their impact on different production and welfare-state regimes, before we can assess chances for successful adaptation of these regimes to the new economic environment.

2. Characteristics and Achievements of Welfare-state Regimes

We take as our point of departure Esping-Andersen's (1990) categorization of welfare states into three basic 'worlds of welfare capitalism', but we modify his scheme in two ways. We include a fourth world, the 'wage-earner welfare states' of Australia and New Zealand, and we rename his 'conservative/corporatist' category 'Christian democratic'

---

* University of North Carolina.

to avoid the misleading connotation that these welfare-state regimes are entirely preserving the inequalities created by the market, and to name the category in a fashion parallel to the social democratic and liberal welfare-state regimes, based on their political origins. With the terminology 'political origins' we refer to the correspondence between welfare-state characteristics and preferences of major political actors, not to the political colouring of the governments that created and expanded the different welfare states. In most cases, there is little or no difference between the two, but in some cases of Christian democratic welfare-state regimes, such as Austria, France, or Switzerland, Christian democratic parties were not the dominant parties in government during the first three and a half decades after the Second World War, when the modern welfare states took their essential form.

The essential characteristics of social democratic welfare states are that they are comprehensive and inclusive (covering the entire population for all major risks), universalistic (covering the entire population with the same programmes), providing basic and income security (with a combination of flat-rate and earnings-related benefits), redistributive (reducing inequality), service heavy (providing a large array of services through the public sector), gender egalitarian (supporting women's employment and shared parental responsibility for child rearing), and active or labour mobilizing (putting strong emphasis on active labour-market policies). Christian democratic welfare states are also comprehensive and inclusive, but fragmented or segmented (covering different segments of the population with different programmes), providing income security (with occupation-based and mainly earnings-related benefits), marginally redistributive (not by design, but simply by reducing poverty and by being so large as to crowd out the even more inegalitarian private alternatives), transfer heavy (providing generous transfers but a minimum of social services outside of health; relying on public financing but private delivery of those services that are provided), male breadwinner based (relying on women to provide care for children and the elderly), and passive (putting emphasis on unemployment compensation and a reduction of the labour force to deal with unemployment). Liberal welfare states are residual (covering only some risks and mainly those unable to insure themselves through the market), fragmented (providing different means-tested programmes for different constituencies), service and transfer poor, and gender indifferent (providing neither decent benefits for traditional families with a male breadwinner nor special benefits to support women's employment and shared parental responsibilities). Wage-earner welfare states primarily provided benefits via labour-market institutions in the context of a highly protected economy and highly regulated labour market; the public social welfare programmes were universalistic but partly means tested (i.e. covering all those eligible with the same programme but excluding upper-middle and upper income earners from eligibility) and they were oriented towards income security and a male breadwinner model.

These are ideal types, of course, and in practice most welfare states showed a mixture of characteristics.[1] In particular, most liberal welfare states had some comprehensive programmes, such as social security in the United States; or Christian democratic welfare states began to emphasize active labour-market policies; or even in social democratic welfare states some people had to rely on means-tested social assistance. Many of these 'atypical' programmes were introduced precisely by governments that had other political preferences regarding the welfare state; for instance, the National Health Service in Britain was introduced by the post-war Labour government, or the active labour-market policies in Germany got a major boost in 1969, when the Social Democratic/Liberal government came to power.

The basic parameters of these welfare states have been shaped by the political commitments of social democratic, Christian democratic, and secular centre or right-wing parties, respectively. The social democratic commitment to solidarity and equality as essential to the promotion of wage-earner interests gave rise to the universalistic and redistributive aspects of the welfare state, to basic security combined with income security, and to the public provision of services with access based on citizenship. As the commitment to equality came to be extended from class to gender, it also generated a variety of gender egalitarian policies, that is, policies designed to integrate women into the labour force, to relieve them of a large part of care-giving obligations, and to put both parents on an equal basis with regard to leave entitlements for child care. The multi-class base of Christian democratic parties, and the commitment of these parties to a project of political mediation and to the principle of subsidiarity, in contrast gave rise to the generous but fragmented structure of the welfare state, satisfying different clienteles with different programmes, to emphasis on occupational bases of programmes, to the public financing but private provision of essential services, such as health care, and to a reliance on the family to provide care for children and the elderly. Care provided by the family, of

---

[1] There is a voluminous literature on characterizations and explanations of these welfare states; see, for example, Stephens (1979), Wilensky (1981), Korpi (1983, 1989), Castles (1985), Palme (1990), Kangas (1991), Hicks and Swank (1992), Castles and Mitchell (1993), Huber et al. (1993), Orloff (1993), van Kersbergen (1995), O'Connor (1996).

course, in practice meant care provided by women, which corresponded to the Christian democratic commitment to the traditional male breadwinner family model. The commitments of secular centre and right-wing parties are more heterogeneous, but a common core includes individual self-reliance, state restraint, and a low tax burden, which are at the root of the comparatively ungenerous, residual welfare state with a restricted range of publicly funded social services.

The figures in Table 1 illustrate these different welfare-state characteristics and their outcomes. Again, the countries are grouped according to welfare-state type, not according to incumbency of the different parties.[2] The data are for 1980 or the closest available date to that year, a point in time before serious cut-backs took effect. Columns 1 and 2 show the total years of rule by social democratic and Christian democratic parties, respectively, from 1946 until 1980.[3] The Scandinavian countries were distinctive in terms of their years of social democratic governance.[4] Liberal welfare states were characterized by the absence of Christian democratic government and, with the exception of Britain, little or no influence of social democracy in government. The 'wage-earner' welfare states were characterized by strong Labour parties, which, none the less, were narrowly defeated in most elections between 1945 and 1980. Since the Christian democratic welfare states were the most heterogeneous, we have broken them down into three sub-groups. The first 'group' contains the lone country of Austria, the only Christian democratic welfare state in which social democracy was more influential than Christian democracy. In the next group, Belgium, Netherlands, and Germany, social democracy was influential but not as influential as Christian democracy. Along with Austria, these countries also were more generous than the other three Christian democratic countries on most of the welfare-state indicators in Table 1.

---

[2] Japan does not fit into any type and is being treated as a case apart. The welfare state comes closest to a residual model, with very low benefits through the public programmes in pensions and health care. The pillars of the system of social provision are private programmes in the large corporations, from which only a minority of the labour-force benefits, and the family.

[3] We assigned a score of 1 for each year that the left or Christian democrats were in power alone, and a fraction for the left's or the Christian democrats' fraction of seats in parliament of all governing parties' seats for coalition governments.

[4] In the mid-1960s Finland experienced a 'system shift' marked by the coming to power of a social-democratic-led government including the communists, and by unification of unions and the development of a corporatist social pact with the employers. In the subsequent two and a half decades, Finland caught up with her Nordic neighbours in terms of welfare-state generosity (Stephens, 1996; Huber and Stephens, 1998).

Table 1
Welfare-state Regimes, Circa 1980

	1 Left cabinet years	2 Christian democratic cabinet years	3 Social security expenditure	4 Transfer payments	5 Total taxes	6 Public HEW employment
Social democratic welfare states						
Sweden	30	0	31	18	56	20
Norway	28	1	20	14	53	15
Denmark	25	0	26	17	52	18
Finland	14	0	17	9	36	9
Mean	24.3	0.3	23.6	14.5	49.4	15.5
Christian democratic welfare states						
Austria	20	15	21	19	46	4
Belgium	14	19	21	21	43	6
Netherlands	8	22	27	26	53	4
Germany	11	16	23	17	45	4
France	3	4	25	19	45	7
Italy	3	30	20	14	33	5
Switzerland	9	10	13	13	33	5
Mean	9.6	16.4	21.6	18.4	42.4	5.0
Liberal welfare states						
Canada	0	0	13	10	36	7
Ireland	3	0	19	13	39	
UK	16	0	17	12	40	8
USA	0	0	12	11	31	5
Mean	4.7	0.0	15.2	11.5	36.5	6.7
'Wage-earner' welfare states						
Australia	7	0	11	8	31	7
New Zealand	10	0	16	10		
Japan	0	0	10	10	28	3

Notes: Column 6, HEW is health, education, and welfare. Further notes and sources to Table 1 are in the Appendix to this chapter.

Table 1 continued

	7 Spending on non-aged	8 Decommod- ification index	9 Support for mothers employment	10 Post- tax transfer Gini	11 % of group in poverty 25-59	12 Single mothers
Social democratic welfare states						
Sweden	12.7	39	62	0.20	4.8	7.7
Norway	8.5	38	43	0.22	3.7	12.1
Denmark	11.2	38	64	0.26	4.8	4.5
Finland	10.5	29	66	0.21	3.0	4.8
Mean	10.7	36.2	58.8	0.22	4.1	7.3
Christian democratic welfare states						
Austria	4.1	31		0.23	2.3	13.3
Belgium	9.9	32	59	0.23	4.4	14.2
Netherlands	10.7	32	34	0.28	6.7	6.6
Germany	7.9	28	36	0.25	4.2	6.0
France	7.7	28	53	0.33	15.9	22.8
Italy	3.3	24	36	0.31	10.5	17.5
Switzerland		30		0.32	6.1	22.4
Mean	7.3	29.3	43.6	0.28	7.1	14.7
Liberal welfare states						
Canada	5.7	22	35	0.29	10.3	42.0
Ireland	5.7	23		0.33	10.9	15.4
UK	6.4	23	22	0.27	5.5	10.8
USA	4.5	14	14	0.31	11.9	42.3
Mean	5.6	20.6	23.7	0.30	9.7	27.6
'Wage-earner' welfare states						
Australia	2.8	13	22	0.29	9.3	44.8
New Zealand	3.1	17				
Japan	2.4	27				

As one can see from the table, both the Christian democratic and social democratic welfare states were much more generous than the other groups in terms of their social expenditure (columns 3 and 4). Indeed, it would appear that the Christian democratic welfare states actually provided more generous transfer payments than the social democratic welfare states. While it is true that they spent more on transfers and they were transfer heavy as compared to the service heavy social democratic welfare states (Huber *et al.*, 1993; Huber and Stephens, 2000), the transfer-spending figures in Table 1 for Christian democratic welfare states were high in part because the target populations (the unemployed and people on early retirement) were large.

Esping-Andersen's decommodification index (column 8) is a better indicator of the generosity of transfer entitlements than the transfer expenditure figure. It is a composite measure of the characteristics of three income-transfer programmes (pensions, sick pay, and unemployment compensation), the components of which are various measures of qualifying conditions and benefit duration and income replacements for two categories of workers, a 'standard production worker' and those qualifying for only minimum benefits (Esping-Andersen, 1990, pp. 49, 54). One can see from the index that social democratic welfare-state transfer systems were more generous than the Christian democratic ones. Other data from the Social Citizenship Indicators Project at the University of Stockholm and other sources indicate that a principal reason for the difference between the social democratic and Christian democratic welfare states on the index was that income-replacement rates among those with minimum qualifying conditions were much better in the Nordic countries (Palme, 1990; Kangas, 1991; OECD, 1994; Carrol, 1999).

It was not, however, in the structure of transfers that the social democratic welfare states and Christian democratic welfare states differed most. As we have shown in an analysis of pooled times series data, the most distinctive feature of the social democratic welfare state was the public funding *and* delivery of social services (Huber and Stephens, 2000). One can see the dramatic differences in this regard from the figures for public health, education, and welfare employment as a percentage of the working-age population in column 6 of Table 1. The expansion of a wide variety of social programmes—day care, elderly care, job training programmes, temporary employment programmes in the public services, after school programmes, to name a few examples—along with improvements of maternal and parental leave programmes, were the main areas of welfare-state innovation in the Nordic countries in the 1970s and they continued in the 1980s. The difference in the level of public social services was the reason why taxation levels in social democratic welfare states were significantly higher than in the Christian democratic welfare states, averaging close to 49 per cent of GDP compared to 42 per cent in the latter group (Table 1, column 5), despite the fact that transfer payments were actually lower on the average in the social democratic welfare states.

Two distinctive features of the social service intensiveness of the social democratic welfare states are worth underlining. First, they were gender egalitarian or 'women friendly' (Hernes, 1987) and promoted the expansion of women's labour-force participation which we examine below. This is reflected in the index in column 9 which measures the extent to which a wide range of social provisions facilitate mothers with young children entering the labour force. Second, they were aimed at the non-aged as can be seen from the OECD figures on spending on the non-aged as a percentage of GDP in column 7 of Table 1.[5] In both cases, these distinctive features involved investment in human capital and in the mobilization of labour.

Columns 10, 11, and 12 paint the picture of poverty and inequality in the four welfare-state types. On the average, the countries with the social democratic welfare states had the lowest post-tax and post-transfer inequality as measured by the Gini index of income distribution; they were followed by the countries with Christian democratic welfare states, then Australia with a wage-earner welfare state and finally those with liberal welfare states. These figures do not include the distributive effects of free or subsidized public goods and services which would increase equality in all welfare states (Saunders, 1994), but particularly in the social democratic welfare states. One has to point out here that inequality in the Northern European tier of Christian democratic welfare states was much closer to the social democratic than to the liberal welfare states, a result heavily influenced by their particular production regimes, to an examination of which we shall turn shortly. The same rank ordering can be found in the poverty levels of the working-age population, though here the Christian democratic average is closer to the social democratic average than the liberal. Poverty is defined as less than 50 per cent of median income in the country in question. Finally, one can see very large differences in the poverty levels among one particularly vulnerable group, single mothers, who are doing best in the social democratic welfare states, worst in Aus-

[5] Theses figures underestimate the differences between the social democratic and Christian democratic welfare states because they include spending on early pensions and disability pensions which were employed as means of labour-force reduction in a number of the Christian democratic welfare states at this time.

tralia, then the liberal welfare states, and in between in the Christian democratic welfare states. Two factors appear to explain variations in poverty rates among single mothers best: child allowances and high levels of labour-force participation among young women which, in turn, is largely a result of policies promoting mothers' employment (Watson, 1996; Gornick et al., 1998). Within the liberal group there were large differences in 1980, with single mothers in Britain being much less likely to end up in poverty, a position that would be eroded in the following decade as the Thatcher reforms let poverty among single mothers rise significantly.

3. Welfare States and Production Regimes

Welfare states are situated in specific economies, and in order to understand the relationship between economic underpinnings and welfare-state characteristics, we need to attempt to understand various types of economic organization in a parallel fashion to the types of welfare-state regimes. We start from the basic distinction drawn by Soskice (1991) between flexibly coordinated and uncoordinated, deregulated, or liberal market economies. His distinction focused investigators' attention on the nature of relations among enterprises, between enterprises and financial institutions, and between enterprises, financial institutions, and the government (Albert, 1991; Soskice, 1991). We expand his notion of coordination to a broader concept of production regimes which has come into use in the literature on varieties of capitalism (Hollingsworth et al., 1993), and we distinguish between coordinated and uncoordinated, or liberal, production regimes. For our purposes here, the aspects of production regimes that are of prime importance are labour-market and wage-bargaining institutions, as well as macroeconomic policies and the role of the central banks.[6]

Table 2 presents data on the labour-market dimensions of production regimes, again for about 1980, grouped in accordance with the welfare-state regime types that are embedded in these production regimes. The Nordic countries and the Northern European tier and Austria can all be classified as coordinated production regimes, though by no means with identical patterns of relationships between business,

[6] For an elaboration of the relationship between welfare-state and production regimes, see Huber and Stephens (in press, particularly ch. 4).

Table 2
Labour-market Regimes, Circa 1980

	1 Female labour-force participation	2 Union density %	3 Union coverage	4 Corporatism index	5 Centralization of wage setting†	6 Wage dispersion†	7 Active labour-market policy spending / unemployment
Social democratic welfare states							
Sweden	74	82	83	4	60	2.0	75
Norway	62	59	75	4	57	2.0	26
Denmark	71	70	95	3	60	2.1	20
Finland	70	73		3		2.5	18
Mean	69.3	71.1	84.3	3.5	59.0	2.2	35
Christian democratic welfare states							
Austria	49	66	71	4	20	3.5	8
Belgium	47	72	90	3	34	2.4	10
Netherlands	35	38	60	4	47	2.5	10
Germany	51	40	76	3	20	2.7	10
France	54	28	92	*	20	3.3	7
Italy	39	51		2	40	2.6	4
Switzerland	54	35		3		2.7	23
Mean	47.0	47.0	77.8	3.2	30.2	2.8	10

Table 2 continued

Liberal welfare states							
Canada	57	31	38	1	9	4.0	6
Ireland	36	68		3			9
UK	58	48	47	2	28	2.8	6
USA	60	25	18	1	6	4.8	4
Mean	52.8	43.0	34.3	1.8	14.3	3.9	6
'Wage-earner' welfare states							
Australia	53	51	80	1	40	2.8	5
New Zealand	45	59	67	1		2.9	20
Japan	54	31	21	*	16	3.0	6

Notes: * Concertation without labour; † mid-1980s data for Belgium, Netherlands, and New Zealand, 1991 for Switzerland.

financial institutions, labour, and the government.[7] The high levels of organization of capital and labour and of coordination between the social partners and the state in coordinated production regimes are visible in the figures for trade union density, contract coverage, corporatism, and centralization of wage setting. Coordinated production regimes had moderate-to-high levels of unionization and high levels of bargaining coverage through negotiated or legislated contract extension, and they were highly corporatist. Wage bargaining was coordinated, either in a highly centralized fashion at the national level, as in the Nordic countries, or at the industrial level, as in Germany. The figures for centralization of wage setting are somewhat misleading, as they code the level at which actual contracts were signed and disregard formal or informal coordination of bargaining. By all accounts, Austria and Germany had highly coordinated systems of bargaining, in Austria through the Austrian Union Confederation and the tripartite Parity Commission (Traxler, 1998, p. 246), and in Germany through the informal pace-setting role of the metalworkers' union (Jacobi et al., 1998, p. 216).

The high degrees of centralization of wage setting and of corporatism have been essential to the economic well-being of the coordinated production regimes, as all of these economies have been highly open to trade and thus needed to be able to produce wage restraint, given the high levels of unionization. The failure of coordinated wage bargaining and wage restraint in the Netherlands in the 1970s, with its heavy cost in terms of unemployment, serves to underline this point. Another essential ingredient for successful competition in high-quality/high-wage international markets is a highly qualified labour force. In the Nordic and Northern tier coordinated production regimes, labour skills are initially generated in companies or with strong company and union participation in public schools. In the Nordic countries and to a lesser extent Germany, they are adapted to changing conditions through continuing training or retraining. Unions play an important cooperative role in organizing working conditions within companies and ensuring quality control.

A further crucial aspect of the coordinated production regimes was the provision of investment capital on preferential conditions, be it through close links between banks and enterprises, as in Germany, or

---

[7] Denmark had different inter-firm relations from the other Scandinavian countries and relied much more on small-to-medium firms for export, but the degree of labour-market coordination and the major policy configurations were similar. The production regime of the Netherlands did not entirely fit into this group as of the 1980s, as coordinated wage setting had broken down; and France had a different production regime with a much more central role for the state.

through state regulations and state-owned banks, as in the Nordic countries and Austria. It is important to note that these arrangements were largely predicated on regulated capital markets. In addition, in the Nordic countries and Austria interest rates were kept low through public-sector surpluses. This same set of countries relied on a combination of supply-side and tax policies to stimulate investment and growth, such as an active labour-market policy (though in Austria only from the 1970s on), regional development policies, support for selected industries, and tax provisions favouring reinvestment of profits over distribution and industrial investors over consumers. Their fiscal and monetary policies were moderately counter-cyclical and backed up by occasional devaluations, with the partial exceptions of Austria, where the schilling was already pegged informally to the German mark in the 1960s, and Finland, where fiscal and monetary policy tended to be more pro-cyclical. The pursuit of these policies was facilitated by the subordination of the central banks to political authority, in stark contrast to Germany, for instance. Economic growth of these small countries was strongly stimulated by their exports to the fast-growing core capitalist economies in North America and Europe.

The Antipodean production regimes also had high union density and contract coverage, but they were essentially different from the coordinated production regimes in Europe in two respects. First, they were based on the primary product export sector, whose earnings supported highly protected domestic manufacturing sectors. Second, wage coordination did not take place through centrally coordinated bargaining, but rather through the courts in the wage-arbitration system. As earnings from primary exports declined and the economies were opened, the entire production regime underwent profound changes.

There is great variation among production regimes and within the category of coordinated production regimes in the levels of women's labour-force participation and thus in overall activity levels. These differences are intimately related to welfare-state characteristics — that is, to the differences in the service intensiveness of welfare states. Women's labour-force participation as of 1980 was highest in the coordinated production regimes associated with social democratic welfare states, followed by the wage-earner and liberal welfare-state and production regimes, and the coordinated production regimes associated with Christian democratic welfare states had the lowest levels. The high levels of women's labour-force participation in the Nordic countries are a result of initial labour-market decisions and a subsequent self-reinforcing process of growth in women's labour-force participation, women's mobilization, demands for an expansion of public social services, alliances with incumbent social democratic parties, and expansion of the public social-service sector. As of 1960, with the exception of Finland, the Nordic countries did not differ much from the others in their levels of women's labour-force participation. With full employment in all of Northern Europe in the 1960s, the Northern Continental countries decided to import foreign labour whereas unions in the Nordic countries successfully resisted such a move, which in turn provided opportunities for women to enter the labour force. The growing numbers of working women then increased women's propensity to organize and become politically active to demand more gender egalitarian legislation in general and more welfare-state services in particular, notably in the area of child care. Growing women's pressure from inside and outside the party moved social democratic parties to adopt gender-egalitarian commitments and, when in office, to pass a range of legislation promoting women's equality and the dual-earner-household model. Prominent among these programmes were a variety of services to care for children and the elderly, as well as parental leave entitlements. The expansion of social services then provided new jobs which in their majority were filled by women.

Given their commitment to the traditional family, Christian democratic governments provided little or no support for the integration of women into the labour force and for the public provision or even public funding of care-giving activities. High union contract coverage prevented the emergence of a low-wage sector in private services, thus obstructing the growth of affordable private care services and the absorption of women into these kinds of jobs. In the liberal production regimes and welfare states, women's labour-force participation increased more rapidly than in the coordinated production regimes with Christian democratic welfare states, precisely because of the expansion of the private service sector. Women entered a dual labour market, and a very large percentage filled low-wage jobs.

A further important difference among the production regimes was their outcome with regards to wage dispersion, as shown in Table 2. The 90/10 ratio, the ratio of the income of the wage and salary earner at the 90th percentile to the income of the one at the 10th percentile, was lowest in the coordinated production regimes with social democratic welfare states and highest in the liberal production regimes and welfare states, with the wage-earner production regimes and welfare states and the average of the Christian democratic welfare states in the middle. However, the coordinated production regimes with Christian democratic welfare states of Northern Continental Europe were closer to their counterparts with social democratic welfare states, with the notable exception of Austria. Clearly, these figures are part of the explanation of the figures for inequality in post-tax/post-transfer income distribution we discussed in the section on welfare-state outcomes.

Our discussion here and the figures in Tables 1 and 2 have revealed that the clustering of welfare-state and production regimes into discrete types is hardly perfect. Nevertheless, if one looks at the total picture, one sees quite consistent patterns of differences between the various types. A similar statement can be made about the fit between production regimes and welfare-state regimes. Whereas there is no necessary one-to-one correspondence, there is a fit between production and welfare-state regimes that we call mutually supportive or enabling. This fit is most obvious between wage levels and benefit levels, or between money wages and social wages, which in turn depend on the type of production prevalent in a given country. Clearly, benefit levels in income-replacement programmes for the working-age population, such as for sickness and unemployment, cannot be higher than prevailing wage levels for given categories of employees, lest perverse work incentives be constructed. By the same token, production regimes with high wages make high benefit levels and the provision of high-quality services affordable. High-quality services in education and labour training, in turn, provide a skilled labour force for the production of exports that occupy a high-skill/high-wage niche in the world economy. Predominance of high-skill/high-wage production and high contract coverage, characteristic of coordinated production regimes, obstruct the expansion of a low-wage sector and thus make it possible to have generous benefit levels in transfer programmes.

4. Welfare-state Retrenchment

As the other chapters in this book make clear, the economic and social environments of the last two decades have not been favourable for social democracy. As a result of changes in domestic social structure and the international economy, as well as the increasing dominance of neoliberal economic doctrines outside and within social democracy, the social democratic model — the welfare-state regime and production regime — has come under attack. Of the components of the model, macroeconomic policies, financial regulation, and central bank subordination were subject to the greatest pressures and underwent the greatest change. The centralized wage-bargaining system also came under stress owing to changes in production techniques and changes in the occupational structure, as Iversen (this volume) points out, but, as Vartiainen (this volume) argues, it was only in Sweden, where these trends combined with radical wage compression policies and a trade union political offensive which alienated employers, that these changes stimulated employers unilaterally to decentralize the wage-bargaining system.[8]

By contrast, the welfare state was the best preserved part of the system and, not incidentally, it enjoys high levels of popular support in all of these countries. Moreover, to the extent that it was cut, it was due to failures in the other parts of the model, not to some internal dynamic in the welfare state. With the exception of a few countries in which conservative governments introduced significant cuts in the welfare state for ideological reasons, most notably the United Kingdom, New Zealand, and, to a lesser extent, the United States, cuts in the welfare state were reluctantly introduced in all welfare-state regime types as a result of large and apparently permanent increases in unemployment. Precisely because the social democratic welfare states other than Denmark were able to avoid rising unemployment until the 1990s, they were also able to avoid cuts. Quite simply, the increase in unemployment meant that more people were dependent on the welfare state and fewer people were contributing to it, so either entitlements had to be cut or taxes had to be raised and, in an environment of slowed growth, it was painful to raise taxes. Elsewhere we have offered an extensive analysis of this rise in unemployment and its consequences (Huber and Stephens, 1998, 1999, 2000, in press). Here it will suffice very briefly to summarize our argument in order to lay the ground for our discussion of social policy developments in the 1980s and 1990s in social democratic welfare-state regimes and in countries which fall in other regime types but were ruled by social democratic parties in this period.

Almost all countries initially responded to the economic turbulence that came in the wake of the end of the Bretton Woods system and first oil shock as if it was just another economic downturn, that is, with demand stimulation by increasing spending and increasing budget deficits. By the early 1980s, governments of all political colourings recognized that they were operating in a changed world and moved towards more austere fiscal policy, as total revenue as a percentage of GDP increased faster than total expenditure in all 18 countries covered in our tables. In countries which experienced a large increase in unemployment, this involved some cutting of entitlements. The rise in

[8] Iversen (1996, this volume) argues that Denmark also experienced such a transition, but Wallerstein and Golden (1997) characterize the change in Denmark as a reorganization rather than an unambiguous decentralization. That is, Danish wage bargaining was never as centralized as in the other Nordic countries and Austria, but a high degree of coordination was maintained through the role of a mediator.

unemployment can in turn be linked to the rising levels of labour-force participation, owing to the entry of more women into the labour force, and to declines in economic growth (Glyn, 1995b; Rowthorn, 1995; Huber and Stephens, in press, ch. 7).[9] Lower growth can, in turn, be linked to lower levels of investment which, in turn, can be linked to higher real interest rates and, for countries in which controlled financial markets were important parts of their Golden-age production regime (including all of the social democratic regimes except Denmark), to financial deregulation.

It is important to recognize that conjunctural factors, which may or may not continue into the future, and policy errors contributed to the rise in unemployment, particularly in the 1990s and most particularly in Scandinavia in the 1990s. While financial deregulation ensured that the steep rise in real long-term rates would spread to all countries, the rising indebtedness of both developed and developing countries in the wake of the oil shocks was the driving force behind the rise. As countries, especially European countries, moved to reduce deficits and even to budget surpluses, interest rates have come down, which in the long run might stimulate higher investment and growth. In the short run, however, this move to budget austerity along with monetary austerity, which is partly a product of European monetary integration, and the austere policies of the Bundesbank imposed in reaction to German reunification, strongly contribute to the high unemployment in Europe (Hall, 1998).

In the cases of Finland, Sweden, and, to a lesser extent, Norway, government policy mistakes strongly contributed to, indeed, may have created the crisis.[10] All three countries deregulated their financial markets in the 1980s, which led to booms in consumer spending and skyrocketing real estate prices and to overheating of the domestic economy and wage inflation. Since all three countries had fixed their exchange rates, this wage inflation translated directly into a deterioration of relative unit labour costs until they were forced to float in the autumn of 1992. In the bust that followed the boom, property values collapsed, which caused bank insolvency and consumer retrenchment, which in turn aggravated the deep recession. The bank bail-out cost the

---

[9] We are aware that many economists argue that GDP growth and employment growth are not linked, but we find Rowthorn's arguments in this regard compelling. Moreover, Rowthorn assumes no wage coordination and, in economies in which unions are relatively centralized and bargaining is coordinated, the argument that higher growth is linked to lower unemployment because unions will be willing to sacrifice some wage growth for employment growth is particularly compelling.

[10] See Huber and Stephens (1998) for a more detailed analysis.

Swedish government 5 per cent of GDP and the Finnish government 7 per cent of GDP, greatly adding to the deficit in both countries. The collapse of Soviet trade which had accounted for 25 per cent of Finnish exports was especially damaging to Finland's economy and goes far in explaining why unemployment rose to 19 per cent, making it a deeper crisis than the Great Depression in that country.

As Pierson (1996) has pointed out, the politics of retrenchment are different from the politics of welfare-state expansion. We have argued that, with a few notable exceptions, welfare-state retrenchment was forced on countries by rising unemployment. Parties of the right, which had opposed the original introduction of generous welfare-state policies, were now reluctant to cut these same policies because they enjoyed widespread popularity. This is particularly true of the generally universalistic policies in the areas of pensions, health care, and education, which form the overwhelming majority of total social expenditure in all countries. The targeted policies, such as social assistance, which do not command such support, are not promising sources of budgetary savings, since they are quite a small portion of the total budget. On the other hand, parties of the left are more reluctant to raise taxes to close the budgetary gap created by rising unemployment. Not only would this be a procyclical measure in an economic downturn, but in the context of the slowed real income growth, there is less room for tax increases which do not cut private consumption in absolute terms. Thus, the era of retrenchment is characterized by declines in partisan effects on social policy, a development which we document in data analysis on a number of indicators of social policy generosity (Huber and Stephens, 1999, in press, ch. 6), though our case studies show that partisan effects have hardly disappeared (ibid., ch. 7).

What has been the impact of the developments of the past two decades on the social policy configurations outlined earlier and on the ability of social democratic parties to put their distinctive mark on social policy? Let us begin our survey with the impact of the new social and economic environment on the Nordic social democratic heartland. In the 1980s only Denmark experienced an unemployment crisis and there the crisis was met by a combination of economizing cuts and some expansion of entitlements to cushion the effects of unemployment. In fact, in the other Nordic countries, particularly in Finland, the 1980s was a decade of welfare-state expansion. The most important area of innovation was in policies which facilitated women's entry into the labour force, such as expansion of day care and parental leave, and even Denmark, which was cutting elsewhere, expanded entitlements in this area.

We do not mean to imply that the 1980s simply replicated the welfare-state politics of the earlier era in the Nordic countries. As in other countries, new thinking on macroeconomic policy meant that what expansion did take place had to do so in the framework of more austere macroeconomic policy, and total revenue and even more so total expenditure grew more slowly than in the 1960s and 1970s. In Sweden, the social democratic government elected in 1982 was explicitly committed not to increase public expenditure as a percentage of GDP. What allowed it to introduce new social policy reforms was the introduction of marketizing reforms in the public sector which resulted in savings. Public enterprises, many of which were losing money, were directed to operate on a profit-making basis and all of them accomplished this by the end of the decade. Public services were increasingly evaluated and funded according to market or market-like criteria, such as payment by output. Similar trends can be detected in all of the Nordic countries.[11]

A second trend in social policy in all four countries was a strengthening of the active or 'work line' with regard to sick pay and work injury policies. As we pointed out above, the Nordic welfare states had always focused on maximal labour-force mobilization, 'work for everyone' (*arbet åt alla*) in the words of the campaign slogan of the Swedish Social Democrats in the 1973 election. In the 1980s, and even more so in the 1990s, the policy response to the rising costs of sick pay and work injury insurance was to try to move the sick and injured back into active work through a combination of disincentives and incentives for both employers (e.g. to improve the working environment) and employees (to return to work).

Finally, as in many countries, the pension systems of the Nordic countries came under pressure in this period. As Myles and Pierson (forthcoming; Myles, 1997) point out, the pressures on pension systems were created by a combination of demographic and economic change. As a result of increasing longevity and declining birth rates, the populations of advanced industrial democracies have aged and will continue to do so as the post-Second-World-War generation moves into retirement. The decline in wage growth and increase in the returns on capital in the present era as compared to the Golden Age made the pay-as-you-go systems designed in the previous era unviable and made more fully funded systems more attractive alternatives. We would add that, to the extent that financial internationalization has contributed to higher interest rates, it contributed to the pressures to restructure the pension systems by raising returns to capital. These pressures resulted

---

[11] See Schwartz (1994*a*, *b*) on Denmark and Sweden as well as the Antipodes.

in the complete restructuring of the Swedish system from a partially funded, but basically PAYG-defined benefit system, to a more fully funded, defined contribution system. The same structural changes, as well as the inability of politicians and labour-market actors to fashion a coalition for supplementary pensions in Denmark, led to the introduction of fully actuarial occupational pensions negotiated by the labour-market parties, which though not mandatory, reached a very high portion of the labour force owing to the high level of unionization (Salminen, 1993).

As the unemployment crisis hit Sweden, Finland, and, to a lesser extent, Norway in the late 1980s and early 1990s, these countries followed Denmark in introducing cuts in entitlements which were aimed at bringing the large budget deficits created by the downturn and the rise in unemployment under control. The depth of retrenchment exactly reflected the depth of the unemployment crisis, with Finland cutting the most and Norway almost not at all. That the immediate motivation for the cuts was the budget deficits is made apparent by the fact that, as the budgets moved into surplus in the late 1990s, further cuts were no longer on the table. Indeed, in the Swedish election campaign of 1998 and in the policy debate which followed, the debate focused on which programmes should be targets for greater spending. While there is no doubt that insistence of all governments on austere fiscal policy represents a neo-liberal turn in economic thinking, we remind the readers that budget surpluses were an established feature of Nordic economic policy in the Golden Age.

While a full review of the changes in entitlements in the four countries would take us too far afield, we can present a very brief examination of the cuts made in Sweden, which is not only considered the prototype of a social democratic welfare state but also, along with Denmark, underwent an intermediate level of retrenchment between Norway and Finland.[12] The replacement rates in the work injury, unemployment, and parental-leave insurance systems, which had been 100 per cent, 90 per cent, and 90 per cent respectively, were lowered to a uniform 80 per cent. For unemployment and work-injury insurance, qualifying conditions were made stricter, waiting days increased, and employee contributions increased. Child benefits were lowered by 15 per cent. In the case of the pension system, there was a clear change in principle as the new supplementary-earnings-related system is a defined contribution system and benefits will depend on lifelong earnings. The citizenship pension is replaced by a supplement for those with

[12] For reviews of the change in the Swedish welfare state, see Palme (1994) and Palme and Wennemo (1997).

low earnings-related benefits. Since the new supplementary system is a defined contribution system, the actual benefits will depend on economic growth and the rate of return on the funded portion. Under standard assumptions about the rate of growth, the new systems will deliver about the same replacement rate and distributive profile as the old system (Palme and Wennemo, 1997, p. 11). In the case of social services, there is no question that the budget cut-backs of the 1990s led to a declining quality of services, and this is quite significant in the case of health care. For this reason, it appears at the time of writing (June 1999) that restoration of service levels in health care will receive special attention.

In assessing the significance of the depth of the cuts for our understanding of the social democratic welfare state, we can observe that while these cuts were significant in Denmark and Sweden and indeed painful in Finland, in no case are the transfer payment entitlements or social service levels significantly below what they were at the outset of the current era, that is, the mid-1970s. Indeed, in most cases, current programmes are more generous than they were at that point in time. Thus, in contrast to the macroeconomic and employment policies discussed in other contributions to this volume, there has been no system shift in social democratic welfare-state policy. Moreover, despite the rise in unemployment, one can detect only a slight increase in inequality in the Luxembourg Income Study (LIS) data and none at all in the poverty levels in the early 1990s, a tribute to the security provided by the Nordic safety nets. In a more detailed study of the annual series on income distribution on which the LIS study is based, Aaberge *et al.* (1999) conclude that the rise in unemployment and the budget cuts in the Nordic countries had very little effect on income distribution.[13]

---

[13] Our reading of the LIS data and Aaberge's data is a bit more guarded. The data on Finland and Denmark do support the thesis that there was little change. The Norwegian data do show a trend to greater inequality, but the decompositions presented by Aaberge *et al.* do support their argument that this is primarily caused by spike-ups in capital income in 1989 and 1993 and 1994. For Sweden, one observes the following trend in the LIS data: 1975 0.217, 1981 0.198, 1987 0.220, and 1992 0.229. But 1981 appears to be deviantly low, because the indexing of pensions led to high increases in pension income that year; more importantly, the changes in Swedish tax law caused by the 1991 tax reform changed the definition of income in a way that increased inequality, above all by counting in-kind perks as income (Sten Johansson, personal conversation, 30 May 1999). This change raised the Gini index by approximately 0.020 (Aaberge *et al.*, 1999). Thus, if the LIS series were adjusted to take account of these factors, it would appear that there is little change, and the Aaberge *et al.* series to 1989 supports this. However, we interpret Aaberge *et al.*'s data for 1989 to 1994 a bit more cautiously, as it appears that even when the spikes for capital income changes are accounted for there was an increase of approximately 0.030, which is substantial, though, even if permanent, it would leave Sweden with one of the most equal distributions of disposable income in the world.

Social democratic governments that held governmental power in essentially Christian democratic welfare states in the era of retrenchment faced an exceedingly difficult situation. We discuss three such cases—Austria, the Netherlands, and France—as they constitute the only appropriate bases for comparison. The German social democrats held power before the 1980s, before there was a general realization that retrenchment was the new agenda, and their return to power is too recent to allow for any serious assessment of policy changes. The socialists in Belgium were partners only in coalition governments led by the Christian democrats from 1979 to 1981 and again from 1988 on. The situations in Spain, Greece, and Portugal are difficult to compare to those of the established democracies of Northern Europe, as they were still facing the difficulties of the post-transition period after authoritarian rule, and they also had much less consolidated welfare-state and production regimes (see the contributions to this volume by Tsakalotos and by Recio and Roca).

The differences outlined above among the production and welfare-state regimes had important consequences for overall activity levels and thus for the resiliency of the welfare states in the changed economic environment of the 1980s and 1990s. Higher activity levels in the Nordic welfare states, heavily due to higher women's labour-force participation, meant that the ratio of people contributing to welfare-state financing to people drawing benefits was more favourable. The differential emphasis on active labour-market policy in the various production and welfare-state regimes, high in the Nordic countries and low in the Continental European countries, further reinforced the differences in this ratio. The approach to the problem of rising unemployment in the coordinated production regimes of Continental Europe was to reduce labour supply by easing older employees into early retirement or disability pensions. This, of course, aggravated the fiscal problems of the welfare state both on the contributions and the benefits side.

This problem was particularly severe in the Netherlands and came to be perceived as a true crisis of inactivity, a crisis that the social democrats were forced to address in the coalition government led by the Christian democrats (1989–94) and then in the coalition with the liberals that they led themselves. The Netherlands experienced a serious economic and unemployment crisis in the 1970s already, as the system of coordinated wage bargaining and government-imposed wage restraint broke down early in the decade and the general economic turbulence was aggravated by the effects of the 'Dutch disease' and a political stalemate. In 1982, employers and unions were capable of concluding a central agreement that entailed wage restraint and set the patterns for subsequent agreements. The 1982–9 Christian democratic–right coalitions made budget consolidation their highest priority and imposed freezes on pensions and family allowances, along with partly significant cut-backs in unemployment, sickness, and disability replacement rates. However, abuses in the generous and lenient disability programme continued to be rampant, with the result that the programme supported some 900,000 people by 1990, having been planned to serve no more than 200,000. Exit from the labour market through this programme, as well as early pensions, long-term unemployment benefits, and social assistance seemed unstoppable (Visser and Hemerijck, 1997, p. 140). The abuses resulted from the fact that employers and unions controlled the social insurance programmes and shared an interest in easing older workers painlessly out of the labour market.

Thus, in the early 1990s, under a Christian democratic–social democratic coalition government, the entire organizational structure of the Dutch welfare state came under scrutiny and was reformed with the central goal of raising activity rates. More and more responsibility for the sickness and disability programmes was shifted on to employers, which gave them an interest in scrutinizing claims and led to greater regulation of these programmes through collective negotiations as well as to a greater role for private insurance. Additional highly unpopular cuts in benefits and an expansion of means testing were imposed, and an independent political body was established to monitor the administration of social insurance schemes. In the 1994 elections, both the social democrats and the Christian democrats lost a large amount of support, but the social democrats emerged as the single largest party and formed a coalition with the liberals and D66. They promised to continue with welfare-state reform, but to protect benefit levels. They did attempt to put more emphasis on active labour-market policy, but with very limited success (Visser and Hemerijck, 1997), which illustrates the difficulties of building social democratic institutions in the context of a well-established Christian democratic welfare state. On the positive side, unemployment declined to 6.5 per cent in 1996 and the job-creation rate from the mid-1980s to the mid-1990s was more than four times better than the average in the European Union (Hemerijck and van Kersbergen, 1997), arguably due to a combination of wage restraint, the development of labour-intensive services, and job redistribution (Visser and Hemerijck, 1997). Both part-time work and women's labour-force participation increased very significantly in this period, and social protection was extended to part-time work. Nevertheless, the full-time-equivalent activity rate is still comparatively very low, at slightly above 50 per cent (OECD, 1997f, p. 35).

The pressures on the Austrian welfare state never even came close to those on the Dutch welfare state, and they were also not as strong as those on the Nordic welfare states, mainly because of the much better unemployment performance. This performance can be attributed in part to structural reasons, including among others the weakness of internationalized firms, continued centralized bargaining and wage restraint, and a comparatively small increase in women's labour-force participation, and in part to the avoidance of the pro-cyclical policy mistakes of the Scandinavian countries.[14] Still, there were fiscal pressures, but through the customary system of consensual policy-making, the budget deficit was reduced from a high of 5 per cent of GDP in 1986 to 3.25 per cent in 1992, through a combination of expenditure cuts and tax increases. It rose again to 5.1 per cent in 1995 and was reduced to below 3 per cent by 1997, this time mainly through expenditure cuts (OECD, 1998, pp. 4, 131). In the 1980s and 1990s Austria was governed by a social democratic–liberal coalition (1983–6) and then a succession of Grand Coalitions between social democrats and Christian democrats. There clearly were partisan differences on policy issues, articulated particularly pointedly before 1986, and thereafter the negotiations in the Grand Coalition were rather arduous at times, leading the Christian democrats even to break up the coalition and force new elections in 1995 over the nature of austerity policies. Yet, part of the very reason for the formation of the Grand Coalition was that both major parties had to come to a compromise on major policy reforms, and once a policy package was adopted, both of them shared the responsibility. Accordingly, cuts in welfare-state entitlements remained moderate and there were even some new programmes being introduced, despite stringent budget constraints (Alber, 1998).

As in Scandinavia, rationalization of the public sector became an important issue. Steps towards professionalization of management, rationalization, and privatization began in the 1980s and were accelerated in the 1990s. Therefore, it became increasingly impossible to use the public sector to shelter employment, and the government attempted to strengthen active labour-market policies. Still, spending on active labour-market policies remained comparatively modest, and

[14] Traxler (1994) mentions the absence of efforts at wage equalization as one of the factors that explain the differences between Austria and Sweden in terms of survival versus decline of corporatist arrangements. Indeed, we saw above the comparatively higher wage dispersion in Austria than in Scandinavia. Other factors are the higher concentration and centralization of both labour unions and business associations in Austria, the structure of business, and the violation of the practice of decision by consent by the Swedish unions in the 1970s (see also Kunkel and Pontusson, 1998).

early retirement became the main tool to reduce unemployment among older workers, leading to one of the lowest labour-force participation rates for workers between 55 and 64 in the OECD (OECD, 1997*f*, p. 143). One of the provisions of the pension reform of 1993 was to move up the average real (as opposed to statutory) retirement age, which had fallen to 58 years, in order to make the system financially sound without increasing government obligations or contributions. The 1990s brought new economic challenges in the form of the influx of foreign workers from former Eastern Bloc countries. The most fundamental challenge, however, is political, as the two major parties have been losing electoral support to the point of losing their joint two-thirds majority in parliament in the 1994 elections. The erosion of the pre-eminent position of the two big parties also weakened the legitimacy of the entire system of incorporation of peak associations into the policy-making process. The opposition parties, lacking the political ties to these associations, have attacked their legitimacy and have been slowly undermining their central role in policy-making (Dachs, 1996, p. 299; Crepaz, 1994). Tálos and Kittel (1999) agree that the government has come to play an increasingly decisive role in social policy formation, but they note significant continuity in the involvement of the peak associations as well.

In France, the socialist governments in the 1980s (1981–6, 1988–93) continued to expand welfare-state protection despite efforts to bring expenditures under control, in large part in order to soften the impact of economic policies, particularly the rationalization of public-sector enterprises (Levy, 1999; Stephens *et al.*, 1999). As Lordon (this volume) makes clear, the turn away from Keynesian policy and nationalization in 1983 toward austerity, a hard currency policy, downward pressure on wages, and modernization of public-sector enterprises brought the desired result only in lowering inflation but was a dismal failure in combating unemployment. Several measures were taken to ease the unemployment pressure and to improve the situation of those affected, such as the provision of full pensions at age 50 for displaced workers, the lowering of the regular retirement age to 60 (which had been done in 1982 already), the establishment in 1988 of the guaranteed minimum income programme tied to a commitment for reintegration (i.e. a contract for a training, or education, or job-search programme), and an expansion of active labour-market policies. One of the results was that the activity rate for workers aged 55–64 fell even lower than those of Germany and the Netherlands in 1996 (Levy, 1999). Since the French welfare state was financed to about 80 per cent on the basis of employment-related contributions, the expansion of spending required increases in contributions (Bonoli and Palier, 1998).

In the 1990s, budget deficits took a significant turn for the worse, and serious efforts at curtailments of welfare-state benefits were added to increases in contributions and a new form of financing. In 1991 the Rocard government introduced a new tax of 1 per cent on all earnings, including capital earnings, to finance social security. At its introduction, the new tax was revenue neutral, as other social security contributions were reduced, but over the course of the decade the tax was raised several times. Major reform efforts affected the pension system for private-sector workers, where the minimum contribution record was raised from 37.5 to 40 years and the basis for the calculation of the replacement rate lengthened, and the health care system, where cost controls were imposed. There were clear partisan differences between left and right in their reform plans. For instance, the right-wing government of Balladur (1993–5) raised the new general social security tax but made it regressive by making it tax-deductible, a practice continued by the next right-wing government of Juppé (1995–7), whereas the socialist/green/communist government under Jospin renewed attempts to shift the tax burden to the affluent. A similar clear difference emerged in the approach to the introduction of pension funds, which the right wanted to construct for workers in large enterprises only and as an alternative to the existing public system by making contributions to the new funds deductible from the contributions to the public system, whereas the left wanted it open to all and complementary to the existing public system (Levy, 1999). In actual policy outcomes, however, the differences have been less pronounced than in policy projects, as the right-wing governments were forced by public protests to retreat several times in their reform efforts. Whether the Jospin government will be more successful in restructuring the welfare state remains to be seen. Certainly, the shift towards greater reliance on the general social security tax is a promising trend as it leads in the direction of greater citizenship-based and thus universalistic social rights, as opposed to employment-based particularistic rights (Bonoli and Palier, 1998), and as it distributes the tax burden more equitably, at least in its left-wing version of not being deductible from other taxes.

In contrast to the European and North American cases, the production regimes of the Antipodes did undergo a system shift as a result of changes in the international economic environment. As a result of long-term secular changes in commodity prices, the Australasian production regimes became unviable because they were based on rents transferred from the primary product sector to a protected manufacturing sector. These rents were highly adversely affected by these changes in international markets. In both countries, the wage-regulation system, which

was the core of the system of social protection, was changed substantially—in New Zealand totally transformed—and this, along with the
rise in unemployment, exposed workers to much higher levels of risk
of poverty than had earlier been the case. Add to this other marketizing
reforms (see Schwartz, 1994a, b, 1998; Castles et al., 1996), and it
becomes apparent that the production regimes of the Antipodes have
converged on the liberal type.

However, there are strong differences between the two countries
with regard not only to the extent of labour-market deregulation but
also changes in the social policy regime proper. In Australia, Labor
attempted not only to compensate those hit hardest by the ongoing
changes with targeted programmes, it also introduced two universalistic
policies, medical care and supplementary pensions, which make the
Australian social policy regime one of the most generous in the liberal
group. Both policies were introduced as a result of the Labor government's 'Accord' with organized labour. The earnings-related superannuation system was actually an agreement between organized labour
and employers, which is probably why it is not mentioned in Quiggin's
(this volume) brief survey of social policy, but it is highly significant
because it was the single most expensive social policy innovation in any
country in this period. It emerged from a 1986 decision of the arbitration system which was subsequently expanded and codified into
legislation by the government and, like other legislation associated
with the Accord, was in part a quid pro quo for wage restraint. When
fully matured in 2031, it would have provided benefits equal to 60 per
cent of pre-retirement income. It was funded by employers' contributions, which were scheduled to rise to 12 per cent of payroll, and
employee and government contributions of 3 per cent each. Similar to
the Finnish earnings-related tier, because it is privately administered,
the pension outlays do not appear as government expenditure and the
employer and employee contributions do not appear as taxes. Thus, the
Labor government managed to introduce, or at least midwife, a very
expensive social policy innovation and yet keep its promise not to
substantially raise taxes.

The continued importance of partisanship for retrenchment-era
social policy in Australia is underlined by the cuts of the Howard
government, which capped the employers' contribution to the new
pension system at 7 per cent and cut active labour-market spending.
More radical neo-liberal changes in social policy and even more so in the
labour-relations legislation were averted only by the government's
minority position in the Australian senate.

Quiggin's (this volume) view of social policy developments in New
Zealand Labour squares with our analysis (Huber and Stephens,

forthcoming, ch. 7). Like in Australia, Labour attempted to cushion the effects of its deregulation of the economy with more tightly targeting programmes at the poor, but it lacked a social policy achievement parallel to the Australian medical care and pension reforms. It also did not make radical changes in the labour-relations system, though the unemployment created by the rapid and thoroughgoing deregulation in other sectors of the economy certainly weakened organized labour. By contrast, the Conservative government elected in 1990 in New Zealand carried out deeply unpopular reforms which completely deregulated the labour market and substantially cut social benefits (Kelsey, 1995).[15] Thus, we do see continued partisan differences in New Zealand, but the whole spectrum has moved abruptly to the right.

In our view, the key reason for the greater success of the New Zealand Nationals compared to the Australian Liberals in implementing their radical neo-liberal attacks on the welfare state and labour-market regulation is the difference in constitutional structure. New Zealand's unicameral unitary system concentrates all power on the parliamentary majority. The plurality single member district electoral system makes it possible for a government to have a large parliamentary majority despite garnering a minority of votes in the election, as in the case of the Bolger government of 1990–3. In Australia, the Senate is elected by a different (proportional) electoral system and thus often has a different political composition from the lower house and, as a result, acts as a check or veto on the government's legislation. Moreover, the states have important powers and are often controlled by the party which is in opposition in Canberra, thus also acting as a check on the ambitions of the national government.

The outcomes with regard to poverty and income distribution in the two countries are what one might expect. Inequality increased modestly in Australia as the post-tax transfer Gini shown in Table 1 rose to 0.32 in 1994, but there was a large decline in poverty among single mothers to 30 per cent in the same period, indicating that the increased targeting of benefits to vulnerable groups had some effect. With the advent of the New Zealand National government, the poverty and inequality figures increased steeply, as New Zealand between 1990 and 1992 showed clearly the combined effect of labour-market deregula-

---

[15] This is not to deny the 'gravedigger thesis' referred to by Quiggin, that is, that Labour's market reforms paved the way for National's welfare-state cuts. However, in comparing Australia and New Zealand under the conservative governments that followed labour, we would emphasize the differences in constitutional structure outlined in the next paragraph in explaining why the Bolger government in New Zealand was able to cut much more deeply than the Howard government in Australia.

tion, the social benefits cuts, and the increase in unemployment (Easton, 1996*b*; see also Podder and Chatterjee, 1998).

5. Conclusion

Let us begin by briefly summarizing our descriptions of the types of welfare-state regimes and the related production regimes. The social democratic welfare-state regimes were characterized by (i) the pre-dominance of universalistic entitlements, (ii) comprehensiveness of their social policy regimes in the sense that programmes existed in all major programme areas, (iii) dominance of citizenship based entitle-ments, (iv) high income replacement rates in transfer programmes, (v) emphasis on high levels of publicly delivered social services, (vi) gender egalitarianism, and (vii) policies aimed at labour-force training and mobilization. The associated production regime was a nationally coor-dinated market economy with strong unions, high levels of union contract coverage, centralized wage bargaining, peak-level corporatist tripartitist policy-making, high levels of wage compression, high levels of female labour-force participation, dependent central banks, highly regulated financial markets, and a strong state role in the economy. Denmark deviated from the coordinated market economy pattern as it lacked a strong bank industry and inter-firm linkages, highly concen-trated industry, and high degrees of financial regulation.

The Christian democratic welfare states were characterized by (i) fragmentation of entitlements with different groups enjoying different entitlements,[16] (ii) predominance of employment-based entitlements, (iii) emphasis on transfers, (iv) moderate to high income replacement rates in transfer programmes, (v) private or 'third sector' delivery of publicly funded services, (vi) reinforcement of the male breadwinner family pattern, and (vii) passive labour-market policy. The associated production regime was a sectorally coordinated market economy with moderately strong unions, high levels of union contract coverage, sectoral wage bargaining, a moderate role for labour in corporatist bargaining, low levels of female labour-force participation, and a modest state role in the economy. The Netherlands, France, and Italy deviated somewhat from the coordinated market economy pattern in different ways.

---

[16] We should note that while fragmentation continues to exist with, for instance, different occupational groups being covered by different legislation and programmes, there has been a definite historical trend toward equalization of entitlements across programmes and groups.

The liberal welfare state was characterized by (i) partial programme coverage, (ii) a significant role for income or needs testing, (iii) moderate to low replacement rates in transfer programmes, (iv) few publicly delivered services outside of education and few publicly funded services outside of health and education, (v) passive family policy, and (vi) passive labour-market policy. The associated production regime was a liberal or uncoordinated market economy with weak to moderately strong unions, low levels of union contract coverage, decentralized wage bargaining, no corporatist policy bargaining, moderately high levels of female labour-force participation, and very little state intervention in the economy.

The Australasian wage-earner welfare state was a male breadwinner system of social protection based on wages and benefits delivered through the arbitration system. The formal welfare state played a backup role and was characterized by (i) partial programme coverage, due, in part, to the social protection delivered through the wage-setting system, (ii) a significant role for income testing but with relatively high income limits, (iii) moderate to low replacement rates in transfer programmes, (iv) few publicly delivered services outside of education and few publicly funded services outside of health and education, (v) reinforcement of the male breadwinner family pattern, and (vi) passive labour-market policy. The associated production regime was a largely uncoordinated market economy with important modifications as the arbitration system rather than markets determined wages and many social benefits and the state provided substantial protection to domestic producers and periodically intervened with active industrial policy.

Changes in the international economy and domestic economic and social structures put these systems under stress, resulting in changes in the production regimes, especially with regard to financial regulation, macroeconomic policies, and central bank dependence. By contrast, though welfare-state retrenchment was widespread, in only two cases, the UK and New Zealand, was it significant enough to speak of a system shift in the regime. We argue that outside of those two countries and the USA, the cuts were unemployment driven—that is, that large and apparently irreversible increases in unemployment increased the number of people dependent on the welfare state and decreased the number of people paying taxes to support the welfare state. Because the welfare state is popular, parties of the right and centre have been reluctant to solve the resultant budget crisis by deep cuts in social expenditure, and, in the context of slowed growth in the post-Bretton-Woods world, parties of the left have been reluctant to solve it entirely by increasing taxes. Thus, there has been a narrowing of partisanship in the field of social policy.

However, our studies of the dynamics in individual countries showed that partisanship has not disappeared. In Scandinavia and Australasia, the left was more reluctant to cut and more likely to raise taxes, and, particularly as budget surpluses re-emerged, to restore entitlements and services which had been cut, or to introduce new policies. Even in the liberal welfare states, where the left has most thoroughly retreated (the UK) or was non-existent (the USA), it is difficult to argue that the right is not more eager to retrench. In the three cases of Christian democratic welfare states we considered, partisan differences were most pronounced in France, which is not surprising given that the Netherlands and Austria were governed by coalitions. Still, on the one hand, in France partisan differences were sharper in the policy proposals and attempted legislation than in actual policy outcomes, owing to popular resistance to cuts, and, on the other hand, the coalition partners in the other two cases frequently disagreed publicly over the desired mix of cuts and tax increases before settling on specific policy packages.

Not only have the cuts in entitlements and services in all but a few cases been modest, the achievements of the welfare state in terms of income equalization and poverty reduction have largely been preserved, despite the increased levels of unemployment. By contrast, the two countries which retrenched dramatically in this period did record large increases in inequality and poverty as a result of social policy cuts as well as the accompanying labour-market deregulation. The UK recorded the largest increases in inequality of any country in the LIS studies, with the Gini index for disposable income rising from the 0.27 shown in Table 1 for 1979 to 0.35 in 1994. Poverty in the working-age population increased from 5.5 per cent in 1979 to 10.9 per cent in 1995. For single mothers, the percentage in poverty increased from 11 per cent to 28 per cent in the same period. Unfortunately, LIS does not have data on New Zealand, but Easton's (1996b) figures show very large increases in poverty and inequality in the early 1990s, and Podder and Chatterjee (1998, p. 17) show an 0.051 increase in the Gini coefficient in the period 1983–96.

We have argued that the resilience of the welfare state is in large part due to its popularity. The welfare state cuts of both the Thatcher and Bolger governments were, indeed, very unpopular. In both cases, the constitutional structures with no veto points and single member districts and plurality elections enabled such unpopular reforms. The single member district, plurality election system allowed governments in both the UK and New Zealand to build large parliamentary majorities on the basis of a minority of voters, thus effectively insulating them from the median voter. Thatcher never received more than 44 per cent of the vote, but amassed huge seat majorities in parliament. The New Zealand National Party received 48 per cent of the vote but 58 of 99 seats in 1990. With no effective second chamber or federalist sub-units controlled by an opposition, the opposition party had little opportunity to exploit the unpopularity of the reforms to block the legislation of the governing party.

Let us close by offering some speculation about the future of social policy in social democratic regimes and possibilities for social democratic reform in other regimes. In the social democratic welfare states, we would venture to say with some confidence that the era of substantial retrenchment is past. In all four countries, either budgets are in surplus or surpluses are projected for the coming year. While unemployment continues to be a problem, particularly for Finland, the other three Nordic countries are now recording unemployment levels well below the European average and their levels of taxation and expenditure have been adjusted to accommodate the now prevailing levels of unemployment. The renewal of reform depends on how much room can be opened up within the prevailing constraints.

For social democratic governments in all types of regimes the central constraints are unemployment, budget deficits, and perceived limits to tax increases. For the European countries, the EMU convergence criteria set additional constraints. Moreover, the development of the EMU presents yet another set of uncertainties because it is unclear how national wage-bargaining systems will respond to the new monetary arrangements (Soskice and Iversen, 1998b). The recent literature on the joint impact of central bank independence and wage-bargaining systems on unemployment indicates two possible combinations which result in low unemployment (Iversen, 1998; Hall and Franzese, 2000). While it is clear that the combination of a dependent and accommodating central bank and centralized bargaining cannot be resurrected, it is not clear what the new European system will be. While the central bank is likely to be independent and unaccommodating, it is unclear whether the bargaining system will be similar to a decentralized system, on the one end, or, on the other end, a coordinated system with the German bargain emerging as wage leader, or something in between. In any case, with the end of any possibility of devaluation or even floating exchange rates, it is clear that restoring social democratic social policy reformism will be dependent on establishing a system of wage bargaining which reliably produces non-inflationary wage agreements, a very uncertain prospect at this point.

The low level of labour-force participation presents an opportunity for reform by social democratic governments in Christian democratic welfare states. Female labour-force participation clearly needs to be increased in the Christian democratic countries in order to increase the tax base of the welfare state. Moreover, as Esping-Andersen (1997; 1999) points out, higher female labour-force participation is needed not only to counteract a deterioration of dependency ratios resulting from an ageing population and declining fertility rates, but also to reduce the household risk of falling into poverty resulting from the spread of non-traditional families and less stable labour markets. (All this is quite in addition to value-based arguments having to do with personal autonomy and power relations in the family.) In order to improve dependency ratios, of course, female labour-force participation needs to be compatible with child-raising; if it is not, it will be accompanied by lower fertility (Esping-Andersen, 1999). This suggests that the Christian democratic welfare states need to be adapted to these requirements and follow the Scandinavian model in the area of welfare-state service expansion, particularly in the areas of child and elderly care. Given the demands of the EMU and the fiscal deficits of most continental countries, this does not appear to be a very likely avenue of reform, since significantly expanding public employment would entail increases in expenditure and taxes. However, small steps in this direction might be taken, and other measures which do not increase the fiscal burden but would facilitate female labour-force participation, such as changing the tax code to individual rather than household taxation, or changing school schedules, might be implemented.

It is rather difficult to venture informed speculation about the possibilities of social democratic social policy reform in the liberal welfare states as we have classified them in Tables 1 and 2, because we have a highly limited number of cases of social democratic governments in power in the retrenchment period, that is, since about 1980. Aside from Irish Labour's participation in government as a decided minority partner, we only have the records of New Labour in Great Britain and of Labor in Australia to analyse.

Glyn and Wood's contribution to this volume suggests that it is extremely difficult for a social democratic government to build a generous social safety net in the context of a liberal welfare state and production regime in the 1990s, at least as long as this government fully accepts the macroeconomic legacy of liberal governments, as the Blair government has done. New Labour has made an active labour-market policy the centrepiece of its approach to poverty and inequality. In contrast to Nordic versions of active labour-market policy, New Labour's version is based on incentives such as tax credits for individuals and reliance on employers to provide training. Except for the group of 18–24-year-olds, there are no tripartite arrangements nor state-provided training, nor state involvement in employment creation in the areas where high unemployment and low skills are concentrated. In the area of benefits, the emphasis on income testing remains, but the limits are more generous for working families. Working families are also helped by the minimum wage and subsidies for child care. The Blair government has been strengthening the one social democratic element in the British welfare state that survived Thatcher's attack, the health system. Otherwise, however, benefits for the lowest income groups outside of the labour market have been improved only slightly; there is no attempt to work towards a generous social safety net. There remains some reasonable doubt about the effectiveness of this policy approach even in reducing poverty, not to speak of inequality.

As a result of the market-oriented reforms of the past decade, Australia and New Zealand have converged on the liberal model in terms of the production regime characteristics, so the long period of Labor government in Australia also offers some lessons for social democrats in liberal welfare states. The first thing to note is that we observed quite important partisan differences in social policy in the two countries, particularly in Australia. Indeed, Australia is the only country which introduced major social policy innovations while attempting to deal with a severe unemployment problem.[17] In fact, since the reforms were part of the Accord process, one can go further and state that the reforms were part of the solution to the unemployment problem since they were quid pro quos for wage restraint. Moreover, the pension reform created a huge pool of savings since the pensions are (or, at least were, before the Howard government's employer contribution reductions) fully funded, which should be a stimulus to investment and thus growth. The sleight of hand here was, of course, the fact that the whole reform is off budget, which suggests that some creative thinking may produce room for policy reform even within tight budget constraints and within the confines of a liberal production regime.

Appendix: Data Definitions and Sources

Table 1

(1) Left cabinet: scored 1 for each year when the left is in government alone, scored as a fraction of the left's seats in parliament of all

---

[17] The reforms in Sweden, Finland, and Norway of the 1970s and 1980s were carried out before the unemployment crisis. The gender egalitarian reforms in Denmark in the 1980s might also qualify as a major social policy innovation carried out during the crisis.

governing parties' seats for coalition governments from 1946 to 1980 (HRS[a]).

(2) Christian democratic cabinet: religious parties' government share, coded as for left cabinet (HRS).

(3) Social security benefit expenditure as a percentage of GDP (HRS, ILO[b]).

(4) Social security transfers as a percentage of GDP (HRS, OECD[c]).

(5) Total taxes as a percentage of GDP (HRS, OECD).

(6) Public health, education, and welfare employment as a percentage of the working-age population (WEEP[d]). Canadian figure provided by John Myles on the basis of Statistics Canada data.

(7) Spending on the non-aged as a percentage of GDP (OECD, 1996d, p. 107).

(8) Decommodification index (Esping-Andersen, 1990, p. 52).

(9) Support for mothers' employment (Gornick et al., 1998).

The data in columns 10–12 are from Luxembourg Income Study (LIS). The calculations were done by David Bradley with household adjustments and other definitions such that the figures are consistent with those in Mitchell (1991), Atkinson et al. (1995), and those periodically updated at the LIS website (http://lissy.ceps.lu).

(10) Gini index for disposable household income.

(11) Poverty—age 25–59: percentage of households in which the household head is aged between 24 and 60 with a disposable income below 50 per cent of the average disposable household income.

(12) Poverty—single mothers: percentage of single mothers with disposable incomes below 50 per cent of the average disposable (post-tax and post-transfer) household income.

Table 2

(1) Female labour-force participation: percentage of women aged 15–64 in the labour force (HRS, OECD).

(2) Union density: union membership as a percentage of total wage and salary earners (HRS, Visser, 1996).

(3) Union coverage: union contract coverage as a percentage of total wage and salary earners (Traxler, 1994).

(4) Corporatism index (Lehmbruch, 1984).

(5) Centralization of wage setting (Wallerstein, forthcoming).

(6) Wage dispersion: 90–10 ratio: the wages of a full-time employee at the 90th percentile of the wage distribution as a multiple of one at the 10th percentile (OECD, 1996a).

(7) Active labour-market spending as percentage of GDP divided by the percentage of the labour force unemployed. Calculated according to Nickell (1997) by David Bradley.

[a] Data from the Huber, Ragin, and Stephens (1997) data set.
[b] Original data source is International Labour Office.
[c] Original data source is OECD.
[d] Data from the Welfare State Exit Entry Project, Science Center — Berlin.

12

How Many Ways Can Be Third?

ADAM PRZEWORSKI*

1. Introduction

Does social democracy make a difference? It is only natural to expect that most of the time it would not. Once particular policies have been tested, most parties will keep offering and implementing these policies regardless of their ideological stripes. The real question is whose policies these are: who leads and who follows?

During the past one hundred years, social democrats repeatedly discovered 'third ways'. Each of these new ways was motivated by a claim that social democracy faced new conditions, and each new strategy was portrayed as the best given the new constraints and opportunities. Several new strategies were path-breaking ideologically and ingenious practically. But third ways do not lead to the first-best. If social democrats sought new ways, it is not only because they believed that the old ways would not bring them closer to their goals, but also because some goals were discovered to be infeasible given the constraints and some were found no longer attractive for other, often electoral, reasons. In any case, as new strategies were invented, some goals were abandoned. Most prominent among them is something that used to be called 'socialism'.

Hence, the achievements and the failures of social democrats cannot be judged by their own historical goals. But if it is not by their own goals, how else can one evaluate social democratic performance? One manner, represented by this volume and innumerable similar studies, is to examine their recent record in office and compare it to that of their opponents. This is a sensible way: as a voter, I want to use my vote to

* New York University.

I appreciate comments by Luiz Carlos Bresser Pereira, Andrew Glyn, Gösta Esping-Andersen, Stephen Holmes, Fernando Limongi, Bernard Manin, Covadonga Meseguer Yebra, José Maria Maravall, Joanne Fox-Przeworski, Molly Przeworski, Kathleen Schwartman, Ignacio Sanchez-Cuenca, and Michael Wallerstein.

select the government that is more likely to avoid war, increase incomes, control inflation, reduce unemployment, keep streets safe, protect health, educate children, win the World Cup, and keep otherwise out of my life. Hence, I do want to know whether social democrats are better at reaching these objectives than their electoral opponents.

This criterion assumes that the objectives and the policies pursued by any one government are independent of those followed by other governments. Yet the newly elected bourgeois government may pursue the same policies as its social democratic predecessor, or vice versa. For example, according to Iversen in this volume, the Danish centre-right majority government embarked between 1968 and 1971 'on an ambitious "spend-and-tax" policy that dwarfed anything the social democrats had done in the past'. In turn, Blair's Labour government in the UK adopted the policies of its Conservative predecessors.[1] In each case, two successive governments differed little in their policies, but the policies are quite different: in the Danish case bourgeois governments pursued social democratic policies, while in the British case the Labour government follows neo-liberal ones.[2] Presumably, in both cases the second government was persuaded that the policies of the first are successful, at least in the sense that voters would like these policies or their outcomes. If indeed, 'the ultimate test of a political movement is whether it can impose its own preferences on the majority of the electorate' (Vartainen, this volume, p. 23), then it makes a difference whether a government induces others to follow its policies even when it is defeated.

Thus differences owing to partisan control cannot be read exclusively from comparing the policies and outcomes of social democratic as compared to bourgeois governments at any moment. To identify the difference due to social democracy, one must decompose policy trends into two components: the changes of 'policy regimes' over time and the differences between social democratic and bourgeois parties at each time. For suppose that, at some time, social democrats and their

---

[1] According to Giddens (1998, p. ix), confronting Thatcher's revolution, 'The Labour Party and its intellectual sympathizers first of all responded largely by reaffirming old left views. The electoral setbacks the party suffered for doing so, however, necessarily stimulated a new orientation.' José Maria Aznar, the right-wing prime minister of Spain, claimed that the Blair–Schroeder declaration of 9 June 1999 was distilled from a letter he sent to Blair (El Pais, Madrid, 12 June 1999).

[2] Note that it may also be the case that a social democratic government initiates right-wing policies which are followed by a bourgeois one. According to Quiggin (this volume, p. 80), 'the shift to the right [by Conservative governments in Australia] is simply an extension of policies initiated by labour governments in the 1980s', even if these were in turn initiated by Margaret Thatcher in Great Britain.

opponents follow exactly the same policies: the question remains whose policies these are. What matters is who sets the tone: who defines the goals, who has more persuasive theories, who has better examples to demonstrate, who can reduce the space for the opponent.

The history of policies may thus have the following dynamic. A government comes to office, makes a major successful policy innovation, and develops a story about the secret of its success. The opposition party campaigns in elections criticizing the incumbent, but everyone knows that, if elected, the new government would follow the same policy. The difference between the two parties is so small that voters base their decisions on accidental issues — a scandal, personalities, a television debate — and at one time the incumbent loses. The victorious party follows the policies of its predecessor. Partisan control alternates without policies changing until, at some time, someone, the right or the left, introduces a major policy innovation, this policy is successful, and the cycle repeats itself.

Obviously, not all major policy innovations are successful; some are unmitigated disasters. If this model is correct, Bayesian learning must drive the policy process.[3] Clearly, Bayesian learning cannot explain the particular form of the policy innovations: these are based either on blueprints or on powerful intuitions. But once a policy is around, and its effects are manifest, other governments, whether in the same or in other countries, update their beliefs about the relative efficacy of different policies, and eventually abandon those that failed and pursue those that are successful. I am not claiming that this adjustment is instantaneous: Lordon (this volume, p. 119) observes that while 'désinflation compétitive appears as the outcome of a painful learning process imposed by external constraints . . . it took almost 10 years for public power to acknowledge this contradiction and to envisage a radical transformation of the economic policy regime'. But, sooner or later, they learn: as Stiglitz (1999a) puts it, 'We are all Bayesians.'

We should thus observe temporary equilibria in which policies are similar regardless of who is in office, punctuated by major policy innovations that temporarily distinguish parties, and followed again by convergence to a new equilibrium in which policies do not differ. I will refer to these equilibria, in which policies differ little across partisan stripes, as 'policy regimes'.

While such a model could be tested empirically, a statistical analysis will not illuminate the question which I find more interesting, namely, the qualitative evolution of the dominant policy regimes and their impact on social democracy. Hence, I adopt a different tack. I want to

---

[3] On Bayesian learning about policies, see Meseguer Yebra (1999).

know which goals, values, and policies were forsaken by social democrats, whether or not it was inevitable that they would be forsaken, and
if it was not inevitable, whether or not it was wise to give them up. But
I do not wish to shy away from the question as it now stands: can social
democracy make a difference? These questions organize the chapter. I
begin by offering a stylized history of 'social democracy'. Then I
characterize the successive policy regimes and discuss how they change.
Finally, I examine the choices facing social democrats today.

2. A Stylized History

At the risk of drawing a caricature, let me sketch a stylized history of
social democracy. Clearly, no student of a particular party will recognize it here. Indeed, the Swedish SAP, the Spanish PSOE, and the Greek
PASOK have so little in common that one can wonder whether the
question as to whether 'social democracy' makes a difference is well
formulated. Hence, first, we need to clear some methodological
underbrush.

One way to understand this question is to ask if the tenure in office
by SAP made a difference in Sweden, by PSOE in Spain, or by PASOK
in Greece, given the conditions of each country at each time, and then
list or average the answers. Formulated in this manner, the question is
about counterfactuals: what would have had happened in Spain if PSOE
had lost in 1982? More generally, if social democrats hold office under
different conditions from their bourgeois opponents, then we have to
isolate the effect of partisan control from that of these conditions.
Methods for doing this exist,[4] but again this is not the approach I adopt
here.

An alternative is to construct a stylized history of 'social democracy'.
This approach hurls itself against several difficulties. One is that the
degree of coordination among the social democratic parties was not the
same at various times: in 1902, when the French SFIO considered
entering into a bourgeois government, the Socialist International polled
leaders of all parties to decide whether this was a correct strategy.
Second, during each period some parties were perceived as
paradigmatically 'social democratic', so that any stylized picture will be
drawn disproportionately from their experience. Yet a stylized history
makes sense if, in spite of all the differences in the timing (SPD rejected
Marxism in 1959, PSOE in 1979) and particular policies (say Rehn–

---

[4] On selection bias and ways of coping with it, see Heckman (1979, 1988).

Meidner Plan versus Austro-Keynesianism), the sequence of policy regimes was similar in different countries.

I believe it was: namely, that the long-term historical evolution of 'social democracy' proceeded from revolution to reformism to remedialism.[5] The question remains is whether it will end in resignation.

3. Reformism

In 1891 the goal was clear: it was socialism understood as the public ownership of the means of production. Whatever else socialists dreamt about would come of itself, once the means of production were socialized: material progress would lead to universal satisfaction of needs, classes and their conflict would disappear, cooperation would become the mode of social life; wars, prejudice, alcoholism, and prostitution would all vanish. This is not a caricature; at least not of the SPD in the 1890s. Only one revolution was needed—nationalization of the means of production—since this revolution would solve all problems for everyone. The internationalism of the movement had both a finalistic and a strategic aspect: socialism was the goal of humanity and it could be reached only by a concerted action of workers in all countries.

The strategy, however, was controversial from the onset. The question was whether an act of violence was necessary. In one analysis, with the advent of universal suffrage, socialists no longer needed stones, just ballots. All that was needed was to wait for the working class to grow inexorably in numbers, until workers would become the numerical majority. Moreover, electoral competition based on extensive suffrage opened to socialists the possibility of aiming at intermediate, partial goals. Even if nationalization of the means of production would solve all the problems, some urgent problems could be solved without it. Thus, social democrats began to compose lists of immediate demands: education and justice were prominent among them. Yet in another analysis, violence was inevitable because the bourgeoisie would never consent peacefully to the expropriation: the revolution had to be violent, whether anyone wanted it to be or not and thus socialists should prepare for it rather than play electoral, bourgeois games.

[5] Since this stylized history is a temporal extension of my (1985) book, I do not cite the evidence and the sources.

The First World War surprised socialists in four ways. First, workers fought against workers. Second, revolution occurred in the least expected country, quickly turned violent, and continued to be repressive. Third, not only did the bourgeoisie not rise in arms against the electoral progress of socialists but, first in Denmark in 1916, and then in Sweden, Norway, the United Kingdom, and France, socialists were either invited to form minority governments or to join multi-party coalitions. Finally, having grown spectacularly until 1914, the electoral support for socialists stagnated short of a majority.

The consequences of these events were profound. They led to a split that separated social democrats from communists. 'Social Democracy' was born of this split. It was 'the third way': neither communism nor capitalism. While Lenin exhorted the Hungarian workers that democracy is just a form of bourgeois dictatorship, by 1919 several Western European social democratic parties eyed electoral victories. Moreover, the separation of paths between the Soviet Union and the West reinforced the damage to internationalism caused in August 1914. Elections were a national institution; workers had national sentiments; appeals to nation won votes. Internationalism became a strategic appeal of the Soviet Union, an instrument for penetrating Western European parties.

Rejecting the Soviet example long before the massive atrocities of the communist regime would become known, social democrats resolutely embraced the democratic road to socialism. This road was to lead to socialism, still understood in terms of 1891: the only economic programme social democrats had was nationalization. But this programme could not be implemented by parties that did not enjoy electoral majorities. Hence, when they formed minority governments or took part in coalitions, social democrats did not know what to do. Moreover, the double threat of communism and fascism led to a clear differentiation of the issue space into two dimensions: economic and political.[6] To defend democracy, social democrats had to compromise on economic issues.[7]

Not being able to implement their programme, social democrats did what they could for their working-class constituency. Specifically, given the high rates of unemployment that punctuated the inter-war period, social democrats focused on two immediate criteria for their

[6] The Chilean coup was an important lesson in Italy, while the defence of democracy was the primary concern of social democrats in Spain after 1977.

[7] For an argument that, under some plausible assumptions concerning income distribution, the left party will moderate on the economic dimension when facing competition in two-dimensional issue space, see Roemer (forthcoming).

actions, namely, employment and insurance. Such measures, even if they favoured workers, were not new: they continued the tradition of reforms of Bismarck, Disraeli, or Giolitti. When in office, social democrats behaved like other parties: with some distributional bias towards their constituency but full of respect for the golden principles of the balanced budget, deflationary anti-crisis policies, gold standard, etc. As for nationalization, they did what governments do with awkward issues: formed study commissions.

The movement continued to pursue a goal, which was socialism, but that goal was relegated to an ill-defined future. Social democrats' embrace of democracy was not just a commitment to abide by its rules and to defend it against enemies, but a constraint on policies parties could pursue in office. Only those policies could be implemented that enjoyed majority support and did not threaten democracy; other projects were deemed 'premature' by the democratic pacemaker. Thus, reformism was an adaptation to political constraints, even if these were self-imposed. The ultimate goals could not be reached immediately, but they could be advanced gradually. And since each reform was a step forward, the steps would one day lead to the realization of the ultimate goals.

For the reformist strategy to work it would have been necessary that (i) the reforms are irreversible, (ii) they are cumulative, (iii) they lead in the same direction. Social democrats realized that some policies they had to pursue only administered the capitalist economy. But other policies would be transformative. Social democrats would introduce reforms once in office; if they made mistakes by advancing too far ahead of the electorate, they would lose, but this would not be a disaster since the opponents would not reverse them; once they won again, social democrats would introduce new reforms; and thus the process would continue until, in Jaures's allegory, the invisible line of the equator would have been crossed, recognized by sailors only from the song of birds and the warmth of winds.

Hence, even if, once in office, social democrats pursued policies that deviated little from those of their bourgeois opponents, they could claim that they were leading the society to a different future.

4. Remedialism[8]

As employment and equality became the goals, nationalization of the means of production was no longer necessary. Public ownership of

---

[8] The term is Robert Dahl's.

some banks, perhaps of transport, or some strategic firms may facilitate government control over the economy, but nationalization is just one among many policy instruments, not a panacea. Capitalist economies could be controlled without state ownership: business cycles could be avoided, or at least attenuated, and unemployment with them; income distribution could be corrected; adversities could be insured. This was the great discovery of social democrats, first in Sweden in the 1930s and then elsewhere.

Whether this answer had a directly social democratic (Wicksell) or a liberal (Keynes) inspiration, it constituted a policy revolution. Moreover, it suited social democrats particularly well: since economic stimulation could be achieved by transferring incomes to workers, the narrow interest of their constituency was the same as the interest of the entire society, so that Léon Blum could say that 'a better distribution . . . would revive production at the same time that it would satisfy justice' (cited in Weil-Raynal, 1956, p. 54).

A full reconciliation of social democrats with capitalism came in the 1950s. In the context of the Cold War, with the experience of fascism, wholesale nationalization would have been politically destabilizing. And capitalist economies functioned well in many aspects. Hence, nationalization of the means of production, 'socialism' in the Marxist sense, was at best unnecessary. 'Socialism' was not some kind of an ·illusive future but *hic et nunc* the opportunity for everyone to realize his or her potential and the security that no one would be abandoned to ill fate.

If productive resources are to remain in private hands, what is the proper role of the state? The answer, not specific to social democrats, was that in many respects competition was a better allocation mechanism than command. But markets created problems: in some respects they were not efficient, they suffered from cycles, generated inequality, and exposed people to various risks. The role of governments was to remedy these imperfections: maintain full employment, promote investment, provide public goods, equalize opportunities, and assure welfare. Specific policies, at times based on innovative, systematic blueprints, varied from country to country, but the combination of private ownership, markets, and corrective interventionism by the state was accepted by almost everyone, not just social democrats.

The result was a spectacular success. Economies grew; social expenditures grew even faster. For the first time in history, there were countries where almost everyone enjoyed basic security. Problems had remedies.

Were social democrats better at coping with problems? Since the literature on this topic is complex and immense, all I can do is to declare that I believe they were. At least, if in 1973 I were to decide, not knowing anything about her future life chances, whether my daughter should be a Swede or an American, I would have chosen social democracy (Lee and Przeworski, 1995). But there were always new problems. Some persisted from the past; some emerged anew. As one compares the problems enumerated by Jaures in 1902 with those mentioned in an exchange of letters among Brandt, Kreisky, and Palme (1976), the list does not get any shorter, in spite of all the remedies.

5. Resignation?

The stagflation crisis of the later 1970s, deepened by the surge of interest rates in 1982, undermined the 'Keynesian welfare state'.[9] Forging farther in the same direction — 'fine tuning' — turned out to be a failure not only economically but also electorally. Social democrats discovered that the constraints their economies faced, internal and external, were much more biting than they had believed. And under these constraints, they could no longer strive for all their objectives. Something had to give.

The imagination of the 'new social democrats' is replete with dilemmas. Giddens, who thinks that the 'Political debate is dominated by worries about declining moral standards, growing divisions between rich and poor, the stresses of the welfare state' (1998, p. 2), finds five of them. But even more serious analyses everywhere find 'dilemmas' or at least 'trade-offs'. Iversen (this volume, p. 275) describes the current 'trilemma' facing Scandinavian — the most successful — social democracy as 'whether it wants to deepen class divisions by accepting greater inequalities, or whether it wants to create a marginalized group of people, excluded from full participation in the economy'. To appear responsible, governments must have the courage to admit that there are trade-offs. And if governments face trade-offs, they cannot promise 'everything'. There are problems that have no remedies.

Faced with the persistence of many old problems and with the emergence of new ones, some, although by no means all, social democrats draw limits to actions of the state. The state faces constraints of a macroeconomic nature: fiscal irresponsibility leads to disasters in

[9] I have been urged by several readers to explain why this policy regime failed. I do not know: there are just too many plausible explanations. They come in three categories: (i) the 'Keynesian welfare state' was in various ways a victim of its own success, (ii) social democratic economic regulation could not resist exogenous shocks, and (iii) bad luck.

the newly global economy. The state must keep reassuring nimble-footed investors. In the words of Felipe Gonzàlez, 'Capital markets charge themselves with reminding that they do not trust an economic policy that does not watch inflation or deficit' (*El Pais*, Madrid, 9 June 1999, p. 15). And since investment responds not only to balances but also to tax rates, the constraint bites on the revenue side. The only way to satisfy it is, thus, to keep a tight control on expenditures.

This economic analysis is accompanied by a new moral tone. The state cannot be responsible for everything; individuals must bear the responsibility for their fate. 'A prime motto for the new politics,' Giddens (1998, p. 65) suggests, is *'no rights without responsibilities.'* The state cannot be responsible for everyone. It can and should help those who are unlucky, but only if they are willing to help themselves. The unemployed must actively look for work; to assure them of income would induce them to be lazy, which is a 'moral hazard', a game-theoretic term transformed into a Protestant sin.

Not only does the state encounter limits to what it can do, often it does damage. Thus Giddens (1998, p. 112) cites Ronald Reagan: 'we have let government take away those things that were once ours to do voluntarily.'[10] Public enterprises must be sold because they are less efficient; public expenditures should be curtailed; control of monetary policy should be placed in the hands of independent central banks to assure credibility—the reader knows the rest, so I stop.

The neo-liberal policy regime at the same time favours globalization and resists its effects. Free trade, free movement of capital, free flow of ideas are the banners of neo-liberals. But while Paul Samuelson had many years ago the courage to tell US automobile executives that 'God may not have willed that automobiles be produced only in Detroit' (I cite from memory), each government resolutely defends its country from the inflow of cheap foreign products and other unwelcome consequences of globalization. Indeed, a few years ago the loss poor countries suffered from protectionism by the OECD area was exactly equal to the total flow of foreign assistance. The slogan seems to be 'Internationalism for exports; the nation for imports.' The new social democrats do not differ. After all,

> Nations are ethical communities, where those involved owe special obliga-
> tions to other members not always owed to others on the outside. Nations
> provide a focus of self-determination: the nation should develop state struc-

[10] There are many aspects of Giddens's book I do not understand, but foremost among them is the subtitle: 'The Renewal of Social Democracy'. What is it that is being renewed by seeking inspiration in Thatcher and Reagan?

tures that allow citizens to decide for themselves matters of general importance. (Giddens 1998, p. 131)

While the degree to which neo-liberal ideas permeated different
social democratic parties is not the same—to cite just one example,
French socialists are successfully pursuing a rather orthodox programme of job creation—policy convergence is again apparent. The
dominant policy regime of our times is the neo-liberal one and, while
the neo-liberal ideas softened as a result of some evident fracas, social
democrats, in government and in opposition, are abandoning even
some of the remedial policies.

6. Analysis

Obviously, if judged by its initial goals, social democracy has been a
dismal failure. But, as nostalgic as one may be about the ideals of one's
youth, it makes no sense to evaluate a movement by goals it had one
hundred years ago. Since I do not want to repeat what has long been
in print (1985, 1991), let me just summarize my conclusions.

(i) Participation in electoral politics was inevitable for any movement that sought a mass following. The only alternative was a revolution by a minority, which had to be and was extremely violent.

(ii) Once socialists accepted the democratic constraint, the policies
they could implement depended on the support they could gain within
the democratic institutions.[11] Since, contrary to the optimistic extrapo-
lations, workers never became the overwhelming majority of any
electorate, social democrats could not implement their original programme of massive nationalization.

The perennial question is which strategy is superior: the 'reformist'
strategy of advancing at each time only as far as the electorate permits,
or a 'radical' strategy of demanding the impossible (and facing defeat)
so as to educate the electorate, waiting until the electorate is ready to
support the maximal programme, and then implementing everything in
one sweep? This, I believe, had been the alternative of social democrats
all along. They have opted for the former strategy and, most likely, they
were right: no single mass movement in history survived unless it
availed itself of the opportunity to improve the immediate conditions
of its followers. But questions entailing counterfactuals always leave a
residuum of doubt.

[11] In Norway in 1928, the Labour government tried to nationalize as a minority.
It lasted 3 days.

(iii) The decision to abandon public ownership of the means of production was perhaps not inevitable but it was wise. The model of a state-owned and command-operated economy did not have political support in Western Europe and, in the light of the recent theory of 'information economics', would have been an economic disaster. Whatever social ills markets may generate, their informational role is crucial in any complex economy (even if it perhaps was not in the Soviet Union in 1928, where planning in physical terms could go a long way). But while allocating most goods by markets was the correct decision, this does not mean that the only choice was the investor-owned economy. Other alternatives were employee ownership, citizen ownership, or various mixtures of the three (three admitting some state-owned firms). Each of these alternatives faces problems: (i) an economy with employee-owned firms may not function differently from one with investor-owned firms and may, in fact, generate less employment; (ii) an economy with citizen-owned firms would generate a better income distribution and perhaps fewer public bads (diffused ownership would mean that the owners would internalize more externalities) but would face problems of monitoring. But these ideas are not quite dead: see Stiglitz's (1999b) recent rediscovery of 'stakeholder privatization'.

But the problem social democrats faced when they gave up Marxism was more profound: would they be able to replace it with a new project of a future society, an alternative vision of socialist transformation? The stake was this. Social democrats could, and did, declare commitment to full employment, equality, and justice. But to use employment, equality, or justice as criteria is not the same as to strive for an equal or a just society. Used as criteria, these values serve to identify the current problems, to choose current policies, and to evaluate their outcomes. To see them as goals, would be to conjure up a vision of society that would not generate unemployment, inequality, or injustice, to identify the mechanisms that generate these ills, and go on to transform them. Without a new project, only remedies would be left.

Let me provide just one illustration. It appears that Western European countries redistribute every year a fair amount of income while the market-generated distribution of income changes little over time within particular countries. If redistributing incomes is costly, this pattern cannot be efficient. Increasing the productive capacity of the poor—a 'transformative redistribution'—would both accelerate growth and equalize incomes.[12]

Social democracy always stood for extending democracy from the political to the social realm. But while democracy in the political realm

[12] For the full argument and evidence, see Przeworski and Gandhi (1999).

was an autonomous value for social democrats, it was only the first step. Equality of earned incomes or of life chances — distinctions came later — was a defining feature of a socialist society. Public ownership of the means of production was the instrument to achieve equality in the Marxist vision of the future and, when nationalization turned out to be a bad idea, something would have to replace it. But what?

The repertory of socialist transformations was not empty: 'abolishing inheritance', 'social ownership' (wage-earners fund), 'freedom from toil' (reduction of labour time), 'citizen's wage' (universal minimal income) were still among the instruments. Yet, except for Sweden and, during a brief period, for France, where socialists arrived from the political wilderness promising to 'change life', the spirit of the time was well summarized by Konrad Adenauer's dictum, *'keinen experimenten'*, no experiments. None of these ideas was embraced by the socialist parties and, perhaps more importantly, none caught the imagination of the electorates. Even in Sweden, where the wage-earner fund was backed by powerful unions, it did not win the support of voters. The French *virage* of 1983 demoralized even the more timid attempts. Hence, while transformative ideas linger within the walls of the academia, the fear that voters would see them as utopian preoccupies social democratic parties.

7. Stability and Change of Policy Regimes

With this historical background, we can pose more analytically questions concerning the dynamics of policy regimes. Specifically, we need to identify these regimes and analyse the mechanisms through which they persist and change.

(a) *Policy Regimes*

Policy regimes are situations in which major parties, regardless of their partisan stripes, propose and implement similar policies. If voters learn from experience, then, after a few periods in which they observe the outcomes of a particular policy, they develop clear views about it. If they think that this policy is better than other alternatives they experienced, they vote for it. In turn, political parties, even if they have policy preferences, seeking to be elected, converge to the almost certain position of the median voter. (On voting models, see Roemer, forthcoming.) Hence, a policy regime is sustained.

For reference, I first summarize the historical description of policy regimes.

(i) Until 1914, that is, before socialists ever held office, their programme was defined by the goal of establishing socialism, even if several parties were not adverse to realizing some immediate goals while they could. Since, except for Alexandre Millerand, who was expelled from the SFIO anyway, socialists never held office, it makes little sense to speak of differences between them and the bourgeois governments, and thus of 'policy regimes'. Note, however, that the danger that socialists would become like all other parties if they played the electoral game was the main argument of the opponents of participation, from the anarchists to Rosa Luxemburg. Roberto Michels saw it as inevitable.

(ii) When socialists held office as minority governments or members of multi-party coalitions during the inter-war period, they followed the economic orthodoxy of the time, with some distributional bias towards their constituency. They adhered to the goal of socialism and, hence, could claim that they led societies to a different future, but their policies while in office were not much different from those of their opponents. Until today, analyses of the MacDonald government as well as of the *Front Populaire* blame them for not breaking with the standard economic wisdom.

(iii) With the rise of Keynesianism (if that is what it was), social democrats found that they no longer needed to nationalize everything and, more influentially, that they could control the capitalist economy and remedy the social ills generated by markets. This policy was highly successful and was embraced, albeit with varying degrees, by other parties. The complaint that parties make no difference was widespread and passionate in the 1960s and 1970s: 'The working class is lost in administering its imaginary bastions. Comrades disguised as notables occupy themselves with municipal garbage dumps and school cafeterias. Or are these notables disguised as comrades? I no longer know' (Konopnicki, 1979, p. 53).

(iv) With the advent of neo-liberalism, social democrats found themselves on the defensive. Their reactions vary from accepting the fiscal constraints while continuing to pursue remedial social policies, to a wholehearted embrace of neo-liberal prescriptions. In any case, policy regimes are converging again, this time to the right. And, again, the perception that choices facing

all governments are narrowly circumscribed and that all have to
follow similar policies is widespread. And so are the voices that
say that globalization deprives national constituencies of the
capacity to make any meaningful political choices.

These successive policy regimes differed principally in three dimensions: forms of ownership, instruments for coping with unemployment,
and international economic arrangements.

While until 1930s social democrats advocated nationalizing the
means of production, they were not able to implement this programme
while in office. And since the idea was anathema to bourgeois parties,
no nationalizations took place (except for creation of municipal companies). Between 1936 and 1984, several banks and industries were
nationalized in a number of countries, by social democrats as well as by
bourgeois governments. But nationalizations were more a matter of
historical accident than of partisan preferences. In fact, Sweden had the
lowest share of state enterprises among the industrialized countries,
while in Austria and Italy the large public sector was a post-Fascist
legacy. Still the idea of selling public assets—'privatization' (I put the
word in quotation marks because it is a neologism)—was inconceivable.
Standard national accounts did not even include changes of the value
of publicly held assets: they had no market value, as no one could think
of selling them. Nevertheless, since 1982 privatizations occurred almost
anywhere governments had something to sell. In turn, no nationalizations
took place, except for states assuming bad debts of private banks.

The second dimension concerns employment and unemployment.
Until the 1930s again, the cyclical movements of economies were seen
as obeying natural laws. Governments could protect incomes, but could
not counteract the cycles. Swedish social democrats lost office twice in
the 1920s over the issue of unemployment compensation but the only
policy difference between the left and the right was whether or not to
compensate the unemployed. At least since the Second World War,
governments of all partisan stripes have become committed to the goal
of 'full employment': with great fanfare, the OECD unveiled a new
blueprint for full employment every 5 years. These blueprints evolved,
but the essential instruments were Keynesian: inflating the economy in
the face of high unemployment, with public works as the most effective
tool. This policy was almost universally abandoned[13], on the grounds

[13] Except for the United States during the Reagan era, where it was an unintended
consequence of divided government.

that demand stimulation increases inflation without having an effect on employment.

The third dimension along which policy regimes experienced profound changes was trade and exchange-rate arrangements. This is, however, a more complex story, and I will not delve into it.

In turn, differences with regard to welfare policies were much less pronounced.[14] The social protection net was built gradually and through varied paths: social christians were as dedicated to protecting material welfare as social democrats, while some bourgeois governments of other inspirations built it in order to thwart a revolutionary threat. And it has not been dismantled. Even Margaret Thatcher did not succeed.

(b) *Policy Innovations*

The major policy innovation of social democrats was the very idea that capitalist economies can be regulated and the effects of markets can be corrected: what is referred to these days as 'the Keynesian welfare state'. In turn, the major innovation of neo-liberals was the claim that well-designed market institutions spontaneously maximize the welfare of society, with only a minimal policy intervention.

Each of these innovations was rationalized by a theoretical blueprint. From Karl Kautsky's *The Class Struggle*, through the last chapter of Keynes's *General Theory*, Friedmans' *Free to Choose,* to the 'Washington Consensus' (Williamson, 1990), each policy regime found a theoretical articulation founded in contemporary economic theories. Even if some ideas were formulated only after the policies they justified were already being implemented, they had an autonomous effect on routinizing the particular policy regimes by persuading the élites, and even the masses, that these policies are based on reason. I remember that in the late 1980s everyone in the United States believed that 'deficits cause inflation' and, even if no one I ever asked, from my father-in-law to taxi drivers, could spell out the causal chain, they all accepted the authority of the economic theory.

But even if new ideas are available, to explain the changes of policy regimes is difficult. Policy innovations can occur in two ways: either some party wins an election offering the old policy and then surprises voters by switching to a new one, or a party campaigns and wins an election proposing a new policy and implements it once in office. Stokes (1999) studied the recent cases in which parties campaigned on traditional platforms and, once elected, switched to neo-liberal policies. I

[14] Perhaps again with the exception of the United States, which is *sui generis,* as it never had a major social democratic party.

will concentrate on the second path. The question, then, is whether and, if ever, under which conditions, would a party offer a new policy, be elected, and implement it with success.

The conclusions of my reasoning (spelled out in Przeworski, 1999), are the following. (i) There are circumstances under which a party would propose a new policy, be elected, and implement it successfully. (ii) This will occur if a combination of particular conditions occurs, specifically, (a) the party is convinced that the new policy is better than the old one, (b) voters think the old policy is not very good, (c) voters believe that the party cares about their welfare rather than about pursuing the new policy for its own sake, and (d) the new policy does not run into bad luck when it is being implemented.

The intuition behind this reasoning is the following. When voters do not know what to think about the new policy, they take a party's proposal to do something new as a signal that this party knows something they (and the other party) do not know, as long as they think that the party which offers the new policy is responsible and they see status quo as not good. Unless the innovating party is unlucky, voters will vote for this policy again. And note that, if the innovating party had in the past followed or proposed the same policy as the other party, voters will tend to think that it is responsible and that it deviates from the old policy because it does believe that the new policy is better.

I think that these conclusions are consistent with the historical experience. To give just a few examples, the Swedish SAP campaigned in the election of 1932 with a programme that was new, even if it realized how new it was only after its initial success, so that the party heralded its policy as revolutionary only in 1936. It was elected in 1932 in the midst of an economic crisis (and a political scandal), so that voters thought the old policy was bad. The SAP was lucky, because demand for Swedish exports was fed by the German rearmament. The elections of Margaret Thatcher and Ronald Reagan also fit this pattern (even if the policy shift in the United States was marked as of 1978, in the middle of Jimmy Carter's term). They both believed that neo-liberal policies are better and advocated them in elections, while voters were experiencing a double-digit inflation with no growth.[15] Moreover, Reagan had the good luck of having a Congress that kept the spending up, while Thatcher gained popularity because of the Malvinas-Falklands war.

More generally, policy regimes changed amidst economic crises, when voters thought that old policies did not work well. The parties that proposed and implemented policy innovations believed that new

---

[15] Moreover, as Kalyvas (1994) argues, British public opinion turned against nationalizations because the Labour government ran into the oil crisis.

policies would be better and their beliefs were founded in ideas of economists. Good luck helped in persuading voters that the new policies were effective.

8. Social Democratic Perspectives

Is a social-democratic-led policy innovation possible today, or is it inevitable that social democrats become 'social liberals' for the foreseeable future? My views are the following. (i) There is an ample room for a policy innovation because the constraints which paralyse social democrats are not as tight as they tend to believe. (ii) Voters' initial enchantment with neo-liberalism is waning in the face of persistently high unemployment in some countries and growing wage disparities in other countries. (iii) Proposing a new policy is a risky bet, since its success depends to some extent on luck. I concentrate on the first point, concerning the purported dilemmas.

The first belief which motivates the current neo-liberal policy regime is that the state is 'too big'. This belief has two versions: the first is a theoretical claim that a big state is bad for economic efficiency, the second is an empirical claim that a big state scares investors. Much of the former is just an ideological fantasy, even if at times mathematically adorned. My favourite is an article which begins by assuming that state expenditures do not enter as inputs into production or as sources of utility for households and then concludes that taxes are bad for growth (Rebelo, 1991). The state can be too big: this much no one will question. But this does not imply that everywhere it is. The following conclusions, I believe, are consistent with the current state of economic theory. (i) There are equilibria in which there is unemployment either because of insufficient supply or insufficient demand. (ii) There are situations in which state subsidies to investment foster growth. (iii) Private insurance markets are never efficient in the presence of differentiated risks: universal compulsory insurance schemes, in which low-risk categories subsidize high-risk categories, dominate markets by efficiency criteria even in the presence of moral hazard.

Hence, (i) demand should be sometimes restricted and sometimes expanded, (ii) some productive role for the state is optimal for growth,[16] and (iii) some compulsory universal insurance schemes are optimal for

---

[16] Barro's (1990) estimate of the optimal size of public productive expenditures is surprisingly high, about 25 per cent of GDP; Cheibub and Przeworski (1997) discovered that the state is too small in most countries by the criterion of equalizing marginal products of the public and the private sector.

current welfare. Since in all the three aspects the optimal solution is an internal one, the state may be too big or too small under the particular conditions. But a blanket programme of reducing the state is just right-wing dogmatism.

The empirical claim that a big state scares the investors is more complicated. In a closed economy, taxes on income are supposed to reduce investment. Almost all economists believe this much, even if Stiglitz (1999b) argued recently that current taxes may forecast lower future interest rates and may in fact stimulate investment. Statistically, the hypothesis that taxes reduce investment almost never fares well, but this may be a matter of data and specification. In any case, closed economies are history: we live in the era of globalization.

Like El Niño, 'globalization' is a God-given gift for all governments. It is a cause that is external, omnipresent, and inexorable. Whatever successes governments achieve, these can be attributed to their wise actions. Whatever failures there are, can be explained residually. There seems to be no politician who does not proclaim that globalization narrowly circumscribes their margin of manoeuvre. Since the entire problematic is a conceptual muddle and serious research is still scarce, summarizing the current state of knowledge is risky. Nevertheless, I think that these are the best beliefs one can hold at the present. (i) Most of the effects attributed to globalization are due to something else, many to technological changes (Glyn, 1998b).[17] (ii) The margin of manoeuvre may be very narrow with regard to some policies but broad with regard to other policies. Specifically, in the light of Mosley (1999), it appears that investors buying government obligations pay close attention to the inflation rate and the current account, but not to other indicators, perhaps surprisingly including the deficit and the tax rates, as well as allocations of expenditure. In turn, direct investment seems insensitive to policies in general. The effect of economic 'fundamentals' on capital flows is hard to determine. (i) Governments were always constrained by the reactions to their policies of private investors; most investment is domestically financed anyway, and globalization has at most an incremental effect. (ii) Reactions to external shocks are not uniquely determined by the nature of these shocks. Even if most governments treat it as inevitable, to cite Stiglitz (1999a) again, it is far from apparent that raising domestic interest rates is the best response

[17] For example, everyone in the less developed countries seems to believe that they are losing jobs owing to the inflow of cheap exports from the technologically advanced economies, while everyone in the developed countries seems to think that they are losing jobs because of the inflow of cheap exports from the low-wage countries. Obviously, without a general technological change, something here does not add up.

to speculative flows against a currency. Effects of external shocks are mediated by the domestic political and economic institutions (Boix, 1999). (iii) Capital flows are subject to multiple ('sunspot') equilibria and the question whether they are driven by economic fundamentals seems wide open. Note that I am not arguing that the volatility of capital flows is costless, nor that open trade has no effect on income distribution, but only that we just simply do not know as of today how 'globalization' works. At the moment it appears to be mostly a smoke screen.

Some constraints, however, are domestic. Two concern the welfare state. The first is that, as it developed in the OECD countries, the welfare state was based on the assumption of a particular demographic and household structure. As this structure changed—and it changed drastically—the current welfare policies are simply poorly designed for the contemporary advanced societies (Esping-Andersen, 1999). Moreover, faced with the combined effect of demographic change and a rise of unemployment, the welfare state suffers from an acute fiscal strain. The second constraint is political. People were willing to support universal compulsory insurance schemes when many of them faced the same risks. As these risks have become differentiated, they are more inclined to opt out for private insurance schemes.

Finally, to implement their programmes, parties must win elections. Hence, they must anticipate who would support their programmes. Class analysis in the Marxist sense—class defined in relation to the ownership of the means of production—illuminates little about contemporary societies. Appeals to 'the exploited' would be anachronistic: a central problem of contemporary societies is that there are millions of people who dream about being exploited. One can obviously think of class in different terms. But while class analysis may elucidate the patterns of voting—income, education, and occupation are still good predictors of partisan orientations—it is irrelevant for understanding who wins elections. The power of class is inframarginal, while political competition takes place at the margin. In most countries, the difference between the electoral support for social democratic and the largest bourgeois parties (or between left and right coalitions) remains very small. Hence, small vote changes at the margin, amplified by disproportionalities of electoral systems, shift partisan control. And this implies that, to the extent to which they can be identified, parties must compete for the same voters.

This much about constraints. I am far from certain that they are exactly what I described them to be: particularly with regard to globalization, it is hard to tell. But many of the 'dilemmas' appear to be just excuses: the famous 'big trade-off' between efficiency and equality is not a trade-off at all if the poor cannot educate their talented offsprings (or, in general, if they are credit-constrained),[18] Iversen's 'trilemma' would vanish if the supply of skills would catch-up with demand for them; Gonzàlez's fiscal constraint can be relieved by administrative reforms that would reduce the cost of delivering social services (Bresser Pereira, 1998); of Giddens's five 'dilemmas' none is that in a logical sense of this term.

The choice facing social democrats is thus which strategy to pursue. One strategy is to accept the diagnosis of the problems and of the constraints by their opponents and to claim that social democrats have better solutions. The problems identified by Thatcher or Reagan are real, but their solutions are wanting, while the old left clings to an outmoded view of the world. Hence, we are the new social democrats: not responsible for the past, better prepared for the new world than the neo-liberals. This is basically a strategy that takes voters' beliefs as they are and accommodates to these beliefs, while staking the political claim at higher competence, honesty, compassion, or whatever the case may be. The alternative strategy is to tell the voters that they are wrong, that they have been misled by neo-liberals, that the problems and the constraints are not what voters believe, and that different policies are possible and will be successful.

The second strategy is obviously much more risky. If social democrats place themselves close to neo-liberal policies, they have a good chance that any minor accident may generate their electoral victory. If once in office they pursue the neo-liberal policies with moderate success, voters will be unable to update their beliefs and will keep voting for them until some new accident occurs. But if social democrats try to persuade voters educated by neo-liberals that they are mistaken, there is going to be a large policy distance between parties. If they are in opposition, social democrats may keep losing; if they are in government and pursue currently unpopular policies, they may be defeated unless they do particularly well. In the past, there were periods when social democrats took the risk and were lucky: Sweden in 1932 is the prime example, but so was Bruno Kreisky's expansionist response to the recession of 1975 (Guger, in this volume) and, if perhaps more timidly, Lionel Jospin's government's current job-creation policy. But many times such policies failed, whether under François Mitterrand in France, who had the bad luck that the world economy did not pick up in time (Lordon, in this volume) or under PASOK in Greece before 1985 (Tsakolotos, in this volume).

---

[18] See the already vast literature that shows that income inequality is bad for economic growth.

The success of the latter strategy requires innovative ideas, the courage of conviction, and luck. Such combinations have been historically rare, which is why policy regimes last for decades and change infrequently. All I can say is that if this reasoning is correct, then the quality of ideas, and the courage to pursue them, matter.

9. Conclusions

Whether or not social democratic and bourgeois governments pursue similar policies is not what matters. If some policies are better than others, if different parties share the understanding of the constraints, and if voters learn from experience, then most of the time parties of different stripes will follow similar policies. Even if parties have different ideal points in the space of outcomes, they will have proximate ideal points in the space of policies if their politicians believe that they face trade-offs between objectives. Policies diverge when there are leaders who find ways of overcoming real trade-offs or who free their imagination from illusory ones. They converge as the experience with new policies accumulates. What does matter is which policy regime dominates everyone's thinking: who leads and who follows.

If this analysis is correct, then the periodic disenchantment with democracy — the widespread perception that elections make no difference — is both justified and misplaced. It is justified because most of the time, no one, whether voter or politician, knows anything better to do. But there are moments when the future is in voters' hands. Whenever a party does propose to do new things, the voters' decision is crucial. Democracy, it seems, works in spurts.

Let me end with a qualification. The focus of my analysis was economic policy. But I think that there has been a persistent difference between social democracy and the right, namely that the right has been traditionally authoritarian, indeed, more statist than social democrats in the political realm. Even today, for all the talk about reducing the state, the main social policy of neo-liberals in the United States is to build more prisons. Hence, I see the language of 'new social democrats' — decline of moral values, strengthening the family, crime — as new indeed. And as ominous.

Bibliography

Aaberge, R., Bjorklund, A., Jantti, M., Pedersen, P. J., Smith, N., Wennemo, T. (1999), 'Unemployment Shocks and Income Distribution: How Did the Nordic Countries Fare During Their Crises?', *Scandinavian Journal of Economics*, **101**.

abo (1990), 'Prywatyzacja w Sieci', *Gazeta Wyborcza*, 16 November.

Adamski, W. W. (1999), 'The Evolution of Acquisitive and Threatened Interests in the Process of Ownership Transformation', in W. W. Adamski *et al.* (eds), *System Change and Modernization*, Warsaw, IfiS.

Agell, J. (1996), 'Why Sweden's Welfare State Needs Reform', *The Economic Journal*, **106**(439), 1760–71.

— Englund, P., and Södersten, J. (1995), 'Svensk Skattepolitik i Teori och Praktik. 1991 års Skattereform', Appendix to SOU (Government Committee Papers) No. 104.

Aghion, P., and Howitt, P. (1998), *Endogenous Growth Theory*, Cambridge, MA, MIT Press.

Aglietta, M. (1995), *Macroéconomie Financière*, Paris, Repères, La Découverte.

— Baulant, C. (1993), 'Le Franc: de l'Instrument de Croissance à la Recherche de l'Ancrage Nominal', in *Du franc Poincaré à l'Ecu*, Colloque Ministère de l'Economie et des Finances, 3–4 décembre 1992, Comité pour l'Histoire Economique et Financière de la France, Imprimerie Nationale.

Aguilar, S., and Roca, J. (1991), 'Economie Politique d'une Grève', *Sociologie du Travail*, **33**(2/1991), 217–38.

Akerlof, G., Dickens, W., and Perry, G. (1996), 'The Macroeconomics of Low Inflation', *Brookings Papers on Economic Activity*, 1–76.

A.K.K. (1992), 'Rozdanie œwiadectw w 1994 r' (Distribution of Certificates in 1994), *Rzeczpospolita*, 20 August.

Alba-Ramírez, A., and Alonso-Borrego, C. (1997), 'Tipo de Contrato y Empleo en el Ciclo Económico, 1987–1996', *Papeles de Economia Española*, **72**, 237–49.

Alber, J. (1998), 'Recent Developments in Continental European Welfare States: Do Austria, Germany, and the Netherlands Prove To Be Birds of a Feather?', paper presented at the 14th World Congress of Sociology.

Albert, M. (1991), *Capitalisme contre Capitalisme*, Paris, Seuil.

Alvarez Aledo, C. *et al.* (1996), *La Distribución Funcional y Personal de la Renta en España*, Madrid, Consejo Económico y Social.

Amable, B., Barre, R., and Boyer, R. (1997), *Les Systèmes d'Innovation à l'Ere de la Globalisation*, Paris, Economica.

Anderson, P. (1994), 'Introduction', in P. Anderson and P. Camiller (eds), *Mapping the West European Left*, London, Verso.

Andrikopoulos, A. A., Prodromides, K. P., and Serletis, A. (1997), 'Electoral and Partisan Cycle Regularities: A Cointegration Test', *Journal of Policy Modeling*, forthcoming.

Apel, M., and Jansson, P. (1997), 'System Estimates of Potential Output and the Nairu', Sveriges Riksbank Working Paper Series, No. 41, Stockholm.

Appelbaum, E., and Schettkat, R. (1994), 'The End of Full Employment? On Economic Development in Industrialized Countries', *Intereconomics*, 122–30.

Archer, R. (1992), 'The Unexpected Emergence of Australian Corporatism', in J. Pekkarinen, M. Pohjola, and R. Rowthorn (eds), *Social Corporatism*, Oxford, Oxford University Press.

Armstrong, P., Glyn, A., and Harrison, J. (1991), *Capitalism Since 1945*, Oxford, Blackwells.

Aronsson, T., and Walker, J. R. (1997), 'The Effects of Sweden's Welfare State on Labor Supply Incentives', in R. B. Freeman, R. Topel, and B. Swedenborg (eds), *The Welfare State in Transition*, NBER, Chicago, IL, and London, The University of Chicago Press.

Arrow, K. (1972), 'Gifts and Exchanges', *Philosophy and Public Affairs*, **1**.

Arsenis, G. A. (1987), *Politiki Katathesi*, Athens, Odysseas.

Artus, P. (1989), 'De la Rigueur Salariale, où Existe-t-il un Salaire Réel Optimal?', *Annales d'Economie et de Statistiques*, no. 13.

Atkinson, A. B. (1996), 'Income Distribution in Europe and the United States', *Oxford Review of Economic Policy*, **12**(1), 15–28.

— Rainwater, L., and Smeeding, T. M. (1995), *Income Distribution in OECD Countries: Evidence from the Luxembourg Income Study*, Paris, Organization for Economic Cooperation and Development.

Attali, J. (1993), *Verbatim*, Paris, Fayard.

Ayala, M., Martínez, R., and Ruiz-Huerta (1995), 'La Distribución de la Renta en España desde una Perspectiva Internacional: Tendencias y Factores de Cambio', *II Simposio sobre Igualdad y Distribución de la Renta y la Riqueza*.

Bade, R., and Parkin, M. (1982), 'Central Bank Laws and Inflation—A Comparative Analysis', mimeo, University of Western Ontario.

Balls, E. (1998), 'Open Economy Macroeconomics in an Open Economy', *Scottish Journal of Political Economy*, **45**(2), 113–32.

Bandrés, E. (1995), 'Política Social y Redistribución de la Renta en España', various authors, *El Estado del Bienestar*, Barcelona, Comisión Obrera Nacional de Catalunya.

Bank of Greece (1999), *Etisia Ekthesi gia to etos 1998* (*Annual Report for 1998*), Athens, Bank of Greece.

Bank Swiatowy (1994), 'Analiza i ocena ubóstwa w Polsce' (Analysis and Evaluation of Poverty in Poland), Warsaw, mimeo.

Barro, R. J. (1990), 'Government Spending in a Simple Model of Endogenous Growth', *Journal of Political Economy*, **98**, S103–26.

Baumol, W. J. (1967), 'The Macroeconomics of Unbalanced Growth', *American Economic Review*, **57**.

— Bowen, W. G. (1966), *Performing Arts: The Economic Dilemma*, New York, The Twentieth Century Fund.

Bel, G. (1999), 'Privatización en España, OPVS y Premio Bursátil: ¿Aprendimos algo de la Experiencia Británica?', *Hacienda Pública Española*, 144, I/ 1998.

Beggs, J., and Chapman, B. (1987), 'An Empirical Analysis of Australian Strike Activity', *Economic Record*, **63**, 46–60.

Benabou, R. (1996), 'Inequality and Growth', *NBER Macroeconomics Annual*, Cambridge, MA, MIT Press.

Bentolila, S, and Blanchard, O. (1990), 'Spanish Unemployment', *Economic Policy*, **10**, 234–81.

— Dolado, J. (1994), 'Labour Flexibility and Wages: Lessons from Spain', *Economic Policy*, **18**, 55–99.

Bergounioux, A., and Grunberg, G. (1992), *Le Long Remors du Pouvoir*, Paris, Fayard.

Berliner, J. (1993), 'The Gains from Privatization', in US Congress, Joint Economic Committee, *The Economies of the Former Soviet Union*, Washington, DC.

Beskid, L. (1998), 'Ubóstwo w Polsce' (Poverty in Poland), in Rada Strategii Społeczno-Gospodarczej, *Podział dochodu i nierównoœci dochodowe. Fakty, tendencje, porównania, Raport 29*, Warsaw.

Bhadhuri, A. (1993), 'The Economics and Politics of Social Democracy', in P. Bardhan, M. Datta-Chaudhuri, and T. Krishnan (eds), *Development and Change: Essays in Honour of K. N. Raj*, Bombay, Oxford University Press.

Białecki, I., and Mach, B. W. (1992), 'Orientacje społeczno-ekonomiczne posłów na tle poglądów społeczeństwa' (Socio-political attitudes of Members of Parliament as Compared with the Attitude of Society), in J. Wasilewski and W. Wesołowski (eds), *Początki parlamentarnej elity. Posłowie kontraktowego Sejmu*, Warsaw.

Biffl, G., Guger, A., Pollan, W. (1987), 'The Causes of Low Unemployment in Austria', *Occasional Papers in Employment Studies*, **7**, University of Buckingham.

Bilbao, A. (1991), 'Trabajadores, Gestión Económica y Crisis Sindical', in F. Miguélez and C. Prieto (eds), *Las Relaciones Laborales en España*, Madrid, Siglo XXI.

Björklund, A., and Freeman, R. (1997), 'Generating Equality and Eliminating Poverty: The Swedish Way', in R. B. Freeman, R. Topel, and B. Swedenborg (eds), *The Welfare State in Transition*, NBER, Chicago, IL, and London, The University of Chicago Press.

Blaas, W., and Guger, A. (1985), 'Arbeitsbeziehungen und Makro-ökonomische Stabilität im Internationalen Vergleich', in P. Gerlich *et al.* (eds), *Sozialpartner-schaft in der Krise*, Vienna, Böhlau, 255–77.

Blair, A., and Schröder, G. (1999), *Europe: The Third Way/Die Neue Mitte*, June, www.labour.org.uk/lp/new/labour/docs/pmspeeches/thirdwaypurplebox.htm

Blanchard, O.-J., and Muet, P.-A. (1993), 'Competitiveness through Disinflation: An Assessment of the French Macroeconomic Strategy', *Economic Policy*, **16**.

— Wolfers, J. (2000), 'The Role of Shocks and Institutions in the Rise in European Unemployment: The Aggregate Evidence', *The Economic Journal*, **110**, C1–C33.

Block, F. (1990), *Postindustrial Possibilities: A Critique of Economic Discourse*, Berkeley and Los Angeles, University of California Press.

Blundell, R., and Reed, H. (1999), 'The Employment Effects of the Working Families Tax Credit', *IFS Briefing Notes* 6/99.

Bochniarz, H., and Wiœniewski, A. (1999), 'Godzina prawdy' (An Hour of the Truth), *Rzeczpospolita*, 5 February.

Boix, C. (1998), 'Partisan Governments and Macroeconomic Policies in OECD Countries', Working Paper 122, Madrid, Instituto Juan March de Estudios e Investigaciones.

Bollard, A., and Buckle, R. (1987), 'Preface', in A. Bollard and R. Buckle (eds), *Economic Liberalisation in New Zealand*, Wellington, Port Nicholson Press, Allen & Unwin.

Boltho, A. (1989), 'Did Policy Activism Work?', *European Economic Review*, **33**, 1709–26.

Bonoli, G., and Palier, B. (1998), 'Restructuring Welfare States: Patterns of Reform in the UK and in France', paper presented at the World Congress of Sociology, Montreal, 26 July–1 August.

Bordes, C., Girardin, E., and Marimoutou, V. (1995), 'Les Effets des Variations de Taux d'Intérêt dans le Nouvel Environnement Financier Français', *Revue Economique*, **46**(3).

Borkowska, S. (1998), 'Zróżnicowanie wynagrodzeń w Polsce w okresie transformacji', in Rada Strategii Społeczno-Gospodarczej, *Podział dochodu i nierównoœci dochodowe. Fakty, tendencje, porównania, Raport 29*, Warsaw.

Bowles, S. (1998), 'Endogenous Preferences: The Cultural Consequences of Markets and Other Economic Institutions', *Journal of Economic Literature*, **36**(1), 75–111.

— Gintis, H. (1993), 'The Revenge of *Homo Economicus*: Post-Walrasian Economics and the Revival of Political Economy', *Journal of Economic Perspectives*, **7**(1), 83–102.

Boyer, R. (ed.), (1988), *The Search for Labour Market Flexibility*, Oxford, Clarendon Press.

— Dore, R., and Mars, Z. (1994), *The Return to Incomes Policy*, London, Pinter.

Bradley, S., and Taylor, J. (1996), 'Human Capital Formation and Local Economic Performance', *Regional Studies*, **30**(1), 1–14.

Brandt, W., Kreisky, B., and Palme, O. (1976), *La Social-Démocratie el l'avenir*, Paris, Gallimard.

Branson, W. (1986), 'Stabilisation, Stagflation and Investment Incentives: The Case of Kenya 1979–80', in S. Edwards and S. Ahamed (eds), *Economic Adjustment and Exchange Rates in Developing Countries*, Chicago, IL, Chicago University Press.

Bresser Pereira, L. C. (1998), *Reforma do Estado para a Cidadania*, Brasilia, ENAP.

Brissimis, S., and Gibson, H. D. (1997), 'Monetary Policy, Capital Flows and Greek Disinflation', *Economic Bulletin*, Bank of Greece, **9**(March).

Brown, W. (1994), 'Incomes Policy in Britain: Lessons from Experience', in R. Dore, R. Boyer, and Z. Mars (eds), *The Return to Incomes Policy*, London, Pinter.

Bruno, M. (1992), 'Stabilization and Reform in Eastern Europe: A Preliminary Evaluation', IMF working paper 92/30, Washington, DC.

Buesa, M., and Molero, J. (1988), *Estructura Industrial de España*, Madrid, Fondo de Cultura Económica.

Bukowski, J. (1995), 'Rola Ministerstwa Przekształceń Własnoœciowych w rozwoju udziału pracowników w prywatyzacji', in L. Gilejko (ed.), *Partycypacja i akcjonariat pracowniczy w Polsce*, Warsaw.

Butschek, F. (1984), *Vollbeschäftigung in der Krise*, Vienna, Orac Verlag.

Cachon, L., and Palacio, J. I. (1999), 'Política de Empleo en España desde el Ingreso en la UE', in F. Miguélez and C. Prieto (eds), *Las Relaciones de Empleo en España*, Madrid, Siglo XXI.

Caciagli, M. (1986), *Elecciones y Partidos en la Transición Española*, Madrid, Centro de Investigaciones Sociológicas.

Calmfors, L. (1993), 'Lessons from the Macroeconomic Experience of Sweden', *European Journal of Political Economy*, **9**, 25–72.

— (1994), 'Active Labour Market Policy and Unemployment — A Framework for the Analysis of Crucial Design Features', *OECD Economic Studies*, **22**, Spring.

— Driffill, J. (1988), 'Bargaining Structure, Corporatism and Macroeconomic Performance', *Economic Policy*, **6**, 13–61.

— Forslund, A. (1990), 'Wage Formation in Sweden', in L. Calmfors (ed.), *Wage Formation and Macroeconomic Policy in the Nordic Countries*, SNS and Oxford University Press.

Calonge, S., and Manresa, A. (1997), 'Consecuencias Redistributivas del Estado del Bienestar en España', *Moneda y Crédito*, **204**.

Calviño, N., and Lorente, J. R. (1996), 'Los Costes del Despido en España', *Economistas*, **69**.

Cameron, D. (1984), 'Social Democracy, Corporatism, Labor Quiescence, and the Representation of Economic Interest in Advanced Capitalist Society', in J. H. Goldthorpe (ed.), *Order and Conflict in Contemporary Capitalism*, New York, Oxford University Press.

Cano, E. (1997), 'Canvi Socioeconòmic i Precarització Laboral en el Sistema Capitalista', PhD thesis, Universitat de Valencia.

Carlin, W., and Soskice, D. (1990), *Macroeconomics and the Wage Bargain*, Oxford, Oxford University Press.

Carroll, E. (1999), *Emergence and Structuring of Social Insurance Institutions: Comparative Studies on Social Policy and Unemployment Insurance*, Stockholm, Swedish Institute for Social Research.

Castañer, X. (1998), 'La Política Industrial, Ajustes, Nuevas Políticas Horizontales y Privatización 1975–1996', in R. Gomà and J. Subirats (eds), *Políticas Públicas en España. Contenidos, Redes de Actores y Niveles de Gobierno*, Barcelona, Ariel.

Castles, F. G. (1985), *The Working Class and Welfare*, Sydney, Allen & Unwin.

— Mitchell, D. (1993), 'Three Worlds of Welfare Capitalism or Four?', in F. G. Castles (ed.), *Families of Nations: Public Policy in Western Democracies*, Brookfield, VT, Dartmouth.

— — (1994), 'An Institutional View of the Australian Welfare State', in Economic Planning Advisory Commission (ed.), *National Strategies Conference, Volume 2*, Canberra, AGPS.

— Shirley, I. (1996), 'Labour and Social Policy: Gravediggers or Refurbishers of the Welfare State', in F. Castles, R. Gerritsen, and J. Vowles (ed.), *The Great Experiment: Labour Parties and Public Policy Transformation in Australia and New Zealand*, Sydney, Allen & Unwin.

— Stewart, J. (1993), 'Towards Industrially Sustainable Development? Industry Policy under the Labor Government', in I. Marsh (ed.), *Governing in the 1990s: An Agenda for a Decade*, Melbourne, Longman Cheshire.

— Gerritsen, R., and Vowles, J. (eds) (1996), *The Great Experiment: Labour Parties and Public Policy Transformation in Australia and New Zealand*, Sydney, Allen & Unwin.

Catalán, J. (1991), 'Del "Milagro" a la Crisis: La Herencia Econòmica del Franquismo', in M. Etxezarreta (ed.), *La Reestructuración del Capitalismo en España 1970–1990*, Barcelona, FUHEM/Icaria.

— (1999), 'Spain, 1936–96', in M. Schulze (ed.), *Western Europe. Economic and Social Change since 1945*, Longman.

Catephores, G. (1983), 'Greece: The Empiricist Socialism of PASOK', *Socialist Economic Review*.

CC.OO (1992), 'Los Despidos en España: Legislación, Evolución y Coste', Madrid, Documentos del Gabinete Técnico Confederal.

Cebrián, I. *et al.* (1992), 'El Paro de Larga Duración en España', in INEM, *El problema del paro de larga duración en España*, Madrid.

— (1996), 'The Influence of Unemployment Benefits on Unemployment Duration: Evidence from Spain', *Labour*, **10**(2), 239–67.

CEC (1992), *Report of the Committee of Independent Experts on Company Tax*, Commission of the European Communities.

Central Statistical Office (1998), *Statistical Yearbook of the Republic of Poland*, Warsaw.

CGP (1989), *La France, l'Europe. Xème Plan, 1989–1992*, Paris, La Documentation Française.

Chapman, B. (1997), 'The Accord: Background, Changes and Aggregate Outcomes', paper presented at CEPR Conference, 4–5 December.

Cheibub, J. A., and Przeworski, A. (1997), 'Government Spending and Economic Growth Under Democracy and Dictatorship', in A. Breton, P. Salmon, and R. Wintrobe (eds), *Understanding Democracy: Economic and Political Perspectives*, Cambridge, Cambridge University Press.

Chennels, L., Dilnot, A., and Emmerson, C. (2000), *The IFS Green Budget January 2000*, London, Institute for Fiscal Studies.

Cohen, G. A. (1997), 'Equality, Equality of Opportunity and the Labour Party', Oxford, mimeo.

Collado *et al.* (1996), *El Empleo en España y Europa. Un Análisis Comparado por Sectores*, Madrid, Argentaria/Visor.

Confais, E., and Muet, P.-A. (1994), 'Les Rigidités du Marché du Travail', in P.-A. Muet (ed.), *Le Chômage Persistant en Europe*, Références/OFCE, Paris, Presses de la Fondation Nationale des Sciences Politiques.

Crean, S. (1995), *Working Nation: The First Year 1994–95*, Canberra, Department of Employment, Education and Training.

Crepaz, M. M. L. (1994), 'From Semisovereignty to Sovereignty: The Decline of Corporatism and Rise of Parliament in Austria', *Comparative Politics*, **27**(1), 45–65.

Crosland, A. (1956), *The Future of Socialism*, London, Jonathan Cape.

Cukierman, A. (1992), *Central Bank Strategy, Credibility, and Independence*, Cambridge, MA, MIT Press.

Dachs, H. (1996), 'Von der "Sanierungspartnerschaft" zur konfliktgeladenen Unübersichtlichkeit. Über politische Entwicklungen und Verschiebungen während der Grossen Koalition 1986 bis 1994', in R. Sieder, H. Steinert, and E. Talos (eds), *Österreich 1945–1995: Gesellschaft, Politik, Kultur*, Vienna, Verlag für Gesellschaftskritik.

Dahl, R. (1985), *A Preface to Economic Democracy*, New Haven.

De Geer, H. (1992), *The Rise and Fall of the Swedish Model*, Stockholm, Carden Publications and the FA Institute.

Deniszczuk, L. (1995), 'Obszary ubóstwa w Polsce', in UNDP, *Polska '95. Raport o rozwoju społecznym w Polsce*, Warsaw.

Departamento de Estadística y Coyuntura de la Fundación FIES (1966), 'Anexo estadístico. Años 1975 a 1995', *Papeles de Economía Española*, **68**.

Department of Employment, Education, Training and Youth Affairs (1996), *Working Nation: Evaluation of the Employment and Education and Training Elements*, Canberra, Evaluation and Monitoring Branch, Economic and Policy Analysis Division, DEETYA.

De Velasco, L. (1996), *Políticas del PSOE, 1982–1995*, Barcelona, Icaria.

DfEE (1998), *The Learning Age: A Renaissance for a New Britain*, February, Department for Education and Employment.

Diamandouros, N. (1994), 'Cultural Dualism and Political Change in Postauthoritarian Greece', Working Paper 1994–50, Centro de Estudios Avanzados en Ciencias Sociales, Instituto Juan March de Estudios e Investigaciones.

Dickens, R. (1999), 'Poverty, Low Pay and the National Minimum Wage', LSE Centre for Economic Performance, May.

Dølvik, J. E., and Stokland, D. (1992), 'Norway: "The Norwegian Model" in Transition', in A. Ferner and R. Hyman (eds), *Industrial Relations in the New Europe*, Oxford, Basil Blackwell.

Domański, H. (1996), *Na progu konvergencji. Stratyfikacja społeczna w krajach Europy Œrodkowo-Wschodniej*, Warsaw.

— (1997), 'Mobilnoœæ i hierarchie stratyfikacyjne' (Mobility and hierarchical stratification), in H. Domański and Rychard (eds), *Elementy nowego ładu*, Warsaw.

Douglas, R. (1980), *There's Got to be a Better Way!*, Wellington, Fourth Estate.

Dowrick, S. (1996), 'Swedish Economic Performance and Swedish Economic Decline: A View from Outside', *The Economic Journal*, **106**(439), 1772–800.

— Nguyen, D. T. (1989), 'OECD Comparative Economic Growth 1950–85: Catch-up and Convergence', *American Economic Review*, **79**(5), 1010–30.

DTI (1998), *Our Competitive Future: Building the Knowledge Driven Economy*, Department of Trade and Industry, CM 4176, London, HMSO.

Due, J., and Madsen, J. S. (1988), *Nur der Slås Søm i: Overenskomstforhandlinger og Organisationsstruktur*, Copenhagen, DJØF.

— — Jensen, C. S., and Petersen, L. K. (1994), *The Survival of the Danish Model. A Historical Sociological Analysis of the Danish System of Collective Bargaining*, Copenhagen, DJØF.

Duncan, T., and Fogarty, J. (1985), *Australia and Argentina: On Parallel Paths*, Melbourne, Melbourne University Press.

Durbin, E. (1985), *New Jerusalems: The Labour Party and the Economics of Social Democracy*, London, RKP.

Easton, B. (1996a), *In Stormy Seas: New Zealand's Economic Performance*, Dunedin, Otago University Press.

— (1996b), 'Income Distribution', in B. Silverstone, A. Bullard, and R. Lattimore (eds), *A Study in Economic Reform: The Case of New Zealand*, Amsterdam, Elsevier.

— (1997), *The Commercialisation of New Zealand*, Auckland, Auckland University Press.

— Gerritsen, R. (1996), 'Economic Reform: Parallels and Divergences', in F. Castles, R. Gerritsen, and J. Vowles (eds), *The Great Experiment: Labour Parties and Public Policy Transformation in Australia and New Zealand*, Sydney, Allen & Unwin.

Edgren, G., Faxén, K.-O., and Odhner, C.-E. (1970), *Lönebildning och Samhällsekonomi*, Stockholm, Rabén and Sjögren.

Edin, P.-A., and Topel, R. (1997), 'Wage Policy and Restructuring: The Swedish Labor Market since 1960', in R. B. Freeman, R. Topel, and B. Swedenborg (eds), *The Welfare State in Transition*, NBER, Chicago, IL, and London, The University of Chicago Press.

Edwards, T., and Whitty, G. (1994), 'Education: Opportunity, Equality and Efficiency', in A. Glyn and D. Miliband (eds), *The Costs of Inequality*, London, Rivers Oram Press.

Egger, P., Hahn, F., Pfaffermayr, M., and Stankovsky, J. (1998), *Herausforderungen durch den Globalisierungswettlauf in der EU*, Vienna, Österreichisches Institut für Wirtschaftsforschung.

Elmeskov, J., Pichlmann, K. (1993), 'Interpreting Unemployment: The Role of Labour Force Participation', in *OECD Economic Studies*, **20**, Paris, Organization for Economic Cooperation and Development.

Elvander, N. (1988), *Den Svenske Modellen: Lönforhandlingar och inkomstpolitik 1982–1986*, Allmanna Forlaget.

Erdem, E., and Glyn, A. (2000), 'The UK Jobs Gap — Lack of Qualifications and the Regional Dimension', evidence to House of Commons, Education and Employment Committee, published in Employability and Jobs: Is there a Jobs Gap?, May 2000, Vol. II, 112–20.

Eriksson, T., Suvanto, A., and Vartia, P. (1990), 'Wage Setting in Finland', in L. Calmfors (ed.), *Wage Formation and Macroeconomic Policy in the Nordic Countries*, SNS and Oxford University Press.

Erixon, L. (1984), 'Den Svenska Modellen in Motgång. En analys av dess effekter och forandrade forutsatninger under Perioden 1974–1984', *Nordish Tidsskrift for Politisk Ekonomi*, **15/16**.

Espina, A. (1990), *Empleo, Democracia y Relaciones Industriales en España*, Madrid, Ministerio de Trabajo y Seguridad Social.

— (1999), 'El Guadiana de la Concertación Neocorporatista en España: de la Huelga General de 1988 a los Acuerdos de 1987', in F. Miguelez and C. Prieto (eds), *Las Relaciones de Empleo en España*, Madrid, Siglo XXI.

Esping-Andersen, G. (1985), *Politics against Markets: The Social Democratic Road to Power*, Princeton, NJ, Princeton University Press.

— (1990), *The Three Worlds of Welfare Capitalism*, Cambridge, Polity Press, and Princeton, NJ, Princeton University Press.

— (1997), 'Welfare States at the End of the Century', in OECD (ed.) *Family, Market and Community*, Paris, Organization for Economic Cooperation and Development.

— (1999), *Social Foundations of Postindustrial Economies*, Oxford, Oxford University Press.

Etxezarreta, M. (1991), 'La Economía Política del Proceso de Acumulación', in M. Etxezarreta (ed.), *La Reestructuración del Capitalismo en España 1970–1990*, Barcelona, FUHEM/Icaria.

Evans, L., Grimes, A., Wilkinson, B., and Teece, D. (1996), 'Economic Reform in New Zealand 1984–95: The Pursuit of Efficiency', *Journal of Economic Literature*, **34**(4), 1856–902.

Favier, P., and Martin-Roland, M. (1990), *La Décennie Mitterrand*, Paris, Seuil.

Faxén, K.-O., Odhner, C.-E., and Spånt, R. (1988), *Lönebildningen i 90-talets Samhällsekonomi*, Stockholm, Rabén and Sjögren.

Featherstone, K. (1986), 'Socialist Parties and European Integration: Variations on a Common Theme', in W. E. Paterson and A. H. Thomas (eds), *The Future of Social Democracy*, Oxford, Oxford University Press.

— (1987), 'PASOK and the Left', in K. Featherstone and D. K. Katsoudas (eds), *Political Change in Greece*, London, Croom Helm.

Feldt, K.-O. (1991), *Alla Dessa Dagar: i Regeringen 1982–1990*, Stockholm, Norstedts.

Flanagan, R. F., Soskice, D. W., and Ulman, L. (1983), *Unionism, Economic Stabilization, and Incomes Policies: European Experience*, Studies in Wage-Price Policy, Washington, DC, The Brookings Institution.

Flood, R., and Kramer, C. (1996), 'Economic Models of Speculative Attacks and the Drachma Crisis of May 1994', *Open Economies Review*, 7, 591–600.

Forslund, A., and Krueger, A. B. (1997), 'An Evaluation of the Swedish Active Labor Market Policy: New and Received Wisdom', in R. B. Freeman, R. Topel, and B. Swedenborg (eds), *The Welfare State in Transition*, NBER, Chicago, IL, and London, The University of Chicago Press.

Forsyth, P. (1992), *Microeconomic Reform in Australia*, St Leonards, NSW, Allen & Unwin.

Freeman, R. B., Topel, R., and Swedenborg, B. (eds) (1997), *The Welfare State in Transition*, NBER, Chicago, IL, and London, The University of Chicago Press.

Frisch, H. (1976), 'Eine Verallgemeinerung des skandinavischen Modells der Inflation: Mit einer empirischen Analyse für Österreich', *Empirica*, 3, 197–218.

Fukuyama, F. (1995), *Trust: Social Virtues and the Creation of Prosperity*, New York, Free Press.

García, J. *et al.* (1997), 'Diferencias Salariales entre Sector Público y Privado en España', *Papeles de Economía Española*, 72, 261–73.

García Serrano, C., Garrido, L., and Toharia, L. (1999), 'Empleo y Paro en España: Algunas Cuestiones Candentes', in F. Miguelez and C. Prieto (eds), *Las Relaciones de Empleo en España*, Madrid, Siglo XXI.

Gardawski, J. (1995), 'Kierunki zmian struktury własnooeci i władzy w spółkach pracowniczych', in M. Jarosz, *Blaski i cienie spółek pracowniczych 1991–1994*, Warsaw.

— (1996), *Poland's Industrial Workers on the Return to Democracy and Market Economy*, Warsaw, F. Ebert Stiftung.

— (1999a), 'Forms and Structure of Ownership', in M. Jarosz (ed.), *Direct Privatization. Investors. Managers. Employees*, Warsaw.

— (1999b), 'Bezpieczne związki', *Gazeta Wyborcza*, 27 August.

Garde, J. A. (1995), 'Reflexiones Sobre el Fraude Fiscal', *Papeles de Economía Española*, 62, 334–40.

Gellner, E. (1975), in E. Gellner and J. Waterbury (eds), *Patrons and Clients in Mediterranean Societies*, London, Duckworth.

Geremek, B. (1990), *Rok 1989. Geremek Bronisław odpowiada, Żakowski pyta* (The year 1989. Geremek tells, Żakowski asks), Warsaw.

Gerlich, P., Grande, E., and Müller, W. (eds), (1985), *Sozialpartnerschaft in der Krise. Leistungen und Grenzen des Neokorporatismus in Österreich*, Vienna, Böhlau.

Gibson, H. D., and Tsakalotos, E. (1993), 'Testing a Flow Model of Capital Flight in Five European Countries', *The Manchester School*, **61**(2), 144–66.

— — (1995), 'The Scope and Limits of Financial Liberalisation in Developing Countries', *Journal of Development Studies*, **30**(3), 578–628.

Giddens, A. (1998), *The Third Way. The Renewal of Social Democracy*, Cambridge, Polity Press.

Główny Urząd Statystyczny (1997a), *Mały Rocznik Statystyczny 1997*, Warsaw.

— (1997b), *Prywatyzacja przedsiębiorstw panstwowych według stanu na 31.12.1996*, Warsaw.

Glyn, A. (1992), 'Corporatism, Patterns of Employment and Access to Consumption', in J. Pekkarinen, M. Pohjola, and R. Rowthorn (eds), *Social Corporatism*, Oxford, Oxford University Press.

— (1995a), 'Social Democracy and Full Employment', *New Left Review*, **211**, 33–55.

— (1995b), 'The Assessment: Unemployment and Inequality', *Oxford Review of Economic Policy*, **11**(1), 1–25.

— (1997a), 'Does Aggregate Profitability Really Matter?', *Cambridge Journal of Economics*, **21**, 593–619.

— (1997b), 'Low Pay and Employment Performance', Corpus Christi College, Oxford, mimeo.

— (1998a), 'The Assessment: Economic Policy and Social Democracy', *Oxford Review of Economic Policy*, **14**(1), 1–18.

— (1998b), 'Internal and External Constraints on Egalitarian Policies', in D. Baker, G. Epstein, and R. Pollin (eds), *Globalisation and Progressive Economic Policy*, Cambridge, Cambridge University Press.

— Salverda, W. (2000), 'Employment Inequalities', in M. Gregory, W. Salverda, and S. Bazen (eds), *Labour Market Inequalities: Problems and Policies of Low-Wage Employment in International Perspective*, Oxford, Oxford University Press.

Goldberg, E. (1996), 'Thinking About How Democracy Works', *Politics and Society*, **24**(1), 7–18.

Goldthorpe, J. H. (1984), 'The End of Convergence: Corporatist and Dualist Tendencies in Modern Western Societies', in J. H. Goldthorpe (ed.), *Order and Conflict in Contemporary Capitalism*, Oxford, Clarendon Press.

— (1987), 'Problems of Political Economy after the Post-war Period', in C. S. Mares (ed.), *Changing Boundaries of the Political: Essays on the Evolving Balance between the State and Society, Public and Private in Europe*, Cambridge, Cambridge University Press.

Golinowska, S. (ed.) (1996a), *Social Policy towards Poverty, Comparative Approach*, Warsaw, IPiSS.

— (ed.) (1996b), *Polska bieda, Kryteria, ocena, przeciwdziałanie* (Polish poverty. Cryteria, evaluation, acting against), Warsaw, IPiSS.

— (1999), 'Nędza, ubóstwo, niedostatek', *Rzeczpospolita*, 9 September.

González Calvet, J. (1991), 'Transformaciones del Sector Publico e Intervención Económica', in M. Etxezarreta (ed.), *La Reestructuración del Capitalismo en España 1970–1990*, Barcelona, FUHEM/Icaria.

— (1998), 'Política Fiscal', in J. Subirats and R. Gomà, *Políticas Públicas en España Contenidos, Redes de Actores y Niveles de Gobierno*, Barcelona, Ariel.

González Páramo, M. (1988), 'Inflación e Impuesto Sobre la Renta en España, 1979–1988', *Actualidad Financiera*, **44**, 28 nov-4 dic.

Gordon, R. J. (1987), 'Productivity, Wages and Prices Inside and Outside of Manufacturing in the US, Japan, and Europe', *European Economic Review*, **31**, 685–739.

Gornick, J., Meyers, M. K., and Ross, K. E. (1998), 'Public Policies and the Employment of Mothers: A Cross-National Study', *Social Science Quarterly*, **79**(1), 35–54.

Gottschalk, P., and Smeeding, T. M. (1997), 'Cross-National Comparisons of Earnings and Income Inequality', *Journal of Economic Literature*, **35**(2), 633–87.

Granovetter, M. (1985), 'Economic Actions and Social Structures: The Problem of Imbeddedness', *American Journal of Sociology*, **91**, 481–510.

Greek Government Programme (1981), General Secretarial for Press and Information, Athens.

Gregg, P., Johnson, P., and Reed, H. (1999), *Entering Work and the British Tax and Benefit System*, London, Institute for Fiscal Studies.

Grilli, V., Masciandoro, D., and Tabellini, G. (1991), 'Political and Monetary Institutions and Public Financial Policies in the Industrialized Countries', *Economic Policy*, **13**(October), 341–92.

Gros, D., and Thygesen, N. (1992), *European Monetary Integration: From the European System to European Monetary Union*, London, Longman.

— Vandille, G. (1995), 'Seigniorage and EMU: The Fiscal Implications of Price Stability and Financial Market Integration', *Journal of Common Market Studies*, **33**(2), 175–96.

Gruen, F. (1986), 'How Bad is Australia's Economic Performance and Why?', *Economic Record*, **62**(177), 180–93.

— Grattan, M. (1993), *Managing Government: Labor's Achievements and Failures*, Melbourne, Longman Cheshire.

Guger, A. (1990), 'Verteilungspolitik als Strukturpolitik', in Beigewum and Memorandum-Gruppe (eds), *Steuerungsprobleme der Wirtschaftspolitik*, Vienna, Bremen, 94–104.

— (1992), 'Corporatism: Success or Failure? Austrian Experiences', in J. Pekkarinen, M. Pohjola, and R. Rowthorn (eds), *Social Corporatism – A Superior Economic System?*, Oxford, Clarendon Press, S 338–62.

Guger, A. (1995), 'Verschlechterung der Wettbewerbsfähigkeit trotz sinkender Lohnstückkosten', *WIFO-Monatsberichte*, **8**, Vienna, Österreichisches Institut für Wirtschaftsforschung, 533–8.

—   (1996), 'Redistribution by the State in Austria', *Austrian Economic Quarterly*, **2**, 185–96.

—   Polt, W. (1994), 'Corporatism and Incomes Policy in Austria: Experiences and Perspectives', in R. Dore, R. Boyer, Z. Mars (eds.) (1994), *The Return to Incomes Policy*, London, Pinter.

—   Walterskirchen, E. (1988), 'Fiscal and Monetary Policy in the Keynes-Kalecki Tradition', in J. A. Kregel, E, Matzner, and A. Roncaglia (eds) *Barriers to Full Employment*, London, Macmillan, 103–32.

Gunnarsson, G., and Lindh, T. (1997), 'Swedish Employment in the 1950s — Filling the Lacuna', University of Uppsala, Department of Economics, Working Paper No. 13.

Gunther, R., Diamandouros, P. N., and Puhle, H.-J. (1995), *The Politics of Democratic Consolidation: Southern Europe in Comparative Perspective*, Baltimore, Johns Hopkins University Press.

Gustafsson, B. (1995), 'Foundations of the Swedish Model', *Nordic Journal of Political Economy*, **22**, 1–26.

Gutiérrez, E. (1994), 'Reflexiones Sobre el Sistema de Protección del Desempleo', *Cuadernos de Relaciones Laborales*, **5**, 57–74.

Gylfason, T. (1990), 'Exchange Rate Policy, Inflation, and Unemployment: The Nordic EFTA Countries', in V. Argy and P. De Grauwe (eds), *Choosing an Exchange Rate Regime: The Challenge for Smaller Industrial Countries*, Washington, DC, IMF.

Hahn, F., (1994), *Kapitalproduktivitäten nach Wirtschaftssektoren im Internationalen Vergleich*, Vienna, Österreichisches Instituts für Wirtschaftsforschung.

—   Walterskirchen, E. (1992), '"Stylised Facts" der Konjunkturschwankungen in Österreich, Deutschland und des USA', *WIFO-Working Paper*, 59, Vienna, Austrian Institute of Economic Research.

Hall, A. (1993), 'Sojusz antylewicowy', *Gazeta Wyborcza*, 26 August.

Hall, P. (1988), 'L'Evolution de la Politique Economique sous Mitterrand', in S. Hoffmann and G. Ross (eds), *L'Expérience Mitterrand, Continuité et Changement dans la France Contemporaine*, Paris, PUF.

—   (1994), 'Central Bank Independence and Coordinated Wage Bargaining: Their Interaction in Germany and Europe', *German Politics and Society*, Autumn, 1–23.

—   (1997), 'Social Capital: A Fragile Asset', *Demos Collection*, Issue 12, 35–7.

—   (1998), 'Organized Market Economies and Unemployment in Europe: Is it Finally Time to Accept the Liberal Orthodoxy?', paper delivered at the Eleventh International Conference of Europeanists. Baltimore, MD, 26–28 February.

—   Franzese, R. (1998), 'Mixed Signals: Central Bank Independence, Coordinated Wage-Bargaining, and European Monetary Union,' *International Organization*, **52**(summer).

— — (2000), 'Mixed Signals: Central Bank Independence, Coordinated Wage-Bargaining, and European Monetary Union', in T. Iversen, J. Pontusson, and D. Soskice (eds), *Unions, Employers and Central Banks: Wage Bargaining and Macroeconomic Regimes in an Integrating Europe*, Cambridge, Cambridge University Press.

Hamilton, C., and Quiggin, J. (1995), 'The Privatisation of CSL', *Economic Analysis and Policy*.

Hansen, B. (1955), *Finanspolitikens Ekonomiska Teori*, SOU (Government Committee Papers) 1995:25, Stockholm.

Hansen, S. A. (1983), *Økonomisk vækst i Danmark*, Copenhagen, Universitetsforlaget.

Harrod, R. (1958), *The Possibility of Economic Satiety, Use of Economic Growth for Improving the Quality of Education and Leisure*, w: *Problems of United States Economic Development*, New York.

Hassler, J., Lundvik, P., Persson, T., and Söderlind, P. (1994), 'The Swedish Business Cycle: Stylized Facts over 130 Years', in V. Bergström and A. Vredin (eds), *Measuring and Interpreting Business Cycles*, Oxford, Clarendon Press.

Hawke, R. J. (1994), *The Hawke Memoirs*, Port Melbourne, William Heinemann Australia.

Hay, C. (1997), 'Anticipating Accommodations, Accommodating Anticipations: The Appeasement of Capital in the "Modernization" of the British Labour Party, 1987–1992', *Politics and Society*, **25**(2), 234–56.

Hayek, F. A. (1944), *The Road to Serfdom*, Chicago.

Heckman, J. J. (1979), 'Sample Selection Bias as a Specification Error', *Econometrica*, **47**, 153–61.

— (1988), 'The Microeconomic Evaluation of Social Programs and Economic Institutions', in *Chung-Hua Series of Lectures by Invited Eminent Economists*, No. 14, Taipei, The Institute of Economics, Academia Sinica.

Hemerijck, A. C., and van Kersbergen, K. (1997), 'A Miraculous Model? Explaining the New Politics of the Welfare State in the Netherlands', unpublished manuscript.

Henderson, G. (1983), 'Fraserism: Myths and Realities', *Quadrant*, June, 33–7.

Henrekson, M. (1996), 'Sweden's Relative Economic Performance: Lagging behind or Staying on Top?', *The Economic Journal*, **106**(439), 1747–59.

Hernes, H. M. (1987), *Welfare State and Woman Power: Essays in State Feminism*, Norwegian University Press.

Hibbs, D. A., and Locking, H. (1991), 'Löneutjamning och Löneokningstakt under den Solidariske Lönepolitiken', *Ekonomisk Debatt*, **19**(8), 653–64.

— — (1995), 'Wage Dispersion and Productive Efficiency: Evidence for Sweden', Trade Union Institute for Economic Research, Working Paper No. 128, Stockholm.

— — (1996), 'Wage Compression, Wage Drift and Wage Inflation in Sweden', *Labour Economics*, **3**, 109–41.

Hibbs, D. A., and Locking, H. (1997), 'Den Solidariska Lönepolitiken och Produktiviteten inom Industrin', in V. Bergström (ed.), *Arbetsmarknad och Tillväxt*, Ekerlids Förlag/FIEF.

Hicks, A., and Swank, D. (1992), 'Politics, Institutions, and Welfare Spending in Industrialized Democracies, 1960–82', *American Political Science Review*, **86**(3), 1–17.

Hilmer, F., Rayner, M., and Taperell, G. (1993), *National Competition Policy*, report by the Independent Committee of Inquiry.

Hine, D. (1986), 'Leaders and Followers: Democracy and Manageability in the Social Democratic Parties of Western Europe', in W. E. Paterson and A. H. Thomas (eds), *The Future of Social Democracy*, Oxford, Oxford University Press.

Hirsch, F. (1977), *The Limits of Growth*, London.

Hirst, P., and Thompson, G. (1996), *Globalization in Question*, Cambridge, Polity Press.

HM Treasury (1999), *Budget 99*.

Hodgson, G. (1988), *Economics and Institutions*, Cambridge, Polity Press.

Hofer, H., and Pichlmann, K. (1996), 'Lohnbildung, Arbeitskosten und Wettbewerbsfähigkeit in Österreich', *Projektberichte*, Vienna, Institut für Höhere Studien.

Holden, S. (1990), 'Wage Drift in Norway: A Bargaining Approach', in L. Calmfors (ed.), *Wage Formation and Macroeconomic Policy in the Nordic Countries*, SNS and Oxford University Press.

— (1991), 'Economic Policy in an Economy with Local and Central Wage Bargaining', memorandum from the Department of Economics, University of Oslo, 1991:8.

Holland, S. (1972), *The Socialist Challenge*, London, Quartet Books.

Hollingsworth, J. R., and Boyer, R. (eds) (1997), *Contemporary Capitalism: The Embeddedness of Institutions*, Cambridge, Cambridge University Press.

— Schmitter, P., and Streeck, W. (1993), *Governing Capitalist Economies: Performance and Control of Economic Sectors*, New York, Oxford University Press.

Holzmann, R., and Winckler, G. (1983), 'Austrian Economic Policy. Some Theoretical and Critical Remarks on "Austro-Keynesianism"', *Empirica*, **10**.

Howell, D. (2000), 'Increasing Earnings Inequality and Unemployment in Developed Countries: A Critical Assessment of the Unified View', mimeo, New School for Social Research, New York.

Huber, E., and Stephens, J. D. (1998), 'Internationalization and the Social Democratic Model', *Comparative Political Studies*, **31**(3), 353–97.

— — (1999), 'Welfare State and Production Regimes in the Era of Retrenchment', Princeton, NJ, Institute for Advanced Study, School of Social Science: Occasional Papers No. 1 (February). Forthcoming in P. Pierson (ed.), *The New Politics of the Welfare State*, Oxford University Press.

— — (2000), 'Partisan Governance, Women's Employment, and the Social Democratic Service State', *American Sociological Review*, **65**(3), 323–42.

— — (in press), *Development and Crisis of the Welfare State: Parties and Policies in Global Markets*, Chicago, IL, University of Chicago Press.

— Ragin, C., and Stephens, J. D. (1993), 'Social Democracy, Christian Democracy, Constitutional Structure and the Welfare State', *American Journal of Sociology*, **99**(3), 711–49.

— — — (1997), Comparative Welfare States Data Set, Northwestern Univeristy and University of North Carolina, http://www.lis.ceps.lu/compwsp.htm

Hutton, W. (1995), *The State We're In*, London, Jonathan Cape.

Ibsen, F., and Stamhus, J. (1993), *Fra Central til Decentral Lønfastsættelse*, Copenhagen, Jurist- og Økonomforbundets Forlag.

Immervoll, H., Mitton, L., O'Donoghue, C., and Sutherland, H. (1999), 'Budgeting for Fairness?', Microsimulation Unit MU/RN/32 Cambridge, March.

Industry Commission (1997), *Assessing Australia's Productivity Performance*, Canberra, AGPS.

INSEE (1994), *L'Economie Française, 1994*, Paris, Le Livre de Poche, Références.

— (1996), *L'Economie Française, 1996*, Paris, Le Livre de Poche, Références.

Iversen, T. (1996), 'Power, Flexibility and the Breakdown of Centralized Wage Bargaining: The Cases of Denmark and Sweden in Comparative Perspective', *Comparative Politics*, **28**(July), 399–436.

— (1998), 'Wage Bargaining, Central Bank Independence and the Real Effects of Money', *International Organization*, **52**(3).

— (1999), *Contested Economic Institutions. The Politics of Macroeconomics and Wage Bargaining in Advanced Democracies*, Cambridge, Cambridge University Press.

— Wren, A. (1998), 'Equality, Employment, and Budgetary Restraint: The Trilemma of the Service Economy', *World Politics*, **49**(July).

Jacobi, O., Keller, B., and Muller-Jentsch, W. (1998), 'Germany: Facing New Challenges', in A. Ferner and R. Hyman (eds), *Changing Industrial Relations in Europe*, Oxford, Blackwell Publishers.

Jacukowicz, Z. (1997), 'Płace w Polsce a zasady wynagradzania w krajach Unii Europejskiej', *Polityka Społeczna*, **11–12**.

Janicki, M., and Władyka, W. (1997), 'Przegrana klasa, Raport', *Polityka*, **5**.

Jensen, J., and Ross, G. (1994), 'France: Triumph and Tragedy', in P. Anderson and P. Camiller (eds), *Mapping the West European Left*, London, Verso.

Jimeno, J. F., and Toharia, L. (1993), 'The Productivity Effects of Fixed Term Employment: Are Temporary Workers Less Productive than Permanent Workers?', FEDEA, WP 9304.

Jobert, B., and Muller, P. (1987), *L'Etat en Action: Politique Publiques et Corporatismes*, Paris, PUF.

Jobert, B., and Théret, B. (1994), 'France: La Consécration Républicaine du Néolibéralisme', in B. Jobert (ed.), *Le Tournant Néolibéral en Europe*, Paris, L'Harmattan.

Jones, E. (1998), 'The Netherlands: Top of the Class', in J. Friden, D. Gross, and E. Jones (eds), *Joining Europe's Monetary Club: The Challenge for Smaller Member States*, New York, St Martin's Press, forthcoming.

Jonsson, B., Thörn, Y., Pettersson, K., Johnsson, G., and Bengtsberg, O. (1997), 'Lönebildning Måste Stramas Upp', *Dagens Nyheter*, Debatt, 2 January.

Junankar, P. N., and Kapuscinski, C. (1997), 'Was Working Nation Working? A Failed Experiment or a Premature Abortion', Public Policy Program, ANU.

Kaitala, V., and Pohjola, M. (1990), 'Economic Development and Agreeable Redistribution in Capitalism: Efficient Equilibria in a Two-Class Neoclassical Growth Model', *International Economic Review*, **31**(2).

Kalecki, M. (1990, [1943]), 'Political Aspects of Full Employment', *Political Quarterly*, **14**, 322–31, in J. Osiatynski (ed.), *Collected Works of Michal Kalecki*, Vol. 1, Oxford, Oxford University Press.

Kalyvas, S. (1994), 'Hegemony Breakdown: The Collapse of Nationalization in Britain and France', *Politics and Society*, **22**, 316–48.

Kangas, O. (1991), *The Politics of Social Rights*, Stockholm, Swedish Institute for Social Research.

Kasper, W., Blandy, R., Freebairn, J., Hocking, D., and O'Neill, R. (1980), *Australia at the Crossroads: Our Choices to the Year 2000*, Sydney, Harcourt Brace Jovanovich.

Katseli, L. T. (1985), 'Greek Experience under PASOK: Lessons for Development Policy', lecture delivered at the Royal Institute of International Affairs, 13 November.

— (1989), 'Economic Integration in the Enlarged European Community: Structural Adjustment of the Greek Economy', in C. Bliss and J. Braga de Macedo (eds), *Unity with Diversity in the European Economy*, Cambridge, Cambridge University Press.

Katzenstein, P. (1984), *Corporatism and Change: Austria, Switzerland, and the Politics of Industry*, Ithaca, Cornell University Press.

— (1985), *Small States in World Markets*, Ithaca, Cornell University Press.

Katznelson, I. (1995), *Liberalism's Crooked Circle. Letters to Adam Michnik*, Princeton.

Kelly, P. (1992), *The End of Certainty: The Story of the 1980s*, Sydney, Allen & Unwin.

Kelsey, J. (1995), *Economic Fundamentalism*, London, Pluto Press.

— (1997), *The New Zealand Experiment: A World Model for Structural Adjustment*, 2nd edn, Auckland, Auckland University Press.

Kienzl, H. (1973), 'Gewerkschaftliche Lohnpolitik und Stabilität', in W. Schmitz (ed.), *Geldwertstabilität und Wirtschaftswachstum*, Festschrift für Andreas Korp, Vienna, Springer.

Kilponen, J. (1999), 'Central Bank Independence and Wage Bargaining Structure — Empirical Evidence', Bank of Finland Discussion Papers (June).

King, A. (1998), 'Why Labour Won — At Last', in D. Denver *et al.*, *New Labour Triumphs: Britain at the Polls*, New Jersey, Chatham House.

King, D. (1999), *In the Name of Liberalism: Illiberal Social Policy in Britain and the United States*, Oxford, Oxford University Press.

—   Wickham-Jones, M. (1998), 'Training Without the State? New Labour and Labour Markets, *Policy and Politics*, **26**(4), 439–55.

Kjellberg, A. (1992), 'Sweden: Can the Model Survive?', in A. Ferner and R. Hyman (eds), *Industrial Relations in the New Europe*, Oxford, Basil Blackwell.

Kochanowicz, J. (1997), 'New Solidarities? Market Change and Social Cohesion in a Historical Perspective', in I. T. Berend (ed.) *Long-term Structural Changes in Transforming Central and Eastern Europe (the 1990s)*, Munich.

Kołodko, G. (1999), *Od szoku do terapii* (From the Shock to the Therapy), Warsaw, Poltex.

Komołowski, L. (1999), 'Comment', *Wprost*, 5 March.

Konopnicki, G. (1979), *Vive le centenaire du P.C.F.*, Paris, CERF.

Korona, D. A. (1999), 'Program powszechnej prywatyzacji a sprawiedliwooeæ dystrybutywna', mimeo.

Korpi, W. (1983), *The Democratic Class Struggle*, London, Routledge & Kegan Paul.

—   (1989), 'Power, Politics, and State Autonomy in the Development of Social Citizenship', *American Sociological Review*, **54**(3), 309–28.

—   (1996), 'Eurosclerosis and the Sclerosis of Objectivity: On the Role of Values Among Economic Policy Experts', *The Economic Journal*, **106**(439), 1727–46.

—   Palme, J. (1997), *The Paradox of Redistribution and Strategies of Equality: Welfare State Institutions, Inequality and Poverty in the Western Countries*, Stockholm, Institutet for Social Forsking.

Kosonen, K. (1992), 'Saving and Economic Growth from a Nordic Perspective', in J. Pekkarinen, M. Pohjola, and R. Rowthorn (eds), *Social Corporatism — A Superior Economic System?*, WIDER Studies in Development Economics, Oxford, Clarendon Press.

Kowalik, T. (1998), 'The Experience of Ownership Transformation of State Firms in Poland', in N. P. Ostojic and N. Scott (eds), *Experiences and Results of Privatization in the Economies of Transition*, Belgrade.

—   (1994), 'Privatization in Poland — Social Process or Another Shock?', in UNDP and Koping Datorg, *Privatization in the Transformation Process. Recent Experiences in Eastern Europe*, Geneva.

Krajewska, A. (1994), 'Opodatkowanie sektora publicznego i prywatnego w Polsce', *Gospodarka Narodowa*, **7–8**.

Krajewski, S., and Piasecki, B. (1999), 'SME Development as a Consequence of the Privatization and Restructuring of State Property in Transition Economies, *Emergo. Journal of Transforming Economies and Societies*, winter, Kraków.

Krawczyk, R. (1990), *Wielka przemiana, upadek i odrodzenie polskiej gospodarki*, Warsaw.

Kreisky, B. (1989), 'Introduction', in *Commission on Employment Issues in Europe, A Programme for Full Employment in Europe in the 1990s*, Oxford, Pergamon Press.

Krugman, P. (1990), *Rethinking International Trade*, Cambridge, MA, MIT Press.

Kunkel, C., and Pontusson, J. (1998), 'Corporatism versus Social Democracy: Divergent Fortunes of the Austrian and Swedish Labour Movements', *West European Politics*, **21**(2), 1–31.

Kurczewski, J. (1995), 'Taka młoda a taka brzydka', *Gazeta Wyborcza*, 15 January.

Kuron, J. (1997), 'Wykluczeni, wyróżnieni, niewidoczni', *Magazyn Gazety Wyborczej*, 22 August.

Lagares, M. (1996), 'Distribución de la Renta en España. Aspectos Fiscales: Datos Fiscales', in B. Pena Trapero (ed.), *Distribución de la Renta en España*, Madrid, Pirámide.

Łagodziński, W. (1999), 'Strach przed biedą', *Rzeczpospolita*, 27 August.

Lancaster, K. (1973), 'The Dynamic Inefficiency of Capitalism', *Journal of Political Economy*, **81**.

Landesmann, M. (1992), 'Industrial Policies and Social Corporatism', in J. Pekkarinen *et al.* (1992), 242–79.

Lange, O. (1931), 'Kryzys socjalizmu', w: O. Lange, *Wybor Pism*, t. 1, Warsaw.

Lange, P., and Garrett, G. (1985), 'The Politics of Growth: Strategic Interaction and Economic Performance in the Advanced Industrial Democracies, 1974–1980', *Journal of Politics*, **47**(August), 792–827.

Langmore, J. (1992), 'Treasury's Modus Operandi and Deregulation: A Critical Look Back', PSRC Discussion Paper No. 25, Public Sector Research Centre, Sydney, University of New South Wales.

Lasheras, M. A. *et al.* (1993), 'Política Redistributiva en el IRPF entre 1982 y 1990', in various authors, *I Simposio Sobre Igualdad y Distribución de la Renta y la Riqueza. Vol. VII. Sector Público y Redistribución*, Fundación Argentaria.

Ławiński, P. (1989), 'Ile wytrzymacie?', *Tygodnik Solidarnooæ*, 29 September.

Layard, R. (1990), 'Varför Överge de Svenska Modellen?', in V. Bergström (ed.), *Varför Överge de Svenska Modellen?*, Trade Union Institute for Economic Research and Tiden.

— (1997), 'Preventing Long-term Unemployment', in D. Snower and G. de la Dehasa (eds), *Unemployment Policy*, Cambridge, Cambridge University Press.

— Nickell, S. J., and Jackman, R. (1991), *Unemployment*, Oxford, Oxford University Press.

Le Cacheux, J. (1994), 'Les Banques Américaines et la Baisse des Taux', *Revue de l'OFCE*, no. 48.

Lecointe, F., Przedborski, V., and Sterdyniak, H. (1989), 'Salaires, Prix et Répartition, ou Comment l'Inflation fut Vaincue', in J.-M. Jeanneney (ed.), *L'Economie Française depuis 1967, la Traversée des Turbulences*, Paris, Seuil.

Lehmbruch, G. (1984), 'Concertation and the Structure of Corporatist Networks', in J. H. Goldthorpe (ed.), *Order and Conflict in Contemporary Capitalism*, Oxford, Clarendon Press.

Lee, J.-H., and Przeworski, A. (1992), 'Cui Bono? Una Stima del Benessere nei Sistemi Corporativisti e in Quelli di Mercato', *Stato e Mercato*, 36, 347–76.

Leventakis, I. A. (1994), 'Tasis sti Diethni Antagonistikotita tis Ellinikis Ikonomias kai Prooptikes', in A. Kintis (ed.), *2004: I Elliniki Ikonomia sto Katofli tou 21 Aiona*, Athens, Ionian Bank.

Levi, M. (1996), 'Social and Unsocial Capital: A Review Essay of Robert Putnam's *Making Democracy Work*', *Politics and Society*, 24(1), 45–55.

Levy, J. D. (1999), 'France: Directing Adjustment?', paper presented to the international research project on 'The Adjustment of National Employment Policy and Social Policy to Internationalization', directed by F. Scharpf, Cologne, Max Planck Institute.

Lewandowski, J. (1999), 'Msza przeciw prywatyzacji', *Gazeta Wyborcza*, 15 January.

Lianos, T. P., and Lazari, A. M. (1994), 'I Ekseliksi ton Basikon Megethon tis Ellinikis Ikonomias kata ti Metapolemikh Periodo', in A. Kintis (ed.), *2004: I Elliniki Ikonomia sto Katofli tou 21 Aiona*, Athens, Ionian Bank.

Lindbeck, A. (1975), *Svensk Ekonomisk Politik*, Stockholm, Aldus.

— (1997), 'The Swedish Experiment', *Journal of Economic Literature*, 35(3), 1273–319.

Lordon, F. (1997), *Les Quadratures de la Politique Economique*, Paris, Albin Michel.

Lundberg, E. (1985), 'The Rise and Fall of the Swedish Model', *Journal of Economic Literature*, 23(2), 1–36.

Lybeck, J. A. (1985), *Devalveringar — Ett Inslag i de Nordiska Ländernas Stabiliseringspolitik*, Stockholm, Liber Förlag.

Lyberaki, A. (1996), 'Greece–EU Comparative Economic Performance at the National and Regional Levels: Why Divergence?', *European Planning Studies*, 4(3), 313–29.

Lyrintzis, C. (1987), 'The Power of Populism: The Greek Case', *European Journal of Political Research*, 15(6), 667–86.

Machin, S., and Van Reenen, J. (1998), 'Technology and Changes in Skill Structure: Evidence from Seven Countries', *Quarterly Journal of Economics*, 113, 1215–44.

McKinnon, R. I. (1989), 'Financial Liberalisation and Economic Development: A Reassessment of Interest Rate Policies in Asia and Latin America', *Oxford Review of Economic Policy*, 5(4).

Malinvaud, E. (1986), 'Jusqu'où la Rigueur Salariale Devrait-elle Aller? Une Exploration Théorique de la Question', *Revue Economique*, 37(2).

Malo de Molina, J. L. (1983), 'El Impacto del Cambio Institucional en el Mercado de Trabajo', *Papeles de Economia Española*, **15**.

Manassaki, A. (1998), 'I Isroes Kinotikon Poron stin Ellada: Istoriki Anadromi kai Prooptikes' ('Inflows of Community Funds into Greece: Historical Retrospective and Prospects for the Future'), *Ikonomiko Deltio (Economic Bulletin)*, Bank of Greece, **12**, 63–89.

Maravall, J. M. (1991), 'Quince Años de Política en España', *Sistema*, **100**, 46–61.

Marglin, S., and Badhuri, A. (1990), 'Profit Squeeze and Keynesian Theory', in S. Marglin and J. Schor (eds), *The Golden Age of Capitalism*, Oxford, Clarendon Press.

Marimon, R., and Zilbotti, F. (1996), '¿Por qué Hay Menos Empleo en España? Empleo "Real" versus Empleo "Virtual" en Europa', in R. Marimon (ed.), *La Economía Española: Una Visión Diferente*, Antoini Bosch.

Marin, B. (1982), *Die Paritätische Kommission. Aufgeklärter Technokorporatismus in Österreich*, Vienna, Manz-Verlag.

Marterbauer, M. (1993), 'Austrian Economic and Social Partnership and European Integration', *Economic and Industrial Democracy*, **14**, 459–72.

Marti, R. (1995), 'Spécification des Préférences Implicites en Matière de Politique Economique Française, 1981–1991', *Economie et Prévision*, **119**.

Martin, A. (1979), 'The Dynamics of Change in a Keynesian Political Economy: The Swedish Case and its Implications', in C. Crouch (ed.), *State and the Economy in Contemporary Capitalism*, New York, St Martin's Press.

— (1984), 'Trade Unions in Sweden: Strategic Responses to Change and Crisis', in P. Gourevitch, A. Nartin, G. Ross, S. Bornstein, A. Markovits, and C. Allen (eds), *Unions and Economic Crisis: Britain, West Germany and Sweden*, London, George Allen & Unwin.

— (1985), 'Wages, Profits, and Investments in Sweden', in L. N. Lindberg and C. S. Mair (eds), *The Politics of Inflation and Economic Stagnation*, Washington, DC, The Brookings Institution.

Martin, C., and Velázquez, F. J. (1996), 'Una Estimación de la Presencia de Capital Extranjero en la Economia Española y Alguna de sus Consecuencias', *Papeles de Economia Española*, **66**, 160–75.

Martin, F. A., and Santos, J. (1994), 'Proyecto del Gobierno Sobre Reforma del Mercado de Trabajo: Garantismo versus Desregulación', *Sociologia del Trabajo*, **20**, 117–49.

Martín Seco, J. F. (1993), *¡La Economía, Estúpidos, la Economía!*, Madrid, Libertarias Prodhufi.

Martinez de Pablos, F. J. (1991), 'La Banca, de los Setenta al Mercado Unico', in M. Etxezarreta (ed.), *La Reestructuración del Capitalismo en España 1970–1990*, Barcelona, FUHEM/ Icaria.

März, E., and Weber, F. (1978), 'Verstaatlichung und Sozialisierung nach dem Ersten und Zweiten Weltkrieg: Eine Vergleichende Studie', *Wirtschaft und Gesellschaft*, **4**, 115–42.

Matsagannis, M. (1999), *Prooptikes tou Koinonikou Kratos stin Ellada (Prospects for the Welfare State in Greece)*, Athens, Ellinika Grammata.

Matthews, R. (1968), 'Why has Britain had Full Employment since the War?', *The Economic Journal*, **78**(3), 555–69.

Mavrogordatos, G. T. (1983), *Stillborn Republic: Social Conditions and Party Strategies in Greece, 1892–1936*, Berkeley, CA, University of California Press.

Meidner, R. (1974), *Co-ordination and Solidarity: An Approach to Wages Policy*, Stockholm, Prisma.

Meseguer Yebra, C. (1999), 'Bayesian Learning About Policies', Ms. Centro de Estudios Avanzados en Ciencias Sociales, Instituto Juan March, Madrid.

Milanovic, B. (1995), *Poverty, Inequality, and Social Policy in Transition Economies*, Washington, DC, The World Bank.

Milic-Czerniak, R. (ed.) (1998), *Gospodarstwa domowe w krajach Europy Œrodkowej*, Warsaw.

Ministerstwo Finansów (1998*a*), 'Œredniookresowa strategia finansowa', mimeo.

— (1998*b*), 'Biała księga Podatków. Analiza obecnego systemu podatkowego. Propozycje zmian. Synteza', mimeo.

Mitchell, D. (1991), *Income Transfers in Ten Welfare States*, Brookfield, Avebury.

Mjøset, L. (1986), *Norden Dagen Derpå*, Oslo, Universitetsforlaget.

— (1989), 'Norway's Full-Employment Oil Economy — Flexible Adjustment or Paralysing Rigidities?', *Scandinavian Political Studies*, **12**(4), 313–41.

Modzelewski, K. (1993), *Dokąd od komunizmu*, Warsaw.

Moene, K. O., and Wallerstein, M. (1993), 'Embodied Technical Progress, Wage Compression and the Centralization of Collective Bargaining', mimeo, April.

— — (1995), 'How Social Democracy Worked: Labor-Market Institutions', *Politics and Society*, June.

Moore, D. (1989), 'Industrial Relations and the Failure of the Accord: What Should be Done?', *Australian Bulletin of Labour*, **15**(3), 153–83.

Morlino, L. (1995), 'Political Parties and Democratic Consolidation in Southern Europe', in Gunther *et al.* (1995).

Moschos, D., and Stournaras, Y. (1998), 'Domestic and Foreign Price Links in an Aggregate Supply Framework: The Case of Greece', *Journal of Development Economics*, **56**, 141–57.

Moses, J. W. (1994), 'Abdication from National Policy Autonomy: What's Left to Leave?', *Politics and Society*, **22**(2), 125–48.

Mosley, L. (1999), 'Room to Move: International Financial Markets and National Welfare States', Department of Government, University of Notre Dame, mimeo.

Mouzelis, N. (1978), *Modern Greece: Facets of Underdevelopment*, London, Macmillan.

Mouzelis, N. (1987), 'Continuities and Discontinuities in Greek Politics', in K. Featherstone and D. K. Katsoudas (eds), *Political Change in Greece*, London, Croom Helm.

— Lipovats, T., and Spourdalakis, M. (1989), *Laikismos kai Politiki (Populism and Politics)*, Athens, Gnossi.

Myles, J. (1997), 'How to Design a "Liberal" Welfare State: A Comparison of Canada and the United States', paper prepared for the Conference on Models of Capitalism and Latin American Development, Chapel Hill, University of North Carolina, May.

— Pierson, P. (in press), 'The Political Economy of Pension Reform', in P. Pierson (ed.), *The New Politics of the Welfare State*, Oxford, Oxford University Press.

Myro, R. (1988), 'La Industria: Expansión, Crisis y Reconversión', in J. L. García Delgado (ed.), *España. Economía*, Madrid, Espasa Calpe.

— (1995), 'Crecimiento y Competitividad de la Industria Española', in various authors, *La Economía Española en un Escenario Abierto*, Fundación Argentaria/Visor, Madrid.

Montes, P. (1993), *La Integración en Europa*, Madrid, Trotta.

Montes, V. J., and Carrasco, A. (1996), 'El Proceso de Localización de la Actividad Industrial en España: La Experiencia de las ZUR', *Economia Industrial*, **309**, 19–26.

Nannestad, P. (1991), *Danish Design or British Decease? Danish Economic Crisis Policy in Comparative Perspective*, Århus, Århus University Press.

Naredo, J. M. (1994), 'Sobre Pobres y Necesitados', *Boletín Igualdad*, **11**, Fundación Argentaria.

— (1996), *La Burbuja Inmobiliario-financiera en la Coyuntura Económcia Reciente (1985–1995)*, Madrid, Siglo XXI.

Nickell, S. (1997), 'Unemployment and Labor Market Rigidities: Europe versus North America', *Journal of Economic Perspectives*, **11**(3), 55–74.

Nilsson, C. (1993), 'The Swedish Model: Labour Markets Institutions and Contracts', in J. Hartog and J. Theeuwes (eds), *Labour Market Contracts and Institutions: A Cross-National Comparison*, North-Holland, Elsevier Science Publishers.

North, D. C. (1990), *Institutional Change and Economic Performance*, Cambridge, Cambridge University Press.

Notermans, T. (1993), 'The Abdication from National Policy Autonomy: Why the Macroeconomic Policy Regime Has Become so Unfavorable to Labor', *Politics and Society*, **21**(2), 133–67.

— (1994), 'Social Democracy in Open Economies: A Reply to Jonathon Moses', *Politics and Society*, **22**(2), 149–64.

Nuti, M. D. (1996), 'Employee Ownership in Polish Privatization', in M. Uvalic and D. Vaughan-Whitehead, *Privatization Surprises in Transition Economies, Employee Ownership in Central and Eastern Europe*, Cheltenham, Edward Elgar.

O'Connor, J. (1996), 'From Women in the Welfare State to Gendering Welfare State Regimes', *Current Sociology*, **44**(2).

OECD (1989), *Economies in Transition*, Paris, Organization for Economic Cooperation and Development.

— (1994), *OECD Jobs Study: Evidence and Explanations*, Paris, Organization for Economic Cooperation and Development.

— (1996a), *Employment Outlook*, Paris, Organization for Economic Cooperation and Development.

— (1996b), *The Fiscal Position and Business Cycles Database*, Paris, Organization for Economic Cooperation and Development.

— (1996c), *Economic Survey, Greece*, Paris, Organization for Economic Cooperation and Development.

— (1996d), *OECD Economies at a Glance: Structural Indicators*, Paris, Organization for Economic Cooperation and Development.

— (1997a), *Employment Outlook*, Paris, Organization for Economic Cooperation and Development.

— (1997b), *Economic Outlook*, December, Paris, Organization for Economic Cooperation and Development.

— (1997c), *Literacy Skills for the Knowledge Economy*, Paris, Organization for Economic Cooperation and Development.

— (1997d), *National Accounts. Volume I, 1960–1995*, Paris, Organization for Economic Cooperation and Development.

— (1997e), *Economic Survey, Greece*, Paris, Organization for Economic Cooperation and Development.

— (1997f), *Economic Surveys: Austria*, Paris, Organization for Economic Cooperation and Development.

— (1998), *Economic Surveys: Netherlands*, Paris, Organization for Economic Cooperation and Development.

— (1999), *Employment Outlook*, Paris, Organization for Economic Cooperation and Development.

OFCE (1995), *L'Economie Française, 1995*, Paris, Repères, La Découverte.

Offe, C., and Ronge, V. (1984), 'Theses on the Theory of the State', in A. Giddens and D. Held (eds), *Classes, Power and Conflict*, London, Macmillan.

Olczyk, E., and Pilczyński, J. (1996), Prawo pracy coraz częœciej łamane. W pracy bardziej niebezpiecznie (Labour Code is More and More Frequently Broken. Job More Dangerous), *Rzeczpospolita*, 22 December.

Orloff, A. (1993), 'Gender and the Social Rights of Citizenship: The Comparative Analysis of Gender Relations and Welfare States', *American Sociological Review*, **58**, 303–28.

Palme, J. (1990), *Pension Rights in Welfare Capitalism*, Stockholm, Swedish Institute for Social Research.

— (1994), 'Recent Developments in Income Transfer Systems in Sweden', in N. Ploug and J. Kvist (eds), *Recent Trends in Cash Benefits in Europe*, Copenhagen, Danish National Institute of Social Research.

Palme, J., and Wennemo, I. (1997), 'Swedish Social Security in the 1990s: Reform and Retrenchment', Centre for Welfare State Research Working Paper 9, Copenhagen.

Pańków, W., and Gąciarz, B. (1999), 'Effective Strategies in Direct Privatization', in M. Jarosz (ed.), *Direct Privatization. Investors. Managers. Employees*, Warsaw.

Pekkarinen, J. (1989), 'Keynesianism and the Scandinavian Models of Economic Policy', in P. A. Hall (ed.), *The Political Power of Economic Ideas*, Princeton, NJ, Princeton University Press.

— Pohjola, M., and Rowthorn, R. (1992), *Social Corporatism – A Superior Economic System?*, WIDER Studies in Development Economics, Oxford, Clarendon Press.

— and a team of experts (1997), 'Finland and EMU', Prime Minister's Office, Helsinki.

Pérez, S. (1999), *Banking on Privilege. The Politics of Spanish Financial Reform*, Ithaca, NY, Cornell University Press.

Perotti, R. (1996), 'Growth, Income Distribution, and Democracy: What the Data Say', *Journal of Economic Growth*, **1**, 149–87.

Pichlmann, K. (1990), 'Unemployment Dynamics, Wage Flexibility, and the NAIRU in Austria', *Empirica*, **17**, 171–86.

Pierson, P. (1996), 'The New Politics of the Welfare State', *World Politics*, **48**(2), 143–79.

Piggott, J., and Chapman, B. (1995), 'Costing the Job Compact', *Economic Record*, **71**(215), 313–28.

Pinto, B., *et al.* (1993), 'Transforming State Enterprises in Poland: Microeconomic Evidence on Adjustment', mimeo.

Pizzorno, A. (1978), 'Political Exchange and Collective Identity in Industrial Conflict', in C. Crouch and A. Pizzorno (eds), *The Resurgence of Class Conflict in Western Europe since 1968*, vol. 1, Macmillan.

Podder, N., and Chatterjee, S. (1998), 'Sharing the National Cake in Post Reform New Zealand: Income Inequality Trends in Terms of Income Sources', paper prepared for the Annual Conference of the New Zealand Association of Economists, Wellington, 2–4 September.

Polanyi, K. (1957), *The Great Transformation: The Political and Economic Origins of Our Time*, Boston, MA, Beacon Press.

Pollan, W. (1992), *Austria's Collective Bargaining System Under Strain*, Vienna, Österreichisches Instituts für Wirtschaftsforschung (mimeo).

— (1997), 'Political Exchange in Austria's Collective Bargaining System: The Role of Nationalised Industries', in M. Sverke (ed.), *The Future of Trade Unionism. International Perspectives on Emerging Union Structures*, Aldershot, Ashgate.

Pontusson, J. (1992a), 'At the End of the Third Road – Swedish Social Democracy in Crisis', *Politics and Society*, **20**, 305–32.

— (1992b), *The Limits of Social Democracy*, Ithaca, Cornell University Press.

- (1997), 'Between Neo-liberalism and the German Model: Swedish Capitalism in Transition', in C. Crouch and W. Streeck (eds), *Political Economy of Modern Capitalism*, London, Sage.
- Swenson, P. (1993), 'Employers on the Offensive: Wage Bargaining, Pay Practices and New Production Strategies in Sweden', mimeo, September.
- — (1996), 'Labor Markets, Production Strategies, and Wage Bargaining Institutions: The Swedish Employer Offensive in Comparative Perspective', *Comparative Political Studies*, **29**(April), 223–50.
- Pridham, G. (1995), 'The International Context of Democratic Consolidation: Southern Europe in Comparative Perspective', in Gunther *et al.* (1995).
- Przeworski, A. (1985), *Capitalism and Social Democracy*, Cambridge, Cambridge University Press.
- (1991), *Democracy and the Markets*, New York, Cambridge University Press.
- (1999), 'Stability and Change of Political Regimes', Ms. Department of Politics, New York University.
- Gandhi, J. (1999), 'Corrective and Transformative Redistributions of Income', Ms. Department of Politics, New York University.
- Wallerstein, M. (1988), 'Structural Dependence of the State on Capital', *American Political Science Review*, **82**(1), 11–30.
- PSOE (1982), 'Por el Cambio. Programa Electoral del Partido Socialista Obrero Español', typescript.
- Pusey, M. (1991), *Economic Rationalism in Canberra: A Nation-building State Changes its Mind*, Cambridge, Cambridge University Press.
- Putnam, R. D. (1993), *Making Democracy Work: Civil Traditions in Modern Italy*, Princeton, NJ, Princeton University Press.
- (1995*a*), 'Bowling Alone: America's Disintegrating Social Capital', *Journal of Democracy*, **6**(1), 65–78.
- (1995*b*), 'Tuning in, Tuning out: The Strange Disappearance of Social Capital in America', *Political Science and Politics*, December, 664–83.
- Quiggin, J. (1987), 'White Trash of Asia?', *Current Affairs Bulletin*, **64**(2), 18–25.
- (1993), *The Industry Commission Approach to Public Sector Reform*, Sydney, Evatt Foundation.
- (1995), 'Does Privatisation Pay?', *Australian Economic Review*, **95**(2), 23–42.
- (1996), *Great Expectations: Microeconomic Reform and Australia*, St Leonards, NSW, Allen & Unwin.
- Rada Strategii Społeczno Gospodarczej (1998), *Podział dochodu i nierównoœci dochodowe. Fakty, tendencje, porównania* (Income Distribution and Income Inequalities. Facts, Tendencies, Comparisons), Raport 29, Warsaw.
- Ramaswamy, R. (1992), 'Wage Bargaining Institutions, Adaptability and Structural Change: The Swedish Experience', *Journal of Economic Issues*, **26**(4).

Rebelo, S. (1991), 'Long-Run Policy Analysis and Long-Run Growth', *Journal of Economic Perspectives*, **99**, 500–21.

Recio, A. (1991), 'Crecimiento Económico y Calidad del Empleo', *Gaceta Sindical*, March, 22–30.

— (1992), 'Economic Internationalisation and the Labour Market in Spain', in A. Castro *et al.*, *International Integration and the Labour Market Organisation*, London, Academic Press.

— (1996a), 'Mercado de Trabajo en España: Comentarios a la Reforma', in F. La Roca and A. Sanchez, *Economia Crítica. Trabajo y Medio Ambiente*, Universitat de Valencia.

— (1996b), 'Welfare State and Labour Market in Spain: Tentative Hypothesis', International Working Party on Labour Market Segmentation, University of Tampere.

— (1998), 'La Política Laboral: Acuerdo y Conflicto en un Contexto de Reform Continua', in R. Gomà and J. Subirats (eds), *Políticas Públicas en España. Contenidos, Redes de Actores y Niveles de Gobierno*, Barcelona, Ariel.

— (1999), 'La Segmentación del Mercado Laboral', in F. Miguélez and C. Prieto (eds), *Las Relaciones de Empleo en España*, Madrid, Siglo XXI.

— Roca, J. (1989), 'Apuntes Sobre la Política de Empleo', *Mientras Tanto*, **36–7**, 169–87.

Rehn, G. (1985), 'Swedish Active Labor Market Policy: Retrospect and Prospect', *Industrial Relations*, **24**, 62–89.

— (1988), *Full Sysselsättning utan Inflation*, Skrifter i urval, presenterade av Eskil Wadensjö, Åke Dahlberg och Bertil Holmlund, Tiden.

Reina, J. L. (1999), *Apuntes Sobre Sindicalismo y Formación Profesional*, Madrid, Trotta.

Roca, J. (1991), 'La Concertación Social', in F. Miguélez and C. Prieto (eds), *Las Relaciones Laborales en España*, Madrid, Siglo 21.

— (1993a), *Pactos Sociales y Política de Rentas*, Madrid, Ministerio de Trabajo y Seguridad Social.

— (1993b), 'Evolución de los Salarios y Evolución del Discurso "Oficial" Sobre los Salarios', in various authors, *La Larga Noche Neoliberal*, Barcelona, Icaria.

— González Calvet, J. (1999), 'Evolución de los Costes Laborales y Diferencias Salariales en España', in F. Miguelez and C. Prieto (eds), *Las Relaciones de Empleo en España*, Madrid, Siglo XXI.

Rodrik, D. (1989), 'Soft Budgets, Hard Minds: Stray Thoughts on the Integration Process in Greece, Portugal and Spain', in C. Bliss and J. Braga de Macedo (eds), *Unity with Diversity in the European Economy*, Cambridge, Cambridge University Press.

— (1997), 'Trade, Social Insurance, and the Limits to Globalisation', NBER Working Paper No. 5905.

Roemer, J. E. (1995), 'An Anti-Hayekian Manifesto', *New Left Review*, **211**, 112–29.

— (forthcoming), *Political Competition*, Oxford, Oxford University Press.

Rojo, L. A. (1981), 'Desempleo y Factores Reales', *Papeles de Economia Española*, **8**, 124–36.

Rosen, S. (1997), 'Public Employment, Taxes and the Welfare State in Sweden', in R. B. Freeman, R. Topel, and B. Swedenborg, *The Welfare State in Transition*, NBER, Chicago, IL, and London, The University of Chicago Press.

Rowthorn, R. (1992), 'Corporatism and Labour Market Performance', in J. Pekkarinen, M. Pohjola, and R. Rowthorn (eds), *Social Corporatism*, Oxford, Oxford University Press.

— (1995), 'Capital Formation and Unemployment', *Oxford Review of Economic Policy*, **11**(1), 29–39.

Sabetti, F. (1996), 'Path Dependency and Civic Culture: Some Lessons From Italy About Interpreting Social Experiments', *Politics and Society*, **24**(1), 19–44.

Salminen, K. (1993), *Pension Schemes in the Making: A Comparative Study of the Scandinavian Countries*, Helsinki, The Central Pension Security Institute.

Sassoon, D. (1996), *One Hundred Years of Socialism*, Cambridge, London, Fontana Press.

Saunders, P. (1994), *Welfare and Inequality: National and International Perspectives on the Australian Welfare State*, Melbourne, Cambridge University Press.

Scharpf, F. (1991), *Crisis and Choice in European Social Democracy*, Ithaca, Cornell University Press.

Schmid, G. (1997), 'The Dutch Employment Miracle? A Comparison of Employment Systems in the Netherlands and Germany', Wissenschaftszentrum Berlin Working Paper Series 202.

Schmidt, F. (1989), *Facklig Arbetsrätt*, Juristförlaget.

Schmitter, P. C. (1995), 'Organised Interests and Democratic Consolidation in Southern Europe', in Gunther *et al.* (1995).

Schneider, R. (1994), *Les Dernières Années*, Paris, Seuil.

Schusselbauer, G. (1999), 'Privatization and Restructuring in Economies in Transition: Theory and Evidence Revisited', *Europe-Asia Studies*, No. 1.

Schwartz, H. (1994a), 'Public Choice Theory and Public Choices: Bureaucrats and State Reorganization in Australia, Denmark, New Zealand, Sweden in the 1980s', *Administration and Society*, **26**, 48–77.

— (1994b), 'Small States in Big Trouble: The Politics of State Organization in Australia, Denmark, New Zealand, and Sweden in the 1980s', *World Politics*, **46**, 527–55.

— (1998), 'Social Democracy Going Down or Down Under: Institutions, Internationalized Capital and Indebted States', *Comparative Politics*, **30**(3).

Scutt, J. (1985), *Poor Nation of the Pacific: Australia's Future?*, Sydney, Allen & Unwin.

Segura, J. (1990), 'Del Primer Gobierno Socialista a la Integración en la CEE: 1983–85', in J. L. García Delgado (ed.), *Economía Española de la Transición y la Democracia*, Madrid, Centro de Investigaciones Sociológicas.

Segura, J., et al. (1991), Análisis de la Contratatación Temporal en España, Madrid, Ministerio de Trabajo y Seguridad Social.

— et al. (1992), La Industria Española y la Competitividad, Madrid, Espasa Calpe.

Seidel, H. (1982), 'Der Austro-Keynesianismus', Wirtschaftspolitische Blätter, 3, 11–15.

Semprich, Ż. (1998), 'Program powszechny z wyjątkami', Rzeczpospolita, 15 December.

Simitis, K. (1989), Anaptiksi kai Eksygxronismos tis Ellinikis Koinonias (Development and Modernisation of Greek Society), Athens, Gnossi.

Simons T. W., Jr (1999), 'Kto może rzucac kamienie?' (Who can Throw Stones?), Rzeczpospolita, 9–10 July.

Socialist Union (1956), Twentieth Century Socialism, London.

Sogo, J. F. (1994), 'Estructura del IRPF por Fuentes de Renta', Hacienda Pública Española, 131, 135–47.

Solchaga, C. (1997), El Final de la Edad Dorada, Madrid, Taurus.

Soskice, D. W. (1990), 'Wage Determination: The Changing Role of Institutions in Advanced Industrialized Countries', Oxford Review of Economic Policy, 6(4), 36–61.

— (1991), 'The Institutional Infrastructure for International Competitiveness: A Comparative Analysis of the UK and Germany', in A. B. Atkinson and R. Brunetta, Economics for the New Europe, New York, New York University Press.

— (1999), 'Divergent Production Regimes: Coordinated and Uncoordinated Market Economies in the 1980s and 1990s', in H. Kitschelt, P. Lange, G. Marks, and J. D. Stephens (eds), Continuity and Change in Contemporary Capitalism, New York, Cambridge University Press.

— Iversen, T. (1998a), 'Central Bank–Trade Union Interactions and the Equilibrium Rate of Employment', Wissenschaftszentrum Berlin Working Paper Series.

— — (1998b), 'Multiple Wage Bargaining Systems in the Single European Currency Area', Oxford Review of Economic Policy, 14(3), 110–24.

Sotiropoulos, D. A. (1991), 'State and Party: The Greek State Bureaucracy and the PanHellenic Socialist Movement (PASOK), 1981–89', unpublished PhD thesis, Yale University, New Haven, CT.

— (1993), 'Ktratike Grafeoikratia kai Laikistiko Komma: He Periptose tou PASOK, 1981–89' (State Bureaucracy and Populist Party: the case of PASOK, 1981–89), Synchrona Themata, 49, 13–24.

SOU (Statens offentliga utredningar, Government Committee Papers) (1998), n. 141, 1998: Medling och lönebildning, Stockholm.

Spourdalakis, M. (1988), The Rise of the Greek Socialist Party, London, Routledge.

Stephens, J. D. (1979), The Transition from Capitalism to Socialism, University of Illinois Press.

— (1996), 'The Scandinavian Welfare States', in G. Esping-Andersen (ed.), Welfare States in Transition, London, Sage.

- Huber, E., and Ray, L. (1999), 'The Welfare State in Hard Times', in H. Kitschelt, P. Lange, G. Marks, and J. D. Stephens (eds), *Continuity and Change in Contemporary Capitalism*, New York, Cambridge, Cambridge University Press.

Sterdyniak, H., Le Bihan, H., Cour, P., and Delessy, H. (1997), 'Le Taux de Chômage d'Equilibre: Anciennes et Nouvelles Approches', *Revue de l'OFCE*, **60**.

Stiglitz, J. E. (1994), *Wither Socialism*, Cambridge, MA, MIT Press.

- (1997), 'The Role of Government in Economic Development', in M. Bruno and B. Pleskovic (eds), *Annual World Bank Conference on Development Economics 1996*, Washington, DC, World Bank.

- (1999*a*), 'Economic Theory, Economic Policy, and Economic Advice', *Annual Bank Conference on Development Economics*, Washington, DC, The World Bank.

- (1999*b*), 'Economic Reforms in Retrospect', The Web.

Stokes, S. C. (1999), 'What Do Policy Switches Tell Us About Democracy?', in B. Manin, A. Przeworski, and S. C. Stokes (eds), *Democracy, Accountability, and Representation*, New York, Cambridge University Press.

Stournaras, Y. A. (1990), 'Public Sector Debt and Deficits in Greece: The Experience of the 1980s and Future Prospects', *Revista di Politica Economica*, **80**(7–8), 405–40.

Streeck, W. (1997), 'Beneficial Constraints: On the Economic Limits of Rational Voluntarism', in J. R. Hollingsworth and R. Boyer (eds), *Contemporary Capitalism: The Embeddedness of Institutions*, Cambridge, Cambridge University Press.

Stromback, T., Dockery, M., and Ying, W. (1997), 'Labour Market Programs and Labour Market Outcomes', Curtin University and Centre for Labour Market Research.

Suppanz, H., and Robinson, D. (1972), *Prices and Incomes Policy. The Austrian Experience*, Paris, Organization for Economic Cooperation and Development.

Surdykowski, J. (1990), 'Między demokracją a polskim piekłem' (Between democracy and the Polish hell), *Gazeta Wyborcza*, 180.

Sutcliffe, R., and Glyn, A. (1999), 'Still Underwhelmed: Indicators of Globalisation and their Interpretation', *Review of Radical Political Economy*, March.

Suwalski, A. (1997), 'Ekonomiczno-społeczne zagadnienia sporu o powszechne uwłaszczenie', *Ruch Prawniczy, Ekonomiczny i Socjologiczny*, **1**.

Svallfors, S. (1995), 'The End of Class Politics? Structural Cleavages and Attitudes to Swedish Welfare Policies', *Acta Sociologica*, **38**(1).

- (1996), *Välfärdsstatens Moraliska Ekonomi – Välfärdsopinionen i 90-talets Sverige*, Boreå.

Swenson, P. (1989), *Fair Shares: Unions, Pay, and Politics in Sweden and Germany*, Cornell, Cornell University Press.

- (1991), 'Labor and the Limits of the Welfare State', *Comparative Politics*, **23**(4), 379–99.

Szafraniec, K., and Adamski, W. W. (1999), 'Polish Peasants: Actors of the Transformation or Clients of the Welfare State?', in W. W. Adamski *et al.* (eds), *System Change and Modernization*, Warsaw, IFiS.

Szostkiewicz, H. (1994), 'Powstanie spółek pracowniczych: nadzieje i doœwiadczenia' (Emergence of Employee Companies, Hopes and Experiences), in M. Jarosz, *Spółki pracownicze*, Warsaw.

— (1996), 'Shareholders and Managers: Labor Relations', in M. Jarosz, *Polish Employee-owned Companies in 1995*, Warsaw.

Taddei, D., and Coriat, B. (1992), *Made in France*, Le Livre de Poche, Essais, Paris.

Tálos, E., and Kittel, B. (1999), 'Sozialpartnerschaft und Sozialpolitik', in F. Karlhofer and E. Talos (eds), *Sozialpartnerschaft*, Vienna.

Taylor, R. (1998), 'The *Fairness at Work* White Paper', *Political Quarterly*, **69**(October–December), 451–7.

Tichy, G. (1984), 'Strategy and Implementation of Employment Policy in Austria', *Kyklos*, **3**, 363–86.

Tilton, T. (1991), *The Political Theory of Swedish Social Democracy*, Oxford, Clarendon Press.

Toharia, L. (1996), 'La Protección por Desempleo en España', in O. De Juan, J. Roca, and L. Toharia (eds), *El Desempleo en España. Tres Ensayos Críticos*, Universidad de Castilla–La Mancha, Cuenca.

— (1997), 'Actives and Passive Labour Market Policies in Spain', *Employment Observatory, Sysdem*, trends 28, summer.

— Malo, J. L. (1997), 'Las Indeminizaciones por Despido: Su Origen, sus Determinantes y las Enseñanzas de la Reforma de 1994', *Documentación Laboral*, **51**, Vol. I.

Toohey, B. (1994), *Tumbling Dice: The Story of Modern Economic Policy*, Port Melbourne, William Heinemann Australia.

Torrero, A. (1993), 'Problemas y Desafíos de una Economía Abierta', in J. L. García Delgado (ed.), *Lecciones de Economía Española*, Madrid, Civitas.

Traxler, F. (1992), 'Austria: Still the Country of Corporatism', in R. Hyman and A. Ferner (eds), *Industrial Relations in the New Europe*, Oxford, Basil Blackwell.

— (1994), 'Collective Bargaining: Levels and Coverage', *OECD Employment Outlook*, July, 167–94.

— (1998), 'Austria: Still the Country of Corporatism?', in A. Ferner and R. Hyman (eds), *Changing Industrial Relations in Europe*, Oxford, Blackwell Publishers.

Tsakalotos, E. (1991*a*), *Alternative Economic Strategies: The Case of Greece*, Avebury, Gower.

— (1991*b*), 'Structural Change and Macroeconomic Policy: The Case of Greece (1981–85)', *International Review of Applied Economics*, **5**(3), 253–76.

Tsakloglou, P. (1993), 'Aspects of Inequality in Greece: Measurement, Decomposition and Inter-temporal Change: 1974, 1982', *Journal of Development Economics*, **40**, 53–74.

— (1996), 'Elderly and Non-Elderly in the EU', *Review of Income and Wealth*, **42**(3).

— (1997), 'Changes in Inequality in Greece in the 1970s and 1980s', in P. Gottschalk, B. Gustafsson, and E. Palmer (eds), *Changing Patterns in the Distribution of Economic Welfare: What Happened during the 1980s?*, Cambridge, Cambridge University Press.

Turok, I., and Webster, D. (1998), 'The New Deal: Jeopardised by the Geography of Unemployment', *Local Economy*, February, 309–28.

Tymowska, K. (1999), *Sektor prywatny w systemie opieki zdrowotnej*, Raport Instytutu Spraw Publicznych, Warsaw.

Undy, R. (1999), 'New Labour's "Industrial Relations Settlement": The Third Way?', *British Journal of Industrial Relations*, **37**, 2 June.

Uusitalo, P. (1984), 'Monetarism, Keynesianism and the Institutional Status of Central Banks', *Acta Sociologica*, **27**.

Vandenbroucke, F. (1998), *Globalisation, Inequality, and Social Democracy: A Survey*, London, Institute for Public Policy Research.

Van Kersbergen, K. (1995), *Social Capitalism: A Study of Christian Democracy and the Welfare State*, London, Routledge.

Viñals, J. (1983), 'El Mercado de Trabajo y sus Implicaciones para las Políticas Macroeconómicas de Ajuste: El Caso de España', *Papeles de Economia Española*, **15**, 258–75.

Visser, J. (1990), 'Continuity and Change in Dutch Industrial Relations', in G. Baglioni and C. Crouch (eds), *European Industrial Relations. The Challenge of Flexibility*, London, Sage.

— (1996), 'Unionisation Trends Revisited', CESAR Research Paper 1996/2, Centre for Research of European Societies and Industrial Relations, Amsterdam.

— Hemerijck, A. (1997), *A 'Dutch Miracle': Job Growth, Welfare Reform and Corporatism in the Netherlands*, Amsterdam, Amsterdam University Press.

Vredin, A., and Ohlsson, H. (1996), 'Political Cycles and Cyclical Policies', *Scandinavian Journal of Economics*, **98**(2), 203–18.

Wallerstein, M. (1999), 'Wage-setting Institutions and Pay Inequality in Advanced Industrial Societies', *American Journal of Political Science*, **43**, 649–80.

— Golden, M. (1997), 'The Fragmentation of the Bargaining Society: Wage Setting in the Nordic Countries, 1950–1992', *Comparative Political Studies*, **30**, 699–731.

— — Lange, P. (1997), 'Unions, Employers' Associations, and Wage-Setting Institutions in Northern and Central Europe, 1950–1992', *Industrial and Labor Relations Review*, **50**(3).

Walsh, P. (1995), *Confessions of a Failed Finance Minister*, Sydney, Random House.

Walterskirchen, E. (1991), *Unemployment and Labour Market Flexibility: Austria*, Geneva, International Labour Office.

Walterskirchen, E. (1997), 'Austria's Road to Full Employment', WIFO-Working Papers, 89, Vienna, Österreichisches Instituts für Wirtschaftsforschung.

Watson, S. (1996), 'Welfare State Regimes and Women's Autonomy', Senior Thesis, Department of Political Science, University of North Carolina, Chapel Hill.

Webster, D. (2000), 'The Geographical Concentration of Labour-Market Disadvantage', *Oxford Review of Economic Policy*, **16**(1), 114–28.

Weil-Raynal, E. (1956), 'Les obstacles économiques à l'éxperience Blum', *La Revue Socialiste*, **98**.

White, S. (2000), 'Social Rights and the Social Contract: Political Theory and the New Welfare Politics', *British Journal of Political Science*, forthcoming.

Wickham-Jones, M. (1997), 'Social Democracy and Structural Dependence: The British Case. A Note on Hay', *Politics and Society*, **25**(2), 257–65.

Wilensky, H. (1981), 'Leftism, Catholicism, and Democratic Corporatism', in P. Flora and A. Heidenheimer (eds), *The Development of Welfare States in Europe and America*, New Brunswick, NJ, Transaction Press, 345–82.

Wilkinson, R. (1994), 'Health, Redistribution and Growth', in A. Glyn and D. Miliband (eds), *Paying for Inequality*, London, Institute for Public Policy Research.

Williamson, J. (1990), 'The Progress of Policy Reform in Latin America', in J. Williamson (ed.), *Latin American Adjustment: How Much Has Happened?*, Washington, DC, Institute of International Economics.

Winch, D. (1988), 'Keynes, Keynesianism and State Intervention', in P. Hall (ed.), *The Political Power of Economic Ideas*, Princeton, NJ, Princeton University Press.

World Bank (1994), *Poverty in Poland*, vols I and II, Washington, DC, World Bank.

Wujec, P. (1993), 'Pejzaż przed PPP' (Landscape before Mass Privatization), *Gazeta Wyborcza*, 17 March.

Wyżnikiewicz, B. (1997), 'Zarabiają coraz lepiej', *Gazeta Bankowa – Magazyn*, May.

Zienkowski, L. (1996), 'Rozpiętoœci społeczne' (Social Disparities), *Nowe Życie Gospodarcze*, 27 October.

—   (1998) (ed.), *Podział dochodów w gospodarstwach domowych* (Household's Income Distribution), 1990–1996, Warsaw.

Index

Anderson, Perry 20
ASKE *see* Representative Assembly of Social
    Control
aspirations:
    equality 5–6
    full employment 3–5
    supply-side intervention 6–8
Australia:
    Accord (wages) 99–100, 302, 309
    constitutional structure 303
    economic performance 81–4, 101–5
    economic rationalism 83
    employment 103–5
    financial deregulation 90–2
    free-market reform 84–7
    health policy 94–6
    ideological shift 87–8
    inflation 103
    labour market 98–101, 103–4
    Medicare 94–5, 99
    political assessment 108–9
    political history 80–1, 105–7
    privatization 97–8
    social policy 302
    superannuation system 302
    taxation 92–4
    wages 99–100, 302, 309
    welfare policy 95–6
    welfare state 302
    Whitlam government 80–1, 83
Austria:
    budget deficit 67–8
    coalition government 299–300
    demand management 64–8
    economic performance 54–8, 78–9
    employment 57, 59
    exchange rate 68–70
    full employment 53–4
    incomes policy 70–3
    inflation 70–3
    Keynesianism 58–60, 74–8
    labour market 57, 69, 72, 299–300
    nationalization 63–4
    political history 53–4
    public sector 299

social partnership 61–3
unemployment 57, 58, 59
unions 70–2
wage bargaining 70–1, 270–1
wage equality 271
welfare state 299–300
see also Austro-Keynesian model
Austro-Keynesian model 58–60
    flaws 74–5
    polarization 77–8
    strain 75–7
AWS *see* Solidarity Action for the Election

Balcerowicz, Leszek 226, 251
Bayesian learning 314
benefit payments:
    Sweden 27
    United Kingdom 210–13
Blair government *see* New Labour
budget deficits 4–5
    Austria 67–8
    France 121
    Greece 148–51, 168–9
    international comparison 114
    Spain 177–8
    United Kingdom 202

capital formation 56
capitalism 319
CC.OO *see* Comisiones Obreras
central bank:
    Germany 269–70
    Sweden 267
    United Kingdom 201–2
Christian democratic welfare states 277, 282–
    3, 297–301, 304, 307–8
coordinated wage bargaining *see* wage
    bargaining
collective agreements, Sweden 42
collective wage bargaining *see* wage bargaining
Comisiones Obreras (CC.OO) 187–8
competitiveness:
    désinflation compétitive 127–30
    France 127–30
    Greece 155

competitiveness (*cont.*):
New Labour 219–20
Sweden 266, 268
United Kingdom 203, 219–20
constitutional structure 303, 306–7
constraints, social democracy 199, 273–5, 329–32
consumer booms 10–11
corporatism 14–15, 270
Denmark 255–6
United Kingdom 209, 215
corruption, Spain 190
credit risk, Australia 91
crisis, economic 291–3

DA (employer association) 254–5
demand management:
Austria 64–8
France 111–12, 113–14
democracy 7, 158–61, 158–66, 323–4
Denmark:
corporatism 255–6
economic history 254–6
employment 261–2
exchange rate 264–5
full employment 265–6
income distribution 296
interest rates 265–6
monetarism 268–9
private sector 259–60
public sector 261–2
wages:
bargaining 257, 263
drift 259
equality 257–8, 260, 263
solidaristic policy 257–9
welfare state 293
depreciation 9
désinflation compétitive 110–11
assessment 123–30
competitiveness 127–30
elements 119–23
European integration 136
inflation 123–5
interest rates 126–7
unemployment 125–7
devaluation:
Spain 176
Sweden 46–7
dismissal, Spain 183–5
Douglas, Roger 83, 88–9, 92

earnings 3–4
economic crisis 291–3
economic growth:
France 113
Greece 147

international comparison 56
Poland 227–8
Spain 175–6
economic rationalism 83
economic trends 8–13
education, United Kingdom 214–16
efficiency 5–6
Swedish welfare state 26–7
EFO model 46
electoral politics 322, 325, 331–3
employee companies 233–7
employment:
Australia 103–5
Austria 59
Denmark 261–3
France 125–7
globalization 11
Greece 158
Holland 262–3
inflation 9–10
international comparison 13–18, 262
Netherlands 297–8
New Zealand 103, 105
Poland 230
social democracy 18–19, 291, 326–7
Spain 176, 179–81
Sweden 26–30, 261–3
training 12–13
United Kingdom 204–9, 217–19
unskilled 11
see also full employment; unemployment
Employment Relations Act 217–18
EMU *see* European Monetary Union
Esping-Andersen, Gösta 276–7, 308, 331
equality:
efficiency 5–6
international comparison 6, 15
social democracy 5–6, 19
Spain 196–7
Sweden 52
United Kingdom 210–13, 221
ERM *see* Exchange Rate Mechanism
European integration 307–8
France 117–19, 131, 134–5, 136–7
Greece 168
European Monetary Union (EMU) 135–7
evolution, social democracy 315–22
exchange rate:
Australia 85–6
Austria 68–70
Denmark 264–6
France 114–15, 126–7, 136
Greece 156–7
Spain 176–8
Sweden 264, 266–8
United Kingdom 203
Exchange Rate Mechanism (ERM) 156–7

France:
    budget deficit 114, 121
    competitiveness 127–30
    demand management 111–12, 113–14
    désinflation compétitive 110–11
        assessment 123–30
        competitiveness 127–30
        elements 119–23
        European integration 136
        inflation 123–5
        interest rates 126–7
        unemployment 125–7
    economic growth 113
    economic programmes 131–2
    employment 125–7
    European integration 117–19, 131, 134–7
    exchange rate 114–15, 126–7, 136
    Franc Fort 120–1, 122
    ideological shift 116–19
    inflation 120–5
    interest rates 126–7
    Jospin 130–7
    Keynesianism 111–14, 119–20, 135
    labour market 128–9, 300–1
    nationalization 122–3
    political crisis 115–16
    privatization 134
    programme commun 111–14
    single currency 127
    social security 301
    structural policy 121–2
    unemployment 114, 124–7
    wage discipline 121, 125–6
    wages 132–3
    welfare state 300–1
    working time 133–4
Franc Fort 120–1, 122
full employment:
    Austria 53–4
    Denmark 265–6
    inflation 4, 28–9
    social democracy 3–5, 17, 273–5
    Sweden 28–9, 37, 40, 264, 267
future of social democracy 20, 329–33

GA *see* gradual adjustment
Germany:
    budget deficit 114
    central bank 269–70
Giddens, Anthony 320–2
Gini index 6, 281
globalization:
    effects 330–1
    employment 11
    Greece 167–8
    international trade 9

    taxation 10–11
Glyn, Andrew 1–20, 200–22, 330
goals *see* aspirations
government intervention 6–8
    Spain 192–6
    United Kingdom 212–13
gradual adjustment (GA) 143–4
Greece:
    balance of payments 151–3
    budget deficit 148–51, 168–9
    civil society 161–3
    competitiveness 155
    current account 151–3
    debt dynamics 148–9
    economic performance 145–8
    employment 147, 158
    European integration 168
    exchange rate 156–7
    globalization 167–8
    inflation 156–7
    investment 156
    political economy 161–5
    political history 138–9
    privatization 144–5
    social capital 161–6
    social democracy 138, 140, 157–8, 161–
        6, 167, 170–1
    taxation 159
    trade unions 162–3
    wages 153–6, 158
    see also Panhellenic Socialist Movement
growth:
    France 113
    Greece 147
    international comparison 56
    Poland 227–8
    Spain 175–6
Guger, Alois 53–79

health policy:
    Australia 94–6
    New Zealand 96
    Poland 250
    Spain 195
    Sweden 296
    United Kingdom 213
history, social democracy 315–22
Holland *see* Netherlands
Holland, Stuart 8
housing, Poland 230
Huber, Evelyne 276–311

ideological shift:
    Australia 87–8
    economic policy 1–2
    extent 305

ideological shift (*cont.*):
  France 116–19
  New Labour 200–1, 222
  New Zealand 303
  PASOK 140–5
  Poland 246–7
  social democrats 1–2
  unemployment 305
ILAs *see* Individual Learning Accounts
impact of social democracy 1, 13–18, 19–20,
  312–13, 322–4
income distribution:
  Denmark 296
  Nordic countries 296
  Poland 229
  Spain 196–7
  United Kingdom 210–13
incomes policy:
  Austria 70–3
  Sweden 28–30
  see also corporatism
Individual Learning Accounts (ILAs) 214
industrial relations *see* labour markets; unions;
  wages, bargaining
Industries Assistance Commission 83
inequality:
  Greece 149–50
  international comparison 306
  United Kingdom 210–13, 215, 221, 306
inflation:
  Australia 103
  Austria 70–3
  France 120–5
  full employment 4, 28–9
  Greece 156–7
  international comparison 120
  New Zealand 103
  Sweden 28–30, 47–8
  unemployment 9–10, 14
inherited conditions:
  social democratic governments 8–10
  United Kingdom 202–3
Institute for Fiscal Studies 211–13
international trade 9
internationalism 317, 321–2
investment 4–5
  Greece 156
  international comparison 287–8
  taxation 329–31
Italy, budget deficit 114
Iversen, Torben 253–75

Jospin, Lionel 130–7

Kalecki, M. 4, 17, 60
Kasper, W. 83
Keynes, Sweden 44

Keynesianism 319–20, 325–7
  Austria 58–60, 74–8
  France 111–14, 119–20, 135
  social democracy 319–20, 325
  Sweden 44–5
Kowalik, Tadeusz 223–52
Kreisky, Bruno 53–4

labour markets:
  Australia 98–101, 103–4
  Austria 57, 69, 72
  compulsion 294
  France 128–9, 300–1
  international comparison 285–6
  long-term unemployed 204–9
  Netherlands 297–8
  New Zealand 101, 103–4, 302–3
  social democracy 16–18
  Spain 181–5, 186–8, 193–4
  Sweden 28–9, 294
  training 287, 290
  United Kingdom 204–9, 308–9
  women 288–9
labour movement *see* unions
labour relations:
  categorization 284–7
  Poland 236–7
Lange, Oskar 223–4
Layard, Richard 204
leasing companies *see* employee companies
liberal welfare states 277, 301–4, 305, 308–9
Lindbeck, Assar 16–17, 26–7
LO (union) 28–9, 32–3, 35, 41, 254–7, 271–2
Lordon, Frédéric 110–37

markets 171, 319
  ideological perspectives 158–60
means of production *see* nationalization;
  privatization
Medicare 94–5, 99
minimum wage, United Kingdom 216–17
Mitterrand, François 118
monetarism 275
  accommodation policy 269–71
  Denmark 268–9
  Netherlands 270
  Sweden 268–9
Monetary Policy Committee (MPC) 201–2
MPC *see* Monetary Policy Committee
multinationals, Spain 189

NAIRU *see* non-accelerating inflation rate of
  unemployment
National Investment Funds (NIFs) 237–9
nationalism 317, 321–2
nationalization 7, 19
  Austria 63–4

France 122–3
   social democracy 19, 316–18, 316–19,
      323, 323–4, 326
neo-corporatism 270
neo-liberal theory 327, 332–3
Netherlands:
   labour market 297–8
   monetarism 270
   unemployment 298
New Deal programmes 204–7
New Labour:
   Clause 4 216
   competitiveness 219–20
   compulsion 205–6
   economic policy 201–3, 220–1
   education 214–16
   egalitarianism 221
   employment 204–9, 217–19, 221–2
   ideological shift 200–1, 222
   inherited conditions 202–3
   New Deal 204–7
   PFIs 220
   social democracy 220–2
   stability 220–1
   state role 222
   unions 216–19
   WFTC 205–7
New Zealand:
   constitution 303, 307
   economic performance 81–4, 101–5
   employment 103, 105
   financial deregulation 92
   free-market reform 88–90
   health policy 96
   ideological shift 303
   inflation 103
   labour market 101, 103–4, 302–3
   political assessment 108–9
   political history 80–1, 107
   privatization 98
   taxation 92–4
   welfare policy 96
   welfare state 302–3
non-accelerating inflation rate of unemployment (NAIRU) 10, 51–2, 203–4
Norway, wages 271–2

objectives see aspirations
oil crisis 291–3
   Austria 53–4

Panhellenic Socialist Movement (PASOK):
   economic policy assessment 166–9
   history 139–45
   ideological clarity 170
   ideological shift 140–5

inequality 149–50
macroeconomic stabilization 144–5
organizational structure 165–6, 169–70,
   172
party organization 165–6
policy assessment 166–9
populism 166
social democracy 138, 140, 157–8, 167,
   172
stabilization through development 143–4
structural dependence 168–9
Papandreou, Andreas 165
Parity Commission for Wages and Prices 61–
   2
Partido Socialista Obrero Español (PSOE)
   economic policy 174–5
   history 174–5
   policy assessment 198–9
   unions 186–8
partisanship 306
PASOK see Panhellenic Socialist Movement
pensions:
   funding difficulties 294–5
   Poland 250
   Spain 194–5, 197
   Sweden 294–5
Poland:
   economic growth 227–8
   economy:
      problems 246, 249
      'shock therapy' 247–8
      transition 248–9
   employee companies 233–7
   employment 230
   enfranchisement programme 243–6
   free-market policy 249–51
   health 250
   housing 230
   ideological shift 246–7
   income distribution 229
   intellectuals 225–6
   labour relations 236–7
   National Investment Funds 237–9
   opposition movement 224–5
   pensions 250
   political history 223–4
   post-communists 226–7
   poverty 228–9
   private sector 231–3, 250
   privatization 231
      employee companies 233–7
      National Investment Funds 237–9
   public sector 240–3
   revolution chronology 251–2
   state firms 240–3
   unemployment 228

Poland (cont.):
    unions 226, 230
    wages 229
policy:
    implementation 327–8
    innovation 327, 327–9
    political parties 313–14
    process 313–15, 333
    regimes 324–7
policy shift see ideological shift
political parties 313–14
    policy 313–14
political preferences:
    shaping 312–13
    Sweden 25–6, 37, 52
post-war consensus 6–7
    Sweden 44–5
poverty:
    international comparison 281
    Poland 228–9
Private Finance Initiatives (PFIs) 220
private sector, Spain 188–90
privatization:
    Australia 97–8
    France 134
    Greece 144–5
    New Zealand 98
    Poland 231–9
    social democracy 326
    Spain 190
    United Kingdom 220
production regimes:
    international comparison 284–90
    investment capital 287–8
    welfare states 290
programme commun 111–14
prospects of social democracy 20, 329–33
Przeworski, Adam 312–33
PSOE see Partido Socialista Obrero Español
public sector:
    Poland 240–3
    Spain 189
    Sweden 23–7, 261–2
Putman, R. D. 159–62

record of social democracy 13–18, 19–20,
    312–13, 322–4
redistribution 5–6, 12–13
    social democracy 5–6
redistribution policy 5–6
reformism 2–3, 316–18
reformist social democracy 2–3
Reagan, Ronald 328
Rehn–Meidner model 28–30, 30–1, 48, 50–1,
    255–6, 260–1
remedialism 318–20, 323

Representative Assembly of Social Control
    (ASKE) 164
resignation 320–2

SAP, policy innovation 328
saving 10–11
Scandinavia see Denmark; Norway; Sweden
Scandinavian model:
    history 254–6
    wage policy 257–63
single currency, France 127
social capital 158–61
    social democracy 158–61
Social Chapter, United Kingdom 218–19
social democratic welfare states 277, 282–3,
    293–6, 304, 307
social regulation theory 159–61
socialism 316–18
Solidarity 224
    transformation 225–6
    union 244
Solidarity Action for the Election
    (AWS) 243–6
Soskice, D. W. 284
Spain:
    budget deficit 177
    corruption 190
    devaluation 176
    dismissal 183–5
    economic history 173–4, 175–8
    employment 176, 179–81
    equality 196–7
    exchange rate 176–8
    government spending 192–6
    health care 195
    income distribution 196–7
    labour market 181–5, 186–8, 193–4
    multinationals 189
    pensions 194–5, 197
    Personal Income Tax 191, 197
    private sector 188–90
    privatization 190
    PSOE history 174–5
    public sector 189
    social democracy 198–9
    taxation 197
    temporary contracts 182–5, 186, 188
    trends, economic 175–8
    UGT 186–8
    unemployment 179–81
    unemployment benefits 192–4
    unions 186–8
    wages 181–2, 187
speculation, Sweden 266–7
stabilization through development
    (STD) 143–4

state role 329-30
STD *see* stabilization through development
Stephens, John D. 276-311
Stiglitz, J. E. 330
stock market 18
strategies, social democracy 20, 332-3
supply-side intervention 6-8
supply-side policy 6-8, 15-18
Sweden:
    attitudes 25-6
    benefit payments 27
    central bank 267
    collective agreements 42
    competitiveness 266, 268
    devaluation 46-7
    economic history 254-6
    economic policy 44-50
    efficiency 26-7
    egalitarianism 21-2, 52
    electoral preferences 37, 50, 52
    employment 26-30, 37, 261-2
    equality 52
    exchange rate 264
    full employment 28-9, 37, 40
    incomes policy 28-30
    inflation 28-30, 47-8
    Keynesianism 44-5
    labour-market model 28
    monetarism 268-9
    policy formation 22-3
    political preferences 25-6, 37, 52
    post-war consensus 44-5
    private sector 259-60
    prospects 50-2
    public sector 23-7, 261-2
    Rehn-Meidner model 28-32, 43, 48, 50-1
    trade unions 23, 28
    unemployment 51-2
    unions 266
    wages:
        bargaining 257, 263
        decentralization 36-44
        drift 259, 264
        equality 257-8, 260, 263
        model breakdown 35-6
        radical policy 32-5
        Rehn-Meidner model 28-32, 43, 48,
            50-1
        solidaristic policy 257-9
        wage-earner funds 32-5, 37
    welfare state 23-7, 294-6
Swedish model *see* Sweden

taxation:
    Australia 92-4
    economic fundamentals 330

globalization 10-11
Greece 159
international comparison 10-11, 280
investment 329-31
New Zealand 92-4
Spain 190-2, 197
United Kingdom 210
Thatcher, Margaret 328
Third Way:
    New Labour 201
    origination 317
trade unions *see* unions
trade-offs, social democracy 320-1, 331-2
training:
    employment 12-13
    United Kingdom 205-6, 214-16, 222
Training and Enterprise Councils
    (TECs) 214-15
trends, economic 8-13
trilemma, social democracy 273-5
Tsakalotos, Euclid 138-72

UGT *see* Unión General de Trabajadores
unemployment:
    Austria 53-458
    France 114, 124-7
    inflation 9-10, 14
    international comparison 115
    Kreisky, Bruno 53-4
    Netherlands 298
    OECD countries 268
    Poland 228
    policy implications 291-2, 295
    rise 291-2
    social democracy 13-14, 326-7
    Spain 179-81
    Sweden 38, 51-2
    United Kingdom 203-5, 208
Unión General de Trabajadores (UGT) 186-8
unions:
    Austria 70-2
    Greece 162-3
    international comparison 16-17
    New Labour 215
    Poland 226, 230
    PSOE 186-8
    Spain 186-7
    Sweden 23, 28, 39, 266
    United Kingdom 209, 215, 216-19
United Kingdom:
    benefit payments 210-13
    budget deficit 114, 202
    central bank 201-2
    competitiveness 203, 219-20
    constitution structure 306-7
    corporatism 209

United Kingdom (*cont.*):
  economic policy 201–3
  education 214–16
  employment 204–9, 217–19, 221–2
  ERM 220–1
  exchange rate 203
  government spending 212–13
  health 213
  income distribution 210–13
  industrial relations 217–19
  inequality 210–13, 215, 221
  interest rates 201–3
  labour market 204–9, 308–9
  long-term unemployed 204–9
  minimum wage 210–11, 216–17
  Monetary Policy Committee 201–2
  North–South divide 208
  privatization 220
  Social Chapter 218–19
  social democracy 220–2
  state role 222
  taxation 210
  training 205–6, 222
  unemployment 203–4, 208, 222
  unions 209, 216–19
  wages 207–9
  welfare state 204–9
  'welfare to work' policy 204–6
University for Industry (UfI) 214

Vartiainen, Juhana 21–52

wage policy:
  social democracy 272–3
  see also incomes policy
wage-earner funds 34–5
wage-earner welfare states 277–8, 305
wages:
  Australia 99–100, 302, 309
  Austria 62–3, 70–3, 270–1
  bargaining:
    Austria 62–3, 70–2
    employment 9–10, 14–15
    European integration 307
    international comparison 287
    Sweden 30–6, 257, 263
  Denmark 257–63
  dispersion 289–90
  drift, Sweden 31–2, 34, 36–7
  equality 271, 289–90
  France 121, 125–6, 132–3

Greece 153–6, 158
Poland 229
social democracy 272–5
Spain 181–2, 187
Sweden 257–63
  bargaining 257, 263
  decentralization 36–44
  drift 259, 264
  equality 257–8, 260, 263
  model breakdown 35–6
  radical policy 32–5
  Rehn–Meidner model 28–32, 43, 48,
    50–1
  wage-earner funds 32–5, 37
United Kingdom 207–9
Wałęsa, Lech 223
welfare state, social democracy 5–6
welfare states 5–6
  Australia 95–6, 302
  Austria 299–300
  categorization 276–7, 304
  characteristics 277–80
  Christian democratic 277, 282–3, 297–
    301, 304, 307–8
  compulsion 205–6
  cuts 290–3, 306
  Denmark 293
  France 300–1
  international comparison 280–4
  liberal 277, 301–4, 305, 308–9
  New Zealand 96, 302–3
  political goals 278–81
  popularity 293
  production regimes 290
  retrenchment 290–3, 306
    Sweden 294–6
  social democracy 5–6, 327
  social democratic 277, 282–3, 293–6,
  304, 307
  Sweden 23–7, 294–6
  types 276–81
  unemployment 291
  wage-earner 277–8, 301–2, 305
'welfare to work' policy 204–6
WFTC *see* Working Families Tax Credit
Wood, Stewart 200–22
Working Families Tax Credit (WFTC) 205–7
working time:
  Directive 218–19
  France 133–4